SOCIAL SERVICE, PRIVATE GAIN

The Political Economy of Social Impact Bonds

The 2008 financial crisis and its subsequent economic impacts generated a challenge for national and regional governments across the world. From this economic ruin, the Social Impact Bond (SIB) was born as an alternative mechanism for government procurement and delivery of social public services.

Social Service, Private Gain examines the evolution of SIBs, how they work, their theoretical motivation, and their global proliferation. The book critically assesses the potential of SIBs to constructively contribute to solving the multifaceted social challenges emerging from a context of entrenched and growing inequality. Claiming to bring incremental resources to the rescue, SIBs have taken up disproportionate space with new legislation, policy, subsidies, institutional supports, lobbyists, and "intermediaries" facilitating SIBs and thriving on their associated transaction costs. Drawing on mainstream and heterodox economic theory, practical case studies, and empirical data, Jesse Hajer and John Loxley generate new insights based on the limited but still suggestive publicly available data on SIB projects. Challenging the assumptions and narratives put forward by proponents of the model, they offer practical policy recommendations for SIBs and explain what the model tells us about the potential for transformational change for the better.

JESSE HAJER is a professor in the Department of Economics at the University of Manitoba.

JOHN LOXLEY was a professor in the Department of Economics at the University of Manitoba and a Fellow of the Royal Society of Canada.

Social Service, Private Gain

The Political Economy of
Social Impact Bonds

JESSE HAJER AND JOHN LOXLEY

UNIVERSITY OF TORONTO PRESS
Toronto Buffalo London

© University of Toronto Press 2021
Toronto Buffalo London
utorontopress.com
Printed in the U.S.A.

ISBN 978-1-4875-0328-4 (cloth)   ISBN 978-1-4875-1762-5 (EPUB)
ISBN 978-1-4875-2691-7 (paper)   ISBN 978-1-4875-1761-8 (PDF)

Library and Archives Canada Cataloguing in Publication

Title: Social service, private gain : the political economy of social impact
  bonds / Jesse Hajer and John Loxley.
Names: Hajer, Jesse, 1980– author. | Loxley, John, author.
Description: Includes bibliographical references and index.
Identifiers: Canadiana (print) 2021014565X | Canadiana (ebook) 20210163410
  | ISBN 9781487526917 (softcover) | ISBN 9781487503284 (hardcover) |
  ISBN 9781487517625 (EPUB) | ISBN 9781487517618 (PDF)
Subjects: LCSH: Bonds. | LCSH: Investments – Social aspects. | LCSH: Social
  service – Finance. | LCSH: Finance – Social aspects. | LCSH: Public-private
  sector cooperation. | LCSH: Public interest.
Classification: LCC HG4515.13 .H35 2021 | DDC 332.6 – dc23

This book has been published with the help of a grant from the Federation
for the Humanities and Social Sciences, through the Awards to Scholarly
Publications Program, using funds provided by the Social Sciences and
Humanities Research Council of Canada (SSHRC).

The Manitoba Research Alliance, through its SSHRC Partnership Grant, also
contributed publishing support.

University of Toronto Press acknowledges the financial assistance to its
publishing program of the Canada Council for the Arts and the Ontario Arts
Council, an agency of the Government of Ontario.

Canada Council   Conseil des Arts
for the Arts   du Canada

ONTARIO ARTS COUNCIL
CONSEIL DES ARTS DE L'ONTARIO
an Ontario government agency
un organisme du gouvernement de l'Ontario

Funded by the   Financé par le
Government   gouvernement
of Canada   du Canada

Canadä

Contents

Figures and Tables

Figures

Tables

Preface

On 10 September 2010, the United Kingdom's Conservative minister of justice, Crispin Blunt, visited HM Peterborough Prison to announce the launch of a new antirecidivism program initiated by the previous Labour government (Sinclair et al. 2014). This program was promoted as the first Social Impact Bond (SIB) project, a new mechanism to deliver prevention-focused social programs based on private sector financing and government repayment, but only in the case of successful outcomes. The Tory minister noted in a press release that, although the government's "priorities are to punish offenders, protect the public and provide access to justice," his government aimed "to initiate a more constructive approach to rehabilitation and sentencing, and re-think whether putting more and more people into custody really does make people safer" (United Kingdom 2010). The press release went on to note that, "at a time of tight public finances, payment by results models, such as the Social Impact Bond, can tap into new sources of funding to reduce reoffending and provide value for money for the tax payer." By generating a new financial instrument to draw on potential future savings of prevention-focused programs and converting these savings into working capital and financial profit for investors, a financial innovation was created seemingly well suited to a context of austerity, high inequality, and growing social service pressures.

At the same time, across the Atlantic, the Financial Crisis Inquiry Commission was wrapping up public hearings as part of its mandate to "examine the causes of the current financial and economic crisis in the United States" (2011, xi), which by that point clearly had grown into a full-blown global downturn of the scale not seen since the Great Depression. The key punctuating events of the financial crisis had taken place twenty-four months earlier, with the US government taking over government-sponsored mortgage lenders Fannie Mae and Freddie Mac on 7 September 2008, followed within a week by the buyout of Merrill Lynch, the bankruptcy of Lehman Brothers, and the government bailout of AIG, all leading corporations in the global financial industry.

The commission's final report, while identifying multiple sources of systematic failure, placed significant emphasis on the emergence of complex financial instruments and the "dramatic failures of corporate governance and risk management" (Financial Crisis Inquiry Commission 2011, xviii) within leading financial corporations at the highest level. Goldman Sachs, one of several named, and a subsequent investor and promoter of SIBs in the United States and elsewhere, had "been criticized – and sued – for selling its subprime mortgage securities to clients while simultaneously betting against those securities," a practice parallel to "buying fire insurance on someone else's house and then committing arson" (236). The report tied these unethical practices of financial industry players and the systematic influence purchased through lobbying and campaign contributions to the methodical undermining of the safeguards put in place after the Great Depression and subsequent efforts designed to restrict the very practices that led to the crisis.

The eventual impact of this crisis, founded on financialization, was intense and widespread, as highlighted in the Financial Crisis Inquiry Commission's report.[1] During the year and half following the October 2008 crisis, US unemployment and underemployment rates more than doubled (Financial Crisis Inquiry Commission 340, 348, 390), and home prices dropped by 30 per cent (475), with owners having to sell their homes at a loss under conditions of extreme hardship, desperation, and adversity. Nearly 40 per cent of households surveyed were without work, had underwater mortgages – mortgages in excess of the market value of their homes – or were behind in their mortgage obligations in this period (Hurd and Rohwedder 2010). These results led to widespread pessimism, illustrated poignantly by the additional 4,750 suicides between 2007 and 2012 attributed to the recession (Stuckler and Basu 2013). Given this context, governments' counterintuitive resort to SIBs, a financialized solution, to address growing social service demands is an irony that has motivated this study.

Despite the acuteness of the events of 2008–9, the crisis was only the most dramatic expression of a growing precariousness amongst the less fortunate majority, who, in the United States for example, had seen stagnant or declining real wage growth going back decades as

---

1 See also Freeman (2010) and Kotz (2017b) for summaries.

inequality had continued to increase since the 1970s. Over this period a shift in welfare state administration has taken place in Western advanced economies, with an accelerated movement towards contracting out in a context of resource constraint, limiting the ability of non-profit organizations to respond. Despite these challenges, non-profit and community organizations have attempted to meet demands, innovate, and expand to take on the increasing roles they have been asked to fill, at times under increasingly restrictive circumstances. As these organizations struggle to meet these challenges, they have developed new operational forms such as social enterprise, cooperative structures to establish an alternative to profit-centred firms, and models that have increasingly become common in social service delivery. These organizations, which continue to adapt, learn, and innovate in how they address social challenges through front-line service delivery, and the public servants who continue to support and enable this work despite growing adversity, are a second motivating source for this study. We hope the knowledge uncovered here can help inform and advance the work of these front-line service providers and their supporters who continue to pursue social justice in increasingly turbulent times.

Acknowledgments

Special thanks to Sanjay Reddy, Duncan Foley, Rachel Meltzer, and Paulo dos Santos, and Ardeshir Sepehri, who provided valuable feedback on the multiple chapters sourced back to Jesse Hajer's PhD, which forms the basis of this book. Appreciation is also expressed to Larissa Ashdown for her multifaceted support and to Zac Saltis for valuable insights and engagements. Gratitude is also expressed to the participants in various conferences who provided valuable feedback and encouragement, including those at the 2017 Progressive Economics Forum sessions at the Canadian Economics Association Meetings in Antigonish, Nova Scotia; the 2017 Canadian Association of Programs in Public Administration and 2017 Manitoba Research Alliance Student Colloquium meetings in Winnipeg; and the 2018 international conference on comparing SIBs and outcomes-based approaches at Oxford University, organized by the Government Outcomes Lab. We also express thanks to the three anonymous reviewers who reviewed the manuscript and provided many valuable proposals for improving the text, and to Lindsay Bain for research assistance in the final stages of manuscript preparation. Special thanks to freelancer Barry Norris for his meticulous copy-editing work and to Jennifer DiDomenico and staff at the University of Toronto Press for leading the publication process. We are pleased to acknowledge the generous financial support of the Social Science and Humanities Research Council of Canada through the Manitoba Research Alliance Grant: Partnering for Change: Community-based solutions for Aboriginal and inner-city poverty. Support from the New School for Social Research Dean's Fellowship is also gratefully acknowledged.

With great sadness, we proceeded through the final stages of publication without John's always-valued insights and guidance. Thank you to Aurelie, Salim, Camille, Raina, Matthew, and their families for sharing John's time, gifts, and dedication with the broader community. I expect John would also want to thank (as would I) our colleagues in the Manitoba Research Alliance and the Economics and Society group at the University of Manitoba for a dynamic and inspiring academic home; the Canadian Centre for Policy Alternatives – Manitoba for bringing our research to a broader audience; and the Canadian Community Economic Development Network Manitoba staff and membership for their enthusiastic engagement in making the world a better place. Finally, John likely would have wanted to highlight the ongoing tragedy and injustice of the very high number of Indigenous children taken into state care, the continued underfunding of services for Indigenous families, and the tireless activism of Cindy Blackstock and First Nations Child & Family Caring Society, which motivated much of John's research and interest in Social Impact Bonds.

Jesse Hajer
February 2021

SOCIAL SERVICE, PRIVATE GAIN

The Political Economy of Social Impact Bonds

Introduction

The 2008 financial crisis and subsequent effects generated a dual challenge for national and regional governments in many advanced economies. In the years following the crisis, governments met new populist movements from both the political left and right. On the left this took its most visible form in the Occupy Wall Street movement, defined in opposition to the growing power, influence, and wealth of the top 1 per cent of income earners, generating renewed expectations for government to deal with the increasingly salient challenges of precarious work, poverty, wealth concentration, and income inequality. From the political right, the Tea Party movement and other voices highly critical of a government captured by elites and calling for austerity spoke to the growing fiscal challenges of falling government revenues and increasing deficits. In the United States these groups coalesced respectively around the unconventional presidential runs of Bernie Sanders and, to a lesser and more chaotic extent, Donald Trump. Similarly unconventional political developments gained momentum in other advanced Western economies.

One new policy tool that emerged and spread in the post-crisis period that appeals to both these perspectives and is driven by macro-level developments is the Social Impact Bond (SIB; see Arena et al. 2016; Whitfield 2015, 8). SIBs have grown as an alternative mechanism for government procurement and delivery of social public services, promising, among other things, to generate social and economic development for marginalized low-income populations while saving the government money (Gustafsson-Wright, Gardiner, and Putcha 2015). Although uptake of the SIB model to date is still limited, with only 122 identified projects up and running as of January 2019, the ambitions of proponents are high, with over one hundred projects in development in the United States alone (Social Finance 2018). Qualitative ambitions are equally aspirational, with one proponent expressing the SIBs' "promise to transform the social sector into a competitive marketplace that efficiently *produces* poverty reduction" (Galloway 2013, 3).

This book examines SIBs as a new model for delivering publicly funded social programs, one that builds on a trend of devolution of public spending authority and an increasing role for non-government entities in the provision of publicly funded services.[1] The main purpose of this book is to explain how SIBs work and to explore their theoretical motivations, providing a foundation for future study of how effective they have been in practice in their short period of existence. The book's main intervention is to summarize systematically the attributes of the SIB model and its dissemination to date. It also constructs and evaluates competing theories that attempt to explain the rise of SIBs – from orthodox economic theories with an emphasis on principal-agent problems and asymmetric information to Marxian-inspired theories of neoliberalism, financialization, and the associated reformulation of state activity. As part of this analysis, we generate new insights based on the limited but still suggestive publicly available data on SIBs projects, challenging some of the assumptions of the narratives put forward by proponents of the model.

A key characteristic of services procured under an SIB is that they are preventative in nature (Deloitte 2012; Mulgan et al. 2011), such that their undertaking could preclude the necessity of some future government expenditures arising from formal legal obligations or informal expectations based on precedent. For example, investment in reintegration services for those exiting prison can reduce recidivism rates, in turn reducing future expenditure obligations on law enforcement, the judiciary, and prison systems (Lipsey and Cullen 2007; Warren 2007). Another example is child welfare services, where investments in income supports, family violence prevention, early social worker intervention, and family reunification can reduce future expenditure requirements associated with child maltreatment and/or placing and maintaining children in the custody of the state.[2] Government-funded investments in early childhood development (Heckman 2006), active labour market programs (Card, Kluve, and Weber 2010), and disease

---

1 McHugh et al. (2013), Joy and Shields (2013), Loxley (2013), and Warner (2013) have placed SIBs in a broader context of longer-term trends with respect to state retrenchment in direct social service delivery and the more recent fiscal pressures linked to the 2008 global financial crisis.

2 See Fang et al. (2012) on the social costs of child maltreatment, and Schweitzer et al. (2015) on the effectiveness of family preservation programs.

prevention (Chokshi and Farley 2012) are all additional cases where effective investments can generate savings for governments and might have the potential to generate savings in excess of their costs in present-value terms. SIBs are a financial innovation in that they create a formal structure to borrow against these projected social savings, potentially allowing more of these unfunded projects to proceed.

The bundling of social program design, finance, and operations into a single outsourced contract between government and the private sector consortium is another defining feature of an SIB. Under an SIB, a government offers to pay an amount to a private sector consortium, with the amount potentially based on the "costs of doing nothing" (Mac-Donald 2013, 32), to address a social problem manifested in an identified population. The consortium then aims to prevent the realization of the negative social outcome, and in turn the costs identified, through an intervention. These consortia often involve private financiers motivated by corporate social responsibility in addition to financial returns (Humphries 2014), service delivery agencies, and often an intermediary that specializes in the development of the SIBs and manages the project. SIBs then involve privatizing some activity that is ordinarily undertaken by the state in conventional social service delivery, including project design, management, and financing.

A third defining feature of SIBs is their pay-by-results structure such that repayment of the investment plus return to the intermediary – and in turn to the financiers – is based on clearly articulated targets and usually arm's-length quantitative evaluations. If the consortium does not meet the targets, it is not paid or its compensation is scaled based by the degree to which targets are unmet. By design, SIBs have internal evaluation processes to determine whether they are meeting their targeted objectives.[3] However, a systematic academic analysis of SIBs, assessing and comparing them to alternative delivery methods such as public delivery and conventional procurement, has yet to be undertaken (Fraser et al. 2018b).[4] The presumption in the SIB proponent literature is that governments face systematic challenges in adopting new ideas and producing innovative solutions to social problems (Liebman and Sellman 2013). SIBs in this view then serve as a mechanism for applying the talents and abilities of the private sector to generate better solutions to social problems (Dubno, Dugger, and Smith 2013).

---

3 See for example Disley and Rubin (2014); Jolliffe and Hedderman (2014); and Vera Institute for Justice (2015).
4 See also Carter et al. (2018); Floyd (2017, 12); Fraser et al. (2018a); and Painter et al. (2018).

Proponents point to the potential of SIBs to involve more diverse stakeholders, generate better incentive structures in government service delivery, more efficiently allocate government spending, and promote program innovations, all while shifting risk to the private sector (Fox and Albertson 2011). Mainstream economists have highlighted that, if SIB contracts are to be efficiency-enhancing solutions relative to alternative procurement models, they need to better address principal-agent problems (Pauly and Swanson 2017; Wong et al. 2016), where hired agents are assumed to put their own interests before those they are hired to serve, which in the presence of asymmetric information provides the opportunity for the agent to take advantage of the principal. This framework has been applied to explain financial innovations analogous to SIBs in applied public finance, such as public-private partnerships (PPPs). These models provide an existing theoretical framework in which to formalize supposed government inefficiency as a justification for SIBs.[5]

There are many reasons to believe impact bonds will continue to grow in number in the medium term. First, there are several impact bonds in development, and the ambitions of proponents to generate new projects are high. As noted above, Social Finance (2018) makes reference to approximately one hundred projects in development in the United States and another sixty-eight projects internationally. The UK minister for civil society predicted a £1 billion market for SIBs by 2019 (Weakley 2016),[6] while there are equally ambitious plans for the development of the impact bond market (Jack 2018). Second, these projects and projections are bolstered by a continually expanding set of legislative, financial, and organizational supports that have been established to promote and expand SIBs. Third, the social policy areas in which SIBs are operating, based on survey studies we review in Chapter 1, have a high potential to generate not only social benefits from a cost-benefit perspective, but also fiscal savings to governments in excess of the cost of programming. This suggests that the universe to which SIBs potentially could be applied on a cost-neutral basis is fairly large.[7] A fourth reason to expect continued growth is that, to date, SIBs appear

---

5 For examples of principal-agent models of public-private partnerships, see, for example, Bennett and Iossa (2006); Hart (2003); Iossa and Martimort (2015); and Martimort and Pouyet (2008).

6 The minister made the projection for the end of Parliament, which would have been 2019 given the fixed election date legislation.

7 This, however, is also true when these same initiatives are implemented directly by government.

to face particularly favourable treatment under standard accounting principles, such that accounting for the expenditures can be deferred, making them attractive to decision makers, allowing them to provide incremental funding for social services in a context of fiscal restraint.[8]

Fifth, unlike views on the waves of privatization that took place in the years following the economic crisis of the 1970s, when both the political left and right arguably had clearly staked out positions, SIBs are ideologically ambiguous (Roy, Hugh, and Sinclair 2018). Their emphasis on social investment and the power of prevention in generating improved outcomes for the disadvantaged speak to those sympathetic to greater government action to reduce socio-economic inequality. Those more critical of government intervention may appreciate their focus on reducing future government expenditure, greater involvement of the private sector and entrepreneurship, and the high-power incentive structure based on paying only for projects that deliver results and demonstrable future savings. This chameleon-like nature or "strategic ambiguity" (Tan et al. 2019, 2–3) of SIBs makes them a particularly appealing tool for political actors. Finally, SIBs fit well with current trends in government approaches to economic inequality, with their emphasis on a laissez-faire approach to labour processes and production instead of intervening directly to mandate or incentivize stable employment and living wages.[9] More often, governments, especially in countries that have been leading in SIB implementation, have continued on a path of growing social public expenditures with a reliance on education, training, and income redistribution measures as the central tools in addressing inequality, thus expanding the scope for applying SIBs. These all suggest the likelihood that SIBs will continue to proliferate in the near future.

---

8 See Chapter 3; not all SIBs take advantage of this – in particular, in the United States, many projects are based on set-aside government allocations.

9 In the post–2008 crisis era, despite rising interest in the issue of inequality, there appears to be minimal interest from or insufficient pressure on governments, particularly in the United States and the United Kingdom, to alter the institutional structure of production as a means of addressing income inequality, if one takes trade union density and minimum wage data as indicators. Trade union density decreased on average in member countries of the Organisation for Economic Co-operation and Development (OECD) by 6.1 per cent between 2009 and 2013 with decreases in the United Kingdom of 6.1 per cent and in the United States of 8.4 per cent. The real value of the minimum wage fell by 5.5 per cent in the United States from 2009 to 2016 and increased by only 1.1 per cent in the United Kingdom over the same period (OECD 2018).

The future trajectory of SIBs, however, is far from certain. Although 2017 was a banner year, with thirty-four new projects 2018 saw the introduction of only ten new SIBs (although seven more were introduced in January 2019). Analysts and stakeholders also appear to be increasingly cautious with respect to the potential of SIBs to overcome their inherent challenges and significant administrative requirements (Carter et al. 2018; Heinrich and Kabourek 2018). Studies have also highlighted the more recent views of proponents who express disappointment with the slow growth and ongoing challenges in expanding the SIB market (Williams 2018, 2019). A more polarized policy discourse based on a resurgence of traditional social democratic policy proposals and right-wing racialized nationalism also might downgrade the usefulness or attractiveness of nuanced policy responses such as SIBs aimed at walking the tightrope of addressing inequality within a rigid neoliberal consensus.

After addressing a number of foundational issues, this book seeks answers to the following questions. First, can the emergence of SIBs be understood as efficiency-enhancing contract structures, founded on optimal contract theory aimed at addressing problems that arise when agents are hired to undertake tasks to further the interests of principals. Second, what are the underlying institutional and behavioural assumptions of this approach, and are they likely to hold in practice? Although we find that SIBs can fit into the mould of the principal-agent construct, providing a useful framework for clearly articulating the potential of SIBs, our analysis suggests that the underlying assumptions of the approach are not self-evident, particularly in the context of public social service delivery, creating doubts as to efficiency-based explanations for the emergence of SIBs. Given this, we then pursue alternative explanations. We argue that, to understand fully the emergence of SIBs, one must consider the broader historical context in which they have emerged, the motivations, interests, and relative power of stakeholders, including the increasing importance and influence of the financial sector, and, further, that SIBs are best understood as a logical extension of neoliberal approaches to state governance.

SIBs are a specific and recent finance-based innovation that is part of two broader and evolving consequences of neoliberal economic policy. The first is in government procurement, where the private sector is gaining further responsibility for delivering and financing services that previously had been either delivered directly or managed by government. At a high level, this is part of the familiar pro-privatization stance associated with neoliberal thinking, but it is also connected to more nuanced developments over the past forty years with respect to government procurement. Although contracting out is a long-standing practice of Anglo-Western governments, new tools that became increasingly prominent in the late 1970s and 1980s have seen an ever-evolving transfer of decision-making power and responsibility to private sector entities (Salamon and Lund 1989, 8–9). The associated deunionization and growing precariousness of the workforce, along with new profit-making opportunities for investors, likely contributed to the growing income inequality seen over this period (Freeman 2005, 137; Gottschalk and Smeeding 1997, 647–58; Jaumotte and Osorio Buitron 2015).

The second trend is financialization, where the role and importance of the financial sector in economic and political affairs have increased, gaining both through growth in its traditional activities and expanding into new areas. Financial innovation produces the tools to facilitate this expansion. Financial innovation applied to government service delivery has generated new venture capital-type mechanisms, with PPPs in infrastructure and now with SIBs. Private capital is being invested directly in public sector activity, generating a new frontier of commodification and profit-making opportunities, often implicitly or explicitly subsidized by the state. This book seeks to understand the emergence of SIBs as a member of this group of financial innovations.

We set out competing theoretical frameworks for understanding the emergence and evaluating the potential of the new and primarily unevaluated SIB delivery model targeted at improving social outcomes, generally for the most marginalized and impoverished segments of society. We propose that a framework which situates SIBs and their precursors historically as arising in the context of advanced capitalist development and political competition for control of the state is the most compelling with respect to explaining the emergence of SIBs. Although in our estimation the principal-agent approach is not a good candidate for explaining the emergence of SIBs, we do believe a modified cost-benefit approach can offer some guidance for those who have been directed by decision makers to implement SIB-type financing mechanisms.

Although we focus on a particular form of privatization, SIBs, the broader lessons and approach aim to contribute to a critical, yet constructive evaluation of neoliberal state governance. The recurrent themes of privatization and financialization as mechanisms to improve economic efficiency are often based on a simple and immutable assertion that the state is less efficient than the private market. This ahistorical approach ignores that public enterprise arose as a part of a broader developmental state and industrial policy approach associated with higher rates of growth and better socio-economic outcomes than under liberal economic development paradigms (Chang 2003). Furthermore, the dismantling of that approach and its replacement with neoliberal variants of governance were not in response to some internal spontaneous development through competitive processes whereby private enterprises outperformed public enterprise. Rather, they were part of a regressive, state-led strategy to restore private sector profitability through measures that marked the beginning of an era of growing income and wealth inequality and an expanding financial sector (Duménil and Lévy 2004, 2011).

SIBs have a logical coherence from an efficiency-based perspective within a framework of neoliberal assumptions. These assumptions, however, are contestable, particularly in a social service context. New Public Management approaches in public administration and its Public Choice counterpart in economics have generated a constrained view of the capabilities of the public sector to engage meaningfully in economic and social development. We put forward an alternative analytical framework based on an institutionalist political economy that recognizes the potential of public service norms as a driving motivator of human behaviour, the ability to build effectiveness in the public service, and a more balanced assessment of the value-adding potential of the financial sector. This produces prescriptions for efficient social service delivery that challenge the need for privatization. For those concerned about growing inequality, and about collective responses to social and economic issues more generally, this approach provides an alternative to the perception "that what really matters is that we learn to outsource our biggest social problems to entrepreneurs, who are the only people capable of using the market to discover really big solutions," and highlights the potential that this "promotion of financial engineering is a willfully ideological project" (Mirowski 2013, 355). We compare and contrast these competing approaches, with the goal of informing evidence-based policy decisions in the area of prevention-focused social investments, aimed at generating social mobility and opportunities for disadvantaged households.

Outline of the Book

In Part One, we provide foundational and historical information regarding the development of the SIB model. Chapter 1 establishes the defining features, and sets up a framework to compare and contrast SIBs to other forms of publicly funded social service delivery based on the scope and scale of private sector involvement and responsibility. We then examine in greater detail the features of the SIB model, exploring examples of social program interventions in various policy areas and their ability to generate value for money and cost savings to governments, integral components of the rhetoric proponents use to advance the model. We show that, independent of the procurement method, a large proportion of social interventions in areas in which SIBs are being implemented demonstrate high social returns on investment and often result in savings to government greater than the cost of the program intervention, laying the foundation for the expansion and viability of the SIB model.

Chapter 2 provides a summary of the characteristics of 122 SIBs launched as of January 2019, including the number of projects, participants, and funds invested, by policy area and host country. We trace back SIB contracts to funding programs and promotional initiatives spearheaded by federal and regional governments and the support of specific intermediary organizations that have advocated for and brokered these contracts. This chapter also compiles – for the first time, to our knowledge – aggregate information on rates of returns investors face on SIB projects and the degree to which SIBs have been meeting their targets and repaying investors. Our analysis suggests that SIBs have maximum rates of return significantly above government borrowing costs and, for the most part, appear to be repaying investors.

In Part Two, we examine efficiency-based explanations of the emergence of SIBs. Chapter 3 outlines the case for SIBs as a vehicle for improving the quality and efficiency of public service delivery. We briefly assess some central propositions that have been made regarding their desirable attributes over conventional procurement models, relying on empirical evidence on SIBs and their precursors. We reduce the case for SIBs to three claimed outcomes: (1) a greater number of beneficial social programs being delivered due to the incremental investment generated; (2) an increase in the quality and efficiency of individual programs delivered due to private sector management and innovation as well as the required collaboration; and (3) improvements to the broader public social service system as a whole. We find that all three of these claims are tenuous and that the most likely benefit of SIBs has little to do with the involvement of the private sector and the payment-by-results structure, but the centrality of strong public sector leadership and coordination required to align incentives across the public service and the associated prioritization of preventative services. Empirical evidence regarding the efficiency-enhancing potential of the contracting out and bundling of public services and privatizations more broadly brings into question the existence of net cost reductions through efficiencies arising from such strategies, undermining the explanatory power of efficiencies as the driving force explaining SIB emergence.

In Chapter 4 we put forward a cost-benefit framework for examining individual SIB projects, based on what we determine to be the pivotal claim of SIB proponents that SIBs lead to higher-quality and more efficient social service delivery, and we draw upon parallels between the SIB model and PPP model of public infrastructure delivery to articulate the efficiency-enhancing potential of SIBs using mainstream economics-based contract theory. The two models have many attributes in common (Gustafsson-Wright, Gardiner, and Putcha 2015; Loxley 2013; Warner 2013). Both involve the bundling of private upfront investment and financing with design and ongoing service provision in a single contract. Agency problems involved in social service delivery contracts are central in SIBs and are similar to those in infrastructure-based projects. Analysing SIBs as a PPP variant allows for the application of theoretical modelling approaches from the PPP literature, which is more established than the existing work on SIBs. It is hypothesized that this theoretical approach will help clarify the source of potential welfare gains under SIBs, pointing to positive economic returns from bundling projects together and better resolution of principal-agent problems, while also having to deal with the potential for quality reductions arising in the delegated contract structure. One implication of our framework is that, for SIBs to be efficiency enhancing, in most cases the SIB structure will need to stimulate changes to the project design and/or operations that would not be achieved under conventional delivery.

In Part Three we draw upon institutionalist and heterodox theoretical perspectives, challenging the explanatory power of efficiency-driven explanations of SIBs put forward in Part Two. Chapter 5 presents original data compiled on the participants in SIB projects, and examines the web of motivations and constraints faced by the institutional players involved in SIBs, including elected officials, civil servants, for-profit and non-profit service delivery agencies, and investors in SIBs, including for-profit investors and non-profit foundations. Chapter 5 highlights how more empirically grounded theories of individual and organizational behaviour that recognize the importance of non-pecuniary intrinsic motivation, the centrality of reciprocity, and individuals as socially embedded can help explain the observed challenges faced by the simple incentive-based schemes we highlight in Chapter 3. While undertaking a similar exercise for the state, in Chapter 6 we also seek to demonstrate how a more careful examination of the motivations of government participants in SIBs could lead to the adoption of the model regardless of its efficiency-enhancing potential.

While Chapters 5 and 6 focus on describing the organizations participating in SIBs and their motivations, Chapter 7 turns to the broader political economic context as a driving factor in SIB emergence. Focusing on changes brought by the adoption of neoliberal governance practices, greater financialization of the economy, and the fallout of the 2008–9 economic crisis, this chapter highlights how the congruence of these factors created an optimal environment for the emergence of the SIB model. We undertake a comparative analysis of countries classified, using Esping-Andersen's (1990) classifications of conservative, liberal, and social democratic regimes. We argue that a number of key structural features of the liberal regime have a logical coherence and have facilitated their leadership role in the adoption of SIBs.

Chapter 8 examines development impact bonds (DIBs). Here we summarize the development of the enabling field for DIBs, provide a recap of the small number of DIB projects launched to date, and review the challenges faced by the DIB model and their parallels with those identified in SIBs. We emphasize situating DIBs in the broader foreign aid context, the larger challenges faced, and the inadequacy of the DIB model to address these challenges.

Chapter 9 concludes the book by recapping our main findings and proposed modifications to the SIB approach, as well as introducing two broad alternatives to the SIB model that aim to reduce socio-economic inequality more effectively, support collaboration and innovation in public social programs, and promote public investment in preventative social services. This is done without what we deem an extraneous reliance on private finance and the contracting out of coordination and management responsibility, functions that we argue rest more appropriately with the state. These alternatives are based on institutionalist and other heterodox perspectives, providing a theoretical framework for how public coordination could result in more efficient delivery outcomes. We also propose that the case of state failure is not an unchangeable reality, but that an effective civil service can be developed with sufficient resources and attention. Given that significant in-kind and financial resource contributions are being made by governments to facilitate SIBs, we raise the question regarding the opportunity cost of not investing those resources in strengthening civil service capacity to deliver and manage services in partnership with the non-profit sector through conventional procurement. Finally, we highlight that the framing effect of SIBs continues a longer-term and larger trend in mainstream economic analysis of social policy and economic development that entrenches a notion of poverty and social exclusion that emphasizes individual deficiencies while marginalizing large-scale universalist approaches that arguably address systematic inequities more effectively. We conclude by advocating for a recognition of poverty, social exclusion, and inequality as structural features of capitalism that will continue to grow in breadth and intensity if left unchecked by countermobilization. Our constructed policy alternatives then contribute to an agenda for that resistance with respect to SIBs, making the case for reforming and restricting the model as well as shifting emphasis to more universalist approaches.

A small number of case studies are distributed throughout the book, provided as illustrative examples of individual SIB projects. Chapter 8 also provides summary information on the first five DIBs. Those looking for additional case studies and specific project information may benefit from consulting the Government Outcomes Lab Project Database (GO Lab 2020), the Social Finance Impact Bond Global Database (Social Finance 2018), Gustafsson-Wright, Gardiner, and Putcha (2015), and the Pay for Success Project Data Tables (Nonprofit Finance Fund 2017).

PART ONE

The Characteristics and Emergence of the Social Impact Bond Model

1 The Structure of Social Impact Bonds

Introduction

Social Impact Bonds are logistically complex contractual arrangements with multiple stakeholders and institutional participants, straddling the boundary between public and private social service provision. This chapter examines in detail the structure of SIBs, and places them in relation to other social service contracting forms. We first introduce the SIB concept by reviewing several definitions that have been put forward by proponents and governments, then classify the defining features that are consistently referenced. After defining the various dimensions along which government and private actors can allocate activities and responsibilities, we set up a framework to compare SIBs to other forms of publicly funded social service delivery. We then examine in greater detail the features of the SIB model, and examine examples of social program interventions in various policy areas and their ability to generate value for money and cost savings to governments, integral components of the rhetoric proponents use to advance the model.

We show that, independent of the procurement method, a large proportion of social interventions in areas in which SIBs are being implemented – anti-recidivism, child welfare, early childhood development, housing and homelessness prevention, active labour market programming, and public health – when using high-quality experimental evidence, demonstrate high social returns on investment and often result in savings to government greater than the cost of the program intervention.

Defining SIBs

Given the complexity of the SIB model, there exists some discrepancy with respect to what exactly an SIB is, with different definitions in some cases including or emphasizing different elements. Table 1.1 summarizes twelve descriptions of SIBs put forward by SIB proponents and governments that have experience with the model. Six defining elements of the SIBs were found in more than one of the definitions reviewed, with four elements consistently found in all definitions reviewed.

First, all definitions highlight that SIBs include government-issued contracts. Three of the definitions note that an SIB can be issued by a non-government entity such as a foundation (Mulgan et al. 2011), a health insurance company (United States 2016), or, in the international aid context, a donor agency (Gustafsson-Wright, Gardiner, and Putcha 2015). In practice, the vast majority of operational SIBs in high-income countries have been issued by governments or public sector entities.[1] We take this as a defining element, and classify *Development Impact Bonds* (DIBs) – SIBs in developing countries issued by aid agencies, including foreign governments – as a distinct instrument.[2] We refer to SIBs and DIBs collectively as *Impact Bonds* (IBs). Second, all definitions emphasize that an SIB contract enables the delivery of a social or human service intervention or project, with the US Office of Social Innovation and Civic Participation also scoping in natural resources as an applicable field. Third, all the definitions emphasize that the contract payment

---

1 Dear et al. (2016) distinguish between entities issuing the contract and the outcomes payers, and claim that "non-governmental outcome payors are not new" (78), pointing to the Big Lottery Fund – established through an Act of Parliament and charged with disbursing the profits of the United Kingdom's national lottery system – and a public university in Israel as examples, but these are both arm's-length or quasi-public sector entities. The authors identify private health care organizations and insurance companies as potential outcome payors in future SIBs. As of January 2019, we identified seven cases of non-government outcome funders, in addition to the Israeli post-secondary institutions referenced. In four of these cases, government entities were also participating as outcome payors. In two of the remaining cases, health insurers, one public and one private, provided the outcome payments. In the latter case the project self-identified as a "Health Impact Bond" (ABN AMRO 2017). The final case was a US blood donation SIB, funded by a foundation in Delaware as a pilot project intended to demonstrate the model's feasibility to state legislators (Levine 2018).

2 These criteria are consistent with Gustafsson-Wright and Boggild-Jones (2017), for whom "a distinguishing feature of a SIB is that the outcome funder is a government entity," and Gustafsson-Wright et al. (2015, 4), who define a Development Impact Bond as an "SIB that is implemented in low- and middle-income countries where a donor agency or a foundation is the outcome funder as opposed to the government (although some combination of government with third party is also possible)." In the case where both aid agencies and local governments are outcomes funders, such as the Colombian Workforce Social Impact D, we classify the project as a DIB.

Table 1.1. Defining Elements of Social Impact Bonds

Source	Contract issued by gov't	Contract issued by gov't or other entity	Funding for social or human service, intervention, or project	Payment to contractor based on performance, results, or outcomes	Financed by external or private investment	Contractor delivers preventative services	Payment of bond from savings to gov't	Presence of intermediary	Presence of independent evaluator
Social Finance (Dear et al. 2016)	x	x	x	x	x				
Deloitte (2012)	x	x	x	x	x	x	x	x	
Deloitte and Mars (Cuifo and Jagelewski 2014)	x			x	x			x*	
Young Foundation (Mulgan et al. 2011)	x*	x	x	x	x*	x	x	x	x
Liebman (2011)	x	x	x	x	x			x	x
Gustafsson-Wright, Gardiner, and Putcha (2015)	x*	x	x	x	x		x*		
United States (2016)	x*	x	x*	x	x*			x*	x*
Harvard Kennedy School (2017)	x		x	x	x				x
United Kingdom (2013)	x		x	x	x				
Australia (New South Wales 2017)	x		x	x	x	x	x		
Canada (2015)	x		x	x	x				
Ontario (2017)	x		x	x	x		x		

*Indicates "may include" or conditional reference.

structure is based on outcomes, as opposed to the undertaking of some specific type of programming or output.

A fourth element present in all definitions is reliance on external investment to finance the project, with investors facing some repayment and return risk contingent on the outcomes achieved. Ten of the twelve definitions reviewed explicitly note that this is private (that is, non-government) investment, in one it is unclear (United States 2016), and in another "local authorities" are included as potential investors (Mulgan et al. 2011, 7), which would include entities owned or created by local or regional governments. Following Mulgan et al. (2011, 8), we term such SIBs *Public Sector Social Impact Bonds*, and define SIBs without the qualifier as those based on private finance, while recognizing that, in practice, some projects include both public and private investment that is paid back with a return.[3]

Two interrelated characteristics that appear explicitly in a minority of definitions are that services procured under an SIB are preventative in nature, such that they prevent negative social outcomes from occurring into the future, and that the payout of an SIB is financed by these future savings over the duration of the contract. These attributes are discussed in other sources as well, while not taken as defining features. A small number of definitions emphasize the presence of an intermediary organization and/or an independent evaluator, which we also deem common but not necessarily definitional features of the SIB model.

With respect to prevention, the Office of Social Innovation and Civic Participation (United States 2016) notes that SIBs "often target prevention of longer-term problems"; a study for Deloitte and MaRS states that "an SIB is often targeted to be preventative rather than remedial in terms of the government objective" (Cuifo and Jagelewski 2014, 6); and Gustafsson-Wright, Gardiner, and Putcha (2015, 36) find that "impact bonds prioritize prevention" and "all but one SIB included in

---

3 As of January 2019, only one SIB had been identified as solely financed by public sector investment: the Nottingham Futures workforce development SIB, where the local council carried the entire investment. Five other SIBs included both public and private sector investment, including two London-based housing/homelessness SIBs, with investment from the UK Department of Health Social Enterprise Investment Fund; the Energise Innovation SIB in Thames Valley, with investment from the Buckinghamshire County Council; the South Carolina healthy pregnancy project, with investment form Medicaid; the Epiqus' KOTO workforce development SIB in Finland, with investment from the European Investment Fund; and a workforce development SIB in rural France, with investment from the Caisse des Dépôts, a public sector lender (Social Finance 2018).

our study are explicitly structured around the prevention of some negative outcome such as returning to prison, remaining homeless, needing remedial education, or being unemployed. The one exception... could indirectly prevent negative outcomes." The UK Cabinet Office (United Kingdom 2016) notes that SIBs "fund early and preventative action on complex and expensive social problems," while Liebman and Feller (2014) similarly note that the SIB model funds programs that may preclude subsequent social program expenditures. Dear et al. (2016), for example, note that "Social Impact Bonds drive funding toward preventative programs and upstream interventions" (16) and that "many governments are interested because [an intervention] delivers direct and immediate savings or because it will reduce future spending by intervening earlier with populations who are likely to incur high costs in the future" (23). The delivery of preventative services based on the above, in addition to the three definitions that explicitly reference it, appears central to the SIB model, and we treat it as an essential characteristic.

Based on the above analysis, we adopt the following definition: *SIBs are procurement contracts, generally issued by government, that enable the delivery of some social service intervention, bundling together design, delivery, and project finance. The contract payment structure is based on the contractor's achieved outcomes, as opposed to the undertaking of some specific programming or service output, requiring a mutually agreed-upon evaluation methodology, which might involve an independent external evaluator and/or a control group to help isolate the impact of the intervention. Private investment is used to finance the project, with investors facing at least some repayment and return risk contingent on the outcomes achieved. SIBs deliver preventative social services such that the intervention prevents some negative social outcome from occurring.*[4]

When SIBs are based on preventative social interventions, they can preclude the need for some future remedial social service, thus generating future cost savings for the government or agency that otherwise would have been required to provide the service. In such cases, SIBs notionally can be, at least partially, paid out of the present value of these projected savings. We call an SIB that generates expected present value savings for its issuer that are greater than or equal to the maximum

---

4 Several widely referenced secondary sources – including Fraser et al. (2018b); Gustafsson-Wright, Gardiner, and Putcha (2015); Joy and Shields (2013); and Warner (2013) – have outlined the basic structure of an SIB, and although there is some variation in nomenclature, they are generally consistent with our definition here.

Figure 1.1. Typical Social Impact Bond Structure

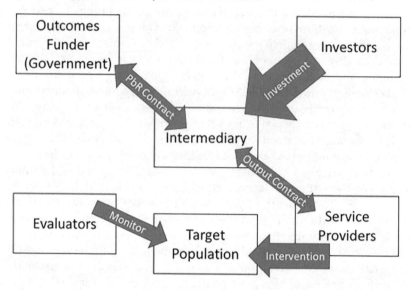

payout under the SIB a *self-funding Social Impact Bond*.[5] Finally, SIBs often include an independent coordinating entity generally termed the "intermediary" to be the lead private entity, sign the contract with government, raise capital from investors, and hire and manage service providers. Figure 1.1 summarizes the typical SIB structure, while Figure 1.2 summarizes a conventional social service procurement structure for comparison.

From a structural perspective, some key distinctions between the typical SIB and conventional procurement models that are illustrated here include: the substitution of a grant or service purchase payment structure from government with a pay-by-outcomes contract; the shift of private sector financial contributions from philanthropic donations to an investment expected to be paid back with a return; and the

---

5 If one of the main advantages of an SIB is its ability to self-finance, this could explain why public sector entities have been the outcomes funders under almost all SIBs. In practice, it is unlikely that any institutional entity other than a regional or national government will have sufficient resources and the incentive to do so. Since it is governments that are responsible – often legislatively bound – to provide some type of assistance to their most vulnerable populations, only governments genuinely can be perceived to have an impending liability of future costs associated with neglect and the foregoing of cost-effective preventative interventions.

Figure 1.2. Conventional Social Service Procurement Structure

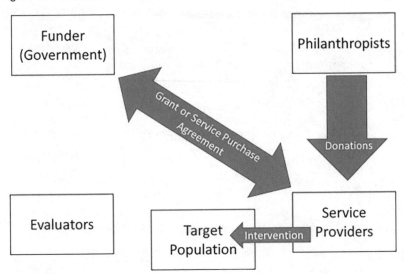

introduction of the intermediary and increased importance of the evaluator in the SIB model, which are not necessarily present or essential
in the conventional model. What is also clear at this point is that an
SIB is not a bond as the definition is generally applied, for at least two
reasons. First, an SIB does not pay out continuous regular payments
to investors at a fixed rate; the investment in an SIB is at risk, and is
more akin to venture capital or equity investments (Callanan, Law, and
Mendonca 2012; Loxley 2013; Shiller 2013; Warner 2015). Second, under
an SIB investors have been encouraged to administer the operations of
the venture, and often do so, whereas typical bond buyers generally are
passive, arm's-length investors (Sinclair et al. 2014).

Figure 1.3 outlines the steps in the redemption of an SIB. This payment process may occur once at the end of the contract or at predetermined points throughout the contract if payment is staggered and based
on cohort or intermediate outcomes, which has become more common
over time (Dear et al. 2016, 27). An evaluation takes place to determine
whether the targeted outcomes have been achieved. This information
is reported back to the government, which issues payment to the intermediary if the project has met its targets. The intermediary in turn pays
out the investors based on the agreed-upon terms. At this point the
government may desire to continue the social program intervention,
and may renew or issue another SIB contract, or contract directly for

Figure 1.3. The Social Impact Bond Outcome Payment Process

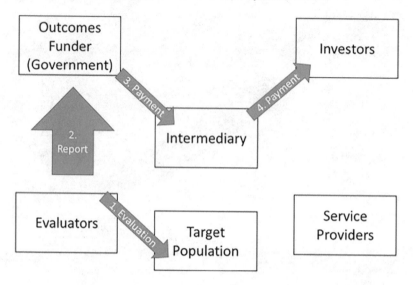

the services using conventional procurement or a government-financed pay-by-results contract (Dear et al. 2016, 80–1).

The above depictions of what a SIB is and how it operates are a stylized or idealized version of how proponents present the concept at an abstract level. In practice, however, projects bearing the SIB label sometimes deviate from these strict criteria. Carter (2020) identifies several dimensions along which SIBs might deviate, including reliance on loan capital or service provider investment, payment based on outputs and milestones as opposed to outcomes, and less stringent evaluation. We explore these issues in more detail in Chapters 2 and 3.

Public versus Private Dimensions in Social Service Provision

SIBs represent a unique approach to social program delivery involving partnerships that crisscross the public-private distinction along numerous dimensions. SIBs are novel and of interest in part due to the way in which they challenge traditional conceptions of the activities that should be undertaken in pubic versus private spheres. Prior to moving deeper into a descriptive analysis of SIBs and their classification and comparing them to other forms of social service delivery, we first define what we mean by "public" versus "private," what we mean by "social" when we are discussing social programs/services and social expenditure, and distinguish between *publicly funded, publicly financed, publicly delivered*, and *publicly controlled* when classifying social service provision.

Definitional issues with respect to the public-private distinction among organizations has been subject to debate and analysis from various entry points and conceptual perspectives, but generally accepted factors of central relevance when defining an organization as public or private include ownership and funding (Perry and Rainey 1988). We apply a similar long-standing definitional approach to social programs (see, for example, Burchardt 1997; Burchardt, Hills, and Propper 1999) and more recently to SIBs (Sinclair et al. 2014), while adding a distinction between how social programs are funded and how they finance expenditures during their lifespan.[6]

We adopt the Organisation for Economic Co-operation and Development's (OECD's) definition of public versus private social expenditure and its categorization of social services as our starting point. This allows us not only to link our analysis to an internationally recognized standard, but also to make use later of the OECD Social Expenditure Database (SOCX) to inform our analysis regarding the approximate universe of relevant public services that theoretically could be subject to SIB-type administration in OECD countries. We then expand on this definition by exploring several other dimensions of the public versus private classification.

Social Expenditure, Benefits, and Programs/Services

The OECD defines social expenditure as "benefits to, and financial contributions targeted at, households and individuals in order to provide support during circumstances which adversely affect their welfare, provided that the provision of the benefits and financial contributions constitutes neither a direct payment for a particular good or service nor an individual contract or transfer ... only benefits provided by institutions are included" (Adema, Fron, and Ladaique 2011, 90). These benefits include "cash benefits (e.g., pensions, income support during maternity leave and social assistance payments), social services (e.g., childcare, care for the elderly and disabled) and tax breaks with a social purpose

---

6 Sinclair et al. (2014) focus on adding a motivational dimension – for-profit versus public service – to a longer-standing three-dimensional classification framework based on finance, delivery, and client/user choice. We address the motivational dimension in Chapter 5.

(e.g., tax expenditures towards families with children, or favorable tax treatment of contributions to private health plans)" (90). *Social services* therefore are considered a subset of a larger definitional concept of *social benefits*. For spending to be consider "social," the programs need "to be intended to address one or more social purposes" and to entail "inter-personal redistribution" or "compulsory participation" (90). The SOCX classifies social benefits in nine categories: "Old-age, Survivors, Incapacity-related benefits, Health, Family, Active labour market policies, Unemployment, Housing, and Other social policy areas," with the "other" category including expenditures such as social assistance and food subsidies, and all categories being subdivided into "cash" and "in-kind" expenditures (90, 96). The OECD tracks education expenditure in a separate database (89, 123).

Public versus Private Funding/Expenditure

Social expenditures are considered "public" when the "financial flows [are] controlled by General Government" (Adema, Fron, and Ladaique 2011, 93); otherwise the expenditure is considered "private," with private social expenditures further classified as either "compulsory" such that they are "stipulated by legislation" or "voluntary" (93–4). Social public expenditures, according to the OECD definition, are "public" when the revenue and expenditure streams used to fund the program are controlled by government, and therefore can be considered *publicly funded*.

Public versus Private Delivery and Management

Within this category of publicly funded social expenditures, variations on delivery structure alter the degree to which private organizations are involved in service provision. Governments may deliver the services directly by hiring staff as government employees and using government-owned assets to deliver the services directly. Under this model, services can be considered to be *publicly funded* and *delivered*. Examples of this direct delivery model, at least at one point in time, include public health care delivery in countries such as Norway, Sweden, Denmark, and Finland (Blanchette and Tolley 2001), and parts of the Job Corps youth training program in the United States (Leaman 1989, 91–2).

Governments also may contract out social service delivery to regulated or unregulated private organizations, either non-profit or for-profit, as an alternative or parallel delivery method to direct delivery.[7] Conventional government procurement in this area is characterized by a direct contractual relationship with service providers, established through partnership, negotiation, or a competitive tendering process (Dehoog 1990), with human services having a long tradition of being contracted out (Martin 2007). In the stylized *conventional procurement model*, government pays the service provider to deliver a particular program or undertake a task that is of primary interest to the government through a service purchase agreement.[8]

A distinction can also be made between the privatization of service delivery through contracting out and the extent to which management decisions and program design are also delegated to private sector actors. For example, under conventional procurement through service purchase agreements, the scope of service activities undertaken is generally specified by the government, whereas in SIBs this is generally delegated to the private sector intermediary.

Public versus Private Financing

Although the service provider might have some existing in-house capital assets and/or use shorter-term bank financing to deal with in-year liquidity constraints, the conventional model is primarily based on public financing, where the government pays the services provider in regular instalments as the work is completed. Publicly controlled and delivered social service models generally are *publicly financed*, such that government funds these services upfront and directly through its standard appropriations and budget processes, supported if necessary by the issuance of state-backed government bonds to support required borrowing.[9]

Long-term *private financing* of social service delivery procured by government contract is a recent development, and is one of the key

---

7 Leaman (1989, 56) notes that many examples of direct government delivery are simultaneously used alongside indirect delivery through contracting with third-party agencies.

8 This is distinct from a grant, where government may fund an organization to advance its mission, but does not lead in specifying the outputs or outcomes of the activity (Pettijohn 2013a). For more information on service purchase models, see van Slyke (2003, n1).

9 See Crain and Miller (1990) for a more detailed description of the federal and state government budget process in the United States.

distinguishing features of SIBs.[10] In this model, private equity or borrowing tied directly to the project being undertaken is mobilized, with, in some cases, repayment terms contingent on certain project-related outcomes.[11]

Public versus Private Ownership of Assets

One additional important distinction with respect to the public versus private divide in the government service delivery context is in regard to control and ownership of the physical assets and intellectual property generated over the duration of the contract. Control and ownership may be aligned with the delivery model, whereby public delivery leads to public ownership and private delivery leads to private ownership, but this might not be the case. In the public-private partnership model of infrastructure delivery, for example, the physical infrastructure asset is often owned by the private sector for the duration of the contract, then transferred back to the public sector at the contract's end. A procurement contract ideally explicitly specifies who has the rights to the assets developed and accumulated throughout the contract. Over and above how formal ownership rights are specified or determined, decisions regarding public versus private delivery will impact the distribution of knowledge between the public and private spheres and their institutional capacity – accumulated through the performance of duties – to deliver social services effectively, which in turn can have implications for the sustainability and accessibility of that knowledge into the future.

Public versus Private Risk

A final distinction with respect to the public-private divide is the allocation of risk between sectors. More recent innovations in payment structures have generated models where contractors are paid based on outcomes as opposed to activities undertaken, increasing payment variability. In economics, contract theory frames this transfer of risk as

---

10 Note that this definition of private finance is different than that used by Hodge (2000), who refers to "charging for previously nonpriced goods and services" (15, table 2.1).

11 Picot et al. (2016), in the public infrastructure context, refer to public financing as "pay as you go" or "cash flow" financing, and private financing as capital market financing (10), and note that the choice between the two models has implications for the intergenerational cost burden of the project (11).

increasing the incentive to undertake greater effort to achieve a higher quality of work, with contracts based primarily on cost reimbursement termed *low powered*, and those based more heavily on outcomes termed *high powered*. This shift of risk to contractors can be considered to be happening parallel to, but distinct from, the "privatization of risk" discussed by authors such as Hacker (2004), where collectivist social insurance programs are being replaced by a regime that places a greater burden of adverse circumstances on individuals and markets.

Based on these public-private distinctions, Table 1.2 summarizes the various public-private dimensions of SIBs and other sample social service delivery models. For each model, the table states whether responsibility for delivery, design/management, financing, outcome risk, and funding fall to the private or the public sector. Included in the table are the publicly funded and delivered and conventional procurement models defined above, as well as some variations on the SIB model, including the pay-by-results contract, the Public Sector Social Impact Bond, and the Human Capital Performance Bond.

As can be seen, SIBs bring publicly funded social service delivery one step closer to fully privatized delivery, with the remaining distinction being that, in an SIB, the government is still the end funder of the service, whereas a fully privatized service would rely on consumer or philanthropic revenues.

Public versus Private Selection by User

Users of social services may or may not have discretion over the service provider or the amount they utilize when seeking support. Burchardt, Hills, and Propper (1999, 9), for example, use a three-dimensional classification framework based on user choice regarding payment and consumption of the service that includes such a distinction. Although the issue of choice to fund is already captured in the OECD definition of voluntary versus compulsory private expenditures, consumption is not. The authors' framework then generates eight categories of classification, with, for example, the "pure public" (9) labelled as publicly funded, delivered, and determined. It is within their framework that, for example, voucher programs for schools and patient choice of physician become important for classification purposes, in addition to whether the providers are themselves publicly funded or operated.

While we briefly address the issue of user choice in later chapters, we abstract from this issue at this point of our analysis, partially for parsimony and partially since this dimension does not feature as a definitional feature of any of the instruments reviewed. Any of the reviewed

Table 1.2. Public-Private Dimensions of Social Service Delivery Models

Delivery Model	Private Sector Delivery of Service/ Operations?	Private Project Management/ Design?	Private Financing? (Source)	Payment Based on Outcomes? (Privatization of Risk)	Reliance Primarily on Private Funding? (Primary source of Funding)
Public delivery	No	No	No (gov't operating budget)	No	No (gov't operating budget)
Conventional input- or output-based contracting	Yes	No	No (gov't operating budget)	No	No (gov't operating budget)
Pay by results[a]	Yes	No	No (gov't operating budget)	Yes (service provider)	No (gov't operating budget)
Human Capital Performance Bond[b]	Yes	No	No (gov't-backed and -issued bonds)	Yes (service provider)	No (gov't operating budget or savings from prevention)
Public Sector Social Impact Bond[c]	Undetermined	No (lower-level gov't entity)	No (gov't operating budget or other public financing)	Possibly (service provider)	No (gov't operating budget or savings from prevention)
Social Impact Bond	Yes	Yes (intermediary or service provider)	Yes (private venture capital investment)	Yes (investor; in some cases service providers)	Generally no, only if project fails to meet targets (gov't operating budget or savings from prevention)
Fully privatized social service	Yes	Yes (service provider)	Yes (equity investment or loans)	Yes (investor)	Yes (consumer or philanthropic revenues)

a Ragin and Paladjain (2013) and Stid (2013) discuss SIBs in relation to the pay-by-results contracting structure. Some critical observers are sceptical of the benefit arising from the involvement of the financial sector in the delivery of social services, yet appear sympathetic to tying payment to outcomes. Stid (2013), for example, sees potential in the pay-by-results model, with a direct relationship between government, well-financed charitable foundations, and service providers as an alternative to the standard SIB model. This maintains results-based payments within the non-profit sector, allowing any surplus to be redeployed for further social purposes. Pauly and Swanson (2017) also note the extent to which the non-profit sector is involved in the issuance of bonds directly to finance its activities, a fact not generally acknowledged in the SIB proponent literature.

b Human Capital Performance Bonds are a variation on the SIB model, but do not use an intermediary or private venture capital–type financing. Instead funds for the projects are raised through a more traditional government bond issue, with the bonds backed by the state, generating a lower cost of borrowing. The bonds are repaid through the savings linked back to the programming, as under an SIB, but it is the service providers who bear responsibility for meeting outcomes in exchange for the opportunity to reap the financial rewards of success, as opposed to external private financiers, who assume risk in the SIB model. See Rothschild (2013) for additional information.

c Mulgan et al. (2011, 8) put forward a concept they call "Public sector Social Impact Bonds" that involves the government contractee paying a lower level of government or a public agency based on outcomes, which in turn finances service delivery through conventional public financing. It is the lower-level government or public agency that then acts as the intermediary.

delivery models listed in Table 1.2 could involve little or significant user choice. For example, under public provision a user might be able to access multiple delivery units or only a single provider. Similarly, fully privatized social service provision might involve multiple providers or the consumer may face a monopoly. Given their small localized scale, SIBs to date have not in practice offered user choice, but this is not due to any intrinsic feature of the model. SIBs have been criticized, however, for excluding and marginalizing users who, in practice, have no role or input into the projects (Warner 2013). This speaks to a weakness in the public-private framing, which sidesteps important distinctions in ownership and decision-making structures of non-government enterprises, with community-based non-profits and cooperative social enterprises facilitating greater democratic representation.[12]

Defining Features of SIBs

SIBs are procurement contracts issued by a government, foundation, or other entity that enable the delivery of some social service intervention. Theoretically any person, corporate or individual, with sufficient resources and desire to see some measurable social outcome for a target population could issue an SIB. In practice, however, restricting temporarily our scope to the developed world, outcome payments under SIBs to date have been undertaken almost exclusively by government or broader public sector entities, falling within the realm of our definition of *social public expenditures*, at least in the case where the bond is paid out,[13] and for the most part are *in-kind* expenditures delivering *social services*.

Several essential and distinctive features of SIBs differentiate the model from conventional publicly controlled and financed government procurement contracts for social service delivery:

- the bundling and contracting out of design, delivery, and project finance into a single contract;
- an outcome-based contract payment structure;
- external multiyear financing of publicly funded social service operations by at-risk for-profit capital; and
- a focus on the delivery of preventative services.

---

12 See Appendix E for further discussion of social enterprise.
13 Social expenditure undertaken under an SIB that was unsuccessful in meeting its targets and in turn did not succeed in triggering payment could be considered private social expenditures, although it is unclear at this point how or if these expenditures would be captured in the SOCX statistics.

In addition, while not universal to all SIBs, other common and notable features of many SIBs projects include:

- the potential to fund SIB outcome payments out of future cost savings to government;
- the presence of an intermediary entity between government and service delivery agents; and
- the presence of an external evaluator and/or randomized control group–based evaluation methods.

We discuss each of these two sets of features briefly below.

Bundled and Contracted-Out Project Design, Delivery, and Finance

The bundling and contracting out of social program design, finance, and operations into a single outsourced contract between government and a private sector–led consortium is a defining feature of an SIB.[14] To the extent that a lead external (private/non-government) agent, either a service provider or an intermediary, takes on the coordinating and management role to determine the scope, type, and arrangement of the intervention, the SIB then involves privatizing some design and management activity that would have been undertaken by the state in conventional social service delivery (Whitfield 2015, 23). Similarly, with the introduction of private financing, the SIB model brings contracting out a step closer to a fully privatized service delivery model.

This bundling and contracting out is similar to the contracting relationship used in a public-private partnership (PPP) model of infrastructure delivery, where bundled contracts are issued for the design, construction, maintenance, and/or delivery of infrastructure-based public services (Gustafsson-Wright, Gardiner, and Putcha 2015; Loxley 2013; Warner 2013). PPPs also have a history of support, promotion,

---

14 In one exceptional case, the Swedish SKL Mission Mental Health - Health Navigator SIB, all service provision was undertaken by a municipal public sector organization generally funded by the national government, with outcome payments committed by municipalities (Backström 2016). Like other SIBs, the project was financed by private investors. Other SIB projects have included public sector partners in private sector–led consortia; for example, public schools have been service delivery agents in several SIBs, including the Utah High Quality Preschool Program, the Chicago Child Parent Centre pay-for-success project, and the Portuguese Junior Code Academy SIB (Social Finance 2018).

and capacity development through arm's-length government and third-party entities, generating what Whiteside (2013, 96) has termed "enabling fields," similar to the SIB case.

PPPs are claimed to save governments money by imposing a life-cycle cost perspective on capital asset procurement and by better aligning incentives while transferring risk from government to the private sector. Based on this rationale, PPP infrastructure projects continue to proliferate, but they are also controversial due to the privatization of public sector assets, high investor profits, reduction in job quality, and lack of evidence of cost reduction or risk transfer of any substance (Loxley 2010; Whitfield 2017). The shared features and applicable experience with and theoretical insights from the PPP model are explored in more detail in Chapter 4.

Payment Structure Based on Outcomes

SIBs rely on sharp distinctions between the inputs, outputs, and outcomes of a social service intervention, as outlined in Morse (2015) and United Kingdom (2014b). Inputs refer to the resources used to implement the intervention, and can include physical assets, paid and unpaid human resources, and knowledge-generated research and development activities. These inputs are combined in service delivery processes, based on existing service production technology, that produce specific service outputs and include competing models and combinations of possible interventions. Outputs include, for example, the number of clients, households, or communities receiving an intervention or reductions in wait times for service, and in general produce measures of specific processes undertaken and completed within a specified timeframe. These outputs are anticipated to generate improved outcomes for stakeholders participating in the interventions, such as a reduction in incidents of recidivism, formerly at-risk children living safely with their family, or sustainable employment for previously unemployed or underemployed workers.

In contrast to outputs, outcomes are of inherent value to the individuals and households served and often to broader society in that they improve the quality of life. They are the targeted objectives of the program that the intervention feasibly can achieve. These outcomes, in turn, might lead to desirable, long-term, widespread societal impacts, but they would require significant scale to translate into improvements in aggregate statistics, such as lower crime rates, improved educational attainment, fewer households living in

Figure 1.4. Inputs, Outputs, and Outcomes

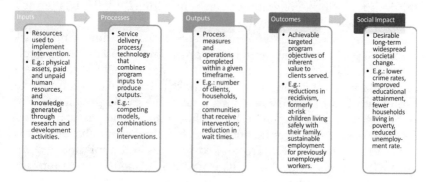

Inputs	Processes	Outputs	Outcomes	Social Impact
• Resources used to implement intervention. • E.g.: physical assets, paid and unpaid human resources, and knowledge generated through research and development activities.	• Service delivery process/ technology that combines program inputs to produce outputs. • E.g.: competing models, combinations of interventions.	• Process measures and operations completed within a given timeframe. • E.g.: number of clients, households, or communities that receive intervention; reduction in wait times.	• Achievable targeted program objectives of inherent value to clients served. • E.g.: reductions in recidivism, formerly at-risk children living safely with their family, sustainable employment for previously unemployed workers.	• Desirable long-term widespread societal change. • E.g.: lower crime rates, improved educational attainment, fewer households living in poverty, reduced unemploy-ment rate.

Source: Adapted from Morse (2015) and United Kingdom (2014b).

poverty, or reduced unemployment.[15] Figure 1.4 summarizes these distinctions.

An SIB contract remunerates a consortium through either a pay-by-results (PbR) or pay-for-success (PfS) structure, based on performance-based contracting (PbC), such that payment to the consortium is based on clearly articulated targeted objectives specified in terms of out-comes. In high-powered incentive versions of PbR, if the consortium does not meet the agreed-upon objectives, the government is under no obligation to pay, or payments are significantly reduced, while lower-powered incentive versions might implement a more tiered or graduated payment structure based on a range of achieved outcomes. Paying only for results is an extreme example of "best to best" bud-get structures, one of the incentive-based tools used in target- and performance-based governance systems; others include reputational or "naming and shaming" approaches, outcome-based management compensation, and organizational independence (Bevan and Hood 2006, 519).

The Partnership for Public Procurement (2012), created by two inter-national procurement professional associations, the Chartered Institute

---

15 Heckman, Heinrich, and Smith (2011b, 40) emphasize an alternative distinction between outcomes and impacts, where outcomes measure the achievement of a benchmark or the level of achievement, while impacts attempt to measure the difference the intervention made relative to where the client would have been without the intervention. Measuring impact is difficult and can be expensive, and comes with a significant time lag.

of Procurement & Supply and the Institute for Public Procurement, defines PbC as "a results-oriented contracting method that focuses on the outputs, quality, or outcomes that may tie at least a portion of a contractor's payment, contract extensions, or contract renewals to the achievement of specific, measurable performance standards and requirements, [...and] may include both monetary and non-monetary incentives and disincentives" (1). In government contracting, the duties of the contractor are specified in either "design" or "performance specifications," with PbC relying extensively if not exclusively on the latter, providing greater discretion in how the objectives are operationalized, "allowing for innovation" (Martin 2015, 65).

The implementation of PbC and PbR contracts has been far from uniform, with much variation with respect to the specific metrics and incentives used (Palameta, Myers, and Conte 2013). The academic and professional literature is also not consistent in its nomenclature with respect to defining PbR, in some cases using the term to refer to contracts based both on outputs and outcomes, particularly in the health care field.[16] In this book, we follow the UK Comptroller and Auditor General (Morse 2015, 11) and reserve PbR to refer to contracts based on outcomes, which appears consistent with the evolution of usage of the term more recently. We use PbR, outcomes-based contracting, and PfS, the more common term in the United States, interchangeably, and use PbC to refer to the larger universe of contracts based on realized quality, outputs, and/or outcomes. This definitional structure is summarized in Figure 1.5.

In the United States since the modern emergence of large-scale social service procurement in the 1960s, there has been a shift from design-based criteria to output specification and, in the 1990s, to PbC (Martin 2007), with the latter now identified as the standard or preferred form of contracting by US government agencies – half of federal government procurement uses this model (Martin 2015). US active labour market programs have used incentive contracts with providers since the 1990s, with the Job Training Partnership Act allocating 6 per cent of its funding to states for incentive bonuses to training providers, and its successor, the Workforce Investment Act, instituting bonuses and penalties to states based on performance outcomes (Courty et al. 2011, 24). More recent expansion

---

16 See, for example, Mason and Goddard (2009, 3), and the discussion in Lagarde et al. (2013, 7).

Figure 1.5. Distinguishing PbC, PbR/PfS, and SIBs

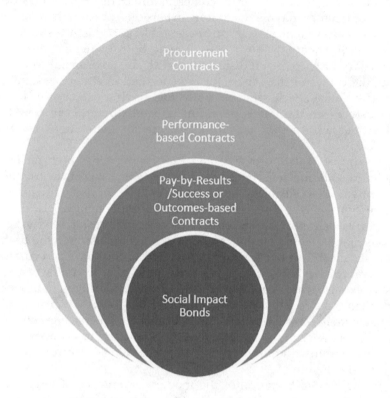

of incentive-based schemes has led to the use of "performance standards systems and bonuses" in "the Supplemental Nutrition Assistance Program ... and welfare-to-work programs, [other] employment and training programs [including adult education; see Palameta, Myers, and Conte (2013)], public school accountability systems under No Child Left Behind, child welfare agencies and child support enforcement programs, Medicaid and SCHIP programs, and other social programs" (Heckman, Heinrich, and Smith 2011d, 2). PbR has also been used in the defence industry (Ng, Maull, and Yip 2009).

In the US health care sector, PbC has proceeded under the guise of "value-based payments" (VbPs) and "accountable care organizations"

(ACOs),[17] with President Barack Obama's last secretary of health and social services prioritizing implementation within Medicaid and Medicare programs, with the objective of having "30% of Medicare payments tied to quality or value through alternative payment models by the end of 2016, and 50% of payments by the end of 2018" (Burwell 2015, 897).[18] The growth of VbPs and ACOs in the United States has been credited to the Patient Protection and Affordable Care Act, which increased electronic patient record collection requirements, enlarging the database on which to set outcomes-based payments, and launched the Medicare Shared Savings Program, which "establishes financial incentives for … ACOs to provide coordinated, well integrated care" (Delbanco et al. 2011, vi). There has also been significant growth of outcomes-based finance at the state level, with PbR used in areas such as active labour market programs, services to persons with disabilities, and adoption (van Slyke 2006, 160). In 2010, nearly 90 per cent of social service non-profits were obligated to report to funding agencies the results, outcomes, and impact of their programs and services, and "17 percent had performance-based payments" (Pauly and Swanson 2014, 8).

In the United Kingdom, PbC initially was implemented on a widespread basis in health care through the Quality and Outcomes Framework, launched in 2004, where pay-by-results-type provisions were integrated into compensation agreements with physicians in the National Health Service (Greene and Nash 2009). It has since been implemented intensively in health care (Epstein, Lee, and Hamel 2004), including mental health (Mason and Goddard 2009), active labour markets programming, and criminal justice (Fox and Albertson 2011; Warner 2013), as well as in family services, welfare, and international aid projects (Morse 2015). PbC is not a recent phenomenon in the United

---

17 VbP models are "defined as financial incentives that aim to improve clinical quality and outcomes for patients, while simultaneously containing (or better yet) reducing health care costs" and "seek to change the behavior of individual providers and provider organizations by aligning payment with value" (Conrad et al. 2015, 2). An ACO is a "provider-led organization whose mission is to manage the full continuum of care and be accountable for the overall costs and quality of care for a defined population" (Rittenhouse, Shortell, and Fisher 2009, 2302), and "emphasizes the alignment of incentives and accountability for providers across the continuum of care" (2301). See Delbanco et al. (2011) for discussion of ACOs focused on shared-risk models, where providers bear some payment risk based on outcomes.

18 The use of the terms "payment by results" and "value-based payments" in the health care field is not always restricted to payments based on outcomes, but has also been applied to some output-based compensation schemes; see Bhattacharyya et al. (2009); Delbanco et al. (2011); and Morse (2015, 11).

Kingdom, going as far back as 2003 in the health care field (Fox and Albertson 2011) and covering the majority of national health services by 2005 (United Kingdom 2005). The implementation in "welfare-to-work" schemes took place in the 2000s, with 60 per cent of payments based on outcomes (Morse 2015, 4). PbR contracts have also become increasingly common in UK management advisory services to government focused on austerity and budget cuts, with payments to management consultants based on a percentage of the savings achieved (Peretti 2016). Recent growth in PbR contracting has been traced back to cabinet direction in the 2011 Open Public Services White Paper, which encouraged their use (Sinclair et al. 2014). As of 2015 the UK government's PbR portfolio included at least fifty-two projects worth £15 billion (Morse 2015).

Australia and the Netherlands have also embraced PbC with outcomes-based contract components, with both countries having used the model for active labour market programming as far back as 1998 and 2002, respectively (Finn 2008).

It is clear that contracts based on outcomes as opposed to simple fee-for-service predate the emergence of SIB-financed projects. Countries that were early adopters of PbR have been the early adopters of SIBs. Over the past thirty years, in countries that have led in SIB implementation, we have seen the emergence of PbC, with movement from contracts with design specifications to contracts based on outputs, followed by an increasing emphasis on contracting based on outcomes, with payments linked to the degree of success with respect to contracted objectives. SIBs, therefore, are only one of the latest iterations of government procurement contracting structures with a stated goal of improving the value government receives for its expenditures flowing to third-party agencies through PbC (Rothschild 2013, 104; Stid 2013, 13).

Project Services Financed by External, For-Profit, At-Risk Capital

The third defining feature of SIBs – the use of multiyear venture capital–type financing to cover project operating expenses for the duration of the project – distinguishes them from other outcomes-based contracting models, where the service provider itself takes on the risk of non-payment. The inclusion of "bond" in Social Impact Bond is somewhat misleading, as there are generally no ongoing regular payments from government to investors during the span of the contract. Rather, SIBs are closer to a venture capital investment or an equity investment than to a traditional bond, with the payment of principal and return semi-periodically throughout the contract or as a lump sum at the end of the contract, but only if agreed-upon objective thresholds are met (Loxley 2013; McHugh et al. 2013; Rothschild 2013, 107).

SIBs have attracted investment directly or through pooled funds primarily from philanthropic charitable foundations, mainstream financial corporations, and wealthy individuals. Pension funds and government entities, to a lesser degree, have also invested in SIBs (Gustafsson-Wright, Gardiner, and Putcha 2015, 58–129).[19] For private investors, SIBs provide an opportunity to receive a financial return while also generating a non-monetary benefit in the form of perceived corporate social responsibility. For charitable foundations, SIBs may allow endowments to be invested in a manner that more closely aligns with their mission relative to traditional investment opportunities. Foundation participation may also signal that a foundation is adopting new trends in philanthropy associated with social entrepreneurship and social finance, to advance its goals and maintain its relevance and attractiveness to donors.[20] We examine the composition and motivations of SIB stakeholders in greater detail in Chapters 5 and 6.

The provision of financial support by philanthropic foundations, wealthy individuals, and corporations for social service interventions is not a new development, and is clearly not limited to SIBs. Earlier models of private sector financial support could include philanthropic investments with repayment obligations, sometimes termed "program-related investment" (PRI; Gustafsson-Wright, Gardiner, and Putcha 2015, 37). One main difference between PRI and SIBs is the former's venture capital–type investment with conditional repayment structure, instead of donations or grants, which are non-repayable, or loans, which must be repaid regardless of outcomes (Pauly and Swanson 2017). With SIBs, this has resulted in investment in "human capital" through social services instead of the more traditional PRI physical assets such as housing and economic development projects (Gustafsson-Wright, Gardiner, and Putcha 2015, 37). This makes SIBs a relatively riskier asset class than PRIs, as they are not backed up by any physical assest that could serve as collateral.

---

19 We were able to identify one SIB project to date has been fully funded by public sector investors: the Nottingham Futures SIB, funded by Nottingham City Council. We identified six other projects that were partially financed by public sources: the London Street Impact, Thames Reach, Energise Innovation in Thames Valley, the South Carolina Nurse Family Partnership, Epiqus' KOTO, and the rural French workforce development SIB projects.

20 The concepts of social finance and social entrepreneurship are discussed further in Appendix E.

SIBs are also structurally riskier for investors than a conventional PbR model. The venture capital model in SIBs generally shifts the PbR mechanism from the service provider to the investor, a key departure from previous PbR contract structures. This has been claimed to allow SIBs to achieve a greater scale, remove operational risk from individual service providers, and enable participation from service providers who could not individually finance upfront costs under conventional payment-by-results schemes (Fox and Morris 2019; United States 2016; Stid 2013).[21] In practice, however, some service providers are compensated partially based on results.[22]

The participation of for-profit, at-risk private finance in the delivery of public services with the expectation of a financial return is not a new concept, with direct private investment in public infrastructure having a long track record going back at least to the development of the first railway systems and electrical utilities (Cassis 2016), if not as far back as Ancient Greece (Goldsmith 2014, 11).[23] The railway and electrical systems, however, were not fully publicly funded enterprises, and it was not until the development of the PPP model of infrastructure delivery that the modern, multiyear private financing for publicly funded and procured service delivery emerged. The promotion of private financing of public infrastructure is also being advanced more broadly through calls for a national infrastructure bank in Canada (Sanger 2017) and in

---

21 Many service delivery agents in the social services sector are incorporated as non-share capital or non-profit organizations, which might affect their ability to borrow based on perceived risk and limited means of collateral security. As Pauly and Swanson (2017) note, however, non-profits still do engage in borrowing, and do in some cases issue bonds directly. Fox and Albertson (2018, 21) note how outcome-based commissioning in the United Kingdom has been used to diversify and attract new service providers, whereas in the United States it is viewed as exclusionary due to the large scale required.

22 Pauly and Swanson (2017) identify fourteen SIBs launched prior to January 2018 in which eighteen service providers or intermediaries are investors and/or are being compensated partially based on results. We identified an additional eleven: the Buzinessclub Rotterdam SIB; the Caritas Fokus Bern Swiss refugee employment SIB; the Age UK Worcestershire Health Reconnections SIB; the Santa Clara Project Welcome Home PfS project; the South Carolina Nurse Family Partnership PfS project; the ASCO ON TRACC New South Wales antirecidivism SIB; the Enschede Werken in Duitsland SIB; the APM Workcare Auckland SIB; the Greater Manchester Homes Partnership SIB; the Ventura County Project to Support Reentry PfS project; and the Kent County Strong Beginnings Pay for Success (Social Finance 2018; Third Sector Capital Partners 2014; Tomkinson 2014).

23 See Wettenhall's (2005) review of the long history of the private provision of publicly funded goods spanning a variety of sectors, including military, trade, treasury services, agriculture, health, education, and infrastructure.

the United States by President Donald Trump's commitment to support private infrastructure investment through generous tax credits (Ross and Navarro 2016, 4).

Within the realm of social programs specifically, for-profit, at-risk private finance of social services has extended precedent – in the international aid context, in particular. The microcredit and microfinance movements, based on the pioneering work of Muhammad Yunis and the Grameen Bank, which aim to reduce poverty through the facilitation of small-scale entrepreneurship and business development, are well-known examples in operation for over three decades (Rahman 1999). Through the more recent but broader movements of social finance and social investment, the mobilization of for-profit, at-risk capital for social good has expanded in both advanced economies and developing countries, although these efforts until recently have operated in parallel to, not through, state procurement and delivery of social services.

Therefore, although private, multiyear, for-profit, at-risk capital has been mobilized and invested in non-government social-purposed initiatives as well as in public sector infrastructure assets, and privately sourced donations have long supported public social service delivery, SIBs are a convergence point of these distinct and evolving trends. SIBs appear to represent the first replicable and distinguishable widespread model for private, multiyear financing of publicly funded social service operations, as opposed to just physical infrastructure, by for-profit, at-risk capital.

Delivery of Preventative Social Services

A key characteristic of services procured under an SIB is that they are preventative in nature (Mulgan et al. 2011; see also Table 1.1), such that their undertaking would prevent some undesirable social outcome from continuing or occurring. Sectors that have been commonly targeted in SIB projects include antirecidivism programming, child welfare, early childhood development, active labour market interventions, housing and homelessness prevention, and disease prevention. There is a large body of literature examining the effectiveness of prevention-focused social program interventions. For illustrative purposes and as a brief introduction to the types of interventions undertaken in SIBs, Appendix A provides examples of research into the ability of social interventions to alter outcomes based on the areas of social interventions with the largest number of SIBs to date, by reviewing select meta-analytical and/or high-quality experimental studies in each area. As of January 2018, the six most common social policy areas for SIB use were criminal justice, early years and education, child and family, housing and homelessness, workforce development, and health (Social Finance 2018). These meta-analytical studies find a track record of prevention-focused interventions improving social outcomes for target populations in social policy areas where SIBs are being implemented.

Financed by Future Savings to Government

Through preventing or discontinuing an undesirable social outcome, a successful social program intervention might preclude the need for some future government expenditures arising from formal legal obligations or informal expectations based on precedent. For example, successful reintegration services for those exiting prison can reduce future expenditure obligations on law enforcement, the judiciary, and prison system (Fox and Albertson 2011; Lipsey and Cullen 2007; Warren 2007). In the field of child welfare services, investments in income supports, family violence prevention, early social worker intervention, and family reunification can reduce future expenditure requirements associated with child maltreatment and/or placing and maintaining children in the custody of the state. Interventions in improved early childhood development opportunities can lead to reduced expenditure requirements on special education services (Blau and Currie 2004, 42) and long-term reductions in social welfare and criminal justice expenditures (Heckman 2006).

Under what we have termed a *self-funding SIB*, governments calculate the costs of a social problem manifested in an identified population, and offer to pay up to that amount to a private sector consortium that contracts to prevent the realization of those costs through an intervention. Under this model, the SIB is restricted to projects that generate cost savings to government, in present-value terms, over and above the initial private sector investment and the return on the SIB. As seen in Table 1.1, some proponent definitions of SIBs explicitly emphasize this ability of government to pay directly for the SIB based on the cost savings achieved – this tending to be the case for earlier definitions of SIBs. In recent years some proponents have attempted to de-emphasize the centrality of savings generation to the model (Carter et al. 2018).[24] Governments have followed suit, with more recent SIB announcements avoiding reference to cost savings as an objective (see, for example, Colorado 2018; Devon County Council 2018; Manitoba

---

24 See, for example, Dear et al. (2016, 22) and Barclay and Mak (2011, 7–9).

Figure 1.6. Net Expected Savings of an SIB-Funded Intervention

2019; Queensland 2017; Sacred Heart Mission 2018; Vlaams minister van Werk 2018).

Determining the projected net savings of an SIB intervention requires three pieces of information that might be of varying difficulty to secure and validate. In addition to (i) the degree to which an intervention is expected to change the probability of occurrence of the negative social outcome, as reviewed in the previous section, also needed is (ii) the estimated cost of treating the negative social outcome in the future if not dealt with preventatively, and (iii) an expected cost analysis of the expenses associated with issuing and paying out the SIB, as summarized in Figure 1.6.

There are various degrees to which an analysis informing whether to proceed with a program intervention incorporates the potential savings of that intervention. How far one "casts the net" is somewhat arbitrary. One approach to classifying the savings is based on the degree to which or how directly government is impacted. For example, the New Economy (2015) Unit Cost Database, endorsed and jointly "quality assured" with the UK government, compiles estimated cost savings of social interventions in areas including criminal justice, employment, housing, and child welfare, with cost saving estimates classified as *fiscal, economic,* or *social* benefits (see Figure 1.7). *Fiscal* benefits are restricted to direct resource savings to government that can be quantified and identified in a government budget line; *economic* costs including forgone economic benefits, specifically "earnings and economic growth" and the associated tax revenue that is lost. *Social* benefits include "wider gains to society such as improvements to health; educational attainment; access to transport or public services; safety; or reduced crime."

A second resource endorsed by the UK Cabinet Office Centre for Social Impact Bonds that speaks to cost-benefit categorization is the publication *Cost Benefit Analysis Guidance for Local Partnerships* (HM Treasury, Public Service Transformation Network, and New Economy 2014). This resource notes that economic and social benefits also might

Figure 1.7. Cashable fiscal vs. economic vs. social benefits

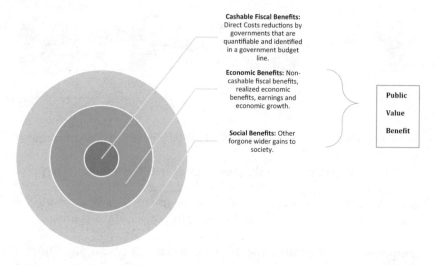

be referred to collectively as "public value benefits" (16), and that fiscal benefits can take the form of cashable and non-cashable with respect to the degree of liquidity of the savings. Cashable benefits include fiscal savings that can readily be realized as an expenditure reduction in a budget line, where non-cashable benefits free up a non-cash resource that can be reallocated to other purposes (17). In general, the quantification of benefits requires a number of assumptions regarding what cost reduction benefits to include and which can genuinely be attributed to the intervention and realistically realized. For example, whether one uses marginal versus average cost reductions, whether one counts capital in addition to operating expenditures, and the discount rate one selects will all affect the outcome of the analysis (Welsh, Farrington, and Gowar 2015). The quantification of benefits for specific outcomes may be published in "rate cards," indicating a government's willingness to pay per outcome, with providers competing under this threshold (Ramsden, Noya, and Galitopoulou 2016, 6).

As one moves from fiscal benefits to social benefits, the greater becomes the set of variables available for inclusion, which increases discrepancy and variation with respect to methodologies. For example, an inclusive cost-benefit framework for a crime prevention intervention presented by Welsh, Farrington, and Gowar (2015, 465) contains six categories of program benefits, including direct costs avoided through reduced crime, benefits arising from reduced substance abuse, and improvements in education, employment, health, and family factors. Each category then has multiple specific benefits that might or might not be quantifiable. For example, the savings from crime reduction include reduced policing, judicial, and incarceration costs, and avoided impact on victims, including "medical care, damaged and lost property, lost wages, lost quality of life, pain, suffering ... funeral expenses, lost wages, lost quality of life" (Welsh, Farrington, and Gowar 2015, 465). If a government rationalizes SIB delivery based on the payout being less than the projected cost savings, the selected notion of "costs prevented" or benefits realized will play a significant role in determining which projects proceed and which do not. A self-funding SIB would be required to generate cashable fiscal savings sufficient to offset the SIB success payout. However, a government could rationalize the SIB model in reference to an alternative, less restrictive notion based on economic or social benefits. A broader definition of costs, including social and economic costs, would allow more projects to proceed, as opposed to using a strict fiscal cost rule, but only under the latter can an SIB be deemed revenue or expenditure neutral.[25]

To what degree can social program interventions deliver benefits greater than their costs? Welsh, Farrington, and Gowar (2015) conduct a meta-analysis of cost-benefit studies from a crime prevention perspective reviewing programs in policy areas where SIBs have been implemented, including early childhood development and youth employment interventions. They restrict their scope to those with randomized control groups or "high-quality quasi-experimental designs" (448). Their review demonstrates that, for preventative social program interventions in program areas where SIBs have been used, there is significant variation in the types of benefits measured, leading to cost-benefit ratios that span from partial cashable fiscal benefit measures to more comprehensive public value measures. Of the fourteen studies reviewed by Welsh, Farrington, and Gowar (2015), based on the "benefit measured" descriptions, eight use measures of benefits limited to fiscal savings and eight uses measure that include broader public value benefits. Only three studies reported a benefit-cost ratio less than 1, with two of these based on fiscal savings, while two-thirds of fiscal

---

25 It should be noted that an intervention may shift cost from one category from another: for example, a reduction in fiscal costs may be offset by an increase economic or social costs. It is also of interest, but perhaps limited practical significance, that any estimate of fiscal costs will be based on the given state of social service entitlements. A relatively more generous social safety net will lead to a higher estimate of fiscal cost savings of a given intervention and vice versa.

benefit-cost ratios were greater than 1. This indicates that a majority of these interventions have the potential to be delivered viably under a self-funded SIB. On average, those studies based on fiscal savings produced a ratio of 2.13, relative to 3.17 for all studies listed.[26]

The advantage of meta-analysis studies such as that of Welsh, Farrington, and Gowar (2015) is that they are based on realized, context-specific evaluations of cost-benefit program effects in precise institutional settings. Other meta-analyses of cost-benefit studies have been carried out in program areas where SIBs have taken place, including health care and disease prevention (see, for example, Nuckols et al. 2017; Sun et al. 2017), housing and homelessness (Ly and Latimer 2015), and workforce development (Jespersen, Munch, and Skipper 2008).

A significant limitation of the meta-analytical approach, however, is that it is difficult to compare and translate the impact of an intervention meaningfully from one jurisdiction or context to another. First, as can be seen in the studies reviewed by Welsh, Farrington, and Gowar (2015), programs in the same policy area can be quite varied with respect to what services are being delivered. Ly and Latimer (2015, 447), for example, describe an "almost bewildering variety of program configurations" in studies of the housing-first approach. Second, as Welsh, Farrington, and Gowar (2015) also note, studies do not consistently use the same set of inclusion criteria with respect to monetizing the benefit generated by the intervention, with significant variation between studies in what is and is not counted. Third, ratios of cashable fiscal benefits to costs of a specific social program intervention will vary from jurisdiction to jurisdiction due to local input costs and entitlement differences.[27]

An alternative approach is to take a single jurisdiction and, based on average treatment effects experienced across jurisdictions, conduct a cost-benefit simulation exercise. The Washington State Institute for Public Policy (WSIPP), a non-partisan entity of the Washington State Legislature, has constructed and applied a cost-benefit model that can form the basis of such an approach. The WSIPP model is peer reviewed, and research produced from it has been published in academic journals

---

26 Averages are based on full sample results. When a cost-benefit range is reported, the low end of the range was utilized to calculate the average.

27 Cost-benefit analyses, based on broader public value benefits, likely would have less variation due to cost savings being counted, regardless of whether they accrue to the government or to society more broadly, assuming uniform programming and treatment integrity; in practice, however, interventions in specific policy areas are far from uniform.

(WSIPP 2017, 9). The institute is well regarded and respected by both academics and policy makers, and is recognized as a leader in cost-benefit policy evaluation, particularly in the analysis of criminal justice and prevention policy evaluation (Farrington and Welsh 2014). It also has been referenced as a potential data source to inform SIB initiatives (Liebman and Sellman 2013, 17).

WSIPP's uniform approach generates cost-benefit ratios that are robust and comparable between program areas, based on meta-analytical averages generated from high-quality analyses of treatment effects, including the inclusion of "linked or indirectly measured" outcomes that might not have been considered in the original set of evaluations, corrected for the double counting of effects (WSIPP 2017, 8).[28] The model accounts for program impacts on a number of health and education variables that are commonly used in micro-level cost-benefit analysis, including high school graduation, standardized student test scores, number of years of completed education, and higher education achievement, as well as morbidity and mortality costs of alcohol and illicit drug disorders, regular smoking, mental health disorders, health care outcomes, and child abuse and neglect (WSIPP 2017, 35). The cost-benefit implications are calculated assuming program implementation in Washington State, in net present-value terms, but the impact of the intervention is drawn broadly from published data using a meta-analytic approach. The estimated effects of the program intervention are classified into four categories based on the ability to assign costs and benefits to one of the following groups: (1) program participants; (2) other individuals; (3) "taxpayers," representing cost and benefits accruing to the state; and (4) those that are more indirect and not clearly attributed to the state or to specific individuals, such as the deadweight loss of taxation (WSIPP 2017, 9). The reporting of benefits and costs accruing solely to the "taxpayer"/state allows for the estimation of cost-benefit ratios based on what we term the fiscal benefits of the program relative to costs. These can serve as an indication of the degree to which intervention models exist that could generate sufficient savings to permit self-funding SIBs, assuming at this level of abstraction that all fiscal savings are cashable.

As of May 2017, the WSIPP had applied its cost-benefit model to 343 program interventions. Table 1.3 summarizes information on the

---

28 For example, improved educational performance might affect multiple indicators, such as standardized test scores or high school graduation rates, that might lead to higher earnings. The WSIPP model counts the effect only once. For more on the double-counting procedure, see WSIPP (2017, 173–4).

cost-benefit outcomes of the program interventions evaluated, with the first row examining the entire suite of interventions and subsequent rows presenting results by social program area. Of the 343 interventions analysed, 76 per cent were predicted to generate positive public value benefits, with justice and education interventions having above-average positive rates – see column 2. Overall, approximately one in five was expected to generate a positive net benefit with a high degree of confidence – 95 per cent or higher, according to the WSIPP Monte Carlo simulations (results presented in column 3) – with justice interventions being the most reliable. Column 4 lists the percentage of interventions with a predicted net fiscal benefit; note that 57 per cent of interventions generated positive net fiscal benefits such that the savings to taxpayers were sufficient to offset the cost of the intervention. This suggests the existence of a large potential population of suitable interventions for self-funded SIB projects.

Of the 343 interventions evaluated, 28, or 8 per cent, were found to produce a gross reduction in costs over status quo treatment, and were removed from the sample for the purpose of calculating benefit-cost ratios, as listed in column 5.[29] Columns 6 and 7 report the percentage of interventions that generated benefit-cost ratios greater than 1, and columns 8 and 9 report on the median ratio values. Removing the interventions with a predicted negative cost marginally alters the share that provided an overall net benefit from 76 per cent to 75 per cent, while those that generated a net fiscal benefit over and above their costs drops from 57 per cent to 53 per cent. The median net benefit value for the entire sample is 4.24, while the median value based only on fiscal benefits is 1.18. Child welfare, public health and prevention, and education all have median net benefits and net fiscal values higher than

---

29 Costs are calculated relevant to either a non-treatment group, where costs are zero, or relative to "treatment-as-usual" when a new intervention is being substituted for an existing suite of services (WSIPP 2017, 175). In the treatment-as-usual case, it is possible for the intervention to have a negative cost if the new intervention package costs less than the status quo service entitlement. Two of the 28 of the interventions where costs were lower for the new intervention resulted in savings to taxpayers but a net cost to society; both of these hypothetical interventions involved reducing prison terms by three months for medium- and high-risk offenders without additional treatment. Another two of the 28 produced negative gross benefits to taxpayers as well as negative total gross benefits, but the cost savings from the shift from the status quo outweighed these negative benefits, resulting in a positive net benefit; these two projects involved reduced jail time for low-risk offenders and diversion from prison of individuals with mental illness. The remaining 24 interventions produced positive net benefits.

Table 1.3. Washington State Institute for Public Policy Benefit-Cost Model Results

Social Program-Area	(1)No. of Interventions Analysed	(2)Benefits minus Costs > 0 (net present value)	(3)95% or Greater Chance Benefits Will Exceed Costs	(4)Taxpayer Benefits minus Costs > 0 (net present value)	(5)No. of Interventions with Costs ≤ 0 (where cost > 0)	(6)Benefit-Cost Ratio ≥1 (where cost > 0)	(7)Taxpayer Benefit-Cost Ratio ≥ 1 (where cost > 0)	(8)Median Benefit-Cost Ratio (where cost > 0)	(9)Median Taxpayer Benefit - Cost Ratio (where cost > 0)
Total	343	76%	21%	57%	28	75%	53%	4.24	1.18
Youth criminal justice	30	83%	37%	53%	4	81%	46%	3.62	0.87
Adult criminal justice	49	80%	45%	59%	10	79%	49%	3.71	0.99
Child welfare	8	75%	25%	75%	2	67%	67%	9.43	3.75
Pre-K–12 education	50	84%	14%	66%	0	84%	66%	6.83	1.91
Children's mental health	25	72%	20%	48%	8	59%	24%	1.38	0.56
Health care	36	64%	25%	42%	1	63%	40%	2.80	0.75
Substance use disorders	39	72%	5%	49%	2	70%	46%	4.93	0.67
Adult mental health	25	68%	28%	60%	1	71%	63%	3.17	1.26
Public health and prevention	64	78%	11%	64%	0	78%	64%	7.48	2.06
Workforce development	10	60%	0%	30%	0	60%	30%	1.48	0.73
Higher education	7	86%	14%	71%	0	86%	71%	13.54	4.09

average. Overall, the WSIPP model provides support for the existence of effective social programs that are able to generate both fiscal and public value net benefits, suggesting significant opportunities for SIB implementation.

Presence of an Intermediary

Instead of a direct contractual relationship between government and front-line service providers, SIBs commonly are distinguished from the conventional procurement model partially by the presence of a distinct coordinating entity. In the United Kingdom and several other countries, this entity is referred to as the *intermediary*. In the United States, this role may be subdivided between a *transactions coordinator* and a *project manager*.[30]

The degree to which the intermediary is independent of investors and service providers in practice can vary between SIB projects, from simply a legal entity or special-purpose vehicle created to facilitate the project partnership, to an independent third-party organization that acts as a lead proponent for the project. In the latter case, a separate legal entity often is established regardless, presumably to limit the legal liability of participating non-government stakeholders. For example, in the Peterborough antirecidivism and Essex child welfare SIBs, Social Finance UK acted as an intermediary (Social Finance 2018), but two separate intermediary entities, Social Impact Partnership Limited (Nicholls and Tomkinson 2013, 12–13) and the Children's Support Services Limited (Social Finance 2014) were formed.

The intermediary finds investors to finance the programming and manages the project. The intermediary is also responsible for selecting the service delivery agents and flowing upfront working capital. The role of an intermediary can be compared to that of a general or prime contractor, but given the responsibility to coordinate private finance, a more accurate comparison would be with that of similar special-purpose vehicles that are used in PPP infrastructure projects. Intermediaries may be competitively solicited, or an intermediary may co-construct the project with government and continue into a project administration role once the SIB has been launched. The former,

---

30 The Nonprofit Finance Fund (2017) defines the role of transactions coordinator as including responsibilities that may include: "design and structure of PFS project and financing model; capital raise; stakeholder management; on-going performance management" while the project manager is the "intermediary during service delivery phase, and/or fiscal sponsor for project funds".

CASE STUDY
The One Service Peterborough Antirecidivism SIB

The One Service Peterborough antirecidivism SIB, the first SIB project, was launched by the United Kingdom's Ministry of Justice in March 2010. It aimed to provide services to three cohorts of one thousand minor offenders over a seven-year period, including mental health supports, trained peer support and mentors, in and outside prison, who would advise and connect participants to existing supports with respect to housing, employment, and health care (Disley and Rubin 2014; Nicholls and Tomkinson 2013). The intervention was based on a previously evaluated program model that was found to provide a ten-to-one social return on investment (Pro Bono Economics and Frontier Economics 2010). The project ran on £5 million from seventeen investors, primarily charitable trusts and foundations, some explicitly focused on inserting social values in financial markets and addressing social disadvantage (Barrow Cadbury Trust 2017). The main stakeholders involved in the project included the Big Lottery Fund and the Ministry of Justice as the outcomes funders, and the lead proponent for the project, Social Finance Ltd., a UK nonprofit that had received a £5 million grant to help develop SIB projects in the United Kingdom (Nicholls and Tomkinson 2013). If reoffending was reduced by at least 7.5 per cent, investors received a minimum repayment of 2.5 per cent, with provisions for early repayment if reoffending was reduced by 10 per cent in the first cohort. A maximum of £8 million was set on total payments, and the internal rate of return (IRR) to investors capped at 13 per cent annually, with an expected IRR of between 7.5 per cent and 11 per cent (Warner 2013). In 2014 the UK government cancelled the last of three planned cohorts in the project due to the introduction of the Transforming Recidivism initiative, a more expansive partial-privatization scheme for antirecidivism programming in England and Wales, based on a payment-by-results compensation structure (Third Sector 2014). In 2017 the SIB was announced to have met its targets, with an average reduction in recidivism of 9 per cent over the first two cohorts, with investors receiving a return of 3 per cent (Owen 2017).

however, is preferred for reasons of "transparency and legitimacy" and the potential to discover new information on program options (Azemati et al. 2013, 28).

The introduction of an intermediary further distinguishes SIBs from conventional procurement, transferring activity from the state to the private sector, including responsibility for project coordination. Where the intermediary is an active proponent organization specializing in SIBs, such as the United Kingdom's Social Finance, its expertise might reduce transaction costs and bring knowledge of best practices from other jurisdictions to the project. The participation of an intermediary, however, creates additional expenses that need to be covered within the project budget or from alternative sources. It has also been claimed that, by adding another layer of administration that likely will develop its own interests, intermediaries increase principal-agent problems with respect to state supervision of service provider performance (Stid 2013). From an efficiency perspective, then, the intermediary – and the SIB approach more broadly – needs to add value equal to or greater than these extra costs to justify its use.

The External Evaluator and Control Group–Based Evaluation Method

Dear et al. (2016, 60) suggest that "measurement is what differentiates Social Impact Bonds from other contracting structures." Martin (2015, 66) notes that PbC "can be thought of as a method of translating performance accountability and performance measurement into performance specifications for use in government contracting." In this sense SIBs substitute a marketized accountability for alternative accountability mechanisms (Carter 2019). Contracting based on outcomes requires specification of the targeted outcomes, and how they will be measured and deemed to be achieved. Based on the centrality of determining the achievement of outcomes, many SIBs use an independent third-party evaluator to conduct the assessment – indeed, some definitions of SIBs include this as an essential feature (see Table 1.1). Such an evaluator is sometimes called an *independent assessor,* and is distinct from an *evaluation advisor,* who might be hired to assist the group managing the SIB and to provide monitoring and analytical assistance while the intervention is being delivered (Burand 2012, 453n9). The Nonprofit Finance Fund (2017) makes a similar distinction between an *evaluator* who will "design and implement [a] plan for determining whether outcomes have been met," and the *validator* who will "verify accuracy of data used in evaluation plan, or evaluation plan itself."

The key role of the evaluator/assessor is to determine the impact of the intervention and to separate out positive changes in outcomes over time that would have occurred without the intervention. This is sometimes referred to as "deadweight," and can be calculated by comparing outcomes for program participants to administrative outcomes in an area outside the intervention's application, or by identifying a control group, drawn from the same population as the treatment group, that does not receive the intervention (HM Treasury, Public Service Transformation Network, and New Economy Treasury 2014, 31).

The control group can be constructed in various ways to isolate the effect of the intervention on the participating population. Welsh, Farrington, and Gowar (2015) and MacKenzie and Farrington (2015) endorse the use of the "scientific methods scale" to classify "the methodological quality of intervention studies":[31]

Level 1: Correlational evidence: [target outcome] correlates with the program.

Level 2: Nonequivalent control group or one-group pre-post design: program group compared with nonequivalent control group; program group measured before and after the intervention (with no control group).

Level 3: Equivalent control group design: program group compared with comparable control group, including pre-post and experimental-control comparisons....

Level 4: Control of extraneous variables: program group compared with control group, with control of extraneous influences on the outcome (e.g., by matching, prediction or propensity scores, or statistical controls).

Level 5: Randomized experiment: units assigned at random to program and control groups. (Welsh, Farrington, and Gowar 2015, 467–8)

The higher levels are more robust and permit stronger conclusions to be drawn from the evaluation evidence, with Level 3 recommended as the cut-off for reliability and inclusion in meta-analytical studies (Welsh, Farrington, and Gowar 2015).

The use of randomized control trials (RCTs) for program evaluation, however, has not been without its critics. Heckman (1992), for example, points out some technical limitations and conceptual challenges with RCTs, such as their restriction to the analysis of mean differences, that randomization can alter participants' behaviour, and that most social programs are multistage in nature and randomization usually only occurs at one stage. Reddy (2012) provides a more fundamental critique of RCTs, given the mediating impact and constitutive role of the political and socio-economic context: it is not possible to isolate the impact

---

31 See Morse (2015, 35) for a similar hierarchy of evaluation quality.

of an intervention and assume that the impact is transferable to other contexts, either to different places or into the future. He notes that it is through comparison of these differing political and socio-economic contexts, "tracing the individual processes that are at play and recognising their commonalities, [that] one can begin to understand how and why policies do or do not work" Reddy (2012, 66). Chernomas and Hudson (2016, 34–6) also point to bigger-picture issues, including the inability of RCTs to determine the motivation or causation of behavioural changes and the limiting perspective that RCTs impose on solutions to social problems. Others have also highlighted the ethical concerns of denying services to an identified population in need (Loxley 2017; Morley 2019; Tse and Warner 2018). We return to these issues in Chapter 9.

Conclusion

In this chapter we laid out the foundational concepts and characteristics of SIBs, with a focus on how SIBs differ from conventional procurement models. We defined SIBs as government procurement contracts that enable social service interventions that bundle together design, delivery, and project finance, and where the contract payment structure is based on outcomes. Private investment is used to finance the project, with investors facing at least some repayment and return risk based on outcomes.

SIBs represent a new frontier for publicly funded social service delivery. They are part of an evolving trend of increased government reliance and devolution of risk and responsibility to the private sector (Warner 2015), bringing social public service delivery one step closer to a fully privatized model (Whitfield 2015, 23). Many of the defining elements of SIBs, including private finance, pay-by-results contracting, and bundled and contracted out design, finance, and operations, have been used before, and extensively in some areas of public service delivery. It is their combination in the social services sphere that makes SIBs a new and unique delivery model.

SIBs are being implemented in a number of policy areas, including antirecidivism, child welfare, early childhood development, housing and homelessness prevention, active labour market programming, and public health. In this chapter, we reviewed evidence that suggests a large proportion of existing social intervention models in these policy areas have been subject to rigorous evaluation and analysis, and are socially beneficial from a cost-benefit perspective, producing high social returns on investment. In many cases these programs not only have produced net social benefits, but also generated fiscal savings to government greater than the cost of the program intervention. In a real sense, these interventions have provided "something for nothing" compared to not intervening or the status quo. If one accepts these results and their transferability, not proceeding with these program interventions suggests some type of collective action failure.

One challenge to transferability is connecting the results from high-quality program evaluations to broad-based programming as it is implemented in practice. Treatment integrity – the adherence to the best practice program design model – is often much more stringently followed in experimental studies, but not well adhered to in practice. In fact, there is evidence to suggest that broad-based social programs in some areas are far from demonstrating best practices. The question, then, is how, in the context of fiscal restraints, should government allocate resources to programs that deliver on the social and fiscal potential of these demonstrated successful interventions? SIBs, by paying based only on results and not requiring upfront government funding, appear to provide a solution.

2 A Short History of Social Impact Bonds and the Development of the Enabling Field

Introduction

The concept of the Social Impact Bond can be traced back to the 1980s (Horesh 1988), but SIBs are a relatively new model for social service delivery. The first SIB project became operational in the United Kingdom in 2010, but not until April 2012 did six new projects begin in that country, followed by the first SIB in the United States in August 2012. The following year, SIB projects were launched in Australia, Germany, and the Netherlands, and in 2014 Canada and Belgium joined the small group of countries with active SIBs. By the end of 2014, these countries collectively had thirty active SIB projects. In 2015 the number of SIBs increased significantly, with twenty-two projects becoming active, and in countries that were launching their first projects, including Austria, Finland, Israel, Portugal, and Switzerland. Based on our survey, the total number of active SIBs worldwide had increased to 122 as of January 2019.[1]

---

1 Data for this chapter on SIB metrics and characteristics are authors' calculations based on data compiled from Gustafsson-Wright, Gardiner, and Putcha (2015), Fraser et al. (2018a), Nonprofit Finance Fund (2017), and primarily Social Finance (2019). SIBs identified and launched as of January 2019 were included in the dataset, and all statistics referenced in this chapter are based on this time frame. Data were cross-referenced with primary source material when available, and adjustments made where required. To be included in our statistics, SIBs had to meet the definition from Chapter 1 and have investors secured. As of February 2019, the SIB database produced by Social Finance listed 130 SIB projects initiated. To arrive at 122, we subtracted eight development impact bonds that we examine separately in Chapter 8, and one Japanese project that did not have a repayable investment component but was funded through non-repayable grants. We then added one UK SIB, the Shared Lives SIB, identified in Fraser et al. (2018a). In some cases operations had

Although the SIB concept thus has generated interest in several countries and with various levels of government, the model is still in the early stages of implementation, in the sense that the total value of contracts is small and most contracts had not reached their conclusion at the initiation of our study.[2] The size of the SIB market remains quite small relative to the overall social impact investing market and the portfolios of investors (Afik et al. 2019, 2; de Gruyter et al. 2020, 227; Wiggan 2019, 108).[3] Various governments, however, are actively exploring the concept, with many instituting upfront incentives to support the development of SIBs for outcome payments, making it likely that the use of SIBs will continue to grow.

We begin this chapter by presenting summary statistics on the size of SIBs by social policy sector based on various measures, including number of SIBs, number of participants, and upfront investment in SIB projects. We then examine the geographic distribution and emergence of SIB projects, with a focus on the facilitating institutional supports. This is followed by a summary of the reported results of the SIB projects to the date of our survey, a review of data on investors' returns, and a conclusion.

The Scale of SIBs by Sector

SIBs have been implemented in a number of policy sectors, including child and family welfare, criminal justice, education and early years, environment and sustainability, health, housing/homelessness, poverty reduction, and workforce development. Table 2.1 summarizes the scale of SIB activity in the various sectors using three different measures: the number of projects, the number of participants receiving

---

begun or pilot runs made based on grant funding, such as the Japanese project noted above, and the Dual Involved Youth PfS project in Illinois, which was seeking investors (Nonprofit Finance Fund 2017). A number of other SIB projects had been announced but not publicly disclosed the securing of investors as of February 2019. These include twenty-five projects spanning multiple policy areas announced by the UK government (United Kingdom 2017b, 2019) and a Canadian child welfare SIB (Manitoba 2019). Two end-of-life care projects, in Waltham Forest and in Hammersmith and Fulham (Big Lottery Fund 2018), were not included as the projects did not appear to have been announced or listed publicly elsewhere.

2 Only forty of the SIBs launched prior to February 2019 were scheduled to have been completed at that time, based on launch date and announced duration.

3 Floyd (2017, 3) estimates that the total contract value of all SIB projects represented less than 0.1 per cent of total US government social spending, and less than 1 per cent of PbR contracts in the United Kingdom.

services, and the total value of upfront investment. Total participant and upfront investment numbers are based on available data and include the vast majority of projects.[4]

Workforce development, which includes programs aimed at improving the labour market outcomes of target groups, has been and continues to be the largest category of SIBs since 2012, making up over one-third of the total. Other areas have been growing rapidly in more recent years, including the housing/homelessness and health sectors, which have the second and forth highest number of impact bonds, respectively. The area of child and family welfare has seen consistent activity since 2012, and is the third most common type of impact bond, while criminal justice and education and early years have a lower but growing number of projects.

With respect to number of participants, health serves the greatest number, with 38,344, while workforce development SIBs serve a slightly lower number. Criminal justice also has a large client base of over 28,000, while child welfare services have just under 9,000. When measured by total upfront investment, health is again the largest, with over $80 million in investment, while the next largest, criminal justice and workforce development, are in the $70– $75 million range.[5] In general, measuring the balance of activity among sectors by total upfront investment results in the more equal distribution of activity among sectors.[6]

---

4 Participant data were identified for 116 of 122 projects and upfront investment data for 104 of 122 projects. Those missing include a Korean workforce development project, a Japanese Health SIB, and a recent German education project. Those missing only participant data include a workforce development project in the Netherlands and a US blood bank SIB. The environment and sustainability SIB also by definition did not have participants. Projects for which only investment data were unreported include three UK workforce development projects, one Australian criminal justice project, two French workforce development projects, one UK child and family project, two UK housing SIBs, one German child welfare project, one US criminal justice project, one Australian criminal justice project, two UK homelessness SIBs, two Dutch workforce development projects, and one Dutch poverty reduction SIB.

5 Following Gustafsson-Wright, Gardiner, and Putcha (2015), SIB investment amounts in different currencies are converted to US dollars using exchange rates in the month the contract was signed or the project announced. All dollar currencies in the book are US unless otherwise specified.

6 Rizzello and Carè (2016) provide a detailed review of investment and the investors in SIBs up until August 2016. Using exchange rates as of 30 August 2016, they calculate the total value of investments at approximately $196.8 million, not including grants. The data used in this chapter include grants when identified, both recoverable and non-recoverable, that are put towards the investment capital of SIB projects

With respect to the size of individual SIB projects, criminal justice and health are the two sectors with the largest number of participants, with approximately 2,600 per project, while workforce development is the third largest at just over 1,000 participants per project. Child and family welfare has approximately 800 participants per project, while poverty reduction, housing/homelessness, and education and early years have lower average participation rates, in the 250–500 range. With respect to average investment, criminal justice is a leader and outlier at over $8 million per project, unless one counts the single environment and sustainability SIB, which is based on a $25 million investment. The remaining policy areas for SIBs are in the $3 million per project range, on average, with the exception of workforce development, which is closer to $2 million.

The Distribution of SIBs by Country

Table 2.2 presents data on the distribution of SIB activity by country of implementation, based on publicly disclosed and indentified data as of January 2019.[7] The United Kingdom continues to be a leading nation with respect to SIB development measured by number of projects, although in three of the last four years prior to our survey other countries had launched more SIB projects, with the United States being a leading developer.[8] Together the United Kingdom and the United States account for 60 per cent of all SIBs launched as of our survey and three-quarters of all participants, with approximately 96,400 participants collectively. Canada and Australia, the next two leading countries by number of participants, have between 7,500 and 8,500 participants each. The average number of participants in SIB projects has been 1,059 per bond, lower but comparable to the UK average of 1,200, while the

---

for operations; we attempt to excluded grants in our investment data that were contributed prior to the SIB launch that supported the development of proposals.

7 Figures in the table totals are based on available data. Not all projects have publicly disclosed data on the number of participants and total upfront investment, as described in footnote 4. Germany, South Korea, Japan, and the United Kingdom are underrepresented in the both investment and participant categories due to missing data, while France, Germany, and the Netherlands are underrepresented in the investment category.

8 The United Kingdom would have led most recently if we had included the ten SIBs announced late in 2017 funded by the Life Chances Fund; however, these projects had not yet identified investors and there was ambiguity regarding whether the projects would proceed as SIBs (Ainsworth 2017).

Table 2.1. Measures of Social Impact Bond Activity, by Sector

	No. of SIBs	%	No. of Clients Served	%	Total Investment($ millions)	%	Participants per Bond[a]	Investment per Bond[b]($ millions)	Avg. Term in months[c]
Child and family welfare	19	16	8,797	7	59.0	14	463	3.5	60
Criminal justice	11	9	28,795	22	75.1	18	2,618	8.3	62
Education and early years	10	8	7,253	6	32.9	8	806	3.3	52
Environment, sustainability	1	1	0	0	25.0	6	n/a	25.0	750
Health	17	14	38,344	30	82.5	20	2,556	3.1	56
Housing/ homelessness	24	20	7,690	6	62.5	15	320	3.0	48
Poverty reduction	1	1	250	0	2.4	1	250	n/a	n/a
Workforce development	39	32	38,062	29	73.2	18	1,029	2.3	49
All sectors	122	100	129,191	100	412.6	100	1,042	3.6	59

[a] Denominator adjusted for six projects not reporting participant data or those with zero participants, including one early childhood, two health, one housing, two workforce development, and the single environment and sustainability SIB.

[b] Denominator adjusted for 16 projects not reporting investment data, including three child welfare projects, one criminal justice, one early childhood, one health projects, three housing, and seven workforce development projects.

[c] This column reports the average length of the SIB contract in months. The average for all sectors with the exception of environment and sustainability, which is an outlier, is 53 months.

United States is delivering larger-sized projects on average, with approximately 1,500 participants per project.

When measured by total upfront investment in SIBs, the United States and the United Kingdom continue to dominate collectively, making up 76 per cent of total investment in SIBs, but the United States is the leader, with just under 55 per cent of total market share. Investment per project in US SIBs dwarfs those in the United Kingdom, with the former averaging $8.2 million, while the latter on average are based on investment of $1.9 million. This is likely partially explained by the prevalence of lower-cost workforce development SIBs in the United

Table 2.2. Data on Social Impact Bonds, by Country

Country	No. of SIBs	% of Total	No. Served	% of Total	Total Investment ($ millions)	% of Total	Average No. Served per Bond[a]	Investment per Bond[b] ($ millions)
Australia	9	7	8,470	7	42.9	11	941	6.1
Austria	1	1	75	0	0.9	0	75	0.9
Belgium	2	2	450	0	0.3	0	225	0.3
Canada	4	3	7,510	6	5.5	1	1,878	1.4
Finland	2	2	4,300	3	12.0	3	2,150	6.0
France	2	2	1,500	1	n.a	0	750	n.a
Germany	3	2	148	0	0.4	0	74	0.4
Israel	2	2	2,850	2	7.6	2	1,425	3.8
Japan	2	2	100	0	0.3	0	100	0.3
Netherlands	11	9	2,850	2	12.9	3	285	1.4
New Zealand	1	1	1,700	1	1.2	0	1,700	1.2
Portugal	4	3	611	0	2.0	1	153	0.5
South Africa	1	1	2,000	2	0.5	0	2,000	0.5
South Korea	2	2	100	0	1.0	0	100	1.0
Sweden	1	1	60	0	1.2	0	60	1.2
Switzerland	1	1	120	0	0.3	0	120	0.3
United Kingdom	48	39	57,516	45	79.4	21	1,198	1.9
United States	26	21	38,831	30	205.2	55	1,618	8.2
All SIBs	122	100	129,191	100	373.5	100	1,114	3.6

[a] Denominator adjusted for six projects without participant data, including one Dutch, one German, one Japanese, one South Korean, and two US projects.
[b] Denominator adjusted for sixteen projects not reporting investment data, including one Australian, one Dutch, two French, one German, one Japanese, one South Korean, eight UK, and one US project.

Kingdom, which make up 29 per cent of SIBs in that country,[9] with workforce development SIBs having a relatively low average dollar value ($1,900 per participant) and contract length, likely reflecting a lower degree of intensity of the intervention. In contrast, the United States has a relatively large concentration of criminal justice projects, which have tended to be more costly interventions both per participant and per project.

9 See Appendix B for a breakdown of sector proportion of SIBs by country.

Figure 2.1. The Emergence of Social Impact Bonds by Region, 2010–19

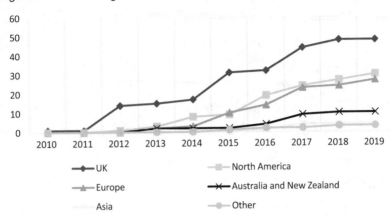

Although SIBs still make up only a miniscule share of overall social expenditure, their use continues to increase, with the highest number of new SIBs launched in 2015–17 since their introduction in 2010. Figures 2.1 and 2.2 present some data on the total number of SIB projects launched over time. Figure 2.1 depicts the cumulative emergence of SIBs by country over time, while Figure 2.2 shows annual growth rates of SIBs from 2013 to 2018 by total number of projects launched, participants, and funds invested. Although there has been a downward trend from very high initial growth rates for investment in 2013 and the peak growth rates for the number of projects and participants in 2015, annual growth rates were strong in years prior to 2018, particularly from 2015 to 2018 – in the 14–72 per cent range. Slower growth occurred in 2018, with only ten new projects launched, although another eight were launched in January 2019. As of our survey, a significant number of SIB projects were in development, with an estimated one hundred projects in the United States alone and at least another one hundred worldwide (Social Finance 2018), suggesting that growth rates will continue to remain positive. However, the declining rate of new project developments suggests that growth rates are failing to live up to proponents' initial expectations (Williams 2018, 2019; Wilson et al. 2020).

The Concept of "Enabling Fields"

The initiation of the SIB model and its subsequent expansion has been buttressed by a suite of initiatives supported by governments, academic institutions, and non-profit organizations. Building on Jooste and Scott

Figure 2.2. Annual Growth Rate of Initiated Social Impact Bonds, 2013–18

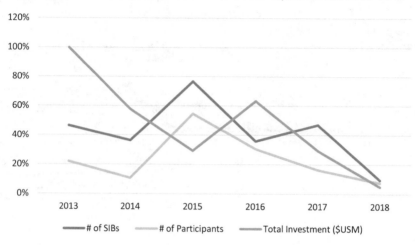

(2012), Heather Whiteside (2013) uses the concept of "enabling fields" to describe the system of institutional supports in the Canadian context to promote public-private partnerships in infrastructure, including the development of new practices and dedicated organizations both outside and within government. These include "important changes within government made to ... planning procedures and bureaucratic decision-making, and new forms of institutional support ... [that] normalize [PPP] use through the routinization, institutionalization, and depoliticization of this policy" Whiteside (2013, 86).

A similar phenomenon has occurred with the emergence of SIBs, demonstrating an abundance of institutional supports to experiment with and to implement the model in terms of proponent institutions, government policy, dedicated funding (Dear et al. 2016, 35), and, in some countries, legislation. Public sector programs have subsidized the design of the SIB as a concept and through specific SIB contracts, with investment supported through tax credits, guarantees, and by topping up outcomes payments, with all four present in the United Kingdom and at least one such support used by all countries with SIBs (Floyd 2017, 14). Outcome funds have been particularly prevalent, with the United Kingdom issuing just under £200 million for this purpose, leading "to a pipeline of over 60 potential future transactions," with supports in several countries also aimed at assisting organizations to increase their capacity to participate in SIBs (Dear et al. 2016, 48). Below we review the evolution of SIB activity in high-income developed countries and outline supports that have been made available for SIB development, as of January 2019.

THE UNITED KINGDOM

The first SIB launched in the United Kingdom was an antirecidivism project implemented for adult offenders serving short-term prison sentences at HM Prison in Peterborough, commissioned by the Ministry of Justice in September 2010 (Disley and Rubin 2014). The Peterborough SIB was developed as a result of a 2007 call by Gordon Brown's Labour government for ideas to promote public-private partnerships to address social issues in the United Kingdom (Eames et al. 2014, 7), and subsequently advanced by the Labour government's Council on Social Action (Whitfield 2015, 7). After a delay of a year and a half, additional SIBs became operational, with six focused on youth employment launched in April 2012. At this point, the United Kingdom was still the only country to have active SIB projects. The next tranche of SIB projects came in November 2012 with a second round of four youth employment projects. That month also saw the launch of two SIBs backed by municipal government payment commitments in addition to the UK government, in the area of housing and homelessness prevention, and the first SIB in the area of child welfare (Dowd 2013). By the end of 2012, fourteen SIB projects were operational in the United Kingdom, along with just one other SIB in the United States. The United Kingdom continues to be the leader today, with forty-eight projects initiated as of January 2019. The UK government has also announced more than a dozen additional projects as receiving support for outcome payments, but the details of operations and investors had not been revealed at the time of writing (Ainsworth 2017; United Kingdom 2017b).

Based on its long experience with outcomes-based payment, the UK government has been a leader in the promotion and financial support of SIBs, acknowledging the substantial public resources it has invested in constructing the SIB market (Cohen 2013).[10] UK government support for SIBs fit well with Prime Minister David Cameron's "Big Society" vision, based on displacing "big government" through the localization of government service provision and a greater reliance on community, volunteer, and non-profit organizations (Cohen 2013; Coote 2011, 1–2). The 2011 Open Public Services White Paper, aimed at focusing and

---

10 See Albertson et al. (2018, 31–60) for a more detailed review of the UK government's use and support of SIBs and outcomes-based commissioning more generally.

disseminating the new government's vision for public sector reform, further articulated this approach, with several references to the use of SIBs specifically and a broader emphasis on restructuring public service delivery towards payment by results, noting that "open commissioning and payment by results are critical to open public services" (United Kingdom 2011b, 29). The government also established an interdepartmental group of staff, which operated from 2010 to 2014, to support the promotion and implementation of PbR and worked to "identify public services where government could make further use of PbR" (Morse 2015, 16). The UK government's promotion of impact bonds has not been limited to the national stage: Prime Minister Cameron advocated and later used his presidency of the 2013 G8 meetings to host a social impact investment forum that included a session on SIBs (Ahmed 2013; United Kingdom 2013), and the United Kingdom continues to be involved in the promotion of Development Impact Bonds through its international development agency (Saldinger 2017; United Kingdom 2014b).

Throughout their existence in the United Kingdom, SIBs have been supported by government development funding (Albertson et al. 2018). Numerous UK public sector dedicated funds have been established and used to support the delivery of SIBs. These include the Commissioning Better Outcomes and Cabinet Office Social Outcomes funds, through which the Big Lottery Fund and the UK government have allocated £40–£60 million for SIB projects (Floyd 2017). The Department for Work and Pension's £30-million Innovation Fund, designed to bolster the social investment market and promote SIBs in the area of youth employment, contributed outcomes payments to ten SIB projects (Insite Research and Consulting 2014, 10). The Cabinet Office Youth Engagement Fund provided an additional £16 million for youth education and training SIBs (United Kingdom 2014a). In 2014 the government introduced the 30 per cent Social Investment Tax Relief tax credit, for which SIB investments by individuals are eligible, resulting in some cases in a more than doubling of effective returns to investors (Floyd 2017). The government also created two dedicated homelessness prevention SIB outcome funds, the Fair Chances Fund in 2014 and the subsequent Rough Sleeping SIB Fund in 2016, which collectively dedicated £25 million in outcome payments through the Cabinet Office and the Department for Digital, Culture, Media and Sport (United Kingdom 2017b). Later the government launched the £80-million Life Chances Fund to support up to 20 per cent of outcomes payments for new SIB projects, with the expectation of leveraging an additional £320 million in outcomes payments from local governments (United Kingdom

2017a). Floyd (2017, 16) estimates that, from 2010 to 2016, the subsidies provided by UK government and quasi-government agencies to support the development and implementation of SIBs totalled £44.7 million, exceeding his estimate of £38.9 million in private investment in UK SIBs over the same period. This is in addition to paid and anticipated outcome payments. Assuming that, on aggregate, SIBs pay back at least their invested capital, this implies that the UK government and its arm's-length agencies will have paid out £2 for every £1 invested in direct service delivery.

As well as grant and outcome payments based on direct public funds, the UK government has established Big Society Capital, a social investment fund seeded with dormant bank account funds, with links back to the Conservatives' 2010 general election platform (Stott 2011, 2–4). The fund is an independent corporation, supplemented with investment from the shareholder banks of Barclays, Lloyds, RBS, and HSBC, whose control of the corporation is limited to 40 per cent. Big Society Trust, a sister organization, holds the remaining shares. Each organization is entitled to voting rights based on share ownership, but the banks have agreed collectively to limit their voting rights to 20 per cent (Big Society Capital 2017). Big Society Trust continues to receive new investment capital through England's share of dormant bank account funds (Big Society Capital 2017). Big Society Capital had invested in seven UK SIBs as of January 2018 (Social Finance 2018). As well, Big Society Capital, along with Barclays Bank, seeded the establishment of the Big Issue Invest Outcomes Investment Fund, a PbR and SIB investment fund, with a £10-million contribution (Big Issue 2018).

SIBs in the United Kingdom have also benefited from the development of proponent organizations that act as technical assistance providers and intermediaries on SIB projects, many supported directly in their efforts by the UK government. Social Finance, incorporated in 2007 as a non-profit, is arguably the leading global proponent of SIBs and the "policy entrepreneur" (Kingdon 2003, 179) behind the SIB model. Overseen by a board with financial sector representatives, the organization is focused on PbR and outcomes-based financing models for social service delivery for vulnerable populations, its website highlighting over £100 million in leveraged investment. Since 2010 the organization has acted as the intermediary in thirteen UK SIBs (Social Finance 2018), and received at least £11.25 million in pubic support for its intermediation activities (Floyd 2017). Social Finance was the organization that drove the creation of Big Society Capital, with several founding members having served on the UK government's Commission on Unclaimed Assets, including the chair, Sir Richard Cohen (Warrell 2008). Social

Finance continues to be a leading global proponent of SIBs, with satellite organizations in the United States and Israel and a network of partners in other countries and regions, including Canada, South Africa, Ireland, and Latin America (Social Finance 2016b). The organization has published numerous reports and technical assistance documents to support the development of SIBs, and maintains a detailed database of impact bond projects in progress and under development.

The Young Foundation was another early promoter of the SIB model, supporting research and development efforts in both in the United Kingdom and Australia (Mulgan et al. 2011; Shergold, Kernot, and Hems 2011). Prevista is another organization that has worked on developing SIBs both inside and outside the United Kingdom, and is "one [of the] very few private companies to act as a social investor, intermediary and managing agent on payment by results contracts" (Prevista 2017).

Within the DCMS, the Centre for Social Impact Bonds was established in 2016 to "provide expert guidance on developing SIBs, share information on outcomes-based commissioning and support the growth of the social investment sector ... in partnership with a range of stakeholders, including local commissioners, service providers, academics, social investors, intermediaries and departments across government" (United Kingdom 2017a). The Centre has also partnered with Oxford University's Blavatnik School of Government to create the Government Outcomes Lab (GO Lab) to provide one-on-one technical assistance to organizations initiating SIBs and other PbR contracts. The GO Lab publishes regularly on developments related to SIBs, and has also sponsored annual international conferences on SIBs and PbR contracting.

The UK government has also been a leader in creating tools and undertaking systems change to facilitate the use of SIBs and other PbR tools. For example, the government partnered with the organization New Economy (2015) to develop the Unit Cost Database, which provides a guide to quantifying costs and savings of various social interventions (United Kingdom 2017a). The government also supported the development of *rate card* systems aimed at facilitating the SIB process, allowing multiple contracts to be issued in the same policy area more effectively and reducing the amount of evaluation required. Rate cards set fixed payments based on a per outcome basis for multiple outcomes, as well as a standardized evaluation process, allowing faster implementation of SIB projects across several service providers and geographic regions (Social Finance US n.d.). The UK government developed and used rate card systems for SIB projects funded through the Innovation Fund, the Youth Engagement Fund, and the Fair

Chances Fund (Gustafsson-Wright, Gardiner, and Putcha 2015, 18). The government also made legislative amendments through the Charities (Protection and Social Investment) Act of 2016, which enabled charities to make "social investments ... that pursue both a financial and social return" (United Kingdom 2016, 4), including SIBs (18–19).

Based on this infrastructure of support and subsequent pools of SIB contracts, the United Kingdom is the undisputed pioneer of SIBs. The UK government continues to drive the model, rolling out tranches of the previously noted Life Chance Fund, announcing £16 million in outcomes payment funding for ten new SIBs in 2017 (United Kingdom 2017a), forty-one separate grants to support the development of new or expanded SIB projects (GO Lab 2017), and support for another twenty-two projects in 2018 (Weakley 2018).[11] Given the experience and foundation laid, the United Kingdom likely will continue to be a leader for some time to come.

THE UNITED STATES

The United Kingdom is the undisputed SIB pioneer, but its rising and nearest rival is the United States. In August 2012, New York City partnered with Goldman Sachs and Bloomberg Philanthropies to deliver the first municipally issued SIB and the first SIB project in the United States, aimed at reducing recidivism (Olson and Phillips 2013). This SIB was unique in that a substantial proportion, $7.2 million of the $9.6 million private sector investment, was backed by a loan guarantee from Bloomberg Philanthropies (Nonprofit Finance Fund 2017; Olson and Phillips 2013), which in the end was executed.[12] In September 2013, over a year after the start of the Riker's Island SIB, came the launch of the second US SIB, the Utah High Quality Preschool Program; another five projects would be established by the end of 2014. Although 2015 saw only one project established, another twelve were launched by January 2018, for a total of eighteen. The United States now has the

---

11 At the time of writing, it was unclear if investors had been identified or when programming would begin (Ainsworth 2017), so these projects are not included in this chapter's SIB statistics reported above.

12 This SIB eventually failed to meet its targets, and was ended earlier than scheduled; as a result, Bloomberg Philanthropies paid back to Goldman Sachs $6.0 million of the $7.2 million it had invested to that point, generating significant discussion and introspection regarding the implications of the results (Anderson and Phillips 2015; Cohen and Zelnick 2015; Milner et al. 2015; Vera Institute for Justice 2015). This is the only SIB to our knowledge that has publicly announced a failure to meet targets and where outcomes payments were not released.

second-largest number of SIB projects and, as noted, is the world's leader in upfront funds invested.

As in the United Kingdom, SIBs in the United States have received financial and promotional support from the national level of government.[13] In 2009 the Obama administration established the Office of Social Innovation and Civic Participation (OSICP), led initially by Sonal Shah, formerly of Google and Goldman Sachs (Cohen 2017), with a mandate to seek a more effective allocation of social service funding and to support a focus on outcomes. In 2011 OSCIP organized a national conference titled "Pay for Success: Investing in What Works" (Lake 2015, 77), and went on to become a leading voice for pay-for-success projects, assembling approximately $100 million in support for project development (United States 2016a). This included $24 million through the US Department of Labor (United States 2013), which issued grants to New York State and the Commonwealth of Massachusetts to support outcomes payments for SIB projects (Nonprofit Finance Fund 2017; United States 2013). It also included approximately $12 million in support through the Corporation for National Community Service's Social Innovation Fund for "Pay for Success planning, feasibility studies, deal structuring, and pipeline development to help grow the field" (United States 2016b, 1). This funding supported several leading proponents and facilitators of SIBs in the United States, many of whom later served as intermediaries and technical assistance providers on projects.[14] The Obama administration also attempted twice to establish a $300-million PfS outcome fund through the budget process, to match local and state government payments (Greenblatt and Donovan 2013; United States 2016b). The legislation that would have enabled outcomes payment partnerships with states passed the House but was referred in 2016 to the Senate Finance Committee, where it stalled. In 2018, however, as part of the budget implementation bill, a Social Impact Partnerships to Pay for Results Act was finally passed and a

---

13 See Bailey and LaBarbera (2018) for a more detailed review of US use and support of SIBs and outcomes-based commissioning more generally.

14 Organizations that received funding from this source included the Corporation for Supportive Housing, the Harvard Kennedy School Government Performance Lab, the Local Initiatives Support Corporation, the National Council on Crime and Delinquency, the Sorenson Impact Center at the University of Utah's David Eccles School of Business, Social Finance USA, and Third Sector Capital Partners (Corporation for National and Community Service 2017), all of whom had formal roles in US SIB projects (Nonprofit Finance Fund 2017). The Institute for Child Success also received funding, and has undertaken a number of feasibility studies for PfS projects (Institute for Child Success 2017).

$100-million fund established, along with a bipartisan Commission on Social Impact Partnerships to oversee the funding (Lester 2018).

In 2016, of the twenty-four US states identified as examining the use of SIB projects, eleven had passed legislation to support their implementation (Hathaway 2016). The majority of these legislative efforts are sector specific, and range from enabling frameworks to develop the model and work with technical assistance providers, to dedicated funds to support contracts, with seven of the legislative efforts including dedicated funding sources to support SIBs and PfS projects. Some of these initiatives involve substantial associated resources. Legislation in Massachusetts enacted in 2012, for example, authorized up to $50 million in PbR outcomes payments with "the "full faith and credit" of the Commonwealth" (Liebman and Sellman 2013, 25). A number of state and local governments – including California, the City of Denver, Colorado, Los Angeles County, Massachusetts, Santa Clara County, South Carolina, and Utah – have also contributed resources to cover program costs not borne by investors, over and above outcomes payments. Several of these include housing costs for participants, which presumably are not an insignificant proportion of total project expenses.

Several organizations in the United States have been promoting the use of PfS and SIBs. Social Finance's US arm has been active as the intermediary on seven US SIB projects and provided technical assistance on another (Nonprofit Finance Fund 2017; Social Finance 2018). It also received a federal grant from the Corporation for National Community Service's Social Innovation Fund to develop rate cards with several state and local governments (Social Finance US n.d.). The Nonprofit Finance Fund, a social finance organization, maintains the payforsucess.org website, which houses an extensive and detailed database on investors, outcomes payors, technical assistance providers, and the structures of US PfS projects. The Fund has also invested in at least five projects and given grant funds to another (Nonprofit Finance Fund 2017). Third Sector Capital Partners, a non-profit PfS intermediary and technical assistance provider, has partnered in at least five US active SIBs, and claims to have supported the development of at least eighteen other PfS projects, mobilized $40 million from the private sector, and leveraged $100 million in public sector funds (Third Sector Capital Partners 2017). The Harvard Kennedy School, through its Government Performance Lab and SIB Lab, has provided similar research and technical assistance services (Harvard Kennedy School 2017), including an *SIB Guide for State and Local Governments* (Liebman and Sellman 2013). For-profit investors also appear to be structuring their support more systematically, with the announcement of a $10-million fund dedicated exclusively to PfS project finance (Reinvestment Fund 2017). Given this growing and intensive infrastructure, and an estimated one hundred additional projects in development (Social Finance 2018), the SIB m arket in the United States is likely to continue its expansion.

AUSTRALIA

Australia is third in the number of participants in SIBs and in disclosed upfront funds invested in SIBs (US$42 million), and fourth in the number of SIBs, at eleven contracts. Australian SIBs have been primarily in the child welfare and housing policy areas, with additional projects in the health and criminal justice sectors. The first Australian SIB, or Social Benefit Bond (SBB) – an equivalent term used in Australia – was launched in 2013, targeted to the successful reintegration of children taken into care by child welfare authorities (Donaldson 2015). Shortly after, a second child welfare SIB began, like the first, in New South Wales (Loxley 2017). Subsequent SBBs were not launched until summer 2016, with two projects, one in the area of homelessness prevention and the other in criminal justice. Australian SIBs have adopted an investment model based on open calls for investors to purchase actual bonds, unlike the practice elsewhere. This has led to the public release of investors' memoranda and annual investors' reports publicizing the progress in meeting SIB-projected performance criteria and specifying returns to date to investors.[15] Although yet to occur, this raises the possibility of marketing the bonds, so that the Australian SBB market is the nearest to a tradable market in SIB investments.

The New South Wales government played a leading role in the first two Australian SIBs, coordinating their development and providing substantial guarantees to investors, including full repayment guarantee plus, for certain investors, an outcomes-based return (Floyd 2017, 15; Loxley 2017, 20). Australian governments have also been leaders in supporting stakeholders in developing their ability to participate in SIB projects (Dear et al. 2016, 48). The government of Queensland, for example, established a AU$1-million "Social Benefit Bonds Readiness Fund" (Rose 2016), and the NSW government has a dedicated Office of Social Impact Investment, "a joint team of the NSW Department of Premier and Cabinet (DPC) and the NSW Treasury … to work with its partners and facilitate growth in the social impact investment market" (New South Wales 2017).

---

15 For sample, see Benevolent Society (2013); New South Wales (2017); and Social Ventures Australia (2013, 2017).

As in the United Kingdom and the United States, SIBs in Australia have benefited from non-profit proponent organizations. Social Ventures Australia (SVA) is an independent non-profit organization established in 2002 by former "senior Macquarie bankers" (Rose 2016) and supported by the investment of four charitable funders and non-profit service providers to support and improve social service outcomes and engagement with social finance through technical assistance and financing (Social Ventures Australia 2013, 2017, 2018). SVA has been an active promoter of SIBs, and four of the six SBBs have been intermediated or coordinated by the organization (Social Finance 2018).

The Centre for Social Impact (CSI), a tri-university research and teaching consortium founded in 2008 on government, corporate, and foundation support (Centre for Social Impact 2017), has also played a role in the development of SBBs. In 2011 CSI undertook a feasibility study funded by the NSW government to examine the introduction of the SIB model in the state, including an assessment of what social service sectors might be suitable, potential investors and service providers, and estimated cost savings (New South Wales 2017; Shergold, Kernot, and Hems 2011). The report concluded that the state government should

> encourage the development of a pipeline of NPOs [non-profit organizations] and programs that are suitable for an SIB by raising awareness and developing NPO capacity and capability to use this new method of funding; ... undertake initiatives to raise awareness across all NSW Government agencies and develop guidelines on how to assess the suitability of policy areas, program interventions and host NPOs; ... [and] also explore the potential for the application of SIBs in policy areas where there is a shared responsibility and shared funding arrangements with the Australian Government. (Shergold, Kernot, and Hems 2011, 11)

In September 2012, the Centre brought together public, private, and international SIB stakeholders at its "inaugural Social Finance Forum" around the same topic and to reinforce planning underway for the first SBB (Loxley 2017; Tomkinson 2012).

Australia has at least four SIBs in development, with service providers identified, in the policy areas of housing, health, and criminal justice, which were initially targeted for launch in 2017, and another four in the conceptual phase, with service providers yet to be identified, and were targeted for launch in 2018 (Social Ventures Australia 2017, 9). The Australian government has also earmarked resources to support SBBs and social investment more broadly, with the 2019 budget proposing AU$5 million to support a new social impact investment advisory committee, AU$14.1 million for three new "social impact investment trials,", and AU$0.5 million to study the potential of PfS projects targeting Indigenous populations (Easton 2019). Given the above activity and government-supported proponent infrastructure, it is likely that the SBB market in Australia will continue to expand.

THE NETHERLANDS

The Netherlands had commissioned the third-highest number of SIBs as of January 2019, with eleven projects, and had the fourth-largest total disclosed upfront investment, at $12.9 million. Eight of these projects have been in workforce development, an area in which the Netherlands has previous experience with in PfS procurement (Finn 2008). The Netherlands also has launched an antirecidivism program, also heavily focused on employment and training, as well as an antipoverty SIB aimed at debt reduction and management, and a health SIB.

The first Dutch SIB was launched in 2013 in Rotterdam, and was coordinated by the Society Impact Platform, a special-purpose intermediary organization focused on the development of impact bonds in the Netherlands (Society Impact 2017).[16] Earlier in 2013, Society Impact Platform and Ernst & Young released a working paper, partially funded by the Ministry of the Interior and Kingdom Relations and the Minister of Social Affairs and Employment, to form the informational basis for the use of SIBs in the Dutch context; the report concluded with a recommendation for further study and the implementation of SIB pilots in the Netherlands (Lunes et al. 2013, 45).

The Dutch bank ABN AmRO has a dedicated Social Investment Fund through which it has supported SIB projects (ABN AmRO n.d.). The bank promotes SIBs through its website, publications, and other public engagement activities, and also acts as a broker for government representatives, investors, and past SIB participants (ABN AmRO n.d). Another lead organization, the Start Foundation, is a "Venture Philanthropy Fund" that provides both repayable and non-repayable support to social programming aimed at integrating the disadvantaged into the workforce. (Start Foundation 2016a). The Start Foundation has published various tools to support SIB development, including fact sheets on the SIBs in which it has participated and an SIB project planning guide. It also planned and hosted a national conference on SIBs in 2015, which opened with a message from the Dutch minister of finance (Start Foundation 2016b). Two domestic specialty consultant service providers, Society Impact and Social Impact Finance, have also emerged to provide intermediary services on Dutch SIBs.

---

16 Society Impact was also the intermediary on a subsequent SIB in Utrecht.

CANADA

Canada had launched four SIB projects by January of 2019, tying it for fifth in the number of projects launched, seventh in upfront funds invested in SIBs, but fourth in the total number of participants, primarily due to a single health SIB with 4,000 participants. Total upfront investment in SIBs in Canada is valued at $5.5 million, leading to a much smaller average project size than in the United States or Australia, and comparable to that in the United Kingdom. The first SIB in Canada, launched in 2014 and commissioned by the provincial government of Saskatchewan, was a relatively small project focused on keeping twenty-two children, who were at risk of coming into care, with their mothers (Loxley 2017). In 2016 Saskatchewan launched a second SIB, in the area of education, and the federal government also launched two SIB projects in the areas of health and workforce development, with programming spanning the provinces of Ontario, Saskatchewan, British Columbia, and Quebec (Social Finance 2018).

The lead non-government proponents of SIBs in Canada have been Deloitte and the MaRs Centre for Impact Investing. In 2012 Deloitte published an information resource targeted at stakeholders to help prepare them for participation and "the arrival of the Social Impact Bond in Canada" (Deloitte 2012, 1). Deloitte has continued to promote SIB investment potential to Canadian investors through staff associated with Deloitte's P3 and other public sector work (MacDonald, Wenban, and Ciufo n.d.). In 2014 Deloitte co-published a report with MaRS examining investor attitudes and interest in engaging in SIBs in Canada (Cuifo and Jagelewski 2014), and MaRS is currently the intermediary in one active Canadian SIB.

Although SIB infrastructure is not as well developed in Canada as in some other countries, there is some indication that more Canadian SIBs are to come. Ontario has a number of projects in the developmental stage and has committed to moving forward with one, Saskatchewan has one project in development, and Manitoba has hired MaRS to launch several SIBs (Loxley and Hajer 2019), with the first announced but without investors (Hajer 2019). Most important, the federal government has announced the availability of the first C$50 million of a larger C$770 million social finance fund to be launched in 2020, supporting government reimbursement of privately financed PbR initiatives (Press 2019). Clearly in line with the enabling field framework, the initial C$50 million fund is earmarked to help organizations prepare to apply to the larger fund when it is launched. The fund came out of a larger social innovation and finance strategy, where social finance was defined as "investments intended to make a measurable social or environmental impact as well as to generate financial returns" (Social Innovation and Finance Strategy Co-creation Steering Group 2018, 13), which recommended a series of policy changes and supports to support social finance as well as social innovation more broadly.

Portugal is tied with Canada with the fifth-highest number of SIBs, although the total amount invested in SIBs as of January 2019 was relatively modest, at $2 million, and the number of participants has been small. Projects to date have been in the fields of education and early childhood development, workforce development, and child and family welfare. SIB development in Portugal is led by MAZE – previously known as the Laboratório de Investimento Social (Social Investment Lab) – which has been the intermediary in all four of Portugal's SIBs. MAZE offers a program for master's students wishing to study SIBs and to generate feasibility studies as part of their research (Laboratório de Investimento Social 2017). The organization is a partnership of the Calouste Gulbenkian Foundation – which also financed the country's first SIB project, the IES Social Business School, an organization formed in 2008 to promote social entrepreneurship (IES - Social Business School n.d.) – and Social Finance UK, with which the current leader of the Social Investment Lab was previously stationed (Laboratório de Investimento Social 2017). Portugal has also been identified as a country with generous government support for building the capabilities of organizations to engage in SIBs (Dear et al. 2016, 48). This support structure continues to evolve. In 2018 MAZE announced, in partnership with the national government, the release of a new social cost database, One Value, to assist with the calculation of cost savings of potential interventions (Maze 2018). A €55 million social innovation fund, based primarily on European support but also on funding from the national government, was also launched in 2018 to provide debt, equity, and "repayable grants," with reference to SIBs as part of the larger program (Hinchliffe 2018).

Finland has only two SIB projects active to date, but one is a relatively large project in the area of workforce development, launched in 2017, with €10 million in upfront investment. This project is unique in that the investor is a public sector entity, the European Investment Fund of the European Investment Bank Group (Finland 2017).[17] SIBs were

---

17 The European Commission is also supporting the development of SIBs (Whitfield 2015, 8), and has committed "to facilitate the exchange of experiences between Member States with social impact bonds" (Davis 2014, 1).

introduced into Finland by SITRA, a publicly resourced investment fund focused on innovation and based on an endowment by the national government (SITRA 2017). SITRA served as the intermediary and as an investor in the first Finnish SIB in 2015 (Social Finance 2018). The growth of the SIB market in Finland is expected to be high, with "approximately 30" SIB projects in development in various sectors at the municipal level (Keltanen 2017).

ISRAEL

Israel had launched two SIBs as of January 2019, a $2.1 million higher education project commissioned in 2015 and a $5.5 million health care SIB launched in 2016. Both SIBs are unique in that the outcome payments are being funded by arm's-length organizations, a university in the first case and health care and quasi-public non-profit insurance entities in the second, as opposed to by government directly. The development of both SIBs was led by Social Finance Israel, the Israeli branch of the UK-based organization, which served as the intermediary in the projects and offers services similar to those of its counterparts in the United Kingdom and the United States.

GERMANY AND AUSTRIA

Germany and Austria together have commissioned four SIBs to date, initially in the area of workforce development. The first German SIB was commissioned by the Bavarian State Ministry of Labour and Social Affairs and Family and Integration, based on €0.3 million in upfront investment. In Austria the first SIB was commissioned by the Federal Ministry of Labour, Social Affairs, Health and Consumer Protection, with €0.8 million of investment. Both SIBs were initiated by the Juvat gemeinnützige GmbH, a non-profit subsidiary of the Benckiser Foundation, which has been promoting the SIB model via its research and development activities (Benckiser Foundation 2016), and invested in and was the intermediary for both initial SIB projects. Germany has since launched a child welfare SIB in the district of Osnabrück (Ruf 2017) and a workforce development project (Social Finance 2018).

FRANCE

In March 2016, after previously avoiding SIBs due to concerns regarding privatization, France's national government issued a call for proposals on "les contrats à impact social" (Mair 2016). Later that year, France's first such projects were announced, commissioned by the Ministry of Economy and Finance. Two workforce development projects were announced, one in rural areas and one in low-income urban neighbourhoods, both centred on microcredit (Social Finance 2018). One project is supported by investment from la Caisse des Dépôts, a public sector lending institution. A further three projects are in development in the areas of child and family welfare and youth employment (Le portail de l'Économie 2016).

Key players in the lead-up to the first French SIBs include Mirova, the "responsible investment division" of Naxis, a large multinational asset management firm (Mair 2016), and the vice-president of Crédit Coopératif, a French credit union, Hughes Sybille, who co-chaired a French government committee on social investment and authored a report recommending the pursuit of SIBs (Mair 2016). Neither Mirova nor Crédit Coopératif, however, ended up investing in these initial SIB projects. Instead these were taken up by IMPACT Partenaires, a social investment company, other traditional lenders, and a foundation. L'Institut de l'entreprise, a French think tank, also played a role in the lead-up to SIBs in France, publishing an extensive report on the potential for SIBs in the French context (Pendeven, Nico, and Gachet 2015).

SOUTH KOREA

South Korea was the first Asian country to adopt the SIB model, where it was pioneered at the municipal government level, with two projects launched to date. The Seoul Metropolitan Government passed the Seoul SIB Act in March 2014, and in October 2015 launched the first South Korean SIB, focused on providing educational supports to children involved in child welfare services, with Pan-Impact Korea serving as the intermediary (Pan Impact Korea 2016, n.d.b). Pan-Impact Korea is an SIB proponent group, organized as a limited liability corporation that offers various services focused on SIB implementation to government and other stakeholders. Although it was formed in 2015, the organization notes that its members have been active in lobbying for SIB-enabling legislative policy since 2011 (Pan-Impact Korea n.d.a). Pan-Impact Korea serves as the secretariat to the Social Impact Bond Local Government Council of Korea, which "provide[s] consultations about SIBs and introduction of related policies, as well as to build partnerships between local governments" (Pan-Impact Korea n.d.a). It also provided technical assistance on South Korea's second and only other SIB to date, commissioned by Gyeonggi province – a workforce development SIB targeted at reducing welfare expenditures (Pan-Impact Korea n.d.a).

JAPAN

Japan launched its first two SIBs in April 2017, both in the policy area of health (Social Finance 2018). The first was commissioned by Kobe

City, and is being led by the Japan Social Impact Investment Foundation (Reuters 2017); the second was commissioned by municipal government of Hachiojia (*Daily Manila Shimbun* 2017). Both have made initial payments to investors (Platt 2018). SIB prototype projects have been operational in Japan since 2015. The Nippon Foundation for Social Innovation initiated three trial SIB-style projects in 2015, focused on adoption, dementia prevention, and youth employment, although these projects were not technically SIBs as the funding was not based on a PbR model (Nippon Foundation 2015). Instead the projects were funded directly by the foundation, which also acted as an intermediary to demonstrate the feasibility of SIB-type interventions focused on prevention, outcomes tracking, and evaluation. Another SIB prototype project, funded by Goldman Sachs, was launched in 2016, targeting disadvantaged youth (Tsukamoto 2017). All four of these prototype projects were at the municipal level and had all the elements of an SIB with the exception of investor repayment. At least one additional Japanese SIB is in the planning stage, with a project in Yokohama being pursued by the UK-based Prevista and Meiji University (Prevista 2017).

Overall there appears to be a growing enabling field in Japan for SIBs. A fund seeded by dormant bank accounts was slated for launch in 2019, modelled on the UK Commissioning Better Outcomes Fund (Sin and Tsukamoto 2018) and based on a 2016 law mandating such funds be allocated to non-profits (Platt 2018). The fund is expected to generate ¥40 billion annually (Ito 2019), creating much scope for future SIB projects. At the national level, SIBs have been prioritized in the cabinet-level "Future Investment Strategy," and approximately twenty municipal governments are engaged in planning SIBs (Ito 2019), although Japan's relatively underdeveloped third sector has been identified as a potential barrier to growth (Sin and Tsukamoto 2018).

NEW ZEALAND

New Zealand has one operational SIB, in the area of workforce development focused on individuals facing mental health challenges, which became active in 2017 (Social Finance 2018). Introduction of the SIB model into New Zealand appears to have been led by the national government, without a strong external proponent driving the process, unlike in most other countries engaged in SIB activities. In 2013 the government approved pursuing the model and seeking interest from investors and other stakeholders, and engaged KPMG to develop a ""business case" for a New Zealand social bonds pilot" (New Zealand 2013, 4). Over the next two years, various activities were undertaken to generate interest and solicit proposals (New Zealand 2017a).

New Zealand has paid particular attention to the transparency and integrity of the SIB procurement and evaluation process, engaging external legal council to undertake a *probity review* to verify that the process was conducted in accordance with best practices with respect to tendering, conflict of interest, etc. (see, as an example, Ambler 2016). The government also referred the work of the Ministry of Health, which has led the process supported by an interdepartmental team, to the Treasury, which commissioned an independent consultant to review the process and identify improvement opportunities (New Zealand 2016, 2017b). The consultant identified some challenges in the process – for example, around the need for "commercial financial expertise" (New Zealand 2017b, 7) and the need for greater senior civil service participation – that highlighted the significant demands of SIB engagement on government staff. According to government analysis, the report also demonstrated that "the requirement to undertake a market-led process has added time and complexity to the procurement process, as well as a loss in negotiation power for the Crown" (8).

The New Zealand government is in the process of developing a second SIB aimed at reducing youth recidivism (New Zealand 2017b, 8). The first SIB was based on only NZ$1.5 million of investment, but the government has now established a fund of NZ$28.3 million for outcome payments for future SIB activity and, latterly, as a source for administrative costs (New Zealand 2017b).

SWEDEN

As of 2017 Sweden had one active SIB, focused on school readiness for children in care, launched in 2016 (Social Finance 2018). Most of the activity of this SIB is delivered directly by the public sector, with a private sector partner providing advisory services (Backström 2016). Two SIB-precursor pilot projects were run prior to the launch of this full SIB. One was implemented by the Center for Social Entrepreneurship Sweden and funded by a public sector innovation agency, Vinnova; the other was run by Fryshuset, a youth-serving social agency, with a grant from a lottery-supported innovation fund (Fryshuset 2014; Mair 2016; Solding 2015). Social Impact Bonds in Sweden appear to have been motivated by interest from a number of stakeholders, with several organizations participating in a larger Nordic network on the topic organized by Mötesplats Social Innovation (MSI; Backström 2015), a government-supported social innovation institute based out of Malmö University. MSI and Vinnova in particular have been engaged in promoting SIBs in Sweden for several years (Lampty 2014).

SWITZERLAND

Switzerland launched its first and only SIB in 2015, a refugee employment project commissioned by the Canton of Bern, with over seventy funding and financing partners participating (Specking 2015). The Swiss federal government has not participated in any domestic SIBs to date, but is an investor in the Humanitarian Impact Bond project of the International Committee of the Red Cross (ICRC), which is being implemented in several African countries; the government is also partnering on a second DIB in Colombia (Social Finance 2018), and in 2018 hosted an international conference on SIBs (Switzerland 2018).

SIBs: Delivering Results

Table 2.3 presents some summary data on the degree to which SIBs are achieving their targeted outcomes and repaying investors (Appendix C provides detailed information by project and data sources). Overall, thirty-five projects were either fully repaid or on track to be repaid, based on the most recent public reports we could find. Three completed projects realized only partial repayment because targeted outcomes were not fully achieved. For two of these projects, the Street Impact and Thames Reach Ace UK homelessness SIBs, we were unable to identify the percentage repaid; for the third, the Portuguese Junior Code Acadamy SIB, only 25 per cent of the investment was repaid. At the time of our review, only one project, the Riker's Island antirecidivism project, had announced that it had not met its targets and the outcome funder had not made any payments to investors. Both the NYC Able and the Junior code academy were the first SIBs in their respective countries, and in many respects were pilot projects, while the two UK homelessness SIBs were relatively early projects, launching in November 2012. Similar circumstances surround Finland's Occupational Wellbeing SIB, the one project still in progress identified not to be on track for full repayment.

Investor Returns

Fully satisfying accounts of investor returns are challenging to assemble, as one needs to rely, for the most part, on publicly announced measures, which are inconsistently reported and calculated. Consistent with broader reported challenges of accessing data on SIBs (Hevenstone and von Bergen 2020), very few projects have revealed actual rates of return paid out to investors for completed projects. As of January 2019,

Table 2.3. Reported Investor Outcomes of 122 Social Impact Bond Projects, as of January 2019

| | Project Investors Reported Repayment Status | | |
	Fully Repaid/ On Track	Not Repaid/ Not On Track	Unknown
Completed Projects*			
Investors repaid in full	7		
Investors at least partially repaid, on track (no final report)	14		
Investors only partially repaid		3	
Investors on track for full repayment (no final report)	2		
Investors not repaid by outcome funder		1	
Investors repayment status unknown			10
Projects in Progress or Unknown Completion Status			
Investors partially repaid, on track for full repayment	8		
Investors on track for full repayment	4		
Investors not on track for full repayment		1	
Investors repayment status unknown			72
Total	35	5	82

* Completed project status based on launch date and announced duration, with the exception of two SIB projects announced terminated prior to scheduled end date.

we were able to identify just three such cases, with annual realized rates of return of 12 per cent, 24 per cent, and a small foundation-funded pilot SIB that did not repay a majority of the investment.[18] Instead, to achieve any meaningful sample size, we had to rely on maximum or

18 The first two were early workforce development SIBs: the T&T Innovation SIB in Manchester, which returned 210 per cent of the £0.8 million initial investment, and the Nottingham Futures SIB, which paid out £2.5 million on £1.7 million invested, both over three and a half years (Social Finance 2018). The negative return was for the €100,000 Junior Code Academy SIB in Lisbon, which paid back only 25 per cent of the investment fronted by the Calouste Gulbenkian Foundation.

expected rates of return as announced at the beginning of the project. Appendix C presents project-level data on projected investor returns for projects where at least one measure of return was identified, while Table 2.4 presents a summary of data on projected rates of returns. It should be noted that, within projects, different investors may have different terms of repayment, with different potential return rates and payment structures.[19] For example, non-profit or foundation investment often faces lower rates of return relative to more conventional equity investor sources in the same project. More conventional investors also may hold preferred shares in the project to be repaid prior to other investors. The use of project average rates of return masks these discrepancies and dampens the variance of the data. Also, our data do not account for the fact that SIB contracts may repay investors at various points throughout the contract as opposed to a lump-sum payment upon completion. Earlier repayment reduces overall capital requirements and increases the real value of payments to investors. These factors are partially accounted for when using the internal rate of return methodology to calculate rates of return, but this is available for only a small number of projects.

Data for most projects are available for total investment, length of project in months, and total maximum outcomes payments available. These can be used to determine the maximum rate of interest paid by outcome funders for the aggregate total investment per project on average, which reflects the financing cost paid by outcome funders in addition to repayment of upfront investment amounts. To the extent that outcomes payments go fully to investors and the repayment of the investment is at the end of the project, this measure then approximates the maximum rate of return to investors. This is typically the case for impact bond projects, but certain projects contain commitments that some outcome payments will be reinvested in future programming. Additionally, if the investment repayment is paid throughout the life of the project or is extended after the programming is completed, then this measure will be higher or lower relative to actual returns, all else being equal. For example, in the Chicago Child Parent Center PfS project, investors repayment is spread out well beyond the completion of the intervention, so this approach overrepresents the rate of return. Caution, then, is advised when interpreting this measure.

With the caveats noted, we present what we call the *maximum aggregate per annum interest rate* in the sixth column of Appendix C. Based

---

19 To calculate average maximum and expected/target rates of return in the presence of multiple investor classes for a single project, we used the unweighted average of reported return rates. In the case of a reported range, we used the midpoint.

on this measure, which we identified for sixty-seven projects, there is a wide range of potential payoffs, ranging from minus 18.5 per cent to 93.5 per cent, where a negative maximum rate suggests cases where investors as a whole are subsidizing projects as opposed to receiving a return, with the unweighted average rate being 17.7 per cent. Column seven of Appendix C lists maximum investor returns, as self-declared and/or reported in public sources. The set of SIBs for which we identified this data is smaller than the previous measure, with only thirty-six identified projects, including projects that reported total return on investment figures, which we converted to annualized return rates. Some of the reported maximum return rates as reported in public sources might be higher than the maximum aggregate per annum interest rate, as some SIBs have different investment classes, where subordinate investors, often foundations or charities, accept less advantageous terms and in effect subsidize the other investors. In addition, in a minority of cases grant funding might be included in total investment, having a similar effect, but we attempted to net out grants when they were explicitly identified. Measurement error and misreporting also might be a factor, as in some cases where there are multiple reference sources and reported information is not identical.[20] Reported maximum rates of return per annum in these thirty-six cases have a more restricted but still substantial range, from 1 per cent to 30 per cent, with an unweighted average return of 9.0 per cent.

The challenge with the above measures is that they do not account for the degree of risk inherent in individual SIB projects and the feasibility of achieving the maximum outcome payments. One possible explanation of large potential returns is the high degree of risk associated with SIB projects, and that SIB projects with higher risk of not meeting their targets are offering higher maximum returns. Table 2.4 thus presents a preferred measure of projected returns, the expected rate of return, which by definition should account for repayment risk. Based on reports from twenty-nine projects, the expected rate of return ranges between 2 per cent and 12 per cent, with the average being 5.9 per cent. Table 2.5 presents data on unweighted average returns conditional on outcomes status, to examine the hypothesis that riskier projects, proxied by those that had yet to repay investors, are more likely to

---

20 For example, there are some small discrepancies between Social Finance (2018) and Nonprofit Finance Fund (2017) with respect to the amount of upfront investment in US projects. Where available, we reviewed original source documentation for confirmation; in cases of discrepancy, we used source documentation.

Table 2.4. Unweighted Average Investor Rates of Return

	Minimum	Average	Maximum	Sample Size
		(per cent)		
Expected/target return, reported	2.0	5.9	12.0	29
Maximum per annum return, reported	1.0	9.0	30.0	36
Maximum per annum aggregate interest rate*	−18.5	17.1	93.5	67

* The maximum aggregate per annum interest rate (i) is the annualized interest rate based on reported maximum outcomes payment available (P_{max}) and total funds invested (I), including in some cases grant funding. Letting t be the contract duration in months, it is calculated as

$$= \left(\frac{P_{max}}{I} \right)^{\frac{12}{t}} - 1.$$

have higher maximum returns. For all measures, rates of return are either higher or comparable for projects where investors were repaid in full or were reported on track to be repaid, relative to projects where results were unknown or investors were not repaid in full. However, based on our constructed maximum aggregate per annum interest rate measure, annual average maximum projected returns for the two projects that paid only partial returns was 32.7 per cent, which is quite high. Some investors also have some (re)payment guarantees with respect to their investment, which changes the risk profile facing investors. For example, the Riker's Island SIB project, which failed to repay any funding to investors, was backed by a 75 per cent loan guarantee (Cohen 2015), so the projected return on at-risk capital would have been much higher at 87.5 per cent, compared to the reported 6.9 per cent maximum rate of return.

Our proxy above for risky projects is clearly imperfect, and many dimensions of SIB project design will influence repayment risk. As the issuer of the SIB, government can structure the arrangements to encourage private investment and mitigate risk. Setting a minimum interest rate for the first few years of the life of an SIB also acts as a form of investor guarantee, in addition to providing or securing more direct principal repayment guarantees. Government can arrange for interest payments to be made annually instead of at the end of the life

Table 2.5. Average SIB Investor Rates of Return, Conditional on Outcome Status, as of January 2019

SIB Investor Repayment Status	Expected/ Target-Return (%)	Number	Maximum per annum Return (%)	Number	Max Aggregate per annum Interest Rate (%)	Number
Repaid in full or on track	7.3	6	11.6	11	25.1	25
Not repaid in full	2.9	2	6.9	1	24.1	3
Status unknown	5.7	21	7.8	24	11.5	29

of the contract. This increases the liquidity of the investors and reduces their risk. Flexibility in selecting participants more likely to succeed in programming and to hit outcome targets will also affect the risk to investors. A systematic analysis of whether there is an appropriate risk-reward balance in SIBs would need to consider these factors.

CASE STUDY
The Benevolent Society and Newpin Social Benefit Bonds: Improving the Profitability of SIBs and Reducing Investor Risk, while Increasing Transparency

The Benevolent Society and Newpin Social Benefit Bonds (SBBs), two similarly structured child welfare SIB projects in New South Wales, Australia, were aimed at reintegrating and keeping with their family children who had been or were at risk of being taken into out-of-home care by child welfare authorities. Both SBBs were based on well-established program intervention models, with parents receiving counselling and parenting support (Loxley 2017). Both projects had similarly sized maximum outcome payments around AU$19 million, but differed significantly in their maximum rates of return: the Benevolent Society SBB, the first Australian SIB, had a maximum rate of return of 30 per cent and was based on AU$10 million of investor capital, while the Newpin SBB was based on AU$7 million in investment, with a maximum return of 15 per cent (Social Finance 2018). The Newpin SBB was expected to produce savings to government of AU$45 million if it met expected targets, well in excess of the maximum outcome payment (Social Finance 2018). Overall, both programs did produce success, improving significantly upon baseline results for the comparison groups (Loxley 2020). Given the use of existing program models and providers, however, the value added of the SIB model itself is unclear.

The two SBB projects implemented several investment enhancement measures that deviate from the simple SIB model described in Chapter 1, with modifications to reduce risk and improve profitability for investors. To some extent, the Benevolent Society SBB did boost investor returns by bringing in more low-risk clients and by excluding more high-risk, especially Indigenous, clients. It offered two bonds, one covering 75 per cent of total financing and offering a 100 per cent principal guarantee with a lower return, the other covering the remaining 25 per cent of financing, and exposed to a potential loss of 100 per cent of the principal in return for a much higher potential return. The former yielded 6 per cent per annum and the latter 10.5 per cent, both very high returns, and each will see 100 per cent of the principal repaid (Loxley 2020).

The Newpin SBB implemented annual interest payments to investors along with a guaranteed minimum rate (Loxley 2017). It also boosted investor returns by limiting the impact of children not staying out of state care by "capping" these reversals. The bond also placed limits on how much investor equity would be at risk at maturity, although this declined in importance in the project's later years (Loxley 2020). At the same time, the bond was not subject to "cherry picking" or "cream skimming" its clients to improve the prospects of success. On the contrary, its focus was on the very high risk sector of the population, which, to some extent, would justify the various measures taken to guarantee minimum investor returns.

Both SBBs, given their broader set of purchasers and greater marketability, serve as exceptional examples of transparency in many respects. The information memorandum for each marketed SIB contained a comprehensive account of the underlying programs to assist parents and children, the terms of loans being made, the metrics by which investors would be repaid and rewarded, and the details of the implementation agreement between the service provider and the government. These very detailed documents were accompanied by annual reviews of performance conducted by independent consultants and by annual progress reports to investors. There is, thus, a plethora of information, typical of Australian SBBs, that is normally hard to get in standard SIBs. Ironically, unlike most SIB projects, often only limited information is released on the identity of SBB investors and the amounts of their investment.

Overall, the data reviewed above highlight that many SIBs offer quite high potential – that is, maximum – rates of return. Using a measure based on total outcome payments collectively, average maximum return rates are substantial at 17.1 per cent per annum. Returns are more modest when looking at projects for which reported maximum and expected/targeted return rates were directly announced. These are more in line with average stock market rates of return, but this raises questions regarding whether investors should be obtaining this level of returns, particularly since they benefit from the publicity and reputational effects of participation. These rates are also significantly higher than government's costs of borrowing, which have been at record lows since the 2008–9 financial crisis and subsequent Great Recession. If one accepts these data as unbiased, such that projects that have publicly reported data are representative of the larger sample, our analysis suggests that investors face a very low rate of projects not meeting targets and of not being repaid. The limited publicly available evidence suggests, rather, that the vast majority of investors have been or are on track to be repaid.[21] This raises additional questions regarding whether government is receiving value for money from the SIB model relative to more conventional procurement or direct pay-by-results models, and underlines the need for greater disclosure and transparency.

Conclusion

The SIB model is still relatively new and in its early stages, and the scale of implementation is relatively modest compared to total social service spending, with 122 projects identified as launched as of January 2019. Workforce development was the leading sector in terms of the number of SIBs launched. Health was the area with the highest investment, while investment in each of criminal justice and workforce development was comparable. In general, a number of social policy areas had multiple operational SIB projects, and there was robust diversity among other project areas, including early childhood development, child and family welfare, and housing and homelessness, while environment/sustainability and poverty reduction had only one project of each type. The United Kingdom, first, and then the United States were the earliest adopters of the model, and continue to be leaders in number of projects, clients served, and funds invested. SIBs are growing rapidly in number,

---

21 One could speculate that stakeholders would be more likely to withhold results if the project did not meet targets for clients; however, they might be equally tentative in releasing results if investors received very high rates of return.

and in countries with a more established SIB market, growth has been driven by an elaborate enabling field of supports, relying extensively on public sector subsidies, both financial and in-kind. Countries more recently engaging seriously with SIBs appear to be replicating this approach.

Although data are limited, SIBs for which results have been announced appear to be repaying investors quite consistently. SIBs face a large variation in maximum return rates, and we were unable systematically to link this to the risk level of projects, although three of the four projects we identified that had not repaid investors fully did have relatively high maximum rates of return for at-risk investment. This variation in return rates is a promising area for future research, likely requiring individual case studies with stakeholder cooperation to determine the underlying factors. Maximum potential overall rates of return to investors for SIB projects are relatively high in many cases, but reported expected returns appear in line with stock market returns. It is unclear if these return rates are justified, however, given the apparent high success rate of SIB projects meeting their repayment requirements. Evaluating this would require greater transparency and the release of investor terms; precise reporting processes of actual returns paid to investors would also aid this process, which, to our knowledge, has occurred in only a small number of cases, notably in Australia.

The status quo leaves much to be desired with respect to the transparency of SIB projects, which was a significant problem in its predecessor, the public-private partnership model, in the public works infrastructure field (Loxley 2010). A standardized and transparent process for public disclosure around SIB projects would help determine whether outcomes payments from public funds are providing value for money relative to more conventional social service models, and whether the interest rates paid to investors, apparently well above the cost of conventional public borrowing, are justified.

PART TWO

Efficiency-Based Explanations of the Emergence of Social Impact Bonds

3 The Rationale of Social Impact Bonds

Introduction

Social Impact Bonds have emerged in response to a number of challenges, including pervasive and ongoing social ills, lack of budgetary resources, and government administrative structures perceived as unresponsive and lethargic. In turn, SIBs claim to offer the promise of increased investment in cost-effective prevention programming, more successful social programs through improved collaboration, reduced risk for government, and a focus on results. Despite the apparent advantages of new resources and the promotion of results-based social investment, SIBs have not been without controversy. Questions have been raised regarding the ability of projected savings to offset the higher costs associated with SIB,s including their more complicated contract and administrative structure, the higher cost of private financing, and the net value added of the intermediary (Loxley 2013; McKay 2013a; Stid 2013; Whitfield 2015). At their foundation, SIBs rest on a notion of the state as unadaptable and incapable of innovation, relative to the private sector, but the evidence on this is not conclusive. If SIBs are a costlier way of delivering interventions, and the total resources available for paying for these services are exogenously determined, then overall welfare may be reduced.

This chapter outlines the case made by proponents of SIBs as a superior vehicle for publicly funded social service delivery, and presents and categorizes some central propositions regarding the desirable attributes of SIBs that lead to improvements over alternative delivery models. This is not a straightforward task, as proponents generally have not framed their arguments by explicitly comparing SIBs to alternative procurement or delivery methods but to a perceived dysfunctional state of affairs with respect to how government approaches social programs more generally. Unlike the more robust literature comparing program intervention models (see Chapter 1 and Appendix A), no experimental studies of the impact of the procurement model used appear to have been undertaken to date.

We evaluate the claims of SIB proponents on their own terms, and attempt to identify which elements of the SIB model are responsible for improvement over conventional practices. We categorize all the claims of proponents, and trace them back to the two main distinguishing features of SIBs reviewed in Chapter 1: private management and finance, and payment-by-results criteria. We use three broad categories of the proposed effects of SIBs: (1) an increase in the number of beneficial social programs delivered; (2) an increase in the quality and effectiveness of individual programs delivered; and (3) improvements to the broader public social service system as a whole. We evaluate each of these claims in turn and the associated attributes of SIBs on which they are premised, but we begin by outlining the case made for SIBs by proponents and their depiction of the status quo. The focus here is to examine the logical consistency of the proponents' case and to review the empirical support of these claims.

SIB Proponents' Narratives of the Status Quo

The literature on SIBs by their proponents often bases the case for SIBs in relation to how government currently approaches social programs more generally. Essentially all proponents begin with a disparaging assessment of the status quo – more specifically, government ineptness at addressing pressing social problems (Whitfield 2015). Take the following statement by Liebman (2011, 1):

> Current approaches to government funding of social services create significant barriers to innovation. Funding streams tend to emphasize inputs rather than program objectives and are often overly prescriptive, requiring grantees to use a particular delivery model. In many cases, program outcomes are not rigorously assessed, allowing unsuccessful initiatives to persist for years.
>
> Meanwhile, the public sector is slow to adopt new program models, even those proven to be highly effective. There is no systematic process through which philanthropically funded interventions with demonstrated success receive the government funding necessary to expand. Investments in preventive services can be particularly difficult to finance.

Liebman and Sellman (2013, 6) present a similar statement, adding that "tight budgets cause us to under-invest in prevention ... [and] threaten to stifle innovation ... [W]e are simply not making rapid enough progress in addressing social problems." Dear et al. (2016, 12) comparably criticize the status quo, describing a context where

> [g]overnment struggled to support or encourage innovation in the social arena, contracts between government and delivery organizations stifled creativity and adaptation, and the social sector had no effective way of being rewarded for successful outcomes. These were and still are huge problems ... services for some of the most vulnerable in society are often bureaucratic, one size fits all solutions ... innovative, holistic services are occasional pinpoints of light ... [W]e are providing an array of services to some of the most vulnerable in society without actually knowing if they work and without gathering the knowledge to improve them or know whether they should be provided in the future.

Although using gentler language, Deloitte (2012, 2) emphasizes the same points, including that "measurable outcomes can be elusive," that there is "limited incentive for innovation," and that "collaboration from a number of groups and perspectives ... [is] often limited in the established structures of our public institutions." Gustafsson-Wright, Gardiner, and Putcha (2015) note "the inability of governments to equitably deliver high-quality services in the education and health sectors ... aris[ing] from lack of resources, ineffective use of such resources, or both" (1), with "undue focus on more expensive curative or crisis-driven interventions, resources not reaching frontline service providers, weak incentives" (2). They also claim that "government systems ... can be bureaucratic and distant from reality," with "insufficient attention to performance and to measuring" and "political and institutional constraints" such as "election cycles, budget silos, and complex or rigid government appropriation systems" (2). The Harvard Kennedy School (2017) points to a "lack of performance assessment, under-investment in prevention, and inability to collaborate effectively with service providers around improving system." Mulgan et al. (2011) are an exception in that they are less critical of government, focusing more on budgetary challenges in the post-2008 financial crisis environment, "incentives [that] are poorly aligned," and noting that it is "difficult to secure funding for initiatives that set out to prevent undesirable outcomes" (15).

Liebman and Feller (2014) formally model the claimed government failure through four channels. First, governments undervalue innovation in social benefits relative to its social value since they consider only the benefit the innovation provides within their jurisdiction. Second, since "governments rarely conduct rigorous evaluations" (8), ineffective programs persist, so experimentation by introducing new programs leads to growing costs as pilot projects become permanent, regardless of outcomes. Third, governments discount future benefits of social innovation too highly due to political considerations and "siloed decision-making" (8). Finally, governments misallocate resources internally, overinvesting in direct delivery of services and underinvesting in management, administration, and evaluation.

Proponents' Claimed Advantages of SIBs

Proponents then highlight the features of the SIB model that help to overcome these barriers. For example, Dear et al. (2016) stress "the values of partnership and collaboration, flexibility and responsiveness, and a focus on data, outcomes, and measurement" (7), later also noting "the payment mechanism, and the delivery oversight" (53). Liebman (2011) points to "performance-based payments and market discipline" (1), "private financing to overcome existing barriers to performance-based pay," and "private investors['] … quality control," both at the project selection phase and during the contract (2), leading to the "rigorous ongoing evaluation of program impacts into program operations, accelerating the rate of learning about which approaches work and which do not" and their "adoption" (3). Liebman and Feller (2014, 18) also highlight how grant support bridges the gap between the returns to the government undertaking the SIB and the broader social return of the innovation, which can then be replicated elsewhere.

Gustafsson-Wright, Gardiner, and Putcha (2015) come closest to a systematic inventory of the claims of SIBs, identifying ten distinct advantages: the ability to "crowd-in private funding, prioritize prevention, reduce risk for government, shift focus to outcomes, achieve scale, foster innovation in delivery, drive performance management, stimulate collaboration, build a culture of monitoring and evaluation, and sustain impact" (36–47). Below we use three categories to classify these claims: SIBs' ability to deliver incremental social services, to produce higher-quality social services, and to have positive system-level effects on the operation of government.

Claim 1: SIBs Allow the Delivery of More Social Programs

One claim of proponents is that SIBs allow additional cost-effective preventative social interventions to proceed (Pauly and Swanson 2017).

Rothschild (2013, 106) speaks to their "incremental investment in high performing social enterprises," while Mulgan et al. (2011, 15) state that SIBs are "unlocking new funding" for important and valuable social initiatives that currently are not going forward due to lack of funding. A related form of this argument is the claim that SIBs facilitate the scaling up of successful interventions (see Burand 2012; Gustafsson-Wright, Gardiner, and Putcha 2015, 41–2). Dear et al. (2016, 44), for example, note that SIB "programs have mainly been additive, not a replacement for existing services, or have changed the contracting framework of services which were already delivered by outside service providers."[1] The degree to which these new programs are incremental as opposed to a change in delivery model for existing programs is an important consideration, one that has not been systematically determined to date.

New Private Funding and Financing

For new prevention programs to be incremental, new money must materialize or be advanced to fund these initiatives. SIBs clearly are designed to attract new private capital into supporting social service delivery. Gustafsson-Wright, Gardiner, and Putcha (2015) conclude that SIBs are attracting capital from "both traditional [philanthropic/foundation] investors and new investors," but that it is not clear if these funds "represent a shift in assets under management from one sector to another or if they equate to some additionality" (38; see also Fraser et al. 2018b 19). Here it is also important to keep in mind the distinction between financing and funding sources, which we discussed in Chapter 1. As Gustafsson-Wright, Gardiner, and Putcha (2015, 37) note, "if outcomes are achieved, outcome funders (governments) will have to pay for the services"; in this case, new funding is not being generated by private investors, only new financing. As Gardiner and

---

1   A related issue is the degree to which SIBs programs rely on existing social infrastructure and services, and the extent to which it is the SIB or the underlying service that is providing the benefit. At least two SIB projects, the Partnering for Family Success Program in Ohio and the Sweet Dreams SIB in Saskatchewan, rely on the use of public or social housing that is not funded under the SIB (Loxley 2017, 20); Pennell (2014). This raises questions regarding the impact of access to housing itself relative to the broader SIB, and the degree to which a limited public or social housing stock is simply being reallocated to families in the SIB projects and away from others. This is a broader issue with SIBs, with many projects connecting clients to existing services. For example, although the Peterborough One Service SIB added some dedicated mental health supports and courses on maintaining family connections, a key component of the project was having mentors and caseworkers connect clients to existing services (Disley and Rubin 2014; Nicholls and Tomkinson 2013).

Gustafsson-Wright (2015) put it, "investors are solving a liquidity problem for government by providing upfront capital and not actually providing new money." SIBs might then just shift payment responsibility into the future (Painter et al. 2018). In fact, the government can end up paying more than it would have under alternative delivery models (Fraser et al. 2018b, 16), potentially reducing the real quantity of preventative social services procured if government resources for this purpose are fixed.

In practice, there are some scenarios where the private sector participants end up being funders. First, if an SIB fails to meet its targets, at-risk capital invested ends up funding the incremental social service. The degree to which this is realized as a new source of funding depends on the availability of socially motivated investors with a high loss tolerance, or the realization of unexpectedly high systematic failure rates. Other than a few high-profile failures, SIB projects appear to be repaying investors, with a large majority of projects that report results publicly having met or appear to be on track to meeting their benchmarks (see Chapter 2).

Second, many SIBs are not based fully on risk capital; some are funded by non-outcomes-based grants or donations. SIBs might attract new grant funding to the total philanthropic donation pool because of their structural characteristics – for example, the strong emphasis on outcomes or the claim of promotion of new innovative approaches. In the stylized SIB model, however, government, not the private sector, funds successful outcomes. Although there are some cases where new funding, as opposed to financing, is generated through private sources, these appear to be exceptional or due to reallocation of traditional funding sources.[2]

New Public Funding

As noted above, SIBs can generate incremental investment by "solving a liquidity problem for government" (Gardiner and Gustafsson-Wright 2015). State leaders face at least two budget constraints. An intertemporal budget constraint must be met such that the expected real present value of government expenditures minus current debt cannot exceed the expected present value of real tax revenues (Romer 2006, 560). This can be considered the "real" budget constraint of government, and is

---

2 This assessment is based on the authors' review of the funding sources and
   participants assembled in a database and discussed in more detail in Chapter 5.

necessarily based on predictions of government behaviour into the future.[3] Standard accounting conventions, however, lead to this budget constraint not being reported publicly. What is reported are measures of current levels of government spending, revenue, and debt.

This publicly reported set of budgetary indicators produce a second set of accounting-based indicators, including the standard reported notions of budgetary balance or deficits or surplus. The effect of specific policy actions on these measures and reported budget balance, such as asset sales and the assumption of unfunded liabilities, is not necessarily indicative of their effect on the real government budget constraint: for example, asset sales generally reduce the deficit and have an ambiguous effect on the budget constraint, while the assumption of unfunded liabilities impacts future expenditures with no effect on standard measures of the debt and deficit (Romer 2006, 562–3). Based on these reported indicators, governments might choose to self-impose, through legislation or policy, budget constraints at the aggregate level and/or at department budget levels. One particularly pervasive expectation is that governments should balance their budgets over some time horizon, giving rise to legislation that requires governments to balance their budget each year or over a longer period.

Unless an SIB provides savings in excess of its cost, it will not loosen a government's real budget constraint, but an SIB may permit the government temporarily to relax self-imposed institutional budget constraints through the PbR structure, which can defer the costs of payment, in some cases to the end of the SIB contract.[4] The contingency-based payment structure of SIBs has been interpreted in such a way that it removes the requirement for government to finance the project upfront, as would be required under more traditional procurement models, generating new resources for social programs that otherwise may go unfunded. This can make SIBs attractive to governments struggling with deficit management due, for example, to ongoing consequences

---

3 The mechanism for enforcement of this constraint is the government issued securities market, in which debt rating agencies play a central role. As governments increase their debt relative to their deemed capacity to repay lenders, they will increasingly be forced to pay a higher rate of interest to issue new bonds. As long as the economy is growing, and that growth rate is greater than the interest rate on debt, governments can continue to borrow and face a stable or declining debt to GDP ratio, and avoid an endogenous debt crisis. See Taylor (2010, 242–6).

4 The logic here parallels that of public asset privatization for the purpose of generating revenues, as summarized by Vickers and Yarrow (1991, 118–19), who highlight the inferiority of this strategy relative to raising funds through the bond market for developed countries with low risk of default.

of the 2008 financial crisis, but looking to increase investment in social programs.

Social Finance, a non-profit organization that specializes in the promotion and creation of SIBs, advises that the business activity of the SIB delivery agency need not be reflected in public accounts if the agency is determined to be separate from government (Social Finance 2011, 23–4, 34–6). Additionally, it notes that government obligations to pay the SIB likely will be accounted for as an executory contract, provision, or contingent liability, all of which are accounted for at time of payment, and therefore costs do not appear as a long-term liability in government accounts unless payments are fixed or fully guaranteed regardless of project outcomes (37–9).[5] If auditors agree, this allows a government to defer accounting for payments for social services delivered under an SIB or other PbR contract that otherwise would have been counted as a current expenditure. This could lead to SIBs supporting incremental social program delivery in the current year, assuming that the government maintains existing expenditure, without affecting the budget balance.

This accounting flexibility might be offset, however, by investors' demands for greater government accountability with respect to its commitment to pay under an SIB. Generally, future governments are not bound by the spending commitments of previous legislatures that span beyond the current fiscal year, which creates uncertainties for investors regarding the reliability of success payments and leads to legislative changes to facilitate future payments (Liebman and Sellman 2013, 25). Some of these legislative approaches compromise budgetary flexibility and set aside current funds for future outcome payments. For example, the State of Utah's School Readiness Initiative Act of 2014 established the School Readiness Restricted Account to fund PfS initiatives. California uses a similar approach with its Recidivism Reduction Fund, part of the Board of State and Community Corrections Act 2013–14.

Other legislative approaches explicitly fund initiatives completely from targeted social service savings such that expenditures need to be reduced in another area, leaving the net impact on overall incremental spending unchanged. Idaho, for example, in its Pay for Success Contracting Act of 2015, requires that SIBs be fully funded by explicitly identified savings and that these savings be set aside in a designated

---

5 Whitfield (2015) also highlights how the off-balance sheet nature of SIBs creates an accounting-based advantage for SIBs, generating an incentive to structure activity through these instruments despite their potentially higher costs and other negative impacts.

account, to be available to fund payments required under the SIB contract. Other states that have established PfS funds in legislation include Oklahoma, Maryland, Colorado, Massachusetts, and Texas, as well as the District of Columbia (Hathaway 2016). While losing accounting flexibility, these legislative funding models, in addition to reassuring investors, also create a source to fund SIBs that otherwise would require an incremental allocation in the year or years in which targeted outcomes are achieved and payments due. Overall, the legislated funds provide for a more transparent process and reliable funding source. The degree to which total preventative funding is affected will depend upon whether these funds are new incremental funds or were previously budgeted for non-SIB prevention-focused programming.

SAVINGS AS A NEW FUNDING SOURCE?

As discussed in Chapter 1, SIBs have the potential to be self-funding. Their proponents argue that, by paying only in the presence of successfully met outcomes and limiting contracts to outcomes with net fiscal savings, governments do not need incremental funds to support SIBs, as they pay for themselves through savings (Fraser et al. 2018b, 10). For this self-financing to be operationalized, governments must commit to identifying and allocating the operating funds saved to an accrual account to recover the cost of the SIB, as is required by some of the SIB legislative frameworks noted above. It is this new financing structure that is at the centre of SIBs as a financial innovation and arguably its most novel attribute.

Self-funded SIBs are a financial innovation in that they create a formal structure to borrow against projected social savings and might allow more unfunded preventative projects to proceed. Governments therefore notionally can finance the contract from the present value of costs they would otherwise incur if the intervention had not taken place, presuming the savings are sufficient to offset the cost fully, apparently creating a new funding source to pay for social programs that did not previously exist.

It important to note that it is not the SIB which is generating the new funding source, but the preventative social service itself. If the probability of the success of the social service outcome is independent of the procurement model, governments alternatively could issue traditional bonds to deficit-finance proven social investments that generate present-value savings greater than or equal to their costs, at government borrowing rates. This would leave the government as the recipient of the benefits, as opposed to investors in the SIB model, and would preclude the additional expenses associated with any additional administrative and transaction costs associated with the SIB structure. This leads to the critique that governments should be financing these services directly given their lower cost of borrowing (Mulgan et al. 2011, 17). Whether funded by an SIB or not, governments benefit from the projected savings used to validate a self-funding SIB. The question then should not be, "are SIBs able to generate savings in excess of their costs?" but "do SIBs deliver the highest net benefit when compared to other service delivery models?" This is complicated by the fact that the procurement model might impact the quality of the service and/or likelihood of success. We explore this issue more formally in Chapter 4 when drawing upon the insights from the theory and experience with public-private partnership infrastructure projects.

Assessment of Claim 1

The evidence that SIBs generate new funding for prevention initiatives is inconclusive. Although private capital is coming forward to finance SIB projects, if the SIBs are successful the government must pay back this investment plus a return (Dear et al. 2016, 20), in addition to any incremental administrative or transaction costs associated with the model (Fraser et al. 2018b, 16), and it is unclear at this point if these funds are simply being reallocated from other philanthropic activities (Gustafsson-Wright, Gardiner, and Putcha 2015, 37–8). There does not appear to date to be significant failure of SIBs resulting in new program implementation that government is not paying for, despite insinuations by some proponents that failure should be expected and part of a government's SIB strategy (see, for example, Liebman and Sellman 2013, 29). The direct savings due to funding only successful projects therefore are likely minimal (MacDonald 2013). SIBs might be attracting more traditional philanthropic support, such as grants or investment guarantees, due to their emphasis on outcomes and prevention, which might be attractive to donors. This also might result in a shift of donations as opposed to incremental new contributions, but to date this has not been verified.

The financing ability feature of the SIB model, however, creates the potential to allow more prevention-focused social programs to proceed than would have been the case otherwise. The combination of private, off-books financing that keeps the expense temporarily outside public accounts, a full outcomes-based payment structure, and limiting projects to those that generate cashable fiscal savings in excess of the SIB payout means that government can use SIBs to skirt self-imposed budget constraints and fund more of these programs. But many governments are setting aside current funds for future SIB payments, creating additional pressure on budgets as opposed to generating new funds (McKay 2013b, 13). If not funded in real time, diligence is required in capturing fiscal savings for these eventual costs, otherwise government will be faced with a large unbudgeted lump-sum cost if the contract is executed successfully by the private partners.

The idea that SIBs can pay for themselves is the most promising source of new funding, but this funding is generated by the social service itself, and is only required because government chose to restrict traditional funding for these activities despite the strong value-for-money case. This becomes particularly transparent where governments set up upfront funding sources for SIB programs. SIB proponents have also moved away from claims of the ability to self-fund (see Chapter 1). In practice self-funding SIBs face the challenge of generating cashable fiscal savings that can be genuinely withdrawn and reallocated, and which generally need to take the form of a real-world service cut that eliminates a social service elsewhere (MacDonald 2013, 30). Indeed, many SIBs no longer aim to meet the standard of generating cashable fiscal savings (Carter et al. 2018; Chiapello and Knoll 2020). More fundamentally the potential value of SIBs then rests on their ability, not to generate new funding, but to promote higher-quality social programs that generate these types of social and fiscal benefits, either directly or by stimulating systematic changes that are more likely to produce such social programs.

Claim 2: SIBs Lead to Higher-Quality and More Effective Outcomes

The second claim proponents make is that SIBs lead to higher-quality outcomes or deliver better results than social programs procured through conventional means, and are therefore more efficient (Albertson et al. 2018; Painter et al. 2018). Several mechanisms produce this proclaimed improvement, including better management and project selection leading to more effective service providers, the promotion of innovation, and greater collaboration, which are leveraged through the introduction of private finance and the PbR structure. The quality enhancement and improved effectiveness potential of an SIB is driven by privatizing management of the project and introducing a high-powered financial incentives payment structure, where the term privatization encompasses any transference of service delivery, including management responsibility, from the public sector to the private sector, through the transfer of assets and/or contracting out.[6] This comes at the expense of greater transaction costs, which we also review in this section.

Better Management and Project Selection

Proponents claim that private finance brings benefits to SIB projects beyond direct financial support, including improved project selection, project management, and transference of business sector skills and practices to the social service delivery sector. In general SIBs are claimed to "introduce the discipline of private capital" (Dear et al. 2016, 51). According to Liebman (2011, 2), "private investors ... perform an important form of quality control ... [S]ervice providers must convince the private investors that their program model and management team are likely to achieve the performance targets." Once the project has been selected, its is claimed that private investors bring more effective project management skills to the program or, as Dear et al. (2016, 80) put it, SIBs "harness the discipline of the private sector and add rigor" through their "active performance monitoring and management." Several evaluations of SIB projects have noted such active involvement of investors (for example, Albertson et al. 2018, 87).

Liebman (2011) captures this concisely and links it back to the PbR structure of the SIB: "the investors and bond-issuing organization ... have strong incentives to rigorously monitor and improve program performance; if performance targets are missed, they will lose the money they invested" (2). The supposed rigour of private sector management leads service providers under an SIB to implement systems changes to track outcomes, as opposed to outputs as required by the PbR model, thus developing and enhancing their capacity in this area (Fraser et al. 2018b, 9–10). This emphasis on data collection creates the basis for other changes to improve operations efficiency.

---

6 Some authors have defined privatization more narrowly. Domberger and Jensen (1997), for example, distinguish between contracting out and privatization, where the latter involves specifically the transfer of assets from public to private ownership. Others have used broader definitions. For example, Starr (2014, 21) settles on a definition of "any shift from public to private of the *production* of goods and services" [emphasis in original], while noting an even more inclusive conception would include "the shift of any activities or functions from the state to the private sector" which would include activities such as deregulation. Vickers and Yarrow (1991, 112) clearly categorize the contracting out of services that were previously undertaken by the public sector as a type of privatization, as does Hodge (2000, 14). We follow these latter authors.

Stakeholders point to how SIBs demand adaptation to a more rigorous, iterative, and flexible management process, which Dear et al.
(2016) refer to as "a new way of working which stretches the service
provider beyond its normal field of view" (32). This requires that, in
general, service providers "accelerate their learning and review cycles
to respond to incoming data and ensure the project is achieving the
desired outcomes," (32) and is an iterative process that may draw upon
all institutional participants in an SIB. Dear et al. (2016, 31) emphasize
that it is these changes at the service delivery level that are the central
channel through which SIBs lead to better outcomes. For this to materialize, evaluation needs to take place throughout the project so that
providers can adapt (Sturla, Shah, and McManus 2018). As Bailey and
LaBarbera (2018) summarize, SIBs are "encouraging delivery organisations to prioritise investment in the infrastructure necessary to track
data and measure the outcomes of social programmes, as well as shifting cultural attitudes around measuring whether service programmes
were truly making a difference in people's lives" (82). SIBs also provide greater stability for service providers given their multiyear nature,
reducing uncertainty around funding and allowing service providers
to focus on meeting well-defined, supposed evidence-based, social
service objectives (Mulgan et al. 2011, 16).[7] In general, the argument
for the better management and project selection case highlights how
SIBs can lead to a more efficient combination of inputs, taking existing
social service production technology as given, and pushing providers
towards their production possibilities frontier. Albertson et al. (2018),
based on their review of SIB project evaluations, suggest that the "SIB
[model] can improve service quality" and "overall, evidence from SIB
programmes tends to be more consistently positive" (108).

Innovation

The focus on outcomes and collaboration also leads proponents to
claim that SIBs generate innovation in social service delivery (Fraser et
al. 2018b, 10; Painter et al. 2018) or improvement in the technology used
in social service production. Social Finance UK founder Toby Eccles has
called SIBs "a highly effective catalyst and momentum builder for innovation ... often ... provid[ing] politicians with a route to encouraging public servants into trying something new" (Dear et al. 2016, 17).

---

7 See Fraser et al. (2020) for a discussion of the degree to which SIBs implement
   "evidence-based" programs.

Liebman and Sellman (2013, 29) claim SIBs are "designed to promote innovation in addressing social problems." Witkin (2019) rationalizes SIBs in a similar manner, assuming that the private sector can provide the innovation that the public sector is presumed unable to deliver, with SIBs being a model of generating new solutions to social problems such as climate change.

Some proponents, however, have argued that SIBs should not be expected to generate innovation but should focus on the right combination of successful interventions (Callanan and Law 2013, 79; Morse 2015, 21). This fits well with the finding of Lipsey and Cullen (2007), 315) that the issue in social service delivery, in areas such as antirecidivism and health care, is not finding what works, but that systems do not implement what works.

Collaboration and Alignment of Incentives

SIBs, by design, generate an intentional realignment of incentives to produce new forms of collaboration within government and between the public and private sectors. Mulgan et al. (2011) highlight how SIBs are "promoting evidence-based action" and "correcting poor incentives," noting that, "in many fields of public policy, incentives are poorly aligned, with those who have the ability to improve social outcomes lacking the incentive to act" (15). Through the construction of the SIB contract, the emphasis on measurement, and the foundation of the PbR contract on preventative savings, SIBs then are claimed to foster better collaboration across government departments to better align incentives. Toby Eccles emphasizes the importance of central government initiative and in particular central government funding support to drive this process (Dear et al. 2016, 17). This increased collaboration generated by PfS structure extends beyond government to include all SIB institutional participants, and is claimed to be "catalyzing systems reengineering in a way that rarely occurs with standard public sector management practices" (Harvard Kennedy School 2017).

There are two distinct arguments or stages through which better incentives and collaboration operate to generate superior outcomes. The first is that, by design, an SIB drives some central government actor which is "above the fray" of supposed siloed, interdepartmental bureaucratic politics to calculate the benefits and cost reductions of an intervention. By doing so it generates an SIB contract that internalizes the externalities that previously led inward-looking government departments to neglect the impact of their action or inaction on other departments or society more broadly. This creates the appropriate "demand" by government for the "right" type of action or activity. The "supply" of service to meet the constructed demand is through the PbR contract structure, which in turn leverages the discipline and innovative capacity of the private sector management. Because the government is paying only for outcomes, it relinquishes the ability to set restrictions on who is part of the service team and how they do their work, generating a flexibility to include new actors – in particular, private finance – and to structure service delivery better to accomplish the targets. This facilitates the second stage of collaboration, now between the private organizations in the SIB – specifically the service providers, including the intermediary and any technical assistance providers, as well as the financiers.

The (Lack of) Direct Evidence Regarding the Effectiveness of SIBs

As we discussed in Chapter 2, the growth of SIBs has proceeded based on a foundation of support and promotion by government, specialized proponent organizations, and other stakeholders. This growth has been supported by the evidence base of preventative interventions and the existence of a client base of who can benefit from these services, not the demonstrated superiority of the SIB model itself. Some proponents have acknowledged this limited evidence base. For example, Dear et al. (2016) note that "projects have mainly reported interim, not final, results and the extent to which they improve outcomes has varied" (26). Academic assessments concur, with Fraser et al. (2018b), in their extensive literature review of both academic and grey literature, referring to a "paucity of evidence about SIBs [with] most of the material identified ... best described as commentary" (14).[8]

This limited evidence base has not stopped proponents from claiming that the model is delivering results. Dear et al. (2016), for example, claim that the SIBs to date have a "promising, if early, record of success," and base this claim on the fact that, "of 22 projects that have shared performance data as of June 2016, 21 indicate positive outcomes for some participants" (26). In general, they claim that "the most critical measure

---

8 Broccardo, Mazzuca, and Frigotto (2020) come to similar conclusions in their review. See also Fox and Morris (2019); Fraser et al. (2018a); Tan et al. (2019). There are efforts systematically to document and evaluate the SIB experience. For example, the Commissioning for Better Outcomes Fund in the United Kingdom is supporting the evaluation of ten SIB projects, with three reports each, conducted at the launch, halfway point, and completion. At the time of writing, only three first-stage reports had been conducted (Big Lottery Fund 2017).

of success in a Social Impact Bond is social impact: did the project lead to better outcomes for participants? Did the intervention improve the lives of people in need?" (23). For example, the first ever SIB contract concluded and was deemed a success for exceeding targets and fully repaying investors plus a 3 per cent annual return (Owen 2017).

This assessment criterion for success is, however, problematic. As we discussed in Chapter 1, great emphasis is placed in SIBs on distinguishing the "results – the reported outcomes of a program – and attributable impact – the outcomes that can be specifically tied to the social intervention," often with sophisticated statistical techniques (Dear et al. 2016, 26). This methodological rigour lends credence to the assertion that the results and the success being generated are genuine and due to the SIB intervention. From a value-for-money perspective, however, this definition of success is problematic when seeking to determine whether the SIB model itself should be considered a success.

The idea that the service being delivered should positively impact participants presents a fairly low standard of "success," and amounts to, in a cost-benefit framework, looking only at the benefits and not the costs. From a public policy perspective, determining the validity of the SIB model should involve a comparative analysis between that model and other feasible service delivery models such as public delivery, conventional procurement, or conventional outcome-based payment schemes. Neglecting to make this comparison and focusing only on participant outcomes is equivalent to looking only at "results" without identifying "attributable impact," an error that SIB proponents, ironically, are highly aware of when it comes to evaluating the impact of a specific intervention, but appear to completely neglect when analysing the delivery model itself. As Fraser et al. (2018b) put it: "To date, across all active SIBs, there has been very little rigorous counterfactual comparison of SIBs versus alternative methods of finance to deliver the same service to the same type of users, and thus a lack of evidence of costs and benefits compared with the alternative approach to procurement" (13).[9] In later chapters we examine in more detail how this can be accomplished and what assessment mechanisms and frameworks exist to undertake this type of analysis, but here we review the limited direct assessments of the track record of SIBs on delivering higher-quality programming as well as the evidence on the effectiveness of

---

9 See also Broccardo, Mazzuca, and Frigotto (2020); Carter et al. (2018); Fox and Morris (2019); Floyd (2017, 12); Fraser et al. (2018a, 2020); and Painter et al. (2018).

privatization and PbR contracting, which have a more robust history and evidence base.

DIRECT ASSESSMENTS THAT SIBS LEAD TO HIGHER-QUALITY OUTCOMES

Gustafsson-Wright, Gardiner, and Putcha (2015) provide one the few systematic reviews of SIBs conducted to date aiming to assess whether SIBs have achieved their goals as articulated by their proponents. Their study, however, does not directly address the question of whether SIBs lead to improved social programs, but assess program characteristics that are presumed to lead to greater effectiveness. Some of their criteria assess whether SIB projects are staying true to the model, given their definition of SIBs. These include verifying that SIBs are: attracting private capital, supporting programs focused on prevention, transferring risk from government to funders, prioritizing outcomes, and generating collaboration between public and private stakeholders. Their criteria that have the most intuitive and plausible connection to improving quality include: the promotion of innovation, increased performance management capacity, collaboration across government stakeholders, a "culture of monitoring and evaluation" in government and service agencies, and the ability to "sustain impact" over time (45–6). They find that innovation has been marginal and limited for the most part to new combinations of existing programs, and that performance management has been enhanced, but there is no evidence that service providers have made program adjustments in response. They do find examples of collaboration within government and early signs of a more rigorous monitoring mentality and longer-term impacts, but it is not clear that these findings are generalizable.

Other studies have confirmed the intensive performance management reforms that take place in SIB projects. An early review of ten SIBs commissioned by the UK Department of Pensions found a "continuous process of monitoring and performance management," with many service providers "not anticipat[ing] the way in which the funding model would drive delivery" (Insite Research and Consulting 2014, 10). In their review, Albertson et al. (2018) find that this result holds more generally across SIB and PbR contracts in the United States and the United Kingdom, and note that, "on balance, more evaluations identified positive effects associated with this increased focus than negative effects" (89).

Edmiston and Nicholls (2018), in a study of four SIB projects in the United Kingdom, find limited evidence that the SIBs promoted innovation relative to previous PbR schemes (66–7) and that "some third sector stakeholders felt that the degree of micro-management built into the SIB was actually reducing their flexibility ... , that the resources and time that went into these additional forms of performance management and measurement could be better spent on front-line services" (64). Two of the SIBs were not "able to produce improved social outcomes relative to previous and other existing service interventions" (68); one had qualitative evidence to support superior performance, and another showed signs of improved outcomes but the baseline comparison was not current with standard intervention practice. They conclude that "the prospective benefits of service innovation appeared to originate more from the novelty, size and experimental nature of the PbR contract ... If anything, the presence of private social investment appeared to stifle the flexibility and autonomy of service providers to innovate and deliver services" (73).[10]

Based on data compiled by the Nonprofit Finance Fund (2017), eleven out of the twenty SIBs launched in the United States to date were based on interventions previously evaluated for their effect on the targeted population, and another seven had been evaluated but not in the specific context applied in the SIB, such that the combination of interventions had been tested separately as opposed to in combination, or the intervention had been tested with a slightly different population. Furthermore, in fifteen of the twenty SIBs, service providers had delivered their interventions to the targeted population prior to the SIB project, and in three other cases only some members of the service provider consortia had delivered the programming previously. The vast majority of US SIBs, then, have been using programming with a strong evidence base of effectiveness and service providers that have previously delivered the same service intervention.

Other recent studies have concluded that minimal innovation is taking place with respect to service interventions provided, which has been rationalized by the fact that investors would be unlikely to participate unless there was an evidence base for the intervention (Arena et al. 2016; Carter et al. 2018; Dayson, Fraser, and Lowe 2020, 167; Fraser et al. 2020; Heinrich and Kabourek 2018; Roy, McHugh, and Sinclair 2018). These studies suggest that the limited innovation that is occurring is either in altering the "mode of delivery" (Albertson et al. 2018, 92) such as by delivering more personalized support, or in delivering services to new participant groups, by increasing the scale of operations, delivering the service in a new geographic region, or targeting a tried

---

10 Edmiston and Nicholls (2018, 69) also highlight the problematic nature of the counterfactuals used in these projects, generally being administrative data as opposed to control groups.

intervention based on a different set of assessed needs. By definition, SIBs are also changing how services are financed. This is sometimes framed as innovation in the financing of social services, with the key benefit being flexible longer-term funding of service providers, increasing stability, and an environment more conducive to longer-term planning and results (Albertson et al. 2018, 93).

Empirical Evidence that Privatization Leads to Better Management and Innovation

PRIVATIZATION EVIDENCE

Arguments for private sector efficiency and privatization can be traced back to the significance of the profit motive and the competitive pressures that private firms face, and that they ignore at the risk of going out of business or being taken over. Specifically, private firms are subject to shareholders demanding maximum lifetime returns on their investment, to the risk of corporate takeover if shares are undervalued due to inefficient management, and to the threat of bankruptcy.[11] This is relative to a monopoly public provider, which, in the Public Choice paradigm, will oversupply services to maximize the potential self-serving opportunities for management (Bel, Fageda, and Warner 2010, 555; Letza, Smallman, and Sun 2004, 165), and will fail to innovate due to lack of the competitive pressure and information that markets provide (Petersen, Hjelmar, and Vrangbæk 2017, 4). The property rights literature emphasizes how public sector employees have little incentive to undertake quality-enhancing investments to stimulate productivity since they lack ownership of productive assets and managers are able to expropriate any gains.

The *a priori* association of privatization with competition is questionable, however, as, depending on the market characteristics, the existence of multiple public sector organizations competing to provide a service is conceptually just as possible as that of a private monopolist (Hart, Shleifer, and Vishny 1997, 1129; Vickers and Yarrow 1988, 45). Even if competition is present, particularly in social services, there is no guarantee that this will drive efficiency enhancements and innovation (Finn 2008, 43).

The assertion that shareholders will hold a firm to account is also tenuous. Chang (2003), for example, notes that private firms face the "problem of 'shareholder collective action'" (209–10) such that, unless

---

11 For a summary and critique, see Vickers and Yarrow (1988, 8–44).

ownership is consolidated, given the diffusion of shares, few individual shareholders will be motivated to provide a high level of oversight due to the free-rider problem associated with better firm outcomes.[12] In the public sector management case, there likely will be a single entity or small number of them responsible for outcomes, held accountable by "institutionalized mechanisms of collective action" unavailable to private shareholders (210). Chang also notes that the proposed rationale for privatization generally reduces to principal-agent problems associated with public governance that idealize the operation of private sector firms while ignoring principal-agent problems within the corporate governance structure of publicly traded corporations. Specifically, privatization often involves the adoption of the privatized service as a subsidiary of an existing corporate structure, replicating the principal-agent structure and associated supervision and information asymmetries. Stiglitz (2008) makes a similar case, noting that, once the neoclassical assumption of perfectly functioning markets – in particular, the assumption of perfect information – is relaxed, "the theoretical case for privatization is weak or non-existent" (xii).

Based on this theoretical ambiguity, one must turn to the empirical evidence (Vickers and Yarrow 1988, 39). Results with respect to efficiency from empirical studies of privatization are mixed, with evidence on the wave of privatization that took place in the 1980s and 1990s often pointing to lower costs but also to lower-quality service (Hart, Shleifer, and Vishny 1997, 1127), with costs savings the primary motivation driving privatization efforts (Auger 1999, 440; Bel and Fageda 2007).[13]

Estimates of cost reductions vary widely and have evolved over time, with some early estimates concluding, with caveats, that privatization leads to greater efficiency. For example, at the US state level, estimated savings in the 1990s were reported to be as high as 20 per cent, but for most states the savings had been minimal – less than 5 per cent – with significant variation depending on service type, with "administrative

---

12 See also Sappington and Stiglitz (1987) and Olson (1965).

13 Costs might be the primary factor noted, but the full set of motivations for privatization is large. Vickers and Yarrow (1988), for example, note the objective of the expansive privatization program that took place under Prime Minister Margaret Thatcher in the 1980s, which included: "(i) improving efficiency; (ii) reducing the public sector borrowing requirement … ; (iii) reducing government involvement in enterprise decision making; (iv) easing problems of public sector pay determination; (v) widening share ownership; (vi) encouraging employee share ownership; [and] (vii) gaining political advantage" (157). Hodge (2000, 18–24) has a similar extensive list, but also has economic efficiency as the priority. We place some non-efficiency explanations of privatization at the centre of the analysis in Chapter 6.

services, mental health and retardation services, and transportation initiatives" generating the highest savings (Auger 1999, 441). Vickers and Yarrow (1988, 39–43) reviewed studies of railroads, electrical utilities, water distribution and waste collection, airlines, water transportation, steel and energy resource appliance production, and, although noting several reservations with existing studies, they concluded that, "where competition is effective, the available evidence suggests that private enterprise is generally to be preferred on both internal efficiency grounds and, subject to the qualification that other substantive market failures are absent, social welfare grounds" (43). Three years later Vickers and Yarrow (1991, 117–18) came to similar conclusions, emphasizing the role of competition over ownership structure in their interpretation of the evidence. They recognized that, in practice, privatization likely is required to create competition, particularly in the case of contracting out, and that the empirical evidence varies when considering competitive and monopolistic industries, with privatization less effective in the latter and regulation playing an integral role with respect to outcomes. Boardman and Vining's (1989) literature review came to similar conclusions, with "an "edge" for the private sector, but results vary[ing] considerably across sectors" (5). Like Vickers and Yarrow, they emphasized the importance of market structure, with monopolistic industries and those subject to high degrees of regulation being favourable to public ownership, but they also highlighted, in the case of contracting out, how low information requirements for supervision are also a key factor for better results under privatization. In their attempt to control for industry concentration and other characteristics, Boardman and Vining found significant and robust performance differences, with private enterprise consistently outperforming public enterprises, including mixed ownership structures, on profitability and efficiency. In a more recent literature review, Villalonga (2000, 5–9) finds that 104 of 168 studies of enterprise privatization supported greater private sector efficiency, but notes that the evidence is not conclusive.

Similar early results were found when looking more narrowly at the contracting out of services, a form of privatization more comparable and relevant to the social service and SIB context. Boyne's (1998) literature review of contracting out in a variety of service areas found that three-quarters of studies show that costs were reduced, although only about half of reviewed studies show efficiency gains associated with privatization after some rudimentary accounting for service levels and quality. Hodge's (2000) review of forty studies of the cost savings associated with contracting for service found that cost reductions on average were in the range of 8 per cent to 14 per cent (123–8), with some substantial variation between service type, with the results being driven by high savings in refuse collection, cleaning, and maintenance (155–6). Hodge makes the important distinction that contracting for services can take place with both private and public sector agents, and includes contracting between public providers and purchasers in addition to private contractors. He finds that the benefits of contracting to a public agent are similar to those of contracting with a private agent, and his results suggest that the cost savings are being driven by the contractual relation, rather than by the firm's ownership status.

Earlier studies of private sector superiority have been questioned on methodological grounds (Boyne 1998). Others have suggested that, once management and administrative costs associated with privatization are considered, savings might be minimal (Globerman and Vining 1996). Empirical studies of the efficiency of privatization continue to be plagued by the problem of limited data and the challenge of accounting for differences in market structure, including the degree of regulation and extent of competition (Bel, Fageda, and Warner 2010, 554; Vickers and Yarrow 1988, 41). More recent studies have raised questions about the earlier consensus on the conditional benefits of contracting out, as these challenges remain primarily unaddressed.

Meta-analyses of cost studies in the area of water and waste, which has seen extensive experimentation with privatization, show only minimal cost differences between public and private provision (see, for example, Letza, Smallman, and Sun 2004, 166–7), despite some earlier results that claimed lower private delivery costs (Bel, Fageda, and Warner 2010; see also Bel and Warner 2008b). Studies have also demonstrated that ceding operations to private sector agents has led to reductions in service quality, a worsening of working conditions, and reductions in responsiveness to end users (Hermann and Flecker 2013; Warner 2013). Zullo (2019, 125) highlights studies showing that, when quality of service and reduced obligations are accounted for, the benefits of privatization disappear. These later findings, in addition to the failure of expected cost savings to be realized, have led to an increase in services being contracted back in and greater reliance on intergovernmental cooperation and mixed public-private models as an alternative to privatization (Bel and Warner 2008a; Dijkgraaf and Gradus 2013; Hefetz and Warner 2004; Warner 2008; Warner and Bell 2008; Warner and Hefetz 2008).

In a particularly relevant recent review, Petersen, Hjelmar, and Vrangbæk (2017) conduct an international literature survey of forty-nine empirical studies published between 2000 and 2014 that examine the cost savings associated with contracting out. Their sample, more diverse than previous reviews, includes studies of "technical services" such as waste collection, transportation, and water services, but also social service areas, including health, education, and training (9–17). Two of their key findings are, first, a steady decline over the study period in the cost advantage of private sector delivery, with studies published between 2010 and 2014 holding an average cost difference of only 0.4 per cent (19); and, second, effectively zero cost difference over the entire period between public and private delivery for social services.[14]

Petersen, Hjelmar, and Vrangbæk (2017) point to advancements in theory based on transaction cost literature to explain their results (19). This work emphasizes how attributes of a particular service can alter the expected benefit of contracting out, where industries with highly specific assets and high cost of performance monitoring – and transaction costs more generally – are less likely to generate savings (4); social service provision is such a case (19). There is also a related temporal case to be made that the benefits of privatization will decline over time as governments first privatize the services where cost reductions are the most likely, leading to diminishing returns to privatization, and as contracting out takes place, public sector competitors will learn, adapt, and become more efficient when faced with the prospect of elimination (5).

A third key finding is a significant difference in effect between English-speaking countries – which face less regulation and relatively low collective bargaining coverage of the private sector workforce – with cost reductions of 6.4 per cent on average, and other countries, which saw average cost reductions of 2.9 per cent (Petersen, Hjelmar, and Vrangbæk (2017, 20), suggesting that privatization might lead to cost reductions simply by reducing workers' wages and benefits. The authors caution that the cost-savings estimates of reviews of earlier privatization studies might have been smaller if the samples had included a greater diversity of service types and geography (20).

The inability of the private sector to outperform the public delivery of social services is also reinforced in country-level comparative studies

---

14 Petersen, Hjelmar, and Vrangbæk (2017, 18) note that many of the studies do not account for the transaction costs associated with contracting out, likely biasing these cost difference estimates in favour of private delivery. They also note that, despite efforts to control for comparability of service, "public sector organizations deliver a broader range of services ... [and] are often required to serve all citizens in a given area, while private companies can often choose their markets and services" (21). They also reference the challenges of comparability, controlling for competition, and methodological challenges with estimating costs (21–4).

of old age security and health care (Stiglitz 2013, 220), the two largest areas of social expenditure in OECD countries.[15] Privatization in the education sector in the United States through the charter schools movement has also been accused of producing dismal results (Fabricant and Fine 2012).

Recent studies of public-private partnerships in infrastructure, a partial privatization model very similar conceptually to SIBs, also show that this form is at best ambiguous from an efficiency perspective. Loxley (2010), in a review of eleven PPP projects in Canada launched between 1994 and 2007, finds that four generated no savings, two did not have a public sector comparator to form the basis of an analysis, and three generated savings, but these came at the expense of lower labour compensations through the substitution of non-union for unionized labour (173). Moreover, in many cases, transaction costs were not properly accounted for (174). Vining and Boardman (2008) provide a similar assessment of ten Canadian PPPs, concluding: "evidence suggests that the benefits are often outweighed by contract costs and externalities" (38). In an international review of PPPs, Hodge and Greve (2007) find that studies looking at value for money were approximately equally split as to whether the PPP model provided superior results; in their 2017 study, they continue to find that reviews of PPPs produce inconclusive results and suffer from methodological challenges (65). The *a priori* evidence on PPPs, then, is inconclusive.

The *ex post* evidence on PPPs also raises doubts. Shaoul's (2005) review of Private Financing Initiatives in the United Kingdom[16] demonstrates that the optimistic projections used in value-for-money analyses to justify the model regularly do not materialize in practice, and finds that the PPP projects faced higher costs with minimal risk transfer than does conventional procurement. In their regression analysis of over five thousand water providers in France, Chong et al. (2006) find that PPPs led to higher prices for consumers, all other things equal, and speculate that this might have been due to reduced competition and high transaction costs. A number of studies highlighting the large number of renegotiations of PPP contracts (Estache 2006; Guasch, Laffont, and Straub 2006, 56; Whitfield 2017) also suggest that value-for-money analyses might have been overly optimistic. Whitfield (2017), for example, reviews a number of problematic cases in the United Kingdom

---

15   Old age security and health care make up, on average, 8.4 per cent and 6.0 per cent, respectively, of the gross domestic product of OECD countries (OECD 2018).

16   In the United Kingdom, PPPs are known as Private Financing Initiatives (PFIs) when private financing is part of the bundled procurement contract.

where government has had to intervene in previously negotiated PPP contracts, finding that a significant proportion – approximately one-third of all agreements, when measured by contract value – have had "buyout, termination or major problems" (7).

Although some early studies of privatization produced significant cost-saving estimates, more recent studies of contracting out and PPPs bring into question the existence of net cost reductions through efficiencies arising from greater reliance on the private sector for public service delivery. SIBs proponents' claims that rely heavily on the superiority of private sector management are not on solid footing in this regard. Social service provision, both empirically and based on theoretical developments with respect to asset specificity, monitoring, and transaction costs, appears to be a poor candidate for efficiencies through contracting out. Proponents' claims become even more tenuous in the cases of SIBs where investors might not have any specific knowledge, management experience, or specialization in social service delivery, and instead might rely on a hired intermediary to manage their interests.

EVIDENCE OF PRIVATE SECTOR INNOVATION

Investigations into the innovative capacity of the private sector also challenge private sector superiority. Mazzucato (2015), for example, makes the case that it is often the state that leads with respect to key technological innovations, with the private sector stepping in to commercialize and mass produce once the innovation's feasibility has been demonstrated, even then often requiring additional subsidies and incentives at the commercialization stage. Rather than the state simply offsetting the gap between social and private returns in technological advancement, or playing a coordinating and facilitating role in creating "systems of innovation," historically revolutionary technological change has been driven by "an entrepreneurial state acting as a lead risk taker and market shaper" (Mazzucato 2015, 16–17). The author points to the development of the Internet, several foundational technologies underpinning the iPhone, the telegraph line, nanotechnology, and green energy as areas where government research led the way. Stiglitz (2015) echoes this message, and supplements it by noting other major technical advancements in the United States, including "the transistor, the laser, the CCD, information theory, … the programming language UNIX," and radio astronomy were made by Bell Labs, a monopoly funded by an effectively universal research tax (9). Stiglitz also points to research showing that scientists are driven more by the recognition of their work by the scientific community than by financial gains, and that increasing the ability to generate private financial gain through patent protection to stimulate new discoveries might actually hinder innovation by reducing the pace of and opportunity for incremental discovery through greater privatization of knowledge and limiting the diffusion of new ideas (Stiglitz 2015, 5).

Chang (2003, 52–7) also highlights how innovation in a modern economy not only must coordinate dispersed knowledge that has been increasingly institutionalized in organizations as opposed to individuals, but also often requires a central agent to formulate a vision, navigate interdependencies, and generate a new institutional structure that might require a reorganization of existing property rights. He points to the "enormous potential gains from good state entrepreneurship" (57) and to the "socialization of risk" (136) as a key factor in the innovation and growth observed in capitalist societies.[17]

Mazzucato's and Stiglitz's research, which focuses on revolutionary technological transformations related to information technology and advanced manufacturing, and Chang's work, which focuses on economic development more broadly, applies equally to the potential for private capital to generate social innovation, and produces an equally if not more critical prognosis in the SIB case. In information technology and advanced manufacturing, intellectual property rights facilitate the private appropriation of financial gains from successful innovation, yet private actors still have been too risk averse to pursue truly transformative innovation. The fact that social service delivery would generate highly dubious, if any, patenting opportunities for successful innovation while still resulting in the privatization of knowledge, and that the only consumer base for services would be government itself, leads one to believe that it would be even more difficult to stimulate any significant innovation through SIBs. Additionally, social innovators could be expected just as much as scientists to experience success through non-pecuniary gains – in particular, the value they derive from the social impact of their discoveries. Finally, resolving social challenges of poverty, social exclusion, and precariousness involves tackling interdependencies associated with the negative outcomes with respect to the policy areas spanned by SIBs. Moving from a state of high inequality and social exclusion to one of greater equality and social integration likely will involve the type of institutional regime shift described by Chang, and is unlikely to be accomplished by parcelling out contracts to address individual symptoms, such as homelessness, unemployment,

---

17 See also Rowthorn and Chang's (1992) discussion of "dynamic efficiency" and the potentially strategic position of the state (12–13).

poor educational outcomes, and unsafe home environments for children, that are tracked as a basis for success.

Pay for Success

Some SIB proponents have depicted the fact that government only pays when projects are successful under an SIB as a self-evident, positive attribute of the model (Greenblatt and Donovan 2013, 19; Butler, Bloom, and Rudd 2013, 58–9), and that funding "what works" over what does not is the "obvious approach" that governments should adopt (Callanan and Law 2013, 80). This is based on the idea that service providers are "street-level bureaucrats" in that they have discretion on the front lines of service delivery (Heinrich 2011, 231; Lipsky 2010), that they respond to financial motivation, and that to better achieve desired objectives they should be paid by results. The financial reward might be valued directly and/or it might be a mechanism to recognize higher achievement, providing a reputational benefit (Heckman, Heinrich, and Smith 2011a, 43).

The general idea of linking individual payment to outcomes in the analysis of production management processes has a long tradition going back at least to Taylor's theory of scientific management (Rinehart 2006, 40), and an even longer tradition historically in practice through the piece-rate–based cottage industry system, and with PbR in social services going back to at least the 1970s in the United States (Pauly and Swanson 2017). In economics, the analysis and rationale for this payment mechanism is often structured in a principal-agent framework, where an agent that is being contracted to do the work will know better than the principal how hard it is working to achieve the goal set by the principal. By setting a compensation structure based on some verifiable, observable outcome, the principal can extract a greater level of effort from the service provider, if, for example, the principal benefits from greater effort and the agent prefers less, *ceteris paribus*. Alternatively, performance-based contracts can arise when the preferences of government and the service provider do not coincide with respect to the type of outcomes desired, including who benefits from the service and to what degree, and a more prescriptive contract detailing provider activity is not efficient or feasible (Heckman, Heinrich, and Smith 2011a, 37–9).[18]

---

18 Heckman, Heinrich, and Smith (2011b, 39) note a third possibility, that performance standards can be implemented as a means to convey data and provide an assessment function.

There are complicating factors that challenge the simple idea that paying fully based on outcomes is optimal for the principal. First, "best-to-best" models are not an uncontested notion, and run counter to needs-based models where poor performance can indicate a higher level of need, calling for greater resource allocation (Bevan and Hood 2006, 519). In other words, there might be diminishing returns to investment in well-performing areas and increasing returns in underperforming areas. Halpern and Jutte (2013) make a parallel argument in the analysis of the ethics of PfS, noting that simply allocating based on efficiency and cost-saving considerations raises significant equity concerns. Considerations such these will affect whether PbR can be a means to improve allocative efficiency. Even if issues of allocative efficiency can be set aside and one accepts that programs that are thriving merit further support at the expense of others, a proper evaluation should look at both the outcomes and the costs of generating those outcomes. Compared to a standard fixed-price contract and typical economic assumptions, the private sector consortia in an SIB will need a financial incentive for taking on the additional risk associated with non-payment under an SIB (Fox and Albertson 2011, 404, 411). This raises the relative cost of the contract. Not only will contractors need to be compensated for any reduction in the expected profit due to the chance the project might fail, but if the private sector investors are risk averse, they will require further additional compensation. This might lead to a costlier intervention than if undertaken under a conventional procurement model, unless it is offset by other efficiencies associated with the SIB model.

Another complicating issue is that high-powered incentives based on selective or narrowly defined performance measures might generate unintended consequences that work counter to program objectives. Dixit (2002), an economist working within the general incentive theory paradigm, summarizes how the unique attributes of public sector operations might undermine the net benefits of PbR-type structures. He notes that, although performance-based incentives might facilitate improvements in some element of the principal-agent relationship between management and service providers, they also might simultaneously generate unintended negative consequences.[19] Some of the public sector attributes he identifies include: (1) the presence of multiple principals due to public goods attributes or externalities associated

---

19 See Prendergast (1999) for a review of some of these and related challenges to the effectiveness of incentives including signal noise, multiple objectives, and the resulting opportunities to "game" indicators, and career concerns.

with goods and services provided by the public sector; (2) concerns of principals with the technique of production in addition to the outputs, including distributional issues and the quality of jobs created; (3) the responsibility of branches of government that deliver services to the public for meeting a number of objectives with attributes that affect consumers on multiple dimensions, many of which might be difficult to measure; (4) the non-existence of competition in many areas in which public services are provided and, when created through privatization or procurement, the problems competition can create due to hard-to-measure multidimensional outcomes of concern to multiple principals; and (5) the presence of career concerns, professional integrity, and a public sector work ethic based on norms of public service that can substitute for private financial incentives (Dixit 2002, 711–17).[20] Although the ideal is to set up targets that are "specific, measurable, achievable, relevant and time-limited," the public sector context creates challenges for effective metrics to be constructed that correspond directly to the often-complex multifaceted goals of public service delivery (Lagarde et al. 2013, 8).

Target-based systems might convert individuals who previously put the best interests of the system first, or at least did not try to conceal negative outcomes, into strategic agents who seek to take advantage of narrow performance indicators (Lowe and Wilson 2017). There is extensive empirical evidence, for example, that the introduction of pecuniary incentives can lead to the displacement of intrinsic motivation, with long-term detrimental effects on performance (Bénabou and Tirole 2003, 490; 2006). The introduction of such schemes might be interpreted as a lack of trust or an expression of non-confidence about the commitment or ability of agents, who in turn might respond reciprocally by behaving in a more self-regarding manner. Performance-based compensation then might generate "incentives to 'cheat' both by target-setters and target managers" (Bevan and Hood 2006, 519). In the narrower case of PbR employment contracts, these and other "dysfunctional behavioral responses" arise, given that payment is based on indicators that at best represent only a subset of the relevant attributes of work performance and that the worker-manager relationship generally cannot be specified fully in a verifiable and enforceable contract (Prendergast 1999, 8).

---

20 Others who have proposed that public service employees might be motivated to provide additional uncompensated labour time or effort stemming from a public service ethic include Francois (2000), Grout and Sonderegger (2006), and Glaeser and Shleifer (2001).

In practice, performance standards often are based on short-term indicators, given the logistical infeasibility of delaying payment to service providers for long periods. In the area of workforce development, examples include using measures such as employment rates or earnings in the first few months after training (Heckman, Heinrich, and Smith 2011a, 33). The outcomes measures used in practice are highly simplified and disconnected from the multifaceted complex realizations of success that programs aim to achieve, resulting in the potential for reported outcomes to diverge from the reality they aim to proxy (Lowe 2013; Lowe and Wilson 2017), particularly when outcomes take an extended time to be fully realized. In this context, one cannot tell if positive performance measures indicate (1) positive outcomes across all service areas, including those not monitored or imperfectly monitored by the chosen indicators; (2) positive outcomes in the well-measured activity area at the expense of poor performance on unmeasured or imperfectly measured activity/cost shifting; (3) poor outcomes and an emergent disassociation between performance measures and outcomes due to strategic gaming; or (4) poor outcomes and outright data fabrication (Bevan and Hood 2006, 522–3).

Gaming in this context refers to the modification of activity or reporting behaviour in response to incentive-based payments or performance standards in a way that might negatively affect service output. For example, contracted service providers might modify the number of clients they serve, which clients they service, and how much effort they dedicate to servicing each client (Heckman, Heinrich, and Smith 2011a). Exclusively self-interested entities will increase their expected compensation by shifting effort from unmeasured to measured indicators (Prendergast 1999, 8). When targets are based on achieving thresholds, strategic players that are underperforming will be incentivized to increase effort to meet the threshold targets if feasible or otherwise abandon efforts altogether until the next round; and overachievers will be incentivized to reduce performance or shift output from the current period to the next (Bevan and Hood 2006; Dixit 2002). Bevan and Hood's (2006) review of performance-based targets in UK health care, for example, identify gaming effects in a "significant minority of service provider units (ranging from 7 to 33 per cent in the studies quoted)" (532). In active labour market programming, there have been some dramatic gaming examples, with private contractors who had paid multi-million-dollar dividends to owners prosecuted for fabricating data on employment outcomes (Syal 2012). Bevan and Hood (2006) suggest an alternative of abandoning specific performance measures, and issuing only general standards, or not specifying thresholds in advance, and auditing to verify data integrity and the coherence of indicator measurement and service objective intent, with in-person evaluations including direct interaction with staff (534–5).

Courty and Marschke (2011a) develop a formal model of the negative and unintended behavioural responses that performance standards can elicit from service providers who take actions to increase reported outcomes, and classify them into three categories: *accounting manipulations*, which are responses that costlessly boost reported metrics, but do not impact outcomes; *gaming responses*, which increase reported performance, but have a direct negative effects on realized but unmeasured outcomes; and *marginal misallocations*, a shifting of resources between activities that individually create a positive impact on reported outcomes, but result in a reduction in the aggregate benefits of the service provided due to the shift of resources away from positive activities that produce unmeasured positive outcomes. Courty and Marschke (2011a, 212–14) cite evidence in their literature review of all of three activities in health and education where performance measures were introduced.

Two specific gaming effects discussed in the studies of PfS social service delivery, especially in the context of active labour market programs, are *cream skimming* and *parking*.[21] Cream skimming refers to the selection by service providers of program intervention participants so as to minimize the effort or resources required to meet the outcome objective, as opposed to "individuals' expected long-run benefits from participation" (Heckman, Heinrich, and Smith 2011a, 30). Parking refers to cases where hard-to-serve clients are provided only low-cost, low-quality interventions, with a minimal chance of generating meaningful positive outcomes for these clients, while focusing effort on those more likely to meet threshold targets (Finn 2008, 11).[22] Parked clients might still end up succeeding due to non-program-related factors, including their own motivation, so the agent might still receive incentive payments for these clients despite not being responsible for their success (Finn 2008, 40).

Heckman, Heinrich, and Smith (2011a) develop a formal model of cream skimming based on the assumption that training providers are

---

21 Carter (2019) distinguishes between "cherry picking," which takes place during client selection, and creaming, which takes place within the assigned or selected client pool. We use "creaming" to refer to both.

22 The concept of parking appears in other PbR contexts, such as in education, where teachers who are reimbursed based on student test scores are incentivized to transfer effort to students whose scores respond strongly to teacher attention away from students whose scores are less responsive (Murnane and Cohen 1986, 5).

driven by the desire to maximize the net present value of intervention impacts. They demonstrate how the introduction of short-term performance incentives can lead to a reduction in the generated benefits of the program in the case that those who are easiest to serve – that is, those who have best outcomes without receiving training supports – are not also those who benefit the most from training services. The introduction of performance incentives in this case might lead to a misallocation of training services away from where they can generate the greatest benefit towards meeting targets, and can also have negative equity impacts, with services being reallocated from those who are worse off to those who are easier to achieve a targeted threshold.[23] In the case where the service provider has preferences other than maximizing benefits – such as having a "social worker mentality" (Heckman, Heinrich, and Smith 2011b, 48), where the trainer provider prefers servicing the worse off regardless of whether they benefit relatively more or less from the training intervention – performance indicators can incentivize trainers to allocate resources more efficiently. Heckman, Heinrich, and Smith (2011b, 57) conclude by highlighting the "the difficulty of designing a performance system that makes things better (rather than making them worse)."

Cream skimming in SIBs can be avoided if a strict randomization of clients is undertaken between the treatment and control group (Liebman and Feller 2014, 26), but this might be challenging in practice. Gaming more broadly can be counteracted by establishing independent and external monitoring and evaluation bodies (Bevan and Hood 2006, 519) and by clearly specifying relevant client characteristics, accepting and categorizing clients according to these criteria, and compensating service providers more for harder-to-serve clients. This can lead, however, to greater administrative requirements, depersonalized service, disputes, and postponement of service to clients (Finn 2008, 40). In general, attempts to address creaming and parking issues arising in PbR schemes might undermine the flexibility and space for innovation that motivated outcomes-based payments in the first place (24, 39). Responding effectively to gaming will also be resource intensive, as agents learn and adapt to PbR schemes, altering their behaviours over

---

23 Although cream skimming includes decisions about whom to accept into programming as well as about allocating individuals to different types of programming, cream-skimming activities can be more covert, including offering services that might appeal to certain groups, strategically locating service delivery, and targeting outreach efforts to increase the odds that easy-to-serve clientele will participate (Heinrich 2011, 236).

time (Heinrich and Marschke 2010, 203). Rather than being of universal benefit to governments, as some proponents claim, PbR structures are complex to implement, might not be suitable in many contexts, and can have a "negative impact on value for money" (Morse 2015, 7). Given the potential negative consequences of PbR payment structures, below we review empirical research on the effectiveness of the PbR contract structure.

Empirical Evidence of the Effectiveness of PbR Initiatives

Although comparative studies of SIBs and conventional delivery are lacking, more traditional PbR models in public service delivery have a long track record, with more comparative analyses of how PbR performs in practice. These studies raise doubts regarding the ability of PbR to generate improvements over more conventional delivery frameworks, and several authors have noted the transferability of problems arising in PfS contracts to SIBs (Fraser et al. 2018b, 15; Lagarde et al. 2013; Maier and Meyer 2017, 5–6). For example, Albertson et al. (2018) conclude that "a recurring theme of PbR evaluation reports is that outcomes-based commissioning has an impact on organisational behaviours; generally, to increase risk-averse behaviour, reduce specialist service delivery and potentially drive down quality" (97). They note that these studies include examination of PbR in the fields of education, health care, active labour market programs, and international development.

EDUCATION
In education, the payment of teachers based on outcomes – specifically, on how students perform on standardized testing or on teacher evaluations – has a long history, going back to the late 1800s in the United States (Podgursky and Springer 2007, 911) and to the 1860s in the United Kingdom (Coltham 1972, 19). Studies of pay-for-performance (PfP) implementation in the late 1800s in the United Kingdom demonstrated that teachers adjusted teaching practice based on what was tested, dropping subjects that were not on the assessment test, increased severity of punishment in the classroom, falsified records, and improperly assisted students during examinations, leading investigators and scholars to berate the PfP system and its detrimental effects on teaching, the curriculum, and the attractiveness of the profession (Coltham 1972, 24–8). In the presence of growing teacher organizing and concern for the state of the profession and working conditions, at the turn of the century the PfP system was eliminated and eventually

replaced by a salary-based system for the vast majority of teachers (Coltham 1972, 30–1; Podgursky and Springer 2007, 911–12).

For similar reasons, in the United States, early PfP incentive systems in education fell in prominence in the mid-1900s, although they persisted in a minority of schools (Murnane and Cohen 1986, 2).[24] An early experimental evaluation of privately provided PbR teaching relative to standard salary-based public education saw both threshold and parking effects (Murnane and Cohen 1986, 5) and minimal to no positive impact (Gramlich and Koshel 1975). Based on interviews in six identified school districts with 10,000 or more students that had used substantial incentive pay for five or more years, Murnane and Cohen (1986) discovered that these districts had modified the structure significantly to alternative systems that provided "extra pay for extra work," "quietly awarded merit pay to almost all teachers," which "make[s] everyone feel special," or were accessed by only a small number of teachers and therefore had minimal salience, with the latter two also requiring significant administrative effort to apply for bonuses (13–14). All of the identified districts were desirable from the perspective of working conditions and baseline salary, and merit pay was de-emphasized, with staff discretion often encouraged with respect to award amounts. Teachers themselves in these districts designed the incentive-based reward structure, with long-standing programs restructuring their PfS systems over time. Murnane and Cohen (1986, 12–17) conclude that these merit pay schemes, as opposed to being typical PfP structures, are one of many options used to facilitate payment tied to hours of work, better communication between teachers and the administration regarding best practices in the classroom and how evaluations should be structured, and leading to higher overall teacher salaries paired with accountability to the broader community. In many contexts, the authors argue that more typical PfP structures will work counter to these goals.[25]

---

24 Murnane and Cohen (1986) refer to many of the same reasons as Dixit (2002) does for the public sector more broadly as to why incentive-based pay would not be effective in a school setting, including team production and the collaboration required to create a positive school learning environment, the pursuit of multiple objectives, many of which are hard to measure, and the potential displacement of intrinsic motivation. The authors emphasize how PbR structures undermine collaboration and how the gains from rewarding top teachers can be offset by discouraging others.

25 Another alternative of these input-based compensation schemes, for example, is "knowledge- and skill-based pay," which rewards teachers based on the acquisition of incremental new teaching capabilities, although studies have not produced evidence of its effectiveness (Podgursky and Springer 2007, 913–14).

PfP payment schemes in US education have seen renewed interest recently, with federal government programs such as the Teacher Incentive Fund launched in 2006 and Race to the Top Fund launched in 2009 encouraging the incorporation of teacher performance into compensation practices. One well-known example of modern PfP teacher schemes is the IMPACT teacher-evaluation system in the District of Columbia, which uses a combination of teacher assessments and student test scores to determine both terminations for low-performing teachers and significant financial bonuses for high-performing teachers, while also providing support for improving performance through professional development resources and helping teachers understand the link between their actions in the classroom and assessment scores (Dee and Wyckoff 2015, 268–9). Many other similar PfP systems are operational, including the North Carolina ABC, the Denver Procomp program, and the Minnesota Qcomp initiatives (Neal 2011, 510–15). PfP systems also saw a resurgence in England with the Performance Related Pay initiative launched by the central government in 1999. This system is based on a threshold application process under which, if the threshold is met, teachers can enter into an annual PfP scheme (Atkinson et al. 2009, 252–3).

Research supports that these incentives are altering teachers' behaviour, with threshold and parking effects having being observed (Koning and Heinrich 2013, 4). Neal (2011, 509–15) summarizes seventeen modern teacher incentive systems aimed at increasing instructional quality, and finds that all but four of fourteen independent evaluations conducted resulted in improved test scores for student subsets in some subject areas. Although the incentives are altering teachers' behaviour, there is minimal evidence with respect to how these compensation schemes are affecting quality (Dee and Wyckoff 2015, 269–70).[26] Neal highlights that one can not be certain if improved test results indicate an overall generalizable improvement in student skills or if teachers simply shift effort towards teaching to the test.[27] Stud-

---

26 Research does suggest, at least in one case, that increased evaluation alone can lead to quality improvements that persist and grow after the year of evaluation (Taylor and Tyler 2012), highlighting the importance of separating the impact of PbR payment structures from the direct benefits of evaluation, paired with improvement guidance that might be part of larger PbR initiatives.

27 Following Koretz (2002), he names three types of teachers' behaviour that can lead to improved test scores but not less to the development of generalizable skills: narrowing of subject matter, coaching to specific testing methods, and straight out cheating. Podgursky and Springer (2007) review a number of documented actions in response to modern PfP incentive structures, including teaching to the test,

ies explicitly examining this issue by comparing alternative student evaluation methodologies show, "in some cases but not all, these gains appear to reflect improvements in general student skills" (Neal 2011, 519). Neal recommends a full separation between testing tools that assess system performance and those used to pay bonuses to teachers, and moving to fixed total award incentive schemes where teachers are paid a bonus based on the pure relative ranking of students on tests that vary substantially with respect to form and content over time to prevent teaching to the test, although he notes these schemes are still vulnerable to cheating by teachers and can generate "wasteful forms of competition" (547).

There is some evidence that creaming effects are also at play in PfP-based school systems. A unique case of mass privatization of the education system took place in New Orleans in the aftermath of hurricane Katrina, with a large proportion of the school system transferred to charter school administration. Subsequent studies have suggested that gaming and creaming activity occurred alongside increasing test scores in this context (Harris and Larsen 2016; Jabbar 2015).

To summarize, incentive pay schemes in the education sector have been fraught historically with challenges and controversy. Although the evidence is clear that financial incentives do alter teachers' behaviour and have been associated with higher test scores, it is not clear if these changes benefit or harm students' acquisition of generalizable knowledge and skills. The literature does, however, point to various adaptations to the PfP framework that might make these schemes more likely to generate beneficial outcomes.

ACTIVE LABOUR MARKET PROGRAMS

Active labour market programs were early modern adopters of PfS programs, with the United States being one of the first adopters (Finn 2009, 40). One program that has been subject to in-depth research, due to high-quality data and control group samples, is the US Job Training Partnership Act (JTPA) – succeeded by the Workforce Investment Act – which allocated funds to training centres across the country, partially based on trainee outcomes (Heckman, Heinrich, and Smith 2011d).

The JTPA directed incentives to be based on identifying the impact of training interventions, but the high cost of isolating the effects of interventions was prohibitive. The incentives used in the JTPA ended

---

moving students into special education streams, helping students on exams, grade manipulation, suspending low-performing students on exam days, increasing student calorie intake on exam days, and administrative manipulation.

up based on employment and earning rates and movement from welfare to employment upon completion and at a three-month follow-up; for youth, completion of training and education benchmarks were also used (Courty and Marschke 2011b, 72–5). Performance standards in some cases were adjusted based on the composition of the trainee pool served by the training centre, creating the potential for trainers to alter their participant pool to reduce thresholds for performance payments (81). Later, individual states, which had some flexibility with respect to performance incentive measures, took steps to take into account demographic considerations aimed at encouraging training centres to enrol harder-to-serve groups and also rewarded centres that spent more of their allocated budget (82–3). The Workforce Investment Act also incorporated similar changes systemwide upon succeeding the JTPA.

This JTPA incentive structure impacted the behaviour of service providers (Heckman, Heinrich, and Smith 2011a, 33) and led to the potential for several incentive problems, including rewarding cream skimming and limiting intake, as well as shifting activities from longer-term training interventions that might have delayed but greater benefits, such as education and training, to interventions that might have more immediate effects on a larger number of participants, such as job search assistance (Courty and Marschke 2011b, 76–8). The system also generated the potential for threshold effects (78), with evidence that training centres were manipulating their client populations temporally to enhance their measured performance (Courty, Kim, and Marschke 2011a, 116).

Heckman and Smith (2011) uncover some "suggestive, but not definitive" (162) evidence in support of "modest" (196) cream skimming in their analysis of program data. Noting that cream skimming has ambiguous effects on efficiency, depending on the correlation between ease to serve and the incremental impact of training services, Heckman, Heinrich, and Smith (2011c) find that the efficiency impact of cream skimming under the JTPA was minimal, although in some cases where resources were allocated away from the hardest to serve, overall efficiency might have increased. The authors conclude that "the cream skimming problem is overstated" and that "administrative discretion … is not the dominant factor" (309).

Courty and Marschke (2011a), in their analysis of JTPA data, also uncover evidence of "strategic reporting" that inflated employment rate outcomes by 11.3 percentage points (215), and threshold effects where participants were shifted between reporting periods with evidence that this came at the expense of productive activity and participant earnings outcomes (218). They conclude that "dysfunctional responses that imperfectly conceived performance measures engender can undermine the organization's mission. These costs make the use of performance measurement systems uneconomical for many public-sector organizations because they raise more management problems than they solve. This may explain why such organizations rarely implement explicit performance measures" (224). These types of behavioural responses have been confirmed by case studies of JTPA training providers (Heinrich 2011).[28]

Additionally, Heckman, Heinrich, and Smith (2011c) find that the use of short-term measures negatively affected programming decisions from an efficiency perspective, as such measures in general had no relation to long-term outcomes: indeed, there is some evidence that they might be negatively correlated, such that positive short-term indicators, such as immediate employment, had negative long-term outcomes in areas such as earnings growth and long-run employment prospects. The authors note that this result, based on their literature review, does "not represent an anomaly in the [employment and training] literature, but rather tells much the same story as the other studies that perform similar analyses" (Heckman, Heinrich, and Smith 2011c, 292). The challenges the JTPA program faced are consistent with previous findings that PfS projects have not performed as expected and have been underresourced with respect to monitoring and evaluation (Heinrich and Marschke 2010, 184), and the underestimation of the inherent challenges as systems and behaviour evolve over time (Heckman, Heinrich, and Smith 2011c).

Finn (2008) reviews two active labour market PbR models, the Austrian Job Network launched in 1998 and refined over a decade of implementation, and the Dutch Reintegration Market, initiated in 2002. These programs differed from the US JTPA program in that incentive payments made up a large proportion of the compensation to service providers (Finn 2008, 17, 33). Both programs were found to reduce costs and increase the number of participants served (5). Successful employment rates in the near term improved in the range of 5–10 per cent, and matches were made in a shorter period than in more conventional programs. Finn's review suggests similar shifts occurred as under the JTPA, with higher employment rates achieved in some cases by focusing on job search assistance at the expense of training programs and

---

28 The Workforce Investment Act implemented changes in reporting structure to reduce manipulation (Courty and Marschke 2011a, 218), and took additional steps to limit creaming through payment schedules based on client characteristics, but selection bias within subgroups persisted (Courty, Kim, and Marschke 2011).

sponsored work placement, with "negative consequences for the quality of service delivery for the most disadvantaged" (39). Although the
cost savings were clear, Finn notes that "relatively little is known about
the extent to which these gains have been offset by high transaction
costs for the purchaser, providers and service users" (5). He further
notes that the movement to PbR systems, in both Austria and the Netherlands, led to government's reduced ability to manage programming
effectively and increased contract management and administration
costs. Parking and creaming effects were observed in both countries,
despite their different payment structures based on classifying clients.
Program modifications to address these problems slowed service delivery, reduced flexibility to pursue innovative solutions, and led to an
increase in administrative costs (40). Finally, Finn highlights how private service providers might cease operations while under obligation
to deliver service, which has occurred in both countries, imposing costs
and requiring reaction from the state to shore up the gaps created (44).

In the United Kingdom, incentive payments in active labour market
programs began in 2002 with the launch of Jobcentre Plus, a revamped
public sector agency delivering job market programming and benefits. A study of the introduction of incentive payments for service
teams based on client outcomes found that, in aggregate, the benefit
of incentive payments was nil, although smaller teams and service
delivery areas had better results (Burgess et al. 2017). The next step to
PfS contracting in active labour market programs in the United Kingdom was triggered by the 2007 Freud report, which recommended
addressing the skills gap for low and unskilled workers relative to
those in other advanced countries by contracting out the service delivery of active labour market programs through PbR contracting. This
was implemented first through the Labour government's Flexible
New Deal, which saw challenges with service provider bankruptcies
(Finn 2008, 44) and later deepened through the Conservative-Liberal
coalition's Work Programme, which made payments almost exclusively based on outcomes (Rees, Whitworth, and Carter 2014, 224).
The Work Programme attempted to address problems of creaming
and parking effects in the previous program by using nine classification categories to determine payment structure, although evidence
suggests that this has not been effective (Morse 2015, 28–9; Rees, Taylor, and Damm 2013; Rees, Whitworth, and Carter 2014, 228–36). A
2014 evaluation of the program determined that outcomes were comparable to its precursors and provided costs savings, although this
was based on a hypothetical counterfactual (Morse 2015, 37). After
being criticized for leaving a large majority of its clients without

labour market success and being poorly suited to the needs of more marginalized and harder-to-serve workers, the program was replaced with the smaller Work and Health Programme aimed exclusively at these groups (Albertson et al. 2018, 37).

Several literature surveys of the relationship between PbR schemes and patient outcomes have taken place in the health care field (Lagarde et al. 2013, 19); their conclusions vary substantially, based on the restrictiveness of their inclusion criteria. Scott et al. (2011) conducted a review of studies examining PbR initiatives in the area of primary care with the goal of assessing the impact on the quality of care provided. Rigorous selection criteria focusing on experimental and quasi-experimental analyses limited their review to five US studies, one German study, and one conducted on services in the United Kingdom. They conclude that the schemes produced "positive but modest effects on a minority of the measures of quality of care included in the study," but express concern with the experimental integrity of the studies – in particular, "selection bias as a result of the ability of primary care physicians to select into or out of the incentive scheme or health plan" (21).

Christianson, Leatherman, and Sutherland (2007) conducted a detailed review of literature surveys, paying significant attention to classifying experimental quality. They conclude that "relatively few significant impacts are reported, and it is often the case that payer programmes include quality improvement components in addition to incentive payments, making it difficult to assess the independent effect of the financial incentives" (21). They note that preventative services have been studied more intensively, but conclude that the "few studies in this area with strong research designs find small, if any, effects of payments to providers that are intended to improve quality" (21). One survey informing this finding is that of Town et al. (2005), who limit their inclusion criteria to randomized control trials that examine PfP incentive programs designed to increase the delivery of preventative interventions – specifically, immunizations and cancer screening – by primary care providers. They observe that only one out of eight studies "found that increasing financial incentives translated into the provision of more preventive care" (235), but qualify their results by highlighting limited sample size and noting that the incentives offered were generally small (148). Other reviews with more stringent criteria or that report separately randomized control or quasi-experimental evidence have produced similar findings, with small or negligible outcome gains (Houle et al. 2012; Mehrotra et al. 2009).

In their review of the United Kingdom's extensive PfP system that emerged as a result of the Quality and Outcomes Framework, and using a less stringent inclusion criteria that took in ninety-four articles, Gillam, Siriwardena, and Steel (2012) find "modest reductions in mortality and hospital admissions in some areas, and where they have been assessed, these modest improvements appear cost-effective" (464). They also note a number of systems changes they associate with the implementation of the Quality and Outcomes Framework, including negative outcomes in unincentivized areas of care, high costs, improved collaboration and knowledge sharing among medical staff, freeing up doctors for more acute problems, and reduced discretion with respect to treatment. They observe that predictions of mechanistic and impersonal care practices have not materialized (464–5).

Greene and Nash (2009), also with more generous scoping criteria, include thirty-six studies, and obtain more optimistic results with respect to the impact of PfP on patient outcomes, finding that "most have produced positive results" (148). They do note, however, that distributional considerations are important, with two studies showing a negative impact, and recommend that steps be taken to ensure that physicians who service disadvantaged populations are not adversely affected. Petersen et al. (2006) come to similar conclusions in their review of seventeen studies going back to 1980, with thirteen producing indicators of quality improvement in the PfP cases. The authors also identified gaming issues with one study, finding reduced access to care, while four studies "suggested unintended effects of incentives" (268).

To recap, survey studies that use narrower scoping criteria that emphasize randomized control trials and quasi-experimental studies find that PfP systems have modest or minimal positive impact on patient outcomes, while studies with more liberal criteria find more positive results. These results should be viewed in light of the number of issues that create challenges for comparing and generalizing results from various health care PbR initiatives. These challenges include merit payments targeted at different administrative levels – individual health care providers, provider groups, or facilities such as hospitals; large variations in the size of incentives between projects; and the co-implementation of various PbR initiatives and quality enhancements reforms (Christianson, Leatherman, and Sutherland 2007, 15). Some studies have been criticized for their poor association between meaningful outcomes for patients and the measures being tested (Bhattacharyya et al. 2009); it is likely that this misalignment is as significant a problem in health care as in education. Studies of health care PfP programs have highlighted many problems found in other program areas, including gaming, the underservicing of hard-to-serve clients, the displacement of intrinsic motivation and professional integrity, and incentive payments to those who were already performing well (Chen et al. 2011; Christianson, Leatherman, and Sutherland 2007, 15; Epstein, Lee, and Hamel 2004, 409–10; Rosenthal et al. 2005, 1788).

INTERNATIONAL DEVELOPMENT

Klitgaard (1997, 495–7) identifies a number of PbR-based public service reform projects in the international development context from diverse sectors, including central government administration in areas such taxation and revenue collection, water treatment, and agricultural credit programs. While arguing that reformed incentive structures are important for developing effective civil services in developing countries, he equally emphasizes the conditional circumstances that are necessary for PbR to be effective, many of which are not present in developing countries. He notes that PbR likely will be successful only in contexts where high effort leads to large incremental gains in performance, public service workers have minimal risk aversion due to a reliable capacity to support themselves and favourable alternative employment opportunities, the state has strong monitoring and evaluation capabilities, and employees are constructively sensitive to pecuniary incentives. PbR reforms then are likely to be effective only as part of a larger package of reforms aimed at generating these conditions.

Klitgaard (1997) suggests that each of these can be enhanced through targeted measures. Outcomes could be made more responsive to efforts by clearly specifying how employee actions impact performance and what actions are expected to lead to better outcomes, by consulting employees when setting goals, and by using participatory methods when designing and undertaking training and evaluation. Employee risk aversion can be reduced "through experiments that can be reversed if they turn out badly, employee self-selection into performance-pay programmes, and credible commitments backed by international organizations"; and evaluation can be improved "through systematic client surveys, peer reviews, benchmarking, detailed studies of performance samples, ratings by superiors, and other techniques" (499). Finally, employee productivity can be improved through human and physical capital investments.

Gaming in SIB Initiatives

There are concerns that the demonstrated gaming problems in PfS and the displacement of intrinsic motivation might carry over to the SIB model (Warner 2013, 13–14), with noted examples in multiple SIB projects. Loxley (2017), who reviews several child welfare SIBs aimed at keeping young children safely with their families, discovers evidence that the Sweet Dreams SIB in Saskatoon, Canada, selected a group of mothers that was more likely to be successful than the potential pool of participants, which, given the lack of a control or comparison group, is particularly problematic. The Benevolent Society Bond in New South Wales, Australia, was also deemed by auditors to have selected families with lower barriers; in this case, however, there were similar findings for the control group, so although investors were not advantaged by the selection bias, it might have made the intensive intervention design less appropriate and cost effective (Loxley 2017, 16–18).[29] The Utah early childhood development SIB, aimed at diverting children from special education services, has also been accused of overstating the impact of services and of selecting clients who were facing fewer barriers than claimed, with educational experts questioning whether the selected children would have ended up requiring special education without the intervention (Popper 2015; Tse and Warner 2018). The Caritas Perspektive SIB in Bern, Switzerland, which works with refugees on employment outcomes, also has been accused of creaming, as its selection criteria is based on the employability of applicants (Sinclair, McHugh, and Roy 2019). In a series of UK employment and training SIBs with multiple payment metrics, evaluations have found evidence of gaming and creaming, with the projects focusing on narrow population groups with easy-to-achieve metrics, and payment based on intermediate outputs instead of outcomes (Wiggan 2019).

Edmiston and Nicholls (2018) find creaming and parking issues in four UK SIBs they reviewed, with some agencies indicating they had to take "measures to 'insulate' their front-line staff from the influence of certain social investors" to avoid the promotion of "dysfunctional practices" (65). Fraser et al. (2020) find similar results in their review of multiple health-related SIB projects. Interviewees reported that the "financial goals of the SIB … conflicted with their professional goals and responsibilities to service users (and intervention fidelity where

---

29 Loxley (2017, 9–10) finds the opposite case for the Newpin Social Benefit Bond, where, out of the program's eligible population, the vast majority was pulled from the hardest to serve – namely, children in care for three or more months – due to court referrals to the program. In this case, the risk for the investors was mitigated through a limit on the number of reversals, where families were reunited but then disintegrated, with the child being taken into out-of-home care, which would count against the number of successful integrations.

CASE STUDY
The Sweet Dreams SIB: Success, or Misattribution and
Selection Bias?

The Sweet Dreams SIB project was a five-year, C$1 million SIB aimed at improving the prospects of twenty-two children remaining with their mothers, in Saskatoon, Canada. These were children of single-parent mothers at risk of requiring services from Child and Family Services. The youth-serving agency EGADZ provided safe shelter at the Sweet Dreams House (financed previously by the federal, provincial, and city governments), along with a suite of supports to develop parenting and job skills. If all twenty-two children remained with their mothers six months after they left the program, the principal would be repaid plus 5 per cent interest per annum. If fewer than twenty-two did so, the payment would be lower, with the whole of the investment at risk. The province of Saskatchewan expected to save between C$0.54 million and C$1.5 million on child welfare costs over five years (Loxley 2017).

The target was virtually met within two years: over five years, the project served thirty-six women and fifty-five children. All but one child remained out of state care and safely with their families – more than twice the initial target. The initial investment was returned fully, and 5 per cent per annum interest was paid (Loxley 2020).

The Sweet Dreams SIB, however, is an example of a project vulnerable to creaming and misattribution of impact. The intake selection was biased by prioritizing mothers who demonstrated a high degree of motivation to keep their children. The project also had no control group against which to assess its performance. Finally, the availability of the Sweet Dreams House was central to the arrangement, but was not part of SIB financing. This raises questions about the project's replicability and whether it was the housing or the SIB programming that led to success. Attribution issues aside, the project is an example of the recommended best practice of government directly funding successful SIB-financed programming upon completion of the SIB, with the province of Saskatchewan committing annual conventional funding of $120,000 a year going forward.

applicable)" (200). Fraser et al. also report evidence of gaming, with data collected "interpreted as a disciplinary device to focus service provider staff on achieving outcomes-related rewards ... as opposed to a collectively devised method to refine service delivery through innovative approaches that reflected a commitment to achieving long term benefits for clients" (200). No such effects were found in the comparison sites.

These findings suggest that the inclusion of dedicated value-based organizations might not be sufficient to prevent gaming incentivized by the PbR aspect of SIBs, although Fraser et al. (2020, 200) note that program staff did push back because of ethical and reputational concerns. What could be considered a form of gaming was also used in anti-homelessness initiatives led by St Mungo's and Thames Reach in the United Kingdom. In addition to helping individuals find housing and employment, the program also worked with immigration authorities to deport homeless individuals who did not meet UK residency requirements (see Bloomer 2016; Ryan and Young 2018).[30]

Some analysts nevertheless dispute that gaming is prevalent. Albertson et al. (2018, 95), for example, in their review of SIB evaluations, note that, unlike in more traditional PbR initiatives, "perverse incentives had not been identified," and more generally, "evaluations of ... SIBs that considered incentives found they had little or no effect," either positively or negatively. An OECD report (Ramsden, Noya, and Galitopoulou 2016) also suggests that early UK SIBs did not appear to face substantial gaming issues, and attributed this to the fact that the contracted service providers were "dedicated social enterprise organisations demonstrating a strong organisational ethos" (16).

Transaction Costs and Windfall Gains

Both the privatization/contracting-out and PfS literature refer to the increased transaction costs of transitioning from the status quo, be it in-house public delivery or conventional procurement, to these alternative delivery models. In general, privatization involves significant transaction costs, related to raising capital, contract preparation, promotion, and other administrative requirements, which can be particularly high relative to raising capital through traditional government borrowing (Vickers and Yarrow 1991, 118). These challenges are similar for SIBs. Privatization also creates a large one-time payoff that effectively captures the net present value of enterprise operations (118), creating potential windfall gains for investors and magnifying the principal-agent problem central to privatization analysis (Stiglitz 2008). Historically, privatization schemes have been marred by questions of legitimacy

---

30 Although this was explicitly part of their strategy to meet targets (Social Finance 2018), it raises questions as to whether deportations should or would normally be part of the charitable mandate of these organizations if not for the PbR structure.

due to undervaluation and the realization of a significant net transfer of public wealth into private hands (Klein 2007; Stiglitz 2008). Although SIBs are time limited, the privatization of a quasi-revenue stream that takes place in SIB contracts over multiyear contracts raises similar potential concerns.

In addition to these more general transaction costs and potential windfall gains for private investors, PbR and SIB approaches face a number of model-specific transaction costs stemming from the identification of appropriate metrics and the implementation of tracking systems and processes, defining the intervention population, generating a control group or counterfactual, and specifying responsibilities under all scenarios. This leads to prolonged negotiation and, in some cases, renegotiation after the contract is signed (Fraser et al. 2018b, 14), resulting in higher administration and transaction costs relative to the conventional model (Albertson et al. 2018, 86–8; Damberg 2009; Maier and Meyer 2017; Muñoz and Kimmitt 2019; Tan et al. 2015; Tse and Warner 2018; Whitfield 2015). In their extensive review of PbR and SIB project evaluations in the United Kingdom and the United States, Albertson et al. (2018) highlight how stakeholders and evaluations consistently reported that "upfront investment in the commissioning process was higher than expected" (86), and note the ongoing costs associated with monitoring and performance management (89).

Data on three individual SIB projects provide some support for this hypothesis. Loxley (2017), for example, finds that, in the case of the Newpin Child welfare SIB, transaction costs were significant, totalling as much as AU\$0.75 million on a AU\$7 million SIB, inclusive of staff time (7–8). Although data are not available, Loxley assesses that the cost of another Australian child welfare project, the Benevolent Society SIB, would be similarly high (15–16). KPMG (2014), also looking at the Newpin SIB, finds the process "very labour intensive for all the stakeholders involved; … [with] six [full-time equivalents] working solely on the development of one social benefit bond over an intensive 12 month period" (28). KPMG does note, however, that transaction costs are expected to fall as the model becomes more common and experience is accumulated over time.

The Reconnections Social Impact Bond in Worcestershire, England, aimed at reducing negative outcomes for older adults due to social isolation also had high developmental costs of £189,000 for a project based on £850,000 of capital raised, which included estimates of government staff time, the salary of a project manager, as well as a cost-benefit model used to estimate the returns to the intervention (Ecorys UK and ATQ Consultants 2015, 5). Although the set-up and transaction costs were high, at 22 per cent, almost half of this went to the cost-benefit analysis and the development of metrics to develop and access the proposed intervention model, which was new and untested to date. The UK Mental Health and Employment Partnership SIB was based on a development grant of £150,000, awarded to Social Finance, for an SIB project financed with £400,000 of private upfront capital (Hickman 2016, 11–13). These partners also appear to have invested approximately £480,000 of public funds in the project service delivery, which would reduce these development costs to 17 per cent of project costs.[31] Neither of these estimates account for any in-house transaction costs borne by the three local commissioning government partners.

Lowe (2020) examines the issue of development costs directly for an unspecified SIB-financed UK health intervention that had been tested and shown to be successful in other UK jurisdictions. The project accumulated £750,000 in development costs prior to providing service to any participants; approximately 55 per cent of this was grant support and the remainder in-kind contributions. This was equivalent to 43 per cent of the social investment in the project. Lowe finds that approximately 41 per cent of the development costs were due directly to accommodating the use of SIB financing. Furthermore, he finds no evidence of efficiencies to offset these costs and that "this SIB programme was not an outlier in terms of development expense" (187), suggesting that SIBs are an "intrinsically expensive ways to fund social programs" (185).

Qualitative assessments also concur that SIBs can be transactionally resource intensive. Ronicle and Stanworth (2015), for example, find that the United Kingdom's first health SIB required "a complex web of contracts" (1) whose negotiation, including the determination of appropriate outcome measures, caused "significant delays" and frustrated the process (13), with the final SIB launching four years after the first development grant funding was secured (6). In their examination of four UK SIB projects, Edmiston and Nicholl (2018, 70) note that "a number of cross-sectoral stakeholders interviewed ... felt that the high transaction costs associated with developing the SIB threatened the future cost savings achievable." Fraser et al. (2020) note, in their case study review of UK health and social care SIBs, that data-collection requirements in some cases "led to increased financial pressure on provider organizations and increased managerial pressure on provider staff, with potentially detrimental implications" (202).

---

31 Authors' calculations based on figures in Hickman (2016, 11–13).

Some SIBs, however, have been found to have relatively low transaction costs. For example, Loxley (2017) finds that such costs were low on the Sweet Dreams SIB, a Canadian child welfare SIB, due to its simple structure and procurement as a directly sourced contract without a request for proposals process, although this SIB has faced criticism with respect to problems that could have been addressed with greater attention at the project design and negotiation phase (2–3).

At the government level, the development of SIB programs can be challenging, given the expertise required. For example, despite the dedication of NZ$29 million in funding for SIBs, the New Zealand government faced significant delays and challenges, partially attributed to the degree of "commercial financial expertise" required, which had to be developed, and the ongoing need for the participation of senior decision makers (New Zealand 2017b, 7). Significant resources have also been expended to cover the cost of intermediaries (Floyd 2017, 24).[32]

Gustafsson-Wright, Gardiner, and Putcha (2015), in their survey of SIBs, conclude that "the first impact bonds have been time-intensive and costly operations" (35), although they and Loxley both suggest that transaction costs might fall over time as the process becomes standardized and capacity is built. There is some precedent for this in PbR contracting: for example, in the United Kingdom, active labour market programming is seeing growth with fewer providers and larger contracts (Finn 2008, 9). Some analysts have argued, however, that SIBs under $15 million cannot overcome fixed transaction costs associated with the model, and that, in general, this threshold is not close to being reached (Floyd 2017, 22).[33]

Assessment of Claim 2

The evidence on the ability of SIBs to generate higher-quality social programs or better outcomes is inconclusive. SIBs have not been tested meaningfully or evaluated against conventional social service delivery methods in a manner that would allow such a determination (Fraser et al. 2020). SIBs are not being evaluated from a value-for-money

---

32 See also examples in Chapter 2.

33 Floyd notes that this is substantially higher than the current size of UK SIBs, and that there is some evidence that SIB proposals in the United Kingdom are getting smaller, based on applications to the Commissioning Better Outcomes fund. See also KPMG (2014, 20) and Azemati et al. (2013), who suggest SIB projects under $20 million are too small to overcome set-up and administration costs associated with the model, which they note are primarily fixed costs.

perspective, a problem with PfS programming more broadly (Morse 2015, 36). A useful counterfactual for future research would be to fund conventional providers directly with an equivalent in incremental resources for enhanced project management and administration, made available through the SIB model to pay out investor returns and higher transaction costs (Whitfield 2015, 34).[34] SIBs, even if successful on their own terms, might not provide value for money; at a minimum, governments that issue SIBs should be required to justify the scheme over standard procurement mechanisms, as has been recommended for PbR schemes more broadly (Morse 2015, 6–8), and the criteria for evaluating value for money should be stated at the beginning of a contract (33).

Although SIBs might produce better outcomes relative to conventional procurement or public delivery, they have higher governance and transaction costs. Their possible advantage over conventional contracting rests on their potential to manage projects effectively, pursue innovation, and adapt. If the argument of private sector superiority in this regard is not conclusive, the burden of proof should fall on the proponents of SIBs, including supportive governments, given the higher financing and transaction costs associated with the model. To date, SIBs are not meeting their proclaimed innovative potential, and it is unclear if the additional resources going towards increasingly intrusive oversight are generating value for program participants.

Examining past experience with privatization and PbR schemes leads to doubts regarding their ability to generate superior outcomes, particularly in the social service context. Standard economic theory suggests that, for privatization to be successful, competition is required, and this is currently not present for SIBs. In fact, given their consortia structure, which often relies on specialist intermediaries and large-scale service providers, SIBs are likely to reduce competition in public social serve delivery. Neyland (2018, 492), for example, labels SIBs an "anti-market device" that restricts competition relative to standard procurement.

The view of social innovation in SIBs focuses solely on increasing efficiency of service provision, which is viewed as a mechanical process, and ignores alternative perspectives that "see social innovation in the shifting dynamics of power and privilege among different groups in society ... identifiable more by the processes of the innovation than the consequences" (Mollinger-Sahba et al. 2020, 252). Instead of empowering

---

34 Liebman and Feller (2014) note that SIBs help reverse a misallocation of resources within governments that underresource management and evaluation of conventional social service delivery.

the vulnerable, SIB participants, already among the most marginalized, are treated as inputs, voiceless and commodified (Cooper, Graham, and Himick 2016; Tse and Warner 2018, 2019; Warner 2013). Service providers are instead subject to "market discipline" (Mollinger-Sahba et al. 2020, 252), where they succeed and demonstrate their virtue by supplying outcomes determined by the lead SIB stakeholders.

PbR schemes, through this disciplinary approach, generate dysfunctional behavioural responses that require additional resources to mitigate. As captured succinctly by the United Kingdom's auditor general, "PbR is a technically challenging form of specialist contracting, and poor design and implementation can have a negative impact on the quality of public services and value for money" (Morse 2015, 22). The challenges of PbR schemes have resulted in many cases in a return to conventional contracting and in some cases to in-house provision (Koning and Heinrich 2013, 2). Both privatization and PbR have the potential to displace public sector motivations of workers and generate rent seeking and/or windfall gains for investors. The limited evidence to date suggests that these concerns are relevant in the SIB context.

Our review of the effectiveness of PbR initiatives in various sectors suggests ways that SIBs could be structured to reduce the negative impacts. These include:

- keeping incentive payments relatively low;
- including front-line service providers in the determination of targets;
- taking time to understanding the motivations of service providers (Heinrich and Marschke 2010, 203);
- verifying and being explicit regarding the link between performance indicators and the actions of front-line staff (Klitgaard 1997; Palameta, Myers, and Conte 2013, 41);
- using incentive payments as a tool to inform and educate service providers regarding the costs and benefit of their actions and impacts;
- clarity regarding what changes could be made by service providers to lead to improved outcomes and successful incentive payments (Murnane and Cohen 1986);
- using incentives where staff are responsible only for the outcome being incentivized (Heinrich and Marschke 2010, 203);
- revisiting contracts and targets in response to new information and to address unforeseen issues (Morse 2015, 33); and
- requiring returns to be earmarked for reinvestment in social causes.

More generally, for PbR to be successful, a broader set of reforms is required, including a participatory process around design, training, and evaluation with the associated required investments (Klitgaard 1997).

The attributes of the SIB model that most convincingly promise improvements are, first, the built-in central coordination within government to break down siloed decision making between departments to determine the net impact of a social service intervention and, in turn, funding initiatives that are expected to produce a social return and potentially a financial return to government. The second attribute is the increased resources provided to improve research, evaluation, and performance management. Neither of these attributes requires the privatization of finance and management or the PbR structure built into the SIB model, and could be pursued independently.

Claim 3: SIBs Lead to a Better Social Service Delivery System

Proponents claim that SIBs are having a positive impact not only through the projects themselves, but also through broader changes to social service delivery systems, both within and between government and private partners. Dear et al. (2016), for example, capture this sentiment in the following passage: "Clear evidence of broader impact is emerging outside the context of individual projects, including improving the capacity of social and public sector organizations and informing policy through the availability of measured outcomes and performance data. Such impact demonstrates the ripple effect of Social Impact Bonds – builds confidence in the values of specific outcomes for government, service providers, and investors, and in doing so, has an impact that extends far beyond the project's domain" (31). This discussion is embedded in the "public sector reform narrative" (Fraser et al. 2018b, 9) as part of the New Public Management approach, highlighting the weaknesses of the status quo state and the potential for private sector practices and values to improve the delivery of public services (Albertson et al. 2018; Painter et al. 2018; Warner 2013, 2015). Two focal points for the analysis include the emphasis on outcomes and evaluation in spending decisions, and a better allocation of risk between sectors.

Focus on Data, Outcomes, and Evaluation

Within government itself, proponents highlight how SIBs have ripple effects beyond the individual projects they enable, by encouraging and building capacity to generate the data and management systems required to track and ultimately to govern, based on outcomes. Liebman and Sellman (2013, 15), for example, note that SIBs

> drive change as part of a broader performance agenda ... A SIB project may also involve the development of systems for linking data across agencies in order to measure outcomes – systems that can be applied to existing spending as well ... [A successful] SIB project could break through the political obstacles and allow not just the incremental SIB spending to be performance-based but also allow for better allocation of base spending – spending that will often be much larger than the incremental SIB spending. These kinds of spill-over benefits to a broader reform agenda could make even a small SIB project worth doing.

Dear et al. (2016) project similar sentiments: "Social Impact Bonds are prompting the development of data systems to help identify the most effective social interventions and to help make optimal public sector resource allocations in the future" (32). They also highlight how SIBs have led to the integration of research and policy on social interventions and to the development of "data clearinghouses which serve as a tool for policymakers when making funding decisions" (32), such as the Unit Cost Database referenced in Chapter 1. Finally, they highlight that the collaboration required in an SIB necessitates intensive research and evaluation which "invariably ... leads to a more detailed understanding of the issue and the way the current system handles it, providing insight into how such systems could be improved beyond the context of one Social Impact Bond" (35). Proponents, then, claim that SIBs not only drive efficiency within projects through incentive alignment; they also improve allocation of spending across government (Fox and Albertson 2011), both through and outside SIB projects.

This is a process that evolves over time and points to the potential of SIBs and PfS to generate a "rigorous feedback loop [...] to correctly allocate government's abundant social sector resources" (Overholser and Whistler 2013, 5). SIBs, if applied more broadly, might serve a discovery-type purpose with respect to resource allocation within government that generates a positive externality in a dynamic setting with an existing bundle of imperfect social service delivery models and incomplete information regarding the optimal delivery structure. Implemented on a large scale, SIBs might systematically allocate resources more efficiently by helping to identify and eliminate wasteful projects and/or delivery models, but at this point such a scale has not been reached.

SIBs in themselves might or might not be more efficient for a particular project in question, but overall they might be efficiency enhancing, as a broad application of their governance structure within government over time could eliminate other wasteful projects whether directly or through the diffusion of outcomes-focused governance.[35] SIBs might have to rely on these externalities to realize the hefty promise celebrated by proponents, as some have pointed out that SIBs cannot be relied upon to provide for "core" government operations, given that "failure to achieve performance targets could lead the providers to cease operations" (Liebman and Sellman 2013, 20), limiting opportunities for scale. Given these challenges, some see SIBs as merely a transitional device towards more extensive outcomes-based commissioning or payment by results, since these avoid the need to pay for an additional intermediary, with the associated transaction costs (Jagelewski 2016). This theory has gained further salience as challenges with the SIB model have led previous proponents, such as the Harvard Government Performance Lab and Third Sector Capital Partners in the United States, to shift focus to more rigorous outcomes-based contracting through direct government funding (Williams 2018, 11). Others doubt, however, whether new institutions will provide loan finance required to bridge the gap SIBs were originally aimed at filling. This reinforces current developments in commissioning, such as the rise of prime contractors organizing supply chains and partnerships, leaving the voluntary sector in a weak position and with low margins (Mulgan et al. 2011, 14).

Risk Transfer

Proponents claim that SIBs can generate a more effective social service system through better allocation of financial risk between government and the private sector. Several have argued that the PbR mechanism is a positive attribute because of the transference of the risk of failure away from government to the private sector (Dear et al. 2016, 17, Deloitte 2012, 3; Fraser et al. 2018b, 10, United States 2016; Mulgan et al. 2011, 16; Painter et al. 2018). This argument is similar to one commonly made for public-private partnerships in infrastructure.

To analyse this proposition, we should first define "risk," and what it means from the perspective of those concerned. In the case of SIBs, there are at least two relevant definitions of risk. The first is a statistical or economic definition of risk – call this "pure risk" – where the

---

35 Dear et al. (2016, 81) highlight SIBs' potential to facilitate conversion to greater outcomes-based procurement by government without private finance, but they see a role for both on an ongoing basis.

term refers to the variance or uncertainty of the predicted value of an event. If one assumes "rational" expectations, all available information would be used to predict the expected value, and the prediction would be unbiased and equal to the average to which the outcome would converge if the event could be repeated over and over again in the identical context. If the individuals or institutions evaluating the event are risk neutral, they will be indifferent to the uncertainty or variance and care only about the expected value of the outcome. If they are risk averse, they will be willing to trade off some of the expected value for greater certainty of achieving the outcome.

Traditionally, in economic analysis, the state is assumed to be risk neutral, since it is able to self-insure fully against risk through its power to raise revenues by taxation. If one evaluates SIBs from the perspective of a benevolent public sector manager who implements policy based on broader social welfare considerations, the idea that risk transfer alone can justify the use of SIBs is erroneous (Liebman and Feller 2014). On the other hand, if one considers the motivations of politicians and assumes that they might be more sensitive about a failed project than a successful one, then SIBs might be a tool for circumventing this risk aversion.[36] This perspective assumes that private sector investors are more willing to accept risk, but this is not self-evident: based on some evaluations of PbR and SIBs projects, service providers also appear to be risk averse and investors require significant compensation to accept risk transfer (Albertson et al. 2018, 94).

Pure risk can be viewed narrowly as statistical random variation in the outcomes of program participants. "Risk" can also be understood more broadly, however, to include treatment integrity – such that prescribed methods are delivered in accordance with an established and tested model – including the logistical and quality risks that accompany the implementation of any complex service delivery requiring the coordination of multiple actors (Dear et al. 2016, 17). One could argue that the private sector consortium under an SIB might be better placed to manage these additional "risks," given the consortium's inclusion of front-line service providers and foundations with better information about and control over the quality of the service being delivered than the government procurer – again, within the "street-level bureaucrat" paradigm (Heinrich 2011, 231; Lipsky 2010). The potential welfare gain here is not from the transfer of risk to a less risk-averse agent,

---

36   This is implied by Toby Eccles, the founder of Social Finance, who states that "Social Impact Bonds provide politicians with a route to encouraging public servants into trying something new" (Dear et al. 2016, 17).

but a better alignment of incentives whereby those with information and control over "what works" are induced to exert effort to deliver a higher-quality service.[37] This claim of broader systemwide benefit from the transfer of responsibility is subject to all the complications and caveats noted above regarding PfS and privatization schemes.

A complete risk analysis would also account for other dysfunctional behavioural responses of service providers, as well as contingencies such as service providers prematurely terminating the contract, either voluntarily or otherwise, leaving clients without services and forcing them to revert to other government or non-profit systems (Gustafsson-Wright, Gardiner, and Putcha 2015, 40). Also, depending on how broadly one defines risk, the degree to which transfer is beneficial will depend on the extent to which transaction costs are incorporated into the analysis (Fraser et al. 2018b, 13). Finally, the above discussion of risk equates the bearing of risk with the allocation of responsibility for the final funding of a project. Given the normative and often legal obligations of government to address social problems, "operational and reputational risks associated with failure" will always remain at least partially with government, further undermining risk transfer in practice (Fraser et al. 2018b, 15; Giantris and Piakiewicz 2013). Within a broader conception of risk, the threat to proper governance and accountability raises challenges in public-private partnership structures (Hodge 2004) such as SIBs.

Assessment of Claim 3

Proponents argue that SIBs benefit the entire social service system primarily by demonstrating success and focusing government practice on evaluation and outcomes more broadly, as well as through a more efficient allocation of risk. These claims are difficult to substantiate. Although there is evidence that capacity is being built within organizations to better track outcomes, and government organizations clearly are assembling support for SIB and PfS projects, the degree to which this is influencing and shifting the broader social service system is unclear (Gustafsson-Wright, Gardiner, and Putcha 2015, 46), and will require further research through case study.

---

37 This argument is central in several economic analyses of public-private partnerships to the case for the superiority of that model over conventional infrastructure procurement. See Bennett and Iossa (2006); Hart (2003); Iossa and Martimort (2015); Martimort and Pouyet (2008).

The United Kingdom is the most likely location where these changes might be occurring, given that country's leading role in piloting the first SIB and its current position as the leader in number of SIB contracts issued (Social Finance 2018). But, as the UK auditor general notes, "neither the Cabinet Office nor HM Treasury currently monitors how PbR is operating across government. Nor is there a systematic collection or evaluation of information about how effectively PbR is working" (Morse 2015, 8). This does not bode well for any broad systematic knowledge dissemination from SIBs. There are also concerns that this knowledge, instead of being accumulated by government, is being captured by private sector intermediaries (Floyd 2017, 24). In their international comparison of SIBs and similar non-SIB interventions delivered by the same provider, Hevenstone and Von Bergen (2020, 211) find "that SIB funding created several obstacles to transparency" and that "contractual targets were never linked to evaluation."

Even with respect to individual projects, there is the danger that SIBs might be overreaching on their ability to drive rigorous research on the effectiveness of policy interventions. Although the establishment of impact through the use of control groups is profiled as the ideal, in practice this has not been pervasive (Carter et al. 2018; Fraser et al. 2020), with the United States, where many projects use control groups and randomized control trials, being more advanced in this regard (Bailey and LaBarbera 2018; Carter 2020). The UK auditor general highlights the importance of control groups in PbR schemes for the effective identification of impact, but notes that, "to date, only a few schemes have monitored performance against a counterfactual" (Morse 2015, 8). Reviews of SIB evaluations in the United Kingdom cite "a paucity of evaluations and those that exist are not of a high standard" (Fox and Morris 2019, 2), where "attribution is often assumed, as opposed to independently proven" (Fraser et al. 2020, 201). Even in the United States, where control groups are more common, their appropriatness/quality has been questioned (Fraser et al. 2018b). Case studies have also demonstrated that few projects hit the high evaluation standards claimed to be central to the SIB model (Albertson et al. 2018, 110–11; Carter et al. 2018; Heinrich and Kabourek 2018). Hevenstone and von Bergen (2020, 210) find that, although SIB projects did track more outcomes over longer periods and undertook more evaluations, "most evaluations did not measure impacts."

Not only are there technical challenges, but getting the contracting parties to agree about the "facts" is not as straightforward as it might appear (Maier and Meyer 2017, 3). Case studies reveal "contested issues related to data collection and interpretation" and challenges with respect to data accessibility among project stakeholders (Fraser et al. 2020, 200–1). A focus on data is resource intensive, and collecting data for outcome payment purposes might divert resources away from productive research and evaluation that could improve genuine outcomes, as opposed to reported output metrics, as has been found in at least one case (Jamieson et al. 2020, 213).

Even if every project met the ideal of a fully randomized control trial, with metrics embraced by all contracting parties, the SIB model rests on the equivalent of a 100 per cent program audit rate, which is unlikely to be efficient even in a standard economic model of self-interested agents, with audits facing diminishing returns. A reallocation of resources away from monitoring to incremental service delivery – with remaining monitoring and accountability of service providers based partially on adherence to a proven program model – likely would be more efficient. This is arguably what the conventional procurement model in practice aims to do, with quality performance reinforced by the prospect of contingent renewal of contracts. As we noted in chapter 1, there are many problems with relying on randomized control trials, including both technical and ethical issues. Alternative forms of evaluation more appropriate to social service delivery for vulnerable populations are available, "but they do not yield clear financial metrics for private investors" (Tse and Warner 2018, 10).

With respect to pure risk transfer, a proxy for the degree of actual risk transfer is the degree to which projects fail to meet their targets and investors do not recoup their investment (Gustafsson-Wright, Gardiner, and Putcha 2015, 40). With few exceptions, SIBs appear to be meeting their targets, and governments in the vast majority of cases are paying out bonds and investors (see Chapter 2). Even if risk were being transferred in practice, there is not a strong case from a social welfare perspective for transferring risk to the private sector. A private sector partner would need to be compensated for accepting risk (Maier and Meyer 2017, 6), and might be even more wary than government in taking on risk (Albertson et al. 2018, 24), leading to high costs to government of transferring that risk. Since government is structurally better equipped to diversify pure risk, for risk transfer to "make sense" in an SIB, it needs to be seen as a response to political risk aversion. But this case for risk transfer raises the question of the degree to which one should accept and cater to the political motivations of elected officials, as opposed to holding politicians better to account for implementing objective and evidence-based improvements in public policy.

The argument that SIBs contribute to broader systems change also ignores much of their negative potential effects. First, greater reliance on the wholesale outsourcing model, on which SIBs and PfP are based, runs the risk of deskilling the public sector and placing government at a disadvantage when procuring social services. As Finn (2008, 7) puts it: "When service delivery is devolved to independent providers, the purchaser loses insight into the 'why' of 'what works.' Contractors and their front-line staff inevitably gain an advantage as they develop greater operational knowledge of how to achieve specified outcomes," and are more likely to keep this information private to gain a competitive advantage. He notes, however, that this can be offset partially through administrative measures to supervise, evaluate, and share information (7).[38] Although this diffusion is already taking place to some degree through conventional procurement relative to direct public service delivery, it is amplified under the contracting out of management that is implicit in SIBs. Additionally, if SIBs replace unionized public service workers with lower-paid private sector consortia and more precarious employment, they could have unintended consequences with respect to income inequality and working conditions in the social service delivery sector (Albertson et al. 2018, 23).

Second, as the system achieves scale, the market for SIBs grows, and SIBs become less relationship based, some gains from scale, standardization, and competition might emerge, but this would be at the risk of the displacement of public service motivation and greater likelihood of rent-seeking behaviour. A cautionary example is provided by the evolution of US prison labour and privatization, leading to what has been termed the *prison industrial complex*. Initially motivated by the desire to provide training opportunities for inmates, undertaken directly and tightly regulated by the state, the use of prison labour expanded rapidly in response to lobbying efforts by large corporations that advocated for deregulation of the use of such labour, including removing minimum-wage requirements and restrictions on the market for prison labour–produced goods (Thompson 2012, 40–1). After the removal of these restrictions, companies turned their efforts to "lobbying for and passing harsher sentencing for non-violent offenses including three-strike laws, mandatory sentencing, and truth-in-sentencing," expending over $32 million between 2000 and 2010 on lobbying activities and campaign contributions (Thompson 2012, 40–1). The initial opening of prison operations to private, for-profit actors in an attempt to make a program more efficient led to an entrenched set of vested interests, rent seeking, and state capture activity that was unlikely to

---

38 In the extreme case, the capacity built up in the private sector may disappear as individual firms fail. For example, Numbers For Good, a London based company that has been an intermediary in three SIB projects to date announced it is dissolving the company due to market pressures (*Pioneers Post* 2019).

have been predicted at the time. The example highlights the potential for unanticipated consequences when previously sheltered public sector activity is opened up to private, for-profit opportunities.

Third, shifting the responsibility to achieve outcomes to private sector partners might weaken the public's ability to hold government to account. Private contractors often are not subject to the same disclosure requirements as public bodies, creating "considerable scope for 'blame shifting,' with the responsibility for poor performance is less obvious" (Finn 2008, 8). As noted above, information disclosure challenges have already been problem in a number of SIBs. Finally, the shift to greater reliance on the private sector ignores the interdependencies of social challenges and the unique position of the state to coordinate strategic responses, as outlined above in the discussion of innovation.

Despite these challenges, there is some evidence that SIBs can be successful in building support for effective social programs, particularly in more conservative political environments where public funding support was previously absent. Tse and Warner (2018), for example, highlight how two US early childhood PfS interventions, supported by a strong network of community stakeholders, were able to leverage longer-term public funding commitments from government to sustain the intervention subsequent to the SIB's demonstrating results. They emphasize, however, the second-best nature of this result, given the well-established evidence regarding early childhood interventions and high transaction and financing costs associated with SIBs relative to conventional delivery, and they point to a counter example where this did not occur, with investors benefiting at the expense of programming for vulnerable families.

Conclusion

In this chapter, we reviewed three central claims of proponents concerning the benefits of SIBs: their ability to generate incremental new resources for cost-effective preventative social programs; their ability to deliver more efficient or higher-quality programs; and the systematic benefits they generate for the larger social service delivery system. The evidence that SIBs generate new funding for initiatives is inconclusive. Private capital is coming forward to finance SIB projects, but this must be repaid by government if the projects are successful. For the most part, SIBs are meeting targets and being paid out, so the private sector generally is not paying for new programs, only financing them at a rate of return on average greater than government borrowing rates. This project finance in theory could allow incremental new projects to proceed by skirting self-imposed government budget constraints if the social interventions are netting cashable fiscal savings to government such that the interventions end up paying for themselves. In practice, however, many governments are setting aside current funds for SIB payments, requiring incremental or reallocated public funding that otherwise could be available for direct financing of prevention-focused social programs.

Similarly, the direct evidence to support claims of increased social program quality or efficiency under SIB delivery is inconclusive at this stage. Part of this is due to the relative newness of the SIB model, but part is also due to the apparent indifference of those involved to determine the model's merits relative to those of other procurement methods. To date there have been no controlled experiments to test whether SIBs provide better outcomes than conventional procurement or public delivery. The quality- or efficiency-enhancing potential of SIBs rests on implicit and explicit assertions that privatization leads to better project management and facilitates innovation, and that the SIB model improves incentives through the PbR payment structure, better coordination within government, and broader stakeholder participation. Theoretically these claims are weak, particularly in the social service context, where contracting out has been shown to have minimal efficiency gains, and financial incentives have generated dysfunctional behavioural responses. The limited case studies that examine SIBs and innovation have found little taking place, except in the financial area. The most intuitively beneficial attributes of the SIB model – government prioritization of cost-effective prevention programming and better alignment of activity across departments – rest on state-led reforms within the public sector itself, based on central government planning that appears to be independent of the procurement model used to deliver programs.

With regard to the ability of SIBs to have beneficial systematic effects on social service delivery more broadly, it is simply too early to tell whether experience with the model is leading to positive changes with respect to a focus on outcomes and evaluation, or negative impacts arising from dysfunctional responses by service providers and questionable practices associated with the introduction of new rent-seeking opportunities. As the scale of SIB use increases, it is likely that more data will emerge; experience with previous privatization and PbR initiatives, however, highlights the potential for both efficiency gains and detrimental effects with respect to both quality and value for money.

Despite their questionable foundation, SIBs appear to be attracting additional public funds and, in the short term, might be permitting incremental preventative social service delivery to proceed by overcoming self-imposed fiscal restraints. Governments appear to be paying for the cost of SIB delivery, including the new administrative structures required and the return to investors. Significant support, both in-kind and financial, is being committed to the SIB model, with an associated opportunity cost. Governments alternatively could be investing these resources in improving public sector service delivery directly. This approach is being advocated, for example, in Australia, where two graduates of the Harvard Kennedy School of Government, home of the formally titled Social Impact Bond Lab, have developed a proposal for a Social Outcomes Fund that would cut out the private investors in SIB contracts and focus on longer time frames of a decade or more to evaluate success (Willis and Tyler 2018). The fund would be replenished by realized savings, as opposed to paying out returns to investors, with a view to overcoming the disadvantages of the SIB model – in particular, the small scale of projects, due to "the need to raise private capital; significant complexity and cost."

Proponents deem SIBs a success because they are meeting their targets. This result is unsurprising, however, since the model is primarily replicating and/or scaling-up proven interventions, with built-in additional supports for evaluation and management capacity not available under other models. To compare the SIB model truly to an appropriate counterfactual, existing non-profit service provision models would need to be equally resourced and studied under similar circumstances.

4 Social Impact Bonds as Public-Private Partnerships

Introduction

In this chapter, we aim to situate the potential of Social Impact Bonds to improve the efficiency of publicly funded social services. We do this by drawing upon the literature that examines public-private partnership models of infrastructure procurement and delivery, and privatization more generally, using the incentive theory, property rights, and transaction costs approaches to the economic analysis of contracts. Our goal is to construct a "best-case scenario" framework for SIBs in a manner that fairly represents the assumptions and claims of proponents in a rigorous and internally consistent manner. As we will see, however, the result is ambiguous when applying modern mainstream theory consistently to the potential superiority of SIB-type models.

SIBs and PPPs share many features relative to more conventional public sector procurement models (Gustafsson-Wright, Gardiner, and Putcha 2015; Loxley 2013; Tse and Warner 2019; Warner 2013, 2015). These include the bundling of design, financing, and operating activities, an increased role for the private sector in project planning and delivery, and a transfer of responsibility and associated risk from the public to the private sector. They also both involve the raising of financial capital for public projects through private consortia as opposed to conventional public borrowing methods. Recognizing SIBs as a variation on the PPP concept and privatization more generally allows for the application of theoretical insights, which we argue can help fill gaps in the existing work on SIBs.[1]

---

1 Formal analytical approaches to modelling PPPs include Bennet and Iossa (2006); Bentz, Grout, and Halonen (2005); Engel, Fischer, and Galetovic (2013); Grout and Sonderegger (2006); Hart (2003); Martimort and Pouyet (2008); Maskin and Tirole (2008); and Menezes and Ryan (2015).

In this context, the potential of the SIB model to deliver superior outcomes is in its ability to better address incentive and agency issues (McHugh et al. 2013; Stid 2013; Maier and Meyer 2017; Pandey et al. 2018; Pauly and Swanson 2017; Wong et al. 2016). Specifically, the challenge is framed as a principal-agent problem, where government is contracting for a service from some private sector agent or contractor, and cannot fully determine the quality of the service being delivered. A few papers have undertaken mainstream, mathematical-deductive economic analyses of the SIB model. Pauly and Swanson's (2017) analysis focuses on how an SIB can be superior to standard PbR contracts based on conventional combinations of borrowing and donation-based finance when the SIB enables financiers to contribute effort to program improvement. In their model, potential financiers include market-based lenders, altruistic donors, and altruistic lenders willing to accept a reduced rate of return. If financiers do not contribute such effort, there will be an equivalence between financing models, where "SIBs provide no advantage over alternative organizational structures" (721). In Pauly and Swanson's model, an altruistic investor exerts greater effort than a traditional donor, since their investment is at risk, in addition to their donation (in the form of a reduced rate of return). The SIB model allows socially beneficial projects to proceed that would not be feasible based on conventional PbR funding arrangements. Wong et al. (2016) also create a model that relies on induced effort through the contracting structure, but the effort is generated by the non-profit provider, who is now supervised by investors. The outcome is similar, however, in that, due to the financial incentives facing the investor – and the assumption that investors have an incentive and the ability to increase program quality that government lacks – the SIB contract generates superior outcomes.

In the incentive or contract theory approach, PPP models parallel the SIB economic models above in that they emphasize how a contract structure that incentivizes greater effort levels from agents can generate more efficient outcomes. Although the SIB models rely on a transfer of greater outcome risk and, in turn, potential financial loss to private partners to motivate effort, PPP models suggest an additional source of efficiency: the bundling of contract components, which generates a more optimal level of upfront investment in design and/or capital asset quality.[2] For example, under a road construction PPP, it is likely that a more durable road will be built, with lower long-run

---

2 Representative samples of PPP models include Bennett and Iossa (2006), Hart (2003), Iossa and Martimort (2015), and Martimort and Pouyet (2008). For a more general discussion of incentive theory, see Laffont and Martimort (2002).

maintenance costs, thus minimizing total present-value costs over the lifespan of the road. This is because a single firm would be responsible for both construction and maintenance costs, and the company would harm only itself by skimping on quality; moreover, under a PPP, the firm often is obliged to return the asset to the public sector in "as new" condition).[3]

This PPP modelling approach, as a multitask principal-agent problem, helps to clarify the sources of potential welfare gains under SIBs, pointing to positive bundling externalities and better resolution of principal-agent problems, in addition to outcomes-based payment. Take, for example, a social program aimed at safely reunifying with their parents children apprehended by child welfare authorities. Under an SIB, where design and operations are bundled, PPP models would suggest that this bundling likely leads to a more optimal amount of research and development in an effective intervention that helps families succeed in providing a safe home environment for their children. This is because designers and financiers, now part of a consortium of firms, have a stake in operational effectiveness, since returns to the consortium are based on outcomes and government compensation is not based on realized costs. Our framework incorporates both risk transfer through outcomes-based compensation and bundling externalities as potential sources of SIB efficiency.

The above models neglect, however, the potential negative effects of the SIB structure. In the PPP literature, it has been noted that these delegated contract structures can lead contractors to reduce service quality while staying within the letter of the contract, and that this aspect should be considered explicitly (Hart 2003). This is one of the downsides of residual-claimant status in PPPs and SIBs in the event of an incomplete contract. Examples in the PPP infrastructure case include denial of public access and lax staff background checks in PPP schools, and sewage spills and health and safety violations in PPP water treatment facilities (CCPA SK 2015). In the case of SIBs, there have been multiple allegations that projects have selected clients who would meet threshold targets most easily, as opposed to those who would benefit most from the programming (Edmiston and Nicholls 2018; Loxley 2017;

---

3 Since payment is predetermined as long as contractual obligations are met, the private sector's status as residual claimant also provides an incentive to achieve this optimum quality at minimum cost, as all savings generate financial returns for the private sector partners. An SIB also provides a similar residual claimant incentive to reduce costs, as payment is based on outcomes and the SIB consortium retains any cost reductions based on more efficient service provision due to, for example, a greater emphasis on performance management.

Tse and Warner 2019). Unlike previous SIB models, our framework explicitly accounts for such negative effects.

The above insights are helpful for understanding the case made for partial privatization models such as SIBs, as well as some challenges, but they still neglect some important features of the debate over the efficacy of SIBs. We also introduce theoretically supported and empirically informed differences in transaction costs and variations in the degree of supplier competition when selecting an SIB over a competing delivery model – other issues that have been raised in the discussion of privatization in the new institutionalist school. This explicitly brings to the fore some additional considerations driving cost differentials between the two models.

This chapter complements the work of analysts such as Pauly and Swanson (2017) and Wong et al. (2016), who use economic methods and who have emphasized how SIBs can be welfare enhancing by helping to resolve agency issues or by helping to internalize externalities. Liebman and Feller (2014), for example, emphasize the internalization of externalities, with SIBs helping to overcome the incentives that a government might lack to invest in evaluation and produce social innovation, given its limited ability to capture the benefits relative to the costs. Pandey et al. (2018) and Burand (2020) also highlight the usefulness of contract theory, with Pandey et al. also noting the applicability of transaction costs and property rights approaches. More generally, this structure might contribute to cost-benefit analyses of the advantages and disadvantages of the SIB model relative to conventional procurement. As previously noted, "there has been very little rigorous counterfactual comparison of SIBs versus alternative methods of finance to deliver the same service to the same type of users, and thus a lack of evidence of costs and benefits compared with the alternative approach to procurement" (Fraser et al. 2018b, 16; see also Carter et al. 2018). Stakeholders, such as the UK auditor general, have also called for more robust and consistent examination of SIBs and other PbR projects relative to more conventional methods, given their challenges and limitations (Morse 2015).

This chapter proceeds as follows. We begin by reviewing the attributes of the PPP infrastructure delivery model, and introduce the suggested benefits of PPPs relative to the conventional infrastructure procurement model from the perspective of a public sector commissioner. We then outline the case for considering SIBs as a type of PPP, and briefly summarize perspectives on privatization in the mainstream economics literature, setting the stage for our cost-benefit framework for SIBs. Before concluding the chapter, we present a comparative framework for evaluating SIBs versus conventional procurement.

Review of the PPP Infrastructure Delivery Model

The phrase *public-private partnerships* in general has been used to encompass a large variety of relations between government and the private sector (Hodge and Greve 2005), but in the physical public infrastructure context, it has a more specific meaning. Under the PPP infrastructure delivery model, infrastructure design and construction are bundled, often with financing, maintenance and/or operations, into a single long-term contract with a private sector partner, which is generally a consortium of individual companies. The private sector partner then might maintain control and ownership of the infrastructure asset over an extended contract, at the end of which the asset is transferred back to the public sector. Governments worldwide, facing fiscal constraints, with growing challenges maintaining existing infrastructure and meeting new demands, have turned increasingly to PPPs for infrastructure delivery for a variety of infrastructure types, including roads, schools, and hospitals (Iossa and Martimort 2015; Loxley 2010), and expanded the procurement model to other areas, such as information technology and military procurement (Parker and Hartley 2003; Kuan 2009). The scope of such operations has reached significant aggregate levels, with total asset investment as of 2010, of at least of \$2.7 trillion worldwide.[4]

PPP contracts are defined primarily by the bundling of investment and service delivery components, and characterized by: their long-term nature; the temporary transfer of assets; and the associated risk, including demand risk in the presence of user fees, that is claimed to be transferred from the public to the private sector, arising from greater contractual obligations (Bennet and Iossa 2006; Bentz, Grout, and Halonen 2005; Engel, Fischer, and Galetovic 2013; Iossa and Martimort 2015; Martimort and Pouyet 2008). This is differentiated from the stylized conventional public procurement model, where design and provision are unbundled, with various components delivered through separate contractors, coordinated and managed by the public sector or directly by the public sector entity that retains ownership and control over assets. Bundling under a PPP, therefore, at a minimum transfers some coordination activity from government to the private sector. Financing, when transferred under a PPP, also devolves activity traditionally undertaken by government to the private sector. A PPP also may transfer to the private sector design, operations, and maintenance

---

4 Authors' calculations based on data in Iossa and Martimort (2015) and the Private Participation in Infrastructure Database (World Bank 2017).

previously done by public sector staff. A PPP, therefore, is an intermediate delivery model between public and private provision of publicly
funded infrastructure, one that results in incremental privatization over
and above conventional contracting-out models.[5] This transfer of both
responsibility and associated risk is used to justify a number of contract
provisions to realize the profits upon which private investment in the
project is based, including in some cases the granting of service monopolies in addition to government lease payment commitments (Istrate
and Puentes 2009; Warner 2013).

Sources of Efficiency Enhancement under the PPP Model

Several sources of efficiency have been put forward to rationalize the
PPP model. In economic models of PPPs, the primary emphasis is on
how the bundling of all components of project delivery imposes a life-
cycle cost perspective on the private sector participants and, therefore,
can result in a more efficient cost and risk allocation in an asymmetric
information environment due to economies of scope or the reduction
in unit costs as more than one product is produced (Iossa and Martimort 2015; Hart 2003; Martimort and Pouyet 2008).[6] It has also been
argued that the PPP model can prevent suboptimal high-cost projects
from proceeding by being passed off by insiders as projects with low
or uncertain costs, and can reduce the catering to special interests that

---

5 From a delivery standpoint, PPPs can appear similar to privatization, particularly as
   design, maintenance, financing, and operations are transferred to the private sector
   partner. In other respects, PPPs maintain some attributes of public delivery. For
   example, asset ownership, if initially transferred to the private sector, is transferred
   at the end of the contract back to government, and the degree of retained risk held
   by the public sector is high. In practice, PPP contract structures have resulted in
   public sector partners carrying substantial retained risk, both initially and through
   subsequent contract revisions and outcomes (Loxley 2010). It has also been argued
   that, from an *a priori* perspective, the optimal risk profile of a PPP is more similar
   to that of public infrastructure provision (Engel, Fischer, and Galetovic 2013). Some
   have argued, in fact, that the PPP terminology and framing is a guise to soften
   resistance to contracting out and privatization (Hodge and Greve 2005, 7).
6 Martimort and Pouyet (2008) highlight two distinct issues with respect to the
   potential gains from bundling and ownership transfer. If contracts are complete
   and exclusively performance based, ownership is irrelevant, and the tasks should
   be bundled if increased asset quality generates a positive operations externality,
   and unbundled if the externality generated is negative. In the case of incomplete
   contracts and asymmetric information regarding quality, transfer of ownership to the
   concessionaire might support increasing asset quality to the socially optimal level.
   This point links back to the insights of Hart (2003).

arises from the preferences of public servants based on ideology or relationships with contractors (Maskin and Tirole 2008).[7]

User fees associated with PPPs have also been identified as a source of efficiency enhancements, and have been claimed to permit a more optimal allocation of demand risk. PPPs can also generate efficiencies in the presence of user fees if one assumes that flowing money otherwise through government into subsidies imposes additional costs (Engel, Fischer, and Galetovic 2013). PPP rationalization that rests on the benefits of user fees requires the assumption that such fees were not feasible or sustainable under the conventional procurement model with public asset ownership, for example, due to the inability of politicians to resist popular opposition to user fees.

Efficiencies in the Conventional Model

Although the efficiency-enhancing potential of the PPP structure is emphasized in economic models of PPPs, potential benefits and efficiencies are also available through conventional delivery. These might arise when the assumptions of complete and fully enforceable contracts, perfectly competitive supplier markets, zero transaction costs, or hyper-rational self-seeking stakeholder motivations are violated, or there exist additional information asymmetries beyond effort-fuelled investments in quality.

The potential benefits and efficiencies of the conventional model include: better targeting construction and operations contracts to specialized contractors through unbundled contracts (Maskin and Tirole 2008; Laffont and Tirole 1988); reducing the size of the payoffs from collusion between the state and contractors and, therefore, reducing the incentive to participate in contracts that are socially suboptimal (Martimort and Pouyet 2008); and providing more flexibility to future governments that might find themselves bound to suboptimal contracts (Laffont and Tirole 1993, 619–36). PPPs can also result in suboptimal levels of service quality where contracts are imperfectly enforceable (Bentz, Grout, and Halonen 2005; Bennet and Iossa 2006; Hart 2003; Martimort and Pouyet 2008). In the case of essential services, suppliers have increased bargaining power in that they can threaten to disrupt service delivery. This effectively reduces risk transfer from government and increases the likelihood of renegotiation in favour of the concessionaire (Grout and Sonderegger 2006), particularly in the presence of

---

7 SIBs have also been put forward by Public Choice–orientated scholars as a means to address political economic problems around governments' not allocating resources in an efficient manner (see, for example, Liebman and Feller 2014; Wong et al. 2016).

an underperforming revenue stream and a credible threat of private partner default (Menezes and Ryan 2015). Alternatively, one of the main benefits of a conventional government procurement contract is that is it based on a contingent renewal basis, like that of contested exchange presented by Bowles and Gintis (1993), and modelled in Bowles (2004, 233–66), where the repeated interaction and associated relationships that develop generate efficiencies. Finally, publicly delivered services also might benefit from additional uncompensated labour time or effort stemming from a public service ethic (Francois 2000; Glaeser and Shleifer 2001), particularly in sectors such as health and education (Grout and Sonderegger 2006), which would be forgone to the extent that PPPs incrementally privatize delivery.

A Note on the Private Financing of PPPs

Although bundling efficiencies are currently the main rationale put forward for PPPs, the rise of the PPP model initially was supported by a more practical and direct advantage for governments or, more specifically, politicians. At first PPPs allowed public sector entities to generate new infrastructure construction without creating a liability on the government balance sheet, which provided a political incentive to use the model as a means to skirt formal and implicit budget constraints based on accounting conventions. This "off-book" accounting of PPPs has been extensive, with, for example, the UK government's holding approximately 87 per cent of its £40 billion PPP portfolio off-books as of March 2010, such that it was not included in official figures for public sector net debt (United Kingdom 2011a, 42; Hodges and Mellet 2012). By 2017 that portfolio had risen to £60 billion (United Kingdom 2018, 4).

The accounting benefit of PPPs was a key component of arguments in both the United Kingdom and Canada for adopting the PPP delivery framework, but increased attention of auditors and the application of accounting conventions such as the International Financial Reporting System (IFRS) have resulted in the recognition of PPPs as capital leases as opposed to operating leases. Many PPP arrangements now must be accounted for as part of public sector debt, leading proponents to shift emphasis to value-for-money considerations (Broadbent and Laughlin 2005; Coulson 2008; Hodges and Mellet 2012; Loxley 2010, 28–33; United Kingdom 2012).[8]

---

8 There is also evidence that more regimented financial oversight leads to greater public borrowing and lower debt costs. See, for example, Baber and Gore (2008), who find that municipalities that use generally accepted accounting principles have higher public borrowing amounts and lower debt costs.

These changes in accounting treatment were based on the fact that PPPs do not generate new incremental resources for infrastructure purely from their financing structure in any "real" – that is, non-accounting – sense, such that government ends up generating new infrastructure without having to finance it either directly or through a revenue-stream concession. PPPs financed fully by a combination of upfront and ongoing transfers generate a fiscal obligation held by government similar to standard debt-financed capital projects. Whether the transaction is "on-book" and accounted for as a capital lease, or "off-book" and accounted for as an operating lease, PPPs have an effect on the real government budget constraint equivalent to that of conventional procurement, regardless of accounting treatment (Engel, Fischer, and Galetovic 2013; Loxley 2010, 30; Vining and Boardman 2008). In the case of user fees, government concedes access to a revenue stream that otherwise could be used as an alternative to distortionary taxation, so there is no new net generation of fiscal capacity (Engel, Fischer, and Galetovic 2013). Only in the case of credit constraints such that government is restricted in its ability to raise public financing for projects – an exceptional circumstance for modern developed economies – could PPPs be deemed a mechanism for allowing projects to go forward that otherwise would not have been possible. Accordingly, and given that the risk structure of PPPs is much closer to that of conventional procurement and that there are ongoing implications for the public budget, it has been argued that PPPs should be accounted for as government liabilities in a manner similar to conventional infrastructure projects (Engel, Fischer, and Galetovic 2013).

Although private financing has not created the windfall of resources originally claimed by early PPP proponents, it still could be a source of efficiency improvements. First, these efficiencies might arise from the type of bundling externalities already noted, for example, due to informational advantages private financiers possess regarding design or asset quality and maintenance that can be extracted by government through bundled contracts (Iossa and Martimort 2015). Second, private financing might have a lower cost in the presence of user fees, if government administration costs and the deadweight loss and distortionary impact associated with taxation are high (Engel, Fischer, and Galetovic 2013), although this result relies on the assumption that the application of user fees is tied to private finance. Regardless, these arguments are clearly distinct from the notion that PPPs generate infrastructure without government having to pay for it. In general, in advanced capitalist societies, governments usually face lower direct borrowing costs, and if one ignores user fees, which are not present in the SIB model, the higher cost of private finance must be offset by efficiencies elsewhere if the model is to produce net benefits.

SIBs as Public-Private Partnerships

SIBs have many attributes in common with the PPP model of infrastructure delivery (Gustafsson-Wright, Gardiner, and Putcha 2015; Loxley 2013; Loxley and Puzyreva 2015; Warner 2015; Whitfield 2015, 22; Tse and Warner 2019). Both models involve the bundling of private upfront investment and financing with design and ongoing service provision in a single contract, although the expenses would be more front-end loaded in a PPP than in an SIB, given the latter's focus on capital investment. Agency problems involved in social service delivery contracts are central in SIBs (Maier and Meyer 2017; Pauly and Swanson 2017) and are similar to those in infrastructure-based projects. Governments face challenges identifying the quality of investments in the design and set-up of a project. Where these investments reduce service delivery costs, governments might induce more effort on the part of contractors to enhance quality by combining initial development with ongoing service delivery in a single contract. Similarly, private financiers might have unique information and/or abilities that government might access only by enlisting their capital to finance the project (Pauly and Swanson 2017). If one interprets the set-up and design elements of a social service intervention as the 'infrastructure' used to deliver the intervention, then economic models of PPPs can be applied to SIBs, with some adaptation.

SIBs have potential drawbacks associated with bundling, related to loss of government discretion and flexibility, that are analogous to those relevant in the PPP decision-making context. Stakeholders face similar incentive structures, as compensation is not tied to realized costs. SIBs also require large upfront investment to develop the program intervention, primarily for research and development, and to establish the project consortium. They similarly require the development of complex legal and administrative structures, leading to higher costs in these areas, as in the PPP case. Both SIBs and PPPs have also been characterized by a need to subsidize or otherwise guarantee a portion of the returns in order to secure private partner participation in the face of the high risk associated with the transfer of obligations and responsibility (Warner 2013). Given all of the above, the task of a public sector decision maker who seeks the socially optimal delivery method is similar for both SIBs and PPPs: to determine if the net expected benefit of bundling, assuming it is positive, is sufficient to offset the expected higher transaction costs of, and loss of discretion over, service provision over the course of the contract (Coulson 2008; Vining, Boardman, and Poschmann 2005).

SIBs, similar to PPPs in their early phases of adoption, are also claimed to have the benefit of generating new funding resources to undertake desired government initiatives without adding to public debt.[9] This "off-book" benefit is facilitated by the particular accounting treatment of SIB contracts, whereby government accounts do not have to reflect the associated liabilities, and does not address the fact that government has incurred an obligation to pay out the contract at a later date. In this case, SIBs might be used to shift expenditures "off-book," as previously was the case for PPPs.

While they have many similarities, SIBs are distinct from PPPs in some important ways. First, SIBs rely heavily on philanthropic considerations, with investment sourced from both for-profit and non-profit charitable sources, and non-profit service providers playing a major role in service delivery. SIBs are also constructed around a PbR model of payment, which is not central to the PPP model. PPPs also last decades, rather than years in the SIB case, and the lack of user fees in SIBs leads to no direct consumer input into the model (Warner 2013). SIBs also operate in core government service sectors – including health, education, and labour market training – where private for-profit participation historically has been more limited, rather than in areas where infrastructure delivery has long been contracted to for-profit providers (Whitfield 2015, 22). Some of these differences, however, are a matter of degree, as PPPs operate in social services fields such as health care and education, where there is also philanthropic investment, and PPPs based on user fees have PbR-like characteristics.

Economic Theory and Modelling of PPPs and SIBs

In this section, we review the theoretical underpinnings of our mainstream framework – principal-agent approaches with asymmetric information in an incomplete contracting setting – as well as our justification for including transaction costs, market power, and a corporate social responsibility (CSR) effect in our SIBs cost-benefit framework.

Asymmetric Information versus Incomplete Contracts

The economic analysis of PPPs and privatization more broadly has drawn upon multiple schools of thought, including Public Choice, industrial organization, transaction costs, and property rights approaches

---

9 See Chapter 3 for further discussion of this point.

(Bel, Fageda, and Warner 2010, 555–6; Clarke and Pitelis 1993; Petersen, Hjelmar, and Vrangbæk 2017, 3–5). More recent models of PPPs, such as those of Iossa and Martimort (2015) and Martimort and Pouyet (2008), focus primarily on the agency issues related to asymmetric information and the resulting moral hazard problem to highlight the benefits arising from bundling project components in PPPs and the life-cycle cost perspective it imposes. These economic analyses of PPPs rely on incentive theory in the presence of agency problems to evaluate the efficiency-enhancing potential of PPPs, drawing on previous work based on the theory of contracts and mechanism design with strategic interaction.[10] The benefit of bundling in a PPP, relative to conventional procurement, is a reduction in both moral hazard and agency costs associated with the observance of asset quality.

In this framework, the procuring government entity faces challenges observing the quality of the infrastructure asset as it is designed – only the contractor has a full and costless understanding of the quality embedded in the asset it is designing and constructing. Since, under conventional procurement, the provider is paid based on delivery of the asset and has no stake in maintaining the asset or delivering services using the asset, it does not invest the resources or effort to improve the quality and efficient provision of the service over the lifetime of the asset. In these models, PPPs can help solve this problem by contracting design, construction, maintenance, and service operations to a consortium of companies that is assumed to operate as a unified firm in relation to government. Here, both the builder and the operator exert effort that directly increases the benefits of the project as a whole, and might either increase or decrease operating costs depending on the nature of the technology employed. In the case where the builder's effort reduces operating costs, bundling provisions into a single contract generally results in superior social welfare outcomes. The effort gap between unbundled and bundled delivery can be bridged by contracting with the builder based on a quality index, but bundling remains superior as long as the index is imperfect (Iossa and Martimort 2015, 19).

The problems arising in this situation from asymmetric information are distinct from those that arise due to incomplete contracts, where some relevant future scenario falls outside the scope of the considerations detailed in the contract and/or is unenforceable at a low cost.

---

10 This approach is referred to as the contract theory or incentive theory approach. For introductory volumes, see Bolton and Dewatripont (2005) and Laffont and Martimort (2002).

There is a case to be made that, in general, government service procurement is prone to incomplete contracts, given the challenges in most service delivery contexts of fully specifying quality considerations (Hart, Shleifer, and Vishny 1997). Incomplete contracts open up the possibility that contractors might exert a second type of effort focused on *quality shading*, such that both social benefit and costs are reduced (Bennett and Iossa 2006; Hart 2003). Quality shading is permitted to occur since contracts are incomplete, and it is assumed that the verifiable and enforceable terms of the contract are still met. The research relying just on quality-enhancing effort leads to a promising case for the superiority of the PPP models over conventional procurement, while the incorporation of quality shading leads to less suggestive implications. The issue of quality shading is of particular significance in the SIB case, as an issue central to SIB design is, as noted earlier, the potential to misrepresent the quality or value added of the service provided by selecting clients from among those who are easiest to serve or most likely to succeed without the intervention (Butler, Bloom, and Rudd 2013; Callanan and Law 2013; Warner 2013).[11] We therefore integrate both quality-enhancing and quality-shading efforts into the cost-benefit framework below.

Transaction Costs

The transaction costs approach also relies on incomplete contracting foundations. Here, contracting out draws upon economies of scale and the associated incentive to invest in efficiency enhancements in exchange for the discretion and flexibility to control production when done in-house. Sappington and Stiglitz (1987) argue that it is primarily within a transactions cost framework with incomplete information that privatization decisions should be analysed. With increasing specialization of the service, or increasing asset specificity, public ownership and delivery become more favourable, while the existence of transparent indicators and a high risk of cost overruns support private delivery (Williamson 1999, 319–23; 2002, 181). This is because, as asset specificity increases, it becomes increasingly important to the principal to contract explicitly for contingent scenarios as the consequences of being "held up" by the agent are increasingly costly. This increases negotiation,

---

11 Zullo (2019) generalizes this problem to the contracting out of public social services more broadly.

administration, and contracting costs, and the benefits of market delivery dissipate (Williamson 1981a, 558–9; 1981b, 1548–9). These two effects are neatly summarized by Williamson (1981a, 559) as "production cost" and "governance cost" effects.

Although the quality-shading approach of Hart (2003) partially accommodates for Williamson's "production cost difference," it does not completely do so, and omits direct variation in "governance cost" between the in-house production and market procurement (Williamson 1981a, 559). Public production might be more costly, due, for example, to higher public sector wages and benefits, but this might be more than offset by higher governance costs. For a great proportion of public services, the assets developed are generally specific to the tasks at hand, which is a plausible explanation for the high administration and transaction costs observed in PPPs (see Chong et al. 2006; Loxley 2010; Shaoul 2005). Given their high degree of asset specificity, their small market, locally defined objectives, and population characteristics, SIBs would be expected to have higher contracting costs, and this has also been documented in practice (KPMG 2014; Loxley 2017; Maier and Meyer 2017; Morse 2015; Tan et al. 2015).[12] Finally, another potential cost associated with private delivery is the threat of default and limited liability, and the associated transaction costs of holding firms accountable in these scenarios (Sappington and Stiglitz 1987). In our framework below, we incorporate exogenously determined differences in transaction costs as administrative costs, and differences in governance costs as part of varying baseline operations costs.

The focus on differences in production (or base costs) and governance (or administrative costs) has been central to an applied cost-effectiveness framework used to evaluate PPPs called value-for-money (VfM) analysis.[13] VfM analysis does not have explicit theoretical micro foundations; it is simply an accounting method to compare variations in cost structure under competing delivery models. VfM analysis provides a clear process for breaking down costs by component, and could serve as an applied approach to evaluate SIBs versus alternative delivery models should a formal analytical selection process be

---

12 See also Chapter 3 in this volume. In general, PbR-based contracting imposes greater administration costs as systems and processes need to be developed to track and assure the quality of data (Damberg 2009).

13 Cost-effectiveness analysis refers to comparing the cost of competing delivery methods where the project characteristics are predetermined or fixed. A full cost-benefit analysis might permit the production/delivery model to vary (Weinrott, Jones, and Howard 1982, 179; Welsh, Farrington, and Gowar 2015, 457).

instituted by government prior to selecting a procurement model. The UK Cabinet Office and Department for Digital, Culture, Media & Sport, for example, refer proponents to cost-benefit analysis tools in the development of SIB proposals to help determine value for money. It should be noted, however, that VfM analyses of PPPs have not been without controversy, and have been criticized for their high sensitivity to the choice of discount rate and tenuous cost estimates of risk transferred to private sector partners (Loxley 2010, 173). It should also be noted that, although VfM is commonly used to appraise PPPs, the UK House of Commons Public Accounts Committee (United Kingdom 2018, 5) concluded: "It is unacceptable that after more than 25 years the Treasury still has no data on benefits to show whether the private financing initiative model provides value for money." We discuss VfM analysis more fully and compare it to the principal-agent framework in Appendix D.

The Significance of Competition

The role of competition has also been of central importance in the economic analysis of privatization (Sappington and Stiglitz 1987). Public Choice theory makes the case against the public provision of goods and services, given the position of the state as a monopoly service provider undisciplined by competitive markets, leading to inefficiencies and overproduction (Bel, Fageda, and Warner 2010, 555; Niskanen 2017). The industrial organization literature, however, highlights that private markets can also have monopolistic tendencies, and public providers may face competition from other public providers and/or be kept in check by the threat of privatization. This literature emphasizes that an analysis of privatization and its benefits requires simultaneously analysing its impact on the degree of competition, and the results of such analysis will depend heavily on assumptions regarding the regulatory environment post-privatization (Vickers and Yarrow 1988).

In 2014, the OECD convened experts and analysts to examine issues with respect to competition and PPPs, and concluded: "The complexity of PPP contracts, caused by the bundling of various project phases, may lead to limited participation in the tender, especially by [small and medium enterprises], and thus favour anticompetitive agreements among the few potential players. Also, bundling and long term contracting, typical for PPPs, could cause market foreclosure" (OECD 2017). It is plausible that similar conditions have arisen in the case of SIBs, and we incorporate the ability of monopoly rents to be present in the case of bundled delivery in our framework below.

Corporate Social Responsibility

The concept of *corporate social responsibility* centres around the notion that not just non-profits, but also for-profit corporations and other businesses should be concerned with factors beyond maximizing returns for owners and shareholders, such as social and environmental concerns, above and beyond what is legally required. McWilliams and Siegel (2001, 117) define CSR as "actions that appear to further some social good, beyond the interests of the firm and that which is required by law," and can be seen as an in-kind dividend to firm owners who value the sought-after social outcomes or as a reputational input into the firm itself. Afik et al. (2019) find supporting evidence that CSR impacts valuation, with a small and temporary increase in share value for SIB investing companies based on a CSR reputational effect. CSR behaviour by large corporations is prevalent across sectors of the economy, and has attracted significant resources (Baron 2008), to the point where a specialized industry of CSR advisory services has developed in response (Graff Zivin and Small 2005, 1).

Economists' scepticism of corporate actions in the public interest goes back at least to Adam Smith, with Milton Friedman a well-known objector to this view arguing back in 1970 that corporate executives have no special ability or insight leading them to better allocate the entitlements of shareholders to charitable causes; shareholders, not management, if they see fit, should allocate any surplus generated from firm operations to charity directly from their dividends (Friedman (2007; 2009, 133–6). Friedman argues that firms should focus on maximizing profits within the constraints "embodied in law and those embodied in ethical custom" (2007, 173–4), a perspective that in the United States has been reinforced by court rulings (Hiller 2013, 288–9). Friedman does distinguish, however, between acts of social responsibility based on the charitable preferences of executives and actions that are construed as charitable, but in fact are taken to increase the profitability of the firm. He notes, for example, that a large employer in a small town might invest in local amenities to help attract and retain employees, or donate in response to tax incentives and the reputational effect that such donations might generate.[14] Other examples of CSR as a profit-maximizing strategy include the ability of producers to differentiate their product

---

14 Although Friedman (2007) notes that he "cannot summon much indignation
    to denounce" these actions, he also notes his "admiration for those individual
    proprietors or owners of closely held corporations or stockholders of more broadly
    held corporations who disdain such tactics as approaching fraud" (177).

and charge higher prices, as well as to divert social pressure and negative publicity (Baron 2009, 8).

We incorporate a CSR effect into our framework such that agents are willing to accept lower compensation because of the socially beneficial nature of the project. This is similar to Pauly and Swanson (2017), who model investors as willing to take a reduced rate of return given their valuing the social benefit of the project. They also assume that all service providers are non-profit and altruistic, which results in their seeking compensation only sufficient to cover their costs. We suggest that the altruism of non-profit organizations would not limit their seeking revenues greater than costs on a particular contract, as this would allow them to fund incremental activity that they intrinsically value outside the contract. In our framework, then, we explicitly model service providers as motivated by incremental revenues, and can generalize service providers as being either for-profit or non-profit.

A Comparative Framework for Evaluating SIBs versus Conventional Procurement

In this section, we provide a comparative framework for SIBs in relation to conventional publicly funded social service provision, from the perspective of a government decision maker who is choosing a procurement vehicle for an unspecified programming intervention in a predetermined social service area. We then temporarily set aside important issues regarding cost and benefits realized outside this public administrator's perspective, such as impacts on transparency and public access to information. We assume this administrator does not value directly the well-being or utility of external agents, but does take into account positive and negative externalities that affect concurrent or future government projects. The framework combines and builds on the insights of existing economic models of SIBs and PPPs, the broader set of considerations reviewed earlier in this chapter with respect to mainstream economic models of privatization, as well as some SIB-specific factors, such as CSR effects and claims regarding the externalities associated with adapting the SIB model in improving internal government operations and funding decisions.[15] We focus on the relative costs and benefits of the SIB model versus conventional procurement as defined in Chapter 1. Within this framework, we classify agents into

---

15 The framework below is based on a more formal model developed in Hajer (2018, 192–8).

Table 4.1. Benefits and Costs of Social Impact Bonds Relative to Conventional
Procurement

Incremental Benefits	Incremental Costs
Efforts of new stakeholders to improve design and delivery	Compensation to stakeholders investing in better design
New efforts from conventional stakeholders	Compensation to agents for risk
Lower profits due to corporate social responsibility effects	Higher cost of private finance
Forgone or deferred cost to government.	Higher administrative costs
Broader increase in project management capacity and focus on outcomes in other projects	Quality shading
	Excess profits/rents due to lack of competition and reduced transparency
	Developmental supports and the broader "enabling field"

three categories: financiers/investors, program designers, and service delivery agencies/operators. The benefits and costs of the SIB model relative to conventional procurement are summarized in Table 4.1, and we review each category in turn below.

Benefits of SIBs

Efforts of new stakeholders to improve design and delivery: Under an SIB, private investors may invest effort in improving the design of the social service intervention and project management, improving the effectiveness of the programming and better enabling service providers to deliver results on desired outcomes. This is incentivized directly by their repayment based on outcomes. New stakeholders also may include social innovation agencies that focus on researching and disseminating social service best practices, outcomes-focused management structures, and associated data collection and analysis.

Efforts from conventional stakeholders: For stakeholders engaged in conventional service delivery, such as existing project designers/consultants and service providers, SIBs might lead to greater effort being exerted to meet objectives, for several reasons. First, SIBs raise the stakes of project success. Project designers who are now intermediaries become more closely associated with the project and are an ongoing part of the project consortium and its management. Second, in general, the greater demands on service providers under an SIB and the more intensive project management and supervision also might increase service providers' work effort. Finally, in a minority of SIB projects, service providers and designers/intermediaries are also partially reimbursed by results, offering a direct financial incentive as well.

Lower profits due to CSR effects: Stakeholder agents, including investors, designers, and service providers, might be willing to accept lower rates of compensation, given the social benefits of the project and reputational or altruistic motivations. This could include a desire specifically to participate in an innovative model of social service delivery or a more general CSR effect.

Forgone or deferred costs to government: Under an SIB, if the project fails to meet its targets, either government will not pay or its financial obligations to agents will be reduced. Government also might defer payments to the end of the project once outcomes are verified, reducing the present value of such expenditures.

Positive externalities: In addition to its benefits, a broader increase in project management capacity and a focus on outcomes are likely to take place outside the project. Stakeholders are likely to develop greater knowledge and an increased capacity to enable and deliver outcomes-focused programming. This includes the ability of government to better procure, account, and budget for successful outcomes, leading to the funding of more effective interventions, the screening out of weaker programs, and an increase in support for cost-effective prevention-focused programming. For service providers, an increase in project management capacity is likely to have spillover benefits to other projects delivered by the organization and, in some cases, can have transformational effects on how the agency approaches its business.

Extra Costs of SIBs

SIBs are also associated with additional costs relative to conventional procurement. These include the need to compensate new and existing stakeholders for greater work effort and the risk of non-payment, the higher cost of private finance, higher administrative costs, increased quality shading by agents, higher costs due to reduced competition, and the costs of the broader enabling field that supports the development of SIBs.

Compensation to stakeholders for investing in better design: Investors and designers of interventions who invest effort and resources in improving the design of the intervention and management of the project, under standard economic assumptions, need to be compensated for these efforts if they are to accept the contract, all else being equal.

Compensation to agents for risk: Relative to a guaranteed return, under an SIB investors need to be compensated for the uncertainty of repayment. The higher the probability of failure, the higher the rate of return needs to be for investors to take the contract. If investors are risk averse, a premium above and beyond this is required, growing with the degree of uncertainty. For the same reasons, any other stakeholders who are paid by results under an SIB require greater compensation levels to participate.

The higher base cost of private finance: The base borrowing costs that private finance faces are generally higher than those that government faces in traditional government bond markets.

Higher administrative costs: Complex procurement structures such as SIBs have higher administrative and transaction costs. These include prolonged negotiations, the need for more complete contracts covering extensive contingencies, and higher tracking and evaluation costs. These materialize as greater demands on existing staffing complements within stakeholder organizations, as well as through the need to hire external legal, financial, and evaluative expertise.

Increased quality shading: By increasing the stakes of failure for agents, SIBs can lead to service quality reductions if they do not affect the measured outcomes used to determine success and pay investors. Similarly, agents might forgo important components of service delivery that are cost effective and beneficial for the service user, but are hard to measure and do not improve the likelihood that investors will be repaid.

Excess profits/rents due to a lack of competition and imperfect information: Given their complex negotiated structure, SIBs reduce the potential for competition among service providers and investors to act as a restraint on costs. SIBs can also reduce transparency by increasing the withholding of information based on claims of commercial confidentiality, thus increasing rent-seeking opportunities and further marginalizing program participants' voices, needs, and oversight.

Developmental supports and the broader "enabling field": As we reviewed in Chapter 2, developmental government and philanthropic supports for SIBs have underpinned their implementation, above and beyond outcome payments by government, including grants for project design, legislative and policy frameworks, and tax subsidies for investors. Although some of these have initial fixed costs that will be spread out among many projects as the number of SIBs increase, others will continue to grow on a per-project basis.

Discussion and Qualifications

For an SIB to be cost effective for government, the benefit generated by the model needs to be greater than the associated costs. When undertaking an analysis to determine whether such is the case, attention must be paid to the degree to which the specific benefits of the SIB model can be disaggregated and added to conventional procurement. Several examples are relevant. Government could increase project management capacity through alternative means by earmarking funds in the contract for training or hiring specialized staff within the service provider, conventionally funding a designer/social innovation organization – that is, intermediaries, technical service providers, etc. – to work with the provider, or better developing the evaluation and management capacity within government to assist service providers. If paying service providers and/or designers by results is a key driver of efficiencies, then government could pay just these agents by results while not involving private investors, negating the higher base cost of private finance. If the management staff of private financiers are key drivers of innovation, rather than the costly private finance itself, these individuals could be sought to assist the project on a philanthropic basis in exchange for a CSR effect or on a fee-for-service basis. From this perspective, there is a spectrum of options as opposed to the simple binary conventional versus SIB decision.

On a related point, it should be noted that costs and benefits are not independent, and in some cases are directly related. For example, the benefit to government of not having to pay in the case of failure is directly tied to the higher compensation costs required to attract investors. This is particularly clear when accounting for the CSR motivations of investors and other agents, which potentially are accessible through conventional means such as traditional philanthropic donation of funds or in-kind support. Any increase in the probability of failure will require a one-for-one increase in compensation to investors once CSR effects are conceptually separated out and treated independently. If the investors are risk adverse, or more risk adverse than government, the cost will be greater than one-to-one. The purported gains from pure risk transfer under an SIB, then, are illusionary, unless the only way to access the CSR-motivated efforts is tied to investment returns. Similarly, any benefits resulting from better project management or/design efforts need to be compensated, or based on a better alignment of PbR incentive mechanisms in the contract.

Finally, it should be noted that our conventional delivery model is not necessarily the public end of the spectrum of options with respect to the public-private delegation of responsibility. Although contracting out has become the standard for many social services, direct government delivery is the norm for services such as policing and fire protection. The transaction costs literature provides a clear case for why this can be the most efficient arrangement in some policy areas, based partially on the asset-specificity argument, but also on the idea that a commitment to public service values is integral to effective delivery. Williamson (1999, 322), for example, refers to this as "probity," based on the norms of "loyalty and rectitude," which are particularly important in areas such as foreign affairs and national defence, making these inappropriate for contracting out. Zullo (2019), in a related argument, highlights how the very logic of contracting out, regardless of the profit status or corporate form of the agent, is based on cost savings founded on excluding some users from service. He concludes that, where universal access is an objective, public services generally suffer when contracted out. The key point here is that both mainstream economists and heterodox economists have made cases for public delivery as the optimal form for some public services. Within the broader mainstream approach, the trade-off in our model can be carried over to the public-versus-private status of the service provider: a public sector provider would have few incentives to exert higher effort to improve quality while also having little incentive to engage in quality shading. In the next chapter, we critique and highlight the limitations of this perspective.

Conclusion

Existing analyses of SIBs highlight how the PbR nature of SIB contracts can generate superior outcomes relative to conventional procurement by giving agents a financial stake in the outcome of the project (Pauly and Swanson 2017; Wong et al. 2016). Studies examining PPPs in infrastructure show how such bundled contracts can also lead to improvements through better-designed projects and reductions in operating costs (Iossa and Martimort 2015; Martimort and Pouyet 2008). SIBs and PPPs, however, can also have negative effects. Other PPPs models point out the greater incentive to engage in hidden quality reductions in the presence of incomplete contracts (Bennett and Iossa 2006; Hart 2003), and this complex, high-stakes contracting structure often faces higher transaction and other administrative costs and the potential for monopolistic rents.

In this chapter, we used these insights to generate a more balanced approach, to provide an analytical framework to better understand the potential of SIBs versus more conventional service delivery contract structures. The superiority of the SIB model relies on the realization of hypothesized efficiencies sufficient to offset any incremental costs. For a public sector decision maker focused on a single project, the decision to proceed with an SIB then will depend on the SIB delivery model's efficiency-enhancing ability to offset quality-shading impacts, additional financing and administration costs, contractor rents due to reduced competition, and higher contractor compensation for effort and risk. The model is expected to accomplish this by facilitating savings through more efficient operations, higher incremental social benefits, and reduced payments to contractors due to non-monetary reputational benefits from participating in the delivery of the project.

We also suggest that these efficiency gains, if they exist, are sourced not from the ability of SIBs to bring in "new money" for social programs, but from their ability to better align incentives such that investment in quality design is closer to the optimum and accounts better for lifetime total project costs. This is similar to the conclusion in the PPP literature, summarized by Engel, Fischer, and Galetovic (2013, 106): "The crisis that started in 2008 has left many countries with large budget deficits. Hence these countries may find PPPs an attractive solution to finance infrastructure projects without increasing their apparent debt burden. We have shown that this should not be a basis for choosing PPPs over conventional provision. PPPs should be favored only when they lead to efficiency gains. To ensure this happens, PPPs should be given the same treatment in budgetary accounting than publicly provided infrastructure."

Although private finance might leverage some in-kind contributions due to CSR effects and bring along expertise that might generate some efficiencies through increased service quality, SIBs primarily generate "new" financial resources to the extent that they allow the government to skirt legislated or informal budget constraints based on accounting convention. SIBs create an expected obligation, albeit a state-contingent one, for government to pay out the bond's liability at some point in the future. In general, the reduction in expected costs due to the state-contingent nature of the SIB requires increasing the transfer to the private partner to ensure participation. Government accounting of SIB liabilities should reflect this if transparency and equivalence between expected and reported financial obligations are priorities. Similarly, the identification and accrual of projected savings are recommended to verify assumptions underlying SIBs' privileged status above other delivery frameworks, such as public delivery and conventional procurement, as evidence of these savings in practice has been questioned (Whitfield 2015, 37).

As we showed in Chapter 2, evidence suggests that SIBs are for the most part paying back investors, and investors are earning rates of returns well above the cost of government borrowing. If this is the case, one implication of our model is that, to provide value for money to government, the quality of services procured under the SIB model must be higher than would be expected from conventional delivery, and that higher quality is due to the model's incentive structure and bundling, as opposed to its subsidization or greater expected access to resources. Specifically, financiers, given their higher costs relative to those of conventional borrowing, must exert effort to improve the project if their participation is to be of value. Although there is evidence that financiers are participating in project governance (Albertson et al. 2018, 87), it is unclear whether these efforts are sufficient to generate a net benefit.

However, the very notion that bundling externalities exist in publicly funded social service delivery, which can be exploited by incentive contracts, is a tenuous claim. The incentive theory approach abstracts away from many features of the real-world context of publicly funded social service delivery that could undermine the effectiveness of rigid, performance-based incentives.[16] Those working within the incentive theory field have noted that the unique attributes of the public sector "make inappropriate the naïve application of magic bullet solutions like competition or performance based incentives" (Dixit 2002, 697). More fundamentally, it is unclear why the moral hazard problem between government and external contractors does not apply equally to relations between consortium members. In the SIB model, an intermediary organization generally coordinates participation of the private sector players, who would face similar principal-agent problems.[17] In general,

---

16 See Dixit (2002) and Chapter 3 for additional discussion.
17 See Sinclair et al. (2014), who highlight the lack of resolution of principal-agent problems in the SIB model, and Chang (2003, 208–38), who makes this point for privatization more broadly.

the principal-agent model makes a number of assumptions – including zero effort expended by public servants, the effectiveness of financial incentives to induce effort, abstraction away from within-firm agency issues, and neglect of non-pecuniary motivation – that undermine the model's predictive power, especially in social service delivery. Empirically, there is also no evidence that SIBs are generating innovation beyond existing social service delivery methods, raising doubts with respect to efficiency as a cause of the emergence of SIBs.

Despite these challenges, we believe our framework is useful for understanding the claims of proponents at the project level, and provides a helpful accounting framework for assessing the merits of SIB delivery relative to more conventional procurement models. Public servants are being asked to pursue SIBs, so the analytical approach introduced here could inform objective assessments of the relative benefits of SIBs. We suggest, however, that a more robust political economy approach is needed to explain the emergence of SIBs.

PART THREE

The Political Economy of Social Impact Bonds

5 Private Institutional Participants in Social Impact Bonds

Introduction

In this chapter, we present some basic empirics about the organizational partners in Social Impact Bond projects, and examine the roles, motivations, and changing contexts of operation and constraints faced by these stakeholders. In the previous chapter, we developed a cost-benefit framework that focused on the efficiency-enhancing potential of SIBs. While we made reference to corporate social responsibility effects on the decisions of private agents, we treated this as an alternative form of compensation to the firm. The framework we introduced relies primarily on typical neoclassical assumptions about the firm as a unitary entity and about the self-regarding behaviour of agents who participate in SIBs, while incorporating some insights from approaches in the new institutionalist tradition, including contract theory, transaction costs, and property rights approaches. Fundamentally, the model relies upon agent effort, including that of designers, financiers, and service providers, responding to greater pecuniary compensation.

Here, we suggest that evaluating SIBs as a publicly funded social service delivery model requires a more sophisticated understanding of what motivates the actions and behaviour of the lead institutional players involved and their workers, and how their decisions are influenced by organizational structural characteristics. Understanding such motivations, including the aims and objectives of those involved, can help predict how they will respond to the change in incentive structure when moving from conventional procurement to an SIB model. This chapter highlights how more empirically grounded theories of individual and organizational behaviour – drawn from a more heterodox institutionalist approach and recognizing the importance of altruistic motivation, the centrality of reciprocity, and individuals as socially embedded – can help explain the observed challenges faced by simple, incentive-based schemes, including PbR and SIBs. We then use this framework to examine briefly how the SIB model affects the sustainability and reproduction of stakeholder organizations more broadly over time, and how their behaviour might adapt. We rely on an approach to modelling cooperative behaviour based on the notion of *strong reciprocity*, a framework well suited to this task, as it embeds how individual norms of behaviour might change in response to policy shifts.

On the private partner side of the SIB relation, one important distinction that helps frame and organize stakeholders based on behavioural norms is between non-profit and for-profit corporate forms, both with respect to investors and service providers (Carter 2019; Chiapello and Knoll 2020). A major component of this chapter is thus dedicated to delineating the differences between these two forms of operation. Within this dichotomy, it is argued that the high prevalence of non-profit stakeholders in social service delivery and the attraction of altruistically motivated workers, executives, and directors to the non-profit sector might undermine the effectiveness of PbR contracting (Francois and Vlassopoulos 2008; Lagarde 2013).[1] If non-profit actors are more likely to value outcomes intrinsically and to share a collective identity and commitment to an organizational mission based on some altruistic social purpose, PbR might improve these agents' efforts, and might even undermine or crowd out intrinsic motivation by signalling a lack of trust and faith in the professionalism and integrity of non-profit workers.[2] Albertson et al. (2018, 94), for example, find that, for SIB projects, "most evaluations of PbR and SIBs that considered incentives found they had little or no effect."

Proponents have defended PbR in the non-profit context by noting that non-profit agents might respond positively to PbR if success under such a contract leads to an increase in resources for client services they intrinsically value (Courty and Marschke 2011b, 71–2). If the incentive generated by this increase in resources is sufficient to offset

---

1 This builds on the insights of Sinclair et al. (2014), who highlight how SIBs transform service delivery by substituting profit for public service motivation, and highlight this as an important dimension of social service delivery model classification.

2 Bénabou and Tirole (2003, 490), for example, make this case for workers more generally. See also Fehr and Gächter (2002b, 1), who show in experimental settings that incentive contracts lead to significant crowding out, to the point where "contracts providing explicit performance incentives are on average less efficient than fixed price contracts that do not provide any performance incentives at all."

any crowding-out effects of PbR, then the net benefit to clients might increase. The SIB payment structure, however, is not a typical PbR structure: SIBs do not usually pay social service providers by results, and therefore service delivery non-profits are not the beneficiaries of the increased resources. At face value, this further weakens the case for the SIB model relative to conventional procurement, particularly if intrinsically motivated social service workers interpret their efforts in meeting targets as primarily enhancing private payouts to investors, as opposed to enhancing the quantity and quality of service provided to clients more broadly. Alternatively, if funders are viewed as part of a larger community of like-minded organizations committed to mission-based service provision, the increased resources incentive might remain intact.

Non-profits and their workers, however, may not be driven only by altruistic motivation to see their clients receive quality services. These workers also may have a preference, for example, to be engaged personally in delivering these services. For such workers, there is an opportunity cost to losing access to this engagement, in addition to employment income, and non-profits might need to rely on SIBs from an organizational sustainability perspective if traditional funding sources are increasingly restrained. Non-profits and their staff then might still value SIBs; additionally, they and their staff might value process fairness and expect others to interact with them based on an assumption that the organization and its staff operate with a high degree of probity and integrity.

In this framework, the effectiveness of the SIB model hinges on the relative strength of three factors: (1) the degree to which SIBs help the individual organization secure resources to do work they intrinsically value undertaking; (2) the extent to which SIBs generate new resources for services for needy targeted populations overall; and (3) the extent to which non-profit workers interpret the motivations of outcome funders and investors as paternalistic and dismissive of their work ethic or altruistic identities. We categorize these as relating to *participation impacts*, *outcome fairness*, and *process fairness*, respectively, with non-profit staff valuing participation and these two types of fairness.

If non-profit organizations and workers see SIBs as a good-faith, cooperative measure to support more effective service delivery and better outcomes for more clients, and as generating incremental productive resources (financial and in-kind) for their organization and the social service delivery they value as a whole, SIBs likely will not crowd out quality-enhancing effort by service workers, and might even enhance them. Alternatively, if SIBs are seen as a paternalistic model that undermines the integrity of non-profit workers and organizations, and reduces available resources through payouts to private for-profit investors and higher administration and transaction costs, quality-enhancing effort likely will decline, even if the organization directly benefits from SIB financing. In the latter case, the SIB then will face an even greater challenge from an efficiency perspective, as it will have to rely fully on the newly solicited effort of financiers to offset this loss and other incremental costs of the SIB model. Actual experience with the model is also likely to affect perception if the promise and the reality of operating an SIB diverge.

This framework generates a number of problematic predictions for the SIB model over time. Here, SIBs are likely to lead to the displacement of intrinsically motivated non-profits that have a comparative advantage in delivering high-quality social services at relatively low cost, while privileging low-quality, higher-cost for-profit providers. Within the non-profit sector, we see a similar shift away from community-based organizations that prioritize both advocacy and service delivery towards larger, more conservative service delivery organizations.

This chapter proceeds as follows: we begin by presenting new data on private partner stakeholder organizations in SIBs, highlighting the high participation of non-profits, and briefly review survey and case study data on their motivations for participating. We then elaborate on the established theory of the non-profit corporate form, emphasizing the centrality of altruism and intrinsic motivation, and also summarize some trends in non-profit and social service delivery. Following this is a selective review of the treatment of altruism and reciprocity in economics, settling on the notion of *strong reciprocity* as our analytical framework for predicting the implications of the SIB model for social service delivery. Before concluding the chapter, we outline the implications of strong reciprocity and high non-profit participation for SIB design, and recommend an SIB model financed by charitable foundations or at low interest rates with targets set in partnership with service agents as the most promising form of the model, on the assumption that non-profit service delivery agents have an affinity with non-profit investors.

Institutional Participants in SIBs

SIBs have several stakeholder groups: (1) government and public agencies, including elected officials, civil servants, and other workers employed by government; (2) investors and other funders, including for-profit investors and non-profit foundations; (3) private for-profit and non-profit service delivery agencies, including those delivering social services, those evaluating the intervention, and those coordinating and/or providing technical assistance on SIB projects; (4) the clients served by the SIB-funded intervention; and (5) the public at large (Callanan, Law, and Mendonca 2012, 7). Not all of these stakeholder groups likely will be involved or consulted in the negotiation or design of an SIB (Maier and Meyer 2017, 3). The most glaring exclusion is that of citizens – more specifically, the client base itself, with participants acted upon rather than engaged in the creation and design of programming.

The stakeholders in SIB development often have conflicting interests (Giacomantonio 2017; Williams 2018), and therefore the negotiating process is of particular significance for determining the distribution of benefits arising from the project. As Chiapello and Knoll (2020, 103) summarize, "what is ultimately implemented needs to be considered as the result of struggles between actors stemming from different back-grounds, each bringing their resources, techniques, and a certain mindset." These differences and interests are reflected in how different stakeholder groups communicate the advantages of SIBs. Ormiston et al. (2020), for example, in their analysis of SIB press releases, find that different institutional participants emphasize different narratives, with government and investors highlighting innovative financing attributes, intermediaries emphasizing new forms of partnerships, and service providers noting better outcomes for program participants. As projects progressed, however, emphasis shifted more towards outcomes, partially due to the fact that "service providers are marginalized particularly in the early stages of SIBs" (244).

Government, intermediaries, and investors are those most directly involved in negotiations, and are more likely to have their interests best represented (Maier and Meyer 2017, 3). The relations that are key for the efficiencies proclaimed by the model, however, are driven by those with service providers, who are also sometimes included in negotiations. We therefore focus our attention primarily on these three groups: government, investors, and service providers, including intermediaries and evaluators. In this section, we present some basic data on these institutional private participants in Impact Bond (IB) projects, including both 122 SIB projects and 8 Development Impact Bond projects, organized by the role of the stakeholder in the IB projects. Data on IB participant organizations were compiled by initially consulting existing databases and reports, including Gustafsson-Wright, Gardiner, and Putcha (2015), Nonprofit Finance Fund (2017), and primarily Social Finance (2018). Data from these sources were further supplemented by a review of stakeholder websites and documentation published by project proponents.

Table 5.1 presents data on the stakeholder organizations participating in IBs as of January 2019, including outcome funders, investors, service providers, intermediaries, evaluators, and technical assistance providers, but excluding law firms providing legal services.[3] We counted individual organizations participating in multiple IBs for each IB in which they participated. With respect to outcome funders, as expected, based on our definition of IBs, the vast majority – 88 per cent – were government entities.[4] Of these government entities, 49 per cent were federal or national governments and 35 per cent were local or municipal governments. State or provincial governments made up approximately 16 per cent, while just over 1 per cent were international government entities.[5]

Of all other categories of participants, private non-profit organizations were the most numerous.[6] Over 70 per cent of social service pro-

---

3 Although we did identify thirty-five cases of named law firms that provided legal services on projects, this information was not consistently reported – and commonly only for US SIBs. Each project generally would have required legal services to prepare and review contracts for each participating party. Legal firms providing other services, such as the role of intermediary, are included in the presented data. Otherwise, legal firms are excluded from our data. If organizations were both investors and service providers, they were counted twice; however, if an organization played the role of intermediary in addition to another role, they were not counted as an intermediary. Similarly, organizations were not counted as technical assistance providers or evaluators if they filled an alternative role. For example, outcomes funders were often explicitly identified as the evaluators. Organizations identified as technical assistance providers and evaluators were only counted as evaluators.

4 Of the twenty-five outcome funders that were not government entities, two were for-profit corporations – one in a DIB and the other a health insurance company in the health impact bond. This latter case is the only identified example of an SIB with outcome payments fully paid by a private for-profit entity – in this case, the De Amersfoortse insurance company. See ABN AMRO (2017) for more details on this project. Four of the eight DIBs had outcome payments funded exclusively by non-government funders.

5 In federal countries where the SIB model has been implemented, SIBs generally have been issued by the state or provincial level of government; in centralized government systems, other levels have taken the lead (Dear et al. 2016, 46).

6 We classified investor organizations as for-profit if they paid out returns to individuals or for-profit companies or businesses. We classified all other organizations based on their incorporation status. Organizations were classified as non-profit primarily from information obtained from their websites. For Australia, Canada, the United Kingdom, and the United States, this was a relatively straightforward task, as corporate form is aligned with tax treatment in these countries. In the United States, non-profits generally post their financial statements and Internal Revenue Service Form 990, which clearly identify their non-profit structure. In the United Kingdom, corporations typically list their status in the footer of their webpage, identifying as a registered charity, and giving their respective registration numbers. Similarly, in Canada and Australia, non-profit

viders were non-profit, which was expected given some definitions of SIBs that emphasize the social motivation of those delivering front-line services (Carter 2020). Non-profits also made up more than two-thirds of service delivery providers, intermediaries, and technical assistance providers, and 58 per cent of investors. Of all participating non-profits, 79 per cent were identified as charitable organizations. Overall, 51 per cent of institutional participants were identified as non-profit, and 22 per cent were public sector organizations. Only 24 per cent of participating organizations were for-profit. Given the large role of non-profit delivery, in the following section, we examine the rationale of the non-profit sector relative to that of conventional private sector delivery of services.

The data reveal some interesting facts relative to the narrative of SIB proponents. First, despite their emphasis on the ability of SIBs to attract new, for-profit investment, the majority of financiers were traditional non-profit organizations, primarily foundations, with a long history of supporting social service delivery on a charitable basis. Second, despite the assumption that social service providers are generally non-profit, we found a significant number of for-profit providers engaged – for example, 44 per cent of evaluators were for-profit entities, and included well-established financial industry players such as Deloitte, Ernst & Young, and KPMG.

Service Providers' Motivations

Under an SIB, the delivery of social services to a target client group is undertaken nearly exclusively by private agents rather than by the public sector, but some SIBs include arm's-length public sector entities such as schools. Surveys indicate that service providers have several motivations for participating in SIBs, reflecting a combination of

---

status was generally straightforward to determine based on disclosed information. Organizations in continental Europe and Asia were more challenging to classify, partly due to different website disclosure norms. In some countries, such as Germany, corporate form is distinct from tax treatment and whether an organization is operating in the public benefit. Where non-profit and charitable status were not explicitly stated, we reviewed organizational descriptors and characteristics to classify the organization. For example, if an organization accepted donations that qualified for a tax credit, we classified it as non-profit (and charitable). Similarly, if an organization paid out dividends to investors, referred to shareholders, and had other characteristics that indicated for-profit status, we classified it as such. In some cases, there was insufficient information to make a classification, and we recorded the status as unknown.

Table 5.1. Organizations Participating in Social Impact Bonds, by Type, as of January 2019

Role	Number	% of Total	% Public	% Non-profit	% For-profit	% Unknown
Evaluator	50	5	2	48	44	6
Intermediary	87	9	0	67	26	7
Investor	373	38	4	57	37	2
Outcome funder	211	21	88	11	1	0
Social service provider	236	24	7	71	16	6
Technical assistance	31	3	0	68	29	3
Total	988	100	22	51	23	3

concerns. Gustafsson-Wright, Gardiner, and Putcha (2015) report that the number one reason indicated in their survey was the "opportunity to scale up intervention that works" (25), while the second was to generate social returns and achieve outcomes, suggesting that intrinsic motivations based on non-self-regarding preferences were driving factors. Service providers also identified the associated flexibility of outcomes-based contracts with the potential for innovation and the testing of new models, as well as funding – specifically, longer-term funding and support for preventative interventions. In their review of UK projects supported by the Commissioning Better Outcomes Fund, Ronicle, Fox, and Stanworth (2016) find that increased and longer-term funding was the primary motivation of service providers, who emphasized access to additional revenues to help their sustainability and continued existence, particularly in a context of fiscal restraint and austerity.

As a related benefit, service providers and intermediaries said that SIBs might give them greater input into the design of the intervention, and more power generally with respect to their operations, than conventional government procurement (Albertson et al. 2018). Ronicle, Fox, and Stanworth (2016) also find support for the model due to its focus on outcomes and how the PbR structure and evaluation allowed providers convincingly to demonstrate the positive effects of their organizations and to improve operations. It appears that some service providers prefer to be part of a funding structure that focuses on outcomes, as opposed to what they see as being subject to rationing or arbitrary decisions under conventional funding. Heinrich and Kabourek (2018), in their interviews with US stakeholders pursuing PfS funding for preschool interventions, also find that funding constraints drive participation. Unlike those of Ronicle, Fox, and Stanworth (2016), however, their interviews reveal a general pessimism about the ability of the SIB model to generate direct auxiliary benefits over time, although many interviewees referenced the model's "aligning program goals with longer-term outcome measures, developing rigorous evaluation methodologies, and attempting financial modelling of program benefits and costs" (Heinrich and Kabourek 2018, 26).

A successful demonstration of outcomes achievement also might help organizations to build future support and scale (Liebman and Sellman 2013, 9). Early success with SIBs might position the organization as a leader in a growing field, and allow it to benefit from early subsidized investments in project management and capacity building in SIB service delivery. All these findings echo previous research examining why non-profits might seek to participate in PbR contracts more generally, which highlights reputational benefits and increased resources (Courty and Marschke 2011b, 71–2).

Several risks have also been identified for service providers that participate in SIBs, even though payment is not tied directly to outcomes. Participating but then failing to meet targets could cause an organization significant reputational damage (Callanan and Law 2013, 79; Fraser et al. 2018b, 12; Giantris and Piakiewicz 2013). The provider also might end up with minimal new flexibility to pursue innovative solutions of its choosing, with any new autonomy from the state usurped by the intermediary or by investors with their own conflicting prescriptions as to how services should be delivered (Dayson, Fraser, and Lowe 2020; Edmiston and Nicholls 2018; Fraser et al. 2018b, 2020).[7]

In 2016 the National Council of Nonprofits in the United States released a set of *Principles for Consideration of New Funding Mechanisms* that constituted a cautious and qualified acceptance of SIBs and PFS funding while implying a number of concerns. For example, the principles state that new financing mechanisms such as SIBs should not displace conventional government funding for proven social services, and that social welfare services are a core responsibility of government that should not be compromised. The principles also highlight the need for all partners to be treated as equals in the project, and that transparency with respect to payments to intermediaries and investors should be required.

---

7 In some cases, the involvement of investors has taken a form that could be deemed intrusive. For example, in at least one SIB, investors became involved in the governance of the organization at the board level (Thames Reach 2015).

Investors' Motivations

The use of private capital to finance project operations is a defining feature of SIBs. However, the sources of that private capital and the institutional investors within these projects are not homogeneous. Investors span the range of philanthropic and more traditional private equity types and motivations, with varying weight placed on the relative importance of private financial returns versus achieving socially beneficial objectives on their own merit (Edmiston and Nicholls 2018).[8] Investors are attracted to the model because of the opportunity to generate a financial return and recycle investments, while simultaneously supporting socially beneficial projects (Fraser et al. 2018b, 10; Mulgan et al. 2011, 16; Social Finance 2011, 4). The demand for social returns might be part of the organization's mission, or the preference of its leadership, or be driven by demands from individual customers or donors (see Kitzmueller 2010). Surveys of investors in SIB projects have found that a combination of social and financial returns, the opportunity to participate in an innovative financing model, and the opportunity to redeploy contributions were important motivations (Gustafsson-Wright, Gardiner, and Putcha 2015, 25; MaRS and Deloitte 2013). Survey respondents noted that gaining public recognition through participating in the SIB was another motivating factor. Respondents also supported the idea that corporate social responsibility was driving participation, while institutional investors who raise capital from clients noted that customer demand was also a factor (Gustafsson-Wright, Gardiner, and Putcha 2015, 26). Investors and financial institutions also seek out SIBs to meet government requirements for social investment – for example, under the Community Reinvestment Act in the United States (Godeke 2013; Jackson 2013). More generally, it was suggested that SIBs do not offer a sufficient risk-reward balance from a financial perspective, so must rely on some combination of financial and social motivations (de Gruyter et al. 2020; Ronicle, Fox, and Stanworth 2016).

Given the risk of non-repayment in SIBs, the weight and priority accorded social impact relative to financial return will influence the degree to which any individual stakeholder values the opportunity to invest in an SIB. All else being equal, investors concerned about return of capital will prefer low-risk, high-return projects, and will seek out

---

8 Initially it was hoped that SIBs would leverage significant private for-profit capital for social programs. In practice, however, SIBs rely heavily on philanthropic foundation support, which to some indicates a "failure of the model" (Bailey and LaBarbera 2018, 79).

evidence-based program interventions to reduce their financial risk, restricting program innovation and service provider flexibility (Fraser et al. 2020). The sources of the funding within an organization will also be an important factor. Although non-profit investors – that is, charitable foundations – and for-profit investors are quite distinct in their corporate forms and *raisons d'être*, they share some similarities in the potential internal sources for SIB investment. Both financial corporations and foundations invest resources through markets to generate purely financial returns. For financial industry stakeholders, this is the core of their business: to generate profits from lending, investment, and trading. Out of the profits generated from this activity, financial corporations might choose to donate a portion to charitable causes, possibly through the establishment of their own corporate foundation. Charitable foundations also engage in these two activities, but the emphasis is reversed. Foundations are established to distribute grant funds to charitable causes, but they also often invest endowments based on generating financial rates of return on their investments. These are sometimes composed of low-risk, program-related investments, where funds are lent to social service projects that have market-based revenue sources sufficient to repay the loan over time (Ragin and Paladjian 2013). The main activities of charities, in contrast, focus on allocating donations to projects. They are sometimes required – in the United States, for example – to disburse a certain amount of their funds per year, leading to support for untested but potentially innovative programs (Kippy 2013). Both charities and traditional investors then engage in both philanthropic and revenue-generating activity, but to different extents.

The expectations of an investor in an SIB and the value of such an opportunity will depend on the source of and motivation behind the funds, which, in turn, will inform the risk-reward mix the investor is willing to accept (Maier, Barbetta, and Godina 2018; Maier and Meyer 2017). If the source of the contribution is a charity, and the investor values the funded program for its social benefits or for reasons of CSR, the opportunity to recover funds based on government outcomes payments is a clear benefit, as it gives the investor the opportunity to recoup the donation and redeploy the funds.[9] In this case, the investor is then more likely to accept a higher degree of risk. The opposite is the case when

---

9 This assumes that the relevant public stakeholders who are responding favourably to the act of corporate social responsibility cannot or do not devalue the SIB investment now that it might be repaid because it is less charitable than a grant. Given the complexity of SIBs for, say, a casual consumer of the firm's services, this might be a realistic assumption, but savvy consumers who value CSR might discount the SIB.

funding sources are based on their ability to generate financial returns; here, the tolerance of risk would be lower.[10] In Appendix E, we explore in greater detail the relevance of socially responsible investment and other related concepts as driving factors for the participation of investors primarily motivated by financial returns.

Early research on contributions from foundations indicates that program-related investment sources, as opposed to grant funding sources, were being used to invest in SIBs (Gustafsson-Wright, Gardiner, and Putcha 2015, 25). Some studies have found financial risk a top concern with respect to participating in SIBs, with investors indicating some guarantees likely would be required to secure their participation, in addition to expecting a market rate of return (Cuifo and Jagelewski 2014). In general, this suggests a relatively low tolerance for risk on the part of private investors, both non-profit and for-profit. In practice in the United States, non-profit participants have assumed subordinate positions on many projects in order to secure the participation of for-profit investors (Dear et al. 2016, 76; Nonprofit Finance Fund 2017), an arrangement that has been suggested as a necessity if the SIB model is to proceed more generally (Liebman and Sellman 2013). As we analysed in Chapter 2, projects appear to be delivering both moderate financial returns and relatively low risk of failure to repay, although this finding is based on relatively limited available data.

Intermediaries, Evaluators, and Technical Assistance Providers

Two private partner roles in SIBs that are newcomers to social service delivery are the intermediary and the evaluator (Maier and Meyer 2017). Some investors have expressed a preference for SIB projects facilitated by an intermediary (Cuifo and Jagelewski 2014), while others have argued that in fact the intermediary "plays perhaps the most important role" (Humphries 2014, 7) – although, since not all SIBs have separate intermediaries, it is questionable that this is the case. Proponents who have served as an intermediary argue forcefully for their benefit, as well as for specialized technical assistance more broadly (Dear et al. 2016, 57;

---

10 Some, such as Burand (2012) have argued that SIBs bring together, from an investor's perspective, the worst of both equity and debt, as they face limited returns and high risk of non-repayment. This would imply a heavy reliance on charitable motives and in-kind CSR compensation of investors to offset these financial disadvantages. Based on the data we reviewed in Chapter 2, however, this did not continue to be the case over time, and likely was a questionable assertion in the first place, even for the earliest SIBs.

Fraser et al. 2018b, 11). Intermediaries not only have played central project-specific roles; they have also been advocates for development of SIB markets more generally (Williams 2018). The intermediary role in an SIB is well suited to be filled by either a for-profit corporation that specializes in finance and project management or a specialized non-profit agency dedicated to these type of social investment structures.

Based on our review, eighty-seven of the IB projects employed an independent intermediary that was not already involved in the project as a service provider, outcome funder, or investor. Of these projects, 67 per cent of the intermediaries were non-profits, and 26 per cent were for-profits. Unlike social service providers, which were tied to a particular geographic location and generally did not participate in multiple projects, several intermediaries and technical assistance providers were often involved in numerous projects. Social Finance was the intermediary in the largest number of projects, leading seventeen of the them.[11] Other organizations that are explicitly special-purpose SIB/PfS organizations or that appear to be developing a niche in SIBs and have participated in multiple IB projects include Kois Invest (international), Laboratório de Investimento Social (Portugal), Numbers4Good (United Kingdom), Quantified Ventures (United States), Sorenson Impact Center (United States), Third Sector Capital Partners (United States), and the Triodos Bank (United Kingdom). Several of these organizations have also acted on other SIB projects solely as technical assistance providers.

In a survey of intermediary stakeholders and their motivations for participation in SIBs, Gustafsson-Wright, Gardiner, and Putcha (2015, 25) identify priorities that included the ability to test innovative solutions to social problems and the focus on outcomes. Respondents also noted that they had left careers in more traditional financial services. It remains to be determined if the motivations of intermediaries turn inward towards both the opportunities to generate revenue and sustainability, as suggested occurs with other service providers, as the organizations become more entrenched over time. Some have suggested that intermediaries, along with evaluators, have a clear vested interest in seeing SIBs succeed, and donate services in anticipation of a growing market for paid services (Maier and Meyer 2017, 5; Whitfield 2017).

Evaluators had the highest proportion of participants from the for-profit private sector. Private for-profit companies that have acted as

---

11 Social Finance was the coordinator of the first SIB, and is the leading proponent organization of SIBs globally, with national organizations in the United Kingdom, the United States, and Israel. For more information, see Chapter 2.

evaluators for multiple IB projects include Deloitte, Ernst & Young, KPMG, and Ecorys, a UK-based research consulting firm. As for technical assistance providers, the single most common player that did not hold other roles in SIB projects was the Harvard Kennedy School Government Performance Lab, previously known as the SIB Lab, which had aided ten US SIB projects. Although only 30 per cent of non-intermediary technical assistance providers were for-profit, the vast majority of these were financial sector firms focusing on accounting services or wealth management, including banks.

The Missing Partner: Service Users and Targeted Participants

The public administration literature is moving "back to a focus on citizenship, participation and public value" (Warner 2008, 165), yet the privatization of social services (Warner 2012, S40) – SIBs, specifically – marginalizes the voices of service users (Warner 2013). Within the SIB design, there is no mechanism to ensure that clients' interests and perspectives are taken into account (Carter 2019; Joy and Shields 2018; Sinclair, McHugh, and Roy 2019). SIBs, then, appear to fit clearly within a New Public Management (NPM) approach, focusing on "contracting, performance measurement, … PPPs, payment for outcomes, … markets and performance management" (Warner 2013, 3–7), while sidestepping the shift to New Public Governance (NPG), which emphasizes "co-creation between the users of services and services at the heart of public service management and delivery" (Albertson et al. 2020, 3). By excluding service users, SIBs clearly do not advance this attribute of NPG, and to the extent that some community-based service providers advocate for their clients, this route is further narrowed through intermediated SIBs, where service providers are marginalized. We explore some of the consequences of this later in the chapter.

Service Providers: The Significance of the Non-profit Form

The high prevalence of the non-profit corporate form among service providers in SIBs and whether investment is coming from a charitable or for-profit source of risk are likely to drive the behavioural motivations of service providers. To better understand the implications of non-profit versus for-profit corporate forms, in this section we review developments in the non-profit sector and mainstream economic perspectives on the rationale of the non-profit corporate form, including the underlying importance assigned to altruism and non-pecuniary motivations.

The Evolution of Non-profit Social Service Delivery

The corporate constitution of a service delivery agent as either for-profit or non-profit likely will alter the balance of motivations leading to participation in an SIB. The two types of providers face different operating contexts and constraints. For-profits often are larger organizations and generally have more working capital and access to credit, leading to greater willingness to undertake risk; non-profits are committed to fulfilling a charitable or social mandate, and are more risk averse and more credit and capital constrained (Morse 2015, 24–6). Non-profits, then, are more likely to benefit from the external finance provided under an SIB than under a standard PbR contract.

Non-profits have faced variations in government policy that have affected the scale of their participation in social service delivery. In many countries, increasing investment as part of a more interventionist and activist state has led to a significant increase in the size of the non-profit sector. For example, in the United States, federal and state spending on non-profits increased by 6.3 per cent annually on average from 1965 to 1980 (Salamon 2015, 31), falling drastically in the subsequent decade to 1.9 per cent annual average growth, partially recovering to 3.2 per cent in the 1990–2007 period, and falling again during the subsequent recessionary period to 2.3 per cent (Salamon 2015, 31). The overall trend, however, has been one of growth, a pattern that appears to be replicated in a number of advanced economies, based on the limited data available (Anheier and Salamon 2006, 99–100).

Historically in the United States, contracted social service work primarily was delivered by the non-profit sector, with government support through grants, but non-profits in that country have faced a drastically changing landscape and scope and scale of operations over the neoliberal era. Service purchase agreements between governments and private sector non-profit social service agencies have existed for centuries (Wedel 1976), but over time these agreements have become more prevalent, and are a growing share of non-profit agency activity (Ascoli and Ranci 2002; Carmel and Harlock 2008; van Slyke 2003). The increased reliance on service purchase agreements has led to greater emphasis on reporting and accountability to government funders, which demands greater administrative work by non-profits (Lipsky and Smith 1989–90; McGregor-Lowndes and Ryan 2009). This trend was part of the broader privatization movement that took place in the 1990s and 2000s, with increasing delivery of government services through non-profit third parties, implemented with the objectives of generating cost savings, state workforce reductions, and increased operational flexibility within government (Auger 1999; Hall and Reed 1998; van Slyke 2003). The result has been that government funding now makes up a significant portion of revenue for non-profit agencies,[12] compromising the independence of the non-profit sector and restraining its advocacy role, while concurrently imposing a greater administrative burden (Evans, Richmond, and Shields 2005). Given the integral nature of demonstrating results under the SIB model, outcomes-related administrative accountability requirements likely will increase.

Despite popular perception, the non-profit sector is heavily reliant on fee revenue. For example, in the United States in 2007, "non-profit service and expressive organizations" fees made up just under 56 per cent of the revenue of these organizations (Salamon 2015, 13). The non-profit sector has also seen increased competition from private sector providers, including for-profits. For example, in the United States in the late 1980s, the non-profit sector saw its market share eroded by the entry of for-profit providers, but non-profits still provided the greater share of services except in the areas of child care, clinics and home health, and nursing home care (Salamon 1993). Between 1997 and 2013, a number of organization types, particularly in the health care sector, but also in other social service sectors, saw the encroachment of private service providers, with the non-profit sector losing market share (Salamon 2015, 40–2). This was partially due to a shift in government policy on tax expenditures, including exemptions, deductions, and credits for income spent on services, as opposed to direct funding of providers, with for-profit entities better placed to compete for customers and gain market share (35–7). At the same time, non-profits more generally became increasingly entrepreneurial in a number of sectors, and more reliant on market-sourced revenue as grant-based funding became increasingly competitive and demanding (Dees 1998). Similar changes have been documented in the European context, with increased competition from for-profit providers, reduced reliance on government funding, and increased marketization of services and reliance on fee revenue (Pape et al. 2019).

Economic Theories of the Non-profit Form

Both mainstream economics and heterodox political economic perspectives have theorized the role and impetus for the existence of non-profit

---

12   In 2011, for example, public charities, which accounted for greater than 75 per cent of the $1.59 trillion in overall revenues of the US non-profit sector, received 23.2 per cent of their revenue from governments for service provision, and another 9.5 per cent through government grants (Pettijohn 2013b, 3).

organizations and the third sector more broadly. Neoclassical and new institutionalist approaches focus on the corporate form of non-profit organizations and how non-profits are generated in response to consumer preferences, imperfect information, and market failure. The defining feature of the non-profit in this framework is its constitution as a non-share capital corporation and the inability of its owners to profit financially from it. A *non-distribution constraint* prohibits the payment of monetary dividends to its directors (Hansmann 1980, 838). Additionally, a *fair compensation constraint* restricts the salaries of executives and staff (Steinberg 2006, 118). The non-profit then is a corporate form that explicitly delinks pecuniary compensation for the owners of the firm from the achievement of objectives (Weisbrod 1989, 542). Non-profits are not restricted in generating "profits," in the sense that they can accumulate revenues greater than their operating costs, but these must be reinvested or maintained within the organization, and the property rights of the firm are limited with respect to the liquidation and redeployment of assets (Steinberg 2006). In exchange for all of these governance restrictions, non-profits are generally exempt from corporate income tax, and may be subsidized in other manners (Weisbrod 1988, 14).

DEMAND-SIDE ADVANTAGES

One rationale for using the non-profit form is based on how it "explicitly divorces rewards from the easily measured aspects of performance when those measures do not accurately reflect the quality of output" (Weisbrod 1989, 542). In cases where benefits have public-good characteristics and there is high potential for consumers to be taken advantage of due to significant asymmetric information problems, non-profit forms might be superior (545). If the quality of the product or service is difficult for the purchaser to discern, this creates the incentive for a for-profit firm to exploit information asymmetries by underinvesting in quality or, more generally, by not delivering on the purchase (Hansmann 1980, 844; Glaeser and Shleifer 2001, 103). This can occur when the end receiver of the service is not the contributor, as in the case of a redistributive charity, where consumption is shared such that the good has public-good characteristics, or where voluntary contributions are necessary to overcome high fixed costs and to achieve scale (Hansmann 1980, 845–51). The latter case is a form of consensual price discrimination, where individuals with a high willingness to pay are more comfortable revealing their preferences given the non-profit status of the firm (Hansmann 1981). Donors might have a specific preference with respect to how goals are achieved, with restrictions on the non-profit giving them greater assurance that their donations will be used in accordance with their wishes (Rose-Ackerman 1996, 716–17).

More concisely, then, there are two types of information asymmetry problems on the demand side that non-profit forms can help overcome: "underinformed consumers" and the case of the "free rider" (Weisbroad 1988, 6). In both cases, the "nonprofit form ... economizes on contracting and enforcement" (Hansmann 1980, 852) which would be required to ensure that the for-profit supplier was spending funds as intended by the contributor, resting on the "trust engendered by the non-distribution constraint" (859). In practice the effectiveness of non-profits in resolving these problems is especially strong in the latter case, since sectors with large redistributive components based on donations, such as charities, education, and arts and cultural services, are often dominated by non-profit provision, whereas in sectors where the consumer is paying primarily to meet private needs, such as health services, there is more likely to be competition from for-profit firms (863).

In the case of market failure, non-profit delivery might be preferable to government delivery where the service is demanded by a small subset of the population; the tax base does not align with the user base; a more streamlined accountability structure between users of the service and management is desirable; and the entry and exit of firms through competitive forces might be beneficial (Hansmann 1980, 895). Government also be might slower to respond to emerging needs, and fail to respond at all when there are diverse preferences among groups representing a minority of the population. Private non-profit delivery, however, faces its own limitations, including: limited resources tied to the free-rider problem; the sector's tendency to focus on subcomponents of the population rather than on public needs more collectively; its decentralized and overlapping nature; its undemocratic functioning, with decision-making power often resting with the well-resourced elite; and lack of professionalization (Salamon 1987, 38–42). Government intervention responds to these limitations from the perspective of the more universal nature of public services, and helps to overcome inequitable and inconsistent access and inefficiencies through economies of scale (Roy, McHugh, and Sinclair 2018). The for-profit sector completes what has been labelled the *three failures approach* – keeping a check on the non-profit sector's inefficiencies through "low-cost production, innovation, and attention to consumer demands" (Steinberg 2006, 127).

SUPPLY-SIDE ADVANTAGES

The three failures approach focuses on demand efficiency considerations based on the reasons consumers of the service or their stewards would prefer the non-profit form. It does so, however, to the neglect of supply-side factors and non-efficiency explanations and motivations, including the desire of non-profit founders, staff, and volunteers to advocate collectively and generate social change (Steinberg 2006). Non-profits have at least two supply-side advantages linked to their mission-centredness and non-distribution constraints. First, it has been suggested that social entrepreneurs form non-profits rather than for-profits because of their ideological or altruistic commitment to a particular goal or cause, with preferences as to how that should be accomplished. The non-profit vehicle provides greater assurance that the organization will sustain commitment to the original vision (Rose-Ackerman 1996, 719) and that founders will reinvest in the enterprise and its mission rather than extract value from the organization.

A second supply-side benefit is that non-profits are positioned more effectively to attract and employ productive staff. Employees with an affinity with the social objectives of the non-profit will self-select, with public service–oriented managers drawn to employment in non-profits (Weisbrod 1988, 31–2). Workers in the non-profit sector, then, are motivated by the non-pecuniary benefits of working collectively towards a purpose they intrinsically value and providing that service at a high quality (Hansmann 1980, 875–6, 899–901)[13]. Empirically, workers in the non-profit sector have been shown to have lower wages than their counterparts in other sectors, which has been rationalized in terms of the willingness of these workers to accept lower wages in exchange for participating in socially beneficial work (Preston 1989).[14] Workers in the non-profit sector also have been shown to have higher overall job satisfaction than those in the for-profit sector that is unrelated to wage differentials and non-pecuniary benefits (Benz 2005; Leete 2006, 165–6). The non-profit sector is also the major attractor of volunteers, who are driven similarly by intrinsic motivations and the wish to see public benefits realized (Leete 2006, 167, 172). Non-profit organizations, then, might develop and entrench norms that strongly dissuade abuse and self-enrichment at the expense of the organizational mission, and reinforced through selective hiring practices at senior levels focused

---

13 See Heckman, Heinrich, and Smith (2011b) for a model of behaviour based on the assumption that service providers aim to maximize the net benefit to clients.

14 This finding has been questioned and qualified, with later studies that control more heavily for industry sector and job characteristics finding that the wage differential is reduced or eliminated; however, given the concentration of non-profits in particular industries, this might result in an identification problem. Since claims that higher-quality service is a defining feature of non-profits, unobservable differences in employee desirability also might be a factor. See Leete (2006, 162–3). For theoretical examinations of why non-profits may or may not pay higher wages, see Francois (2000, 2003, 2007).

on individuals who demonstrate attributes and commitment to charitable objectives (Hansmann 1980, 875–6). All of this leads to a more efficient and productive social service environment from a fiscal-cost perspective.

This intrinsic motivation of non-profit workers could be considered an example of *public service motivation* (PSM). This concept originated in the public administration literature, but has been adopted in economics, human resource management, and other disciplines. It is the idea that individuals might demonstrate an altruistic preference for working in service of broader public interests, and there is convincing survey-based evidence of its existence (Francois 2000; Perry and Vandenabeele 2015). This literature highlights how individuals who are motivated by such factors will self-select into public service and, in turn, bring intrinsically motivated effort, reducing the cost or otherwise producing public goods and services.[15] PSM has been used to explain public service efficiency and the failure of PbR in the public sector.[16] Experimental studies examining the impact of PbR payment schemes for government workers have invoked the crowding out of intrinsic motivation and PSM as a mediating factor to help explain the ineffectiveness of financial incentives to leverage effort from these workers (Bellé 2015; Bellé and Cantarelli 2015; Frey, Homberg, and Osterloh 2013). Correspondingly, it has been argued that PSM in turn can help sidestep principal-agent problems (Gailmard 2010).

Many of the arguments behind the notion of PSM in the public sector context are transferable to the non-profit sector. Francois and Vlassopoulos (2008) highlight that both government and the non-profit sector are strategically positioned, given the lack of a residual claimant

---

15 There is debate in this literature whether PSM and intrinsic motivation are separable and distinct, similar to the warm-glow versus altruism classification of Andreoni (1989). Those who argue for separability measure the former based on self-evaluations of how pleasurable and interesting workers finds their specific job, while the latter is based on revelations of commitment more generally to public service and others. See Bellé and Cantarelli (2015) for examples and discussion of this point. This links back to Perry and Wise's (1990) and Perry's (1996) delineation of the various dimensions of PSM, with *attraction to public policy making* a rational or self-serving motivation that fits the intrinsic warm-glow-type motivator, where the other dimensions of self-sacrifice, commitment to public service and social equity, and compassion are more altruistic in nature.

16 Rainey and Steinbauer (1999, 5–6), for example, outline several historical examples of US public agencies that have been assessed and found highly efficient, in multiple sectors such as old age security, military, natural resource management, business administration, customs, and personal identification documentation. See also Chang (2003).

to benefit from altruistic and intrinsic motivation, particularly in the delivery of social services, and that this can negatively affect the appropriateness of high-powered pecuniary incentives. They note that "prosocial behaviour" (23) based on the intrinsic and altruistic motivations of leaders, managers, and workers helps provide the non-profit form a supply-side efficiency advantage based on their willingness to accept lower pecuniary compensation. In the economic study of the literature on non-profits, this has been referred to as the "donative labor hypothesis" (Leete 2006, 161), which also suggests that PfP compensation of executives would be less appropriate in the non-profit sector, and wage differentials within organizations would be more condensed (164).[17] The non-profit sector then is supply constrained by "religious, ideological and political entrepreneurship" (Kendall 2003, 3), reliant upon "the public-spirited generosity of philanthropists who feel that contributions to the commonwealth are spiritual or moral imperatives" (Robbins 2006, 13), as well as by limited government distributions to the sector.

Given the preponderance of intrinsic motivation, the non-profit form paired with the contingent renewal of contracts might be a particularly appropriate response to asymmetric information in an incomplete contracting environment, since contingent renewal is facilitated by the formation of personalized relationships and interactions and the development of trust between parties over repeated transactions.[18] Others have suggested that one might even go farther, given that the intrinsic motivation of non-profit actors might result in a significant alignment of goals with governments that are seeking to maximize the social benefit of expended funds. Here, a conflict of interests with a profit-maximizing agent might not exist when contracting with a non-profit. Van Slyke (2006), for example, argues that, rather than agency theory based on a conflict of interest between stakeholders, contractual relations within and with non-profits are better understood within a *stewardship theory* framework based on aligned interests, where "long-term contractual relations are developed based on trust, reputation,

---

17 Not all mainstream economists rely on altruistic motivations to justify the non-profit form. Glaeser and Shleifer (2001), for example, also emphasize the importance of incomplete contracts and how non-distribution constraints paired with donations more likely will lead to quality enhancement in non-profits than in for-profit enterprises, highlighting how even a fully self-regarding entrepreneur might chose the non-profit form. See also Steinberg (2006) for a more comprehensive review.

18 Bowles and Gintis (1993) and Bowles (2004, 233–66) review models of this type more generally as a solution to principal-agent contracting problems.

collective goals, and involvement where alignment is an outcome that results from relational reciprocity" (164).[19] This overlaps with the heterodox institutionalist critique of neoclassical and new institutionalist theories of the non-profit firm: while these mainstream approaches emphasize market failure and optimality, they neglect the fundamental distinction between activities to advance common interests and societal gain and those aimed at advancing private pecuniary interests (Valentinov 2011, 2012). We explore this idea further in the following section.

A more fundamentalist critique of the neoclassical approach and heterodox alternative is the social origins approach (Salamon and Anheier 1998; Salamon, Sokolowski, and Haddock 2017), based on the empirical weakness of the neoclassical theory.[20] Social origins theory emphasizes power relations, class structure, historical compromises and alliances between classes, and their persistence over time as determining factors of the size and role of the non-profit sector, as opposed to explanations of neoclassical theory based on market failure and consumer preferences. We pursue the importance of the broader political economic context as an explanatory factor for the emergence of SIBs in Chapter 6.

Altruism, Intrinsic Motivations, and Reciprocity

Understanding the motivations of non-profit sector labour and service within a stewardship theory framework requires going beyond the standard textbook presentation of the individual in neoclassical economics, with self-regarding individuals forming the standard. Neoclassical economics for the most part recognizes only one type of agent, the "rational egoist," who focuses only on their own material gains, and this is the model of human behaviour primarily found in mainstream policy analysis (Ostrom 2005, 253). Heterodox economists, especially institutionalist and feminist economists, have long criticized this neglect (Folbre 1995; Hodgson 1993). Folbre (1995), for example, puts

---

19 See also Donaldson and Davis (1991) and Davis, Schoorman, and Donaldson (1997). Zullo (2019) uses a related distinction comparing classical contracting to relational contracting. A similar parallel exists when using New Public Management versus New Public Governance approaches in public administration; see Dayson, Fraser, and Lowe (2020).

20 For example, neoclassical approaches emphasize the substitutability of private non-profit services for public social welfare provision, whereas in practice many Western European states have both large public and non-profit sectors, and overall there appears to be a positive correlation between public good provision and the size of the non-profit sector. See Salamon and Sokolowski (2017) for additional details and examples of empirical challenges for the neoclassical approach.

forward three categories of alternative motivations: "altruism ..., long-run reciprocity and the fulfillment of obligation or responsibility." She highlights the importance of these alternative motivations in explaining caring labour, which characterizes much of the work undertaken by non-profit direct client service providers through SIBs. These schools and heterodox approaches more generally also reject the methodological individualist approach and assumption of exogenous preferences in neoclassical theory, highlighting individuals as socially embedded, operating in a structure-agent framework, with institutionally shaped preferences (Davis 2003, 108–66).[21] Although methodological individualism is fundamental to neoclassical economics (Colander 2000), examples on the periphery, however, incorporate altruistic behaviour within a setting of exogenous preferences.

Altruism in Neoclassical and Institutionalist Economics

Within neoclassical economics itself, the dependence of preferences through the specification of individual utility to include the well-being, consumption, or behaviour of others is long-standing, going back to Pareto, Fisher, and Marshall, and later systematically formalized by Gary Becker (1974, 1064–5). Two distinct forms of altruism have been analysed, one towards one's close genetic relations and close friends, and the other generosity more broadly (Rose-Ackerman 1996, 710). Economists have attempted to construe both approaches as enlightened self-interest, such that altruism might be *fitness enhancing* in that it improves the odds of survival of one's genes or more broadly one's material outcomes. Becker (1976), for example, constructs a model showing how altruists can end up with consumption equal to or higher than that of self-interested "egoists" (822), as rational egoists will consider the effect of the altruist's generosity on them in social interactions, and will support higher income for the altruist as they in turn benefit – in effect, also appearing to engage in benevolent behaviour. This leads to Becker's (1974, 1080) "rotten kid" theorem, where even a purely self-regarding

---

21 Institutionalists, for example, emphasize how the "individual is socially and institutionally constituted ... molded by cultural or institutional circumstances" (Hodgson 2000, 327). See also Hodgson (1993, 2014) and Rutherford (1996) for a summary of the "old" institutionalist economics, as distinguished from new institutionalist economics, which is methodological individualist and based on the assumption of exogenously determined preferences (Hodgson 1993). Some have argued that the institutionalist approach has been partially incorporated into mainstream economics (Hodgson 2007), as mainstream economics has become more eclectic (Davis 2007).

child maximizes utility by behaving as if it was an altruist, in a family with a parent who sufficiently values the well-being of other family members. Collard (1978) points out that enlightened self-interest is simply utility maximization under uncertainty, and can be handled with standard economic approaches, as can the case of "reciprocity or implicit exchange" (4), although he believes that true altruism is common and does exist.

Others come to similar conclusions regarding the benefits of altruistic behaviour, but operate from a more institutionalist-evolutionary perspective, and model individuals as norm followers with ethical commitments as opposed to hyperrational utility maximization.[22] Others, with one foot back in the neoclassical school and remaining within the utility-maximizing framework, highlight the complexity of preference structures, incorporating and distinguishing between self-interest moral-ethical values and considerations. For example, Andreoni (1989, 1990) puts forward a "warm glow" theory of "impure altruism" (1989, 1447) distinguishing the personal enjoyment individuals experience when contributing to others from the direct valuation of the well-being of others, which has generated support through experiments (Harbaugh, Mayr, and Burghart 2007).[23] Alternatively, individuals might be motivated by inequality aversion (Fehr and Fischbacher 2005; Fehr and Schmidt 1999).

---

22 Bergstrom and Stark (1993) demonstrate how cooperators, while losing out on one-time interactions, can still prevail over time in evolutionary settings if they interact primarily with other cooperators and can end up with greater rewards, although the authors briefly situate this approach also in a utility-maximizing framework. Smith (2003), for example, discusses altruism and reciprocity as efficiency-enhancing institutions arising through trial and error. Gintis et al. (2005) argue that there is a genetic-evolutionary disposition in the human species towards cooperation, and that evolutionary group selection pressures resulted in the development of levelling institutions that minimized within-group competition to increase the likelihood of survival in inter-group competition. See also Bowles (2004, 441–68) who develops an inter-group model of the evolution and survival of altruistic norms based on its enhancement of group fitness despite its individual fitness-reducing character.

23 Sen (1977) similarly distinguishes acts of sympathy from acts of commitment, where the former can be understood as self-regarding, while the latter are based on selflessness. Margolis (1982) models individuals as having two utility functions, one that is selfish and one that is for the individual's social group with which he or she identifies, with the value on the two determined by a "fair share ... principle" (36–7). Others have suggested that utility maximization is constrained by a Kantian ethical norm or duty of cooperation (see Collard 1978, 14–15, 43–4; Laffont 1975), or a less stringent obligation not to free ride in a public-goods scenario where others are expected to contribute (for example, Sugden 1984).

Simon (1991), whose work has been central to the modern hetero-dox institutionalist school, puts forward a particularly relevant theory as to the functionality of altruism in institutional settings. He sug-gests that unselfish behaviour facilitates integration in human society, where advantages arise to non-egoist behaviour due to the "docility" of altruists such that they are "tractable, manageable, and above all, teachable" (35). Docility is "used to inculcate individuals with orga-nizational pride and loyalty" (36), facilitating an affinity between the individual and larger institutions, allowing the individual to value intrinsically the achievement of the collective's identified goals. This identification of workers within organizations reduces shirking or inat-tention to quality, for example (41). Within this framework, organiza-tions and government can be "highly effective," with minimal and at best indirect motivation of market forces and/or the profit motive (43).

Individuals, then, might be motivated intrinsically as opposed to requiring external impetus to deliver high levels of effort that might not appear to reward the individual directly in a material or self-serving manner (Kreps 1997). An attempt to introduce rewards and incentives tied to outcomes in this case might not be effective and might even be counterproductive in situations where agents view such actions as evidence of a lack of trust or low confidence in their abilities, or an indi-cator of the undesirability of the work (Bénabou and Tirole 2003, 490). Frey (1997 20) emphasizes the importance of intrinsic motivation and how the "price effect" of pecuniary reward might not outweigh this crowding-out effect.[24]

The presence of displaceable intrinsic motivations has significant implications for the principal-agent framework, as highlighted by Fran-cois and Vlassopolous (2008). They situate the importance of this in the social service delivery context, noting that, in the case of impure altru-ism, corporate form is irrelevant, whereas, in the case of pure altruism, non-profit and government delivery is advantageous given the ability

---

24 Although the introduction of monetary incentives and/or controlling regulation into relationship-based transactions can lead to the crowding out of intrinsic motivations, it does not necessarily do so. Frey (1997) notes several conditions that affect the degree to which intrinsic motivations are crowded out (26–33, 92–6). The less impersonal the exchange, the more enjoyable or interesting the task, and the greater scope for possible variation and participation of the agent in how work is done, the more likely intrinsic motivation will be crowded out. Crowding out also increases to the degree the intervention is based on controlling regulation, as opposed to rewards, ignores the input and specific capabilities of the individual, and is strict and rigid in imposition and enforcement. See also Frey and Oberholzer-Gee (1997).

to attract donated labour effort. Based on an extensive literature review, they present a representative utility function of an agent who is motivated by both outcomes-based altruism and intrinsic warm glow–type motivation, modelled as increasing quality-enhancing effort. If an agent directly values both contributing quality-enhancing effort towards an intervention and the benefit generated, it is possible that crowding out can occur and the introduction of the payment-by-results incentive at the individual agent level might be counteracted fully. The introduction of the PbR incentive might have no impact on the net effort levels selected by the service provider. PbR, however, generates higher administration costs and further increases the risk premium, reducing overall welfare.

In the context of school quality and incentive pay for teachers, Besley and Ghatak (2005) similarly adopt the assumption that agents are intrinsically motivated, but assume that motivation is conditional on the type of organization by which the individual is employed. More specifically, intrinsically motivated individuals hold a preference for a specific "mission" (617), which is broadly defined as relating to how the organization goes about accomplishing its objectives. They use this framework to demonstrate how this, combined with competition between organizations to deliver service and attract staff, has efficiency-enhancing qualities. Staff are attracted to the organizations best aligned with their mission, minimizing quality-adjusted labour costs. Besley and Ghatak (2005) also highlight the implications of funders who provide support aimed at altering how organizations go about doing their work, noting that "mission changes come at a cost, since the agent ... will become demotivated and the organization will become less productive" (626).[25]

Below we attempt to situate the above insights regarding intrinsic and altruistic motivations into a framework that acknowledges a preponderance of altruistic and reciprocal behaviour, but that also accommodates the presence of some rational egoists, where policy decisions can shift behaviour. We then use this framework to analyse the shift SIBs might induce.

Strong Reciprocity Theory

One modern critique of the self-regarding *homo economicus* and enlightened self-interest explanations of non-self-regarding behaviour that

---

25 See also Besley and Ghatak (2006), who build on this framework, examine more explicitly the issue of teacher pay, and highlight how incentive pay might increase productivity but can have negative equity considerations.

builds on the insights above and incorporates altruism, reciprocity, and obligation as motivators of human behaviour is the theory of *strong reciprocity*. Strong reciprocity theory emphasizes that individuals have preferences over social processes and outcomes for others in addition to their own personal outcomes. Gintis et al. (2005) define strong reciprocity as "a predisposition to cooperate with others and to punish (at personal cost, if necessary) those who violate the norms of cooperation, even if it is implausible to expect that these costs will be recovered at a later date" (8). Strong reciprocity differs from typical models explaining altruism that depend on self-interest and relationships between individuals and allow for punishment to be implemented and subsequent rewards to be recouped.[26] It is argued that strong reciprocity is a more general notion and can be applied when agents are anonymous and partake only in one-time interactions. The theory of strong reciprocity implies that individuals are primarily *"conditional cooperators"* and *"altruistic punishers"* (8). Conditional cooperators by definition are altruistic when they anticipate that the individuals they are relating with are also altruistic. Altruistic punishers will punish individuals, even at a significant net cost to themselves, if they feel those individuals have violated what they consider the "prevalent norms of cooperation" (8). Strong reciprocity highlights that it is the intention of the interacting parties that matters, as opposed to outcomes (Bowles et al. 2005, 18–19), such that this behaviour is distinct from an aversion to inequality (Fehr and Fischbacher 2005, 153). A number of experimental studies have demonstrated that individual behaviour aligns closely with the strong reciprocity thesis (Carpenter et al. 2009; Fehr and Fischbacher 2005; Fehr and Gächter 2000, 2002a, 2002b; Gintis 2000; Gintis et al. 2005; Ostrom 2005).

Based on their review of experimental studies, Fehr and Fischbacher (2005, 81) suggest that it is reasonable to assume that between 40 per cent and 50 per cent of agents are strong reciprocators. They note that strong reciprocity is only one possible alternative behavioural type, but they also note that there is much evidence supporting the strong reciprocal type and that the presence of strong reciprocators fundamentally changes the first-best behaviour of purely self-interested agents (155). For example, in a sequential game where there are gains from

---

26 These models of group "reciprocal altruism" often end up being unstable and converging to universal defection when a small number of participants choose to defect, due, for example, to random behaviour; see Bowles (2004, 441–4). For additional discussion of strong reciprocity theory, see Fehr, Fischbacher, and Gächter (2002).

cooperation, if a self-interested individual identifies that he or she is engaging with a strong reciprocator, cooperating in response maximizes the selfish player's payoff – a result with parallels to Becker's rotten kid theorem. The presence of strong reciprocators effectively transforms prisoner dilemma–type games, where self-interested agents always defect into coordination or assurance games, with the threat of altruistic punishment reinforcing the mutually beneficial coordination equilibrium.

The strong reciprocity literature most relevant to SIBs are experiments of contracting models based on employment relationship settings. Fehr and Fischbacher (2005), for example, review this literature and the implications of strong reciprocity for the standard moral hazard model in which the principal sets a compensation structure for an agent that exerts quality-enhancing effort. They find that, if the relationship involves strong reciprocators, implicit contracts based on trust can outperform explicit contracts tied to effort levels (176–8). Fehr, Klein, and Schmidt (2007), building on these studies, examine the standard explicit contract relative to two trust-based contracts, one where the employer pays a generous wage in advance, and the other with an implicit contract based on an optional bonus structure. They find that the implicit contract based on the bonus structure has the highest take-up rate in experimental settings and generates the highest total surplus, while the standard explicit contract model dominates the trust contract based on a high wage. This result again could help rationalize the conventional social service procurement model, where a bonus could be generated through repeated selection and rents in an implicit contingent renewal relationship.

Strong reciprocity theory suggests that neoclassical economics' ignorance of the conditional cooperator and altruistic punisher aspects of human behaviour has led to significant mistakes and lost opportunities when forming public policy. Ostrom (2005) highlights that the number of strong reciprocators and rational egoists, however, is not static, and the degree to which community members are willing to cooperate is influenced by the characteristic of the given policy intervention. Specifically, interventions deemed "controlling" by community members will crowd out cooperative behaviour, while interventions seen as "supporting" will encourage cooperation (258).[27] After reviewing a vari-

---

27 See also Frey (1997, 18), who highlights that this determination is subjective and therefore the same action might be interpreted differently – that is, controlling by one and supporting by another – by different individuals. This does not imply, however, that measures cannot be objectively evaluated as relatively more

ety of experimental evidence, Ostrom prescribes a policy framework involving a multifaceted approach, including the participation of government, community organizations, and the private sector, to increase the degree to which community members perceive control over the policy intervention and encourage cooperative behaviour.

Ostrom notes a worldwide public policy trend away from local decision making towards a more centralized regulatory bureaucracy, with several problematic messages being conveyed to the public, including that the state expects citizens to behave as rational egoists, which has created a self-fulfilling prophecy through the crowding-out effect discussed above (see also Bowles and Hwang 2008). Ostrom reviews evidence regarding the effectiveness of policy frameworks designed to manage shared resource use, and from this concludes that the most effective framework is not a centralized system of regulation but a "polycentric system" of management (Ostrom 2005, 269). Polycentric systems are composed of several semi-autonomous decision-making bodies at different levels of governance, which include public and private entities.

Bowles and Gintis (2005) build on Ostrom's polycentric system of management, focusing in particular on community governance and providing theoretical foundations for the social-solidarity economy (see Appendix E). After reviewing several case studies, they make certain generalizations. One is that community governance can address not just market failures, but also the state's failures to deal with several types of community-level problems. In particular, community governance facilitates the provision of local public goods, risk sharing, credit markets, and, most relevant to SIBs, the monitoring of work effort in cooperative ventures. Community governance is able to address these problems as repeat interaction among members is high, leading to the development of relationships and trust that reduces information asymmetries. Over time individual interactions will develop into networks which will further reduce transaction costs, increase the benefits of socially beneficial behaviour, and ostracize free riding.

Bowles and Gintis (2005) also suggest that the way the distribution of property rights is assigned at the local level will contribute to whether community governance is crowded in or crowded out. The key argument here is that, for community governance to be successful, local community members need to own the rewards and consequences of their

---

controlling or supportive, but this should be empirically informed by responses from agents.

management of local issues. Also, the management and distribution of the rewards of successful cooperation should be highly transparent and public, so that the altruistic punisher mechanism can function to avert the breakdown of the cooperative process. This requires legal and governmental support to foster the environment necessary for effective community governance that complements, rather than replaces, competent state governance.

Implications for the Implementation and Design of SIBs

The strong reciprocity thesis provides a framework for assessing how SIBs will affect the delivery of social services, with both static and dynamic implications. Like the literature reviewed above on the non-profit form, strong reciprocity suggests that individuals in practice are likely to be intrinsically motivated to provide a high level of work effort, particularly in a social setting related to local public-good provision. This intrinsic motivation, however, can be crowded out by public policies and contract structures that undermine trust and imply that individuals will behave as rational egoists.

Even if the introduction of an SIB is seen as an unfair act, it is unclear whether the participating non-profit would respond by giving up the opportunity to participate or by withdrawing effort. SIBs have the potential to generate improved outcomes for clients and additional resources for the non-profit organization and for the sector more broadly. The non-profit's response will depend on a variety of factors, including the degree to which it expects the SIB to generate such new resources. Evidence suggests that, in bilateral experimental settings, although strong reciprocators value equitable outcomes, the desire to punish could take priority (Falk and Fischbacher 2004). The adding of warm-glow considerations further complicates the analysis.

The multifaceted nature of the preferences and behaviour of strong reciprocators creates challenges for predicting the crowding-in or crowding-out response in any specific applied scenario. Once one determines that agents value participation, equitable outcomes, and fair processes, and that individuals will engage in altruistic punishment, one must judge how these tendencies interact and are respectively valued. These issues become more challenging in our case study, as non-profit participants are acting in reference to multiple partners, including government, intermediary, and investors, as well as the client base they might intrinsically value servicing. Here we suggest that the relevant factors include: *participation impacts*, the degree to which the intervention affects the ability of the non-profit to participate in service delivery;

process fairness, whether the intention of the SIB model is deemed fair or unfair; and *outcome fairness*, whether the outcome implications for client pools are deemed fair or unfair. The determination of fairness might be based on expected outcomes either for the organization or for the sector more broadly, or on norms that value sovereignty and self-determination and the degree to which stakeholders in the non-profit see investors as part of a larger group of community insiders. In the remainder of this section, we discuss these three factors and the implications of these contextual attributes, and, based on this, offer recommendations on how to structure SIBs. We then explore the dynamic implications and two remaining potential critiques of our analysis.

Participation Impacts

Non-profit organizations and their workers might value being personally engaged in delivering services as per the "warm glow" theory of "impure altruism" (Andreoni 1989, 1447), where givers value the act of contributing to others in addition to and independent of the outcomes it generates. For paid workers, losing access to employment that provides a warm glow in addition to income can generate a strong incentive for sustaining their particular organization. Also, non-profits, particularly in a context of austerity and constrained in their funding options, might need to rely on SIBs from an organizational sustainability perspective. As one provider put it succinctly, "we do not adapt services to financing but seek financing for services" (Hevenstone and von Bergen 2020, 207). Non-profit organizations thus might value SIBs because the bonds allow them to access additional resources immediately and to be seen as willing to engage in innovative approaches based on new partnerships, further positioning themselves in a highly competitive funding environment.

Process Fairness

If the intentions of SIBs are interpreted as punitive or paternalistic and SIBs themselves are identified as a mechanism of control, they will more likely displace intrinsically motivated effort and spur stakeholders in non-profits to engage in costly reciprocal punishment. Alternatively, if SIBs are deemed supportive and complementary to the values of such stakeholders, they might crowd in effort. The reference point is important here: if non-profits are engaged in funding arrangements that involve a high degree of micromanagement and limited discretion for agencies, then SIBs might be seen as an improvement. If the arrangements are flexible, based on a partnership or stewardship approach, SIBs might be interpreted as less fair. To improve the likelihood of crowding in, governments could work with non-profit funders and service providers to set targets with investors and the intermediary to build program metrics deemed reflective of clients' well-being, not just government savings. In general, a participatory approach would build on the advantages of community governance.

Outcome Fairness

If stakeholders in non-profit organizations intrinsically value the well-being of clients, the degree to which the SIB model leads to more or less quality-adjusted support will be of direct concern. SIBs might be viewed as increasing total resources available by circumventing self-imposed budget constraints within government through drawing upon future cost savings due to prevention, and by taking steps to keep these resources dedicated to improving social service delivery. If stakeholders in non-profits see SIBs as a tool that increases resources available for front-line service delivery, SIBs should crowd in effort, and vice versa.

Design features to improve the likelihood of crowding in might include reducing rates of return to or below the cost of government borrowing, or requiring investors explicitly to commit to reinvesting any returns in social service projects (Tse and Warner 2018). This would provide reassurance that government was not transferring rents in the form of interest payments to the private sector investors, attracting investors motivated primarily by CSR concerns; and provide reassurance to stakeholders of non-profits that SIBs were not diverting funds from social service delivery (Tse and Warner 2018). Alternatively, government could limit investors to those from the non-profit sector with reputations for social and fiduciary responsibility based a track record of supporting high-performing social service delivery. The latter could require the establishment of an independent non-profit to receive and reallocate outcomes payments. In general, crowding-in grows as non-profits increasingly share an affinity with funders and believe their involvement will improve outcomes.[28]

Design in Practice

Some SIBs have adopted the above-noted measures to address process and outcomes fairness, in some cases explicitly in response to criticisms

---

28 These recommendations are similar in some way to those of Williams (2018, 2019), who recommends that SIBs return to a philanthropic funding base and to projects focused on meaningful innovation.

of the model. For example, the chief executive of YMCA Scotland, Peter Crory (2013), criticized the first pilot SIB, emphasizing how a subsequent SIB delivered by the Scotland YMCA "create[d] a more localised community model that would enable local relationships to grow between investor and provider and participant... [and] reject[ed] distant investors whose sole interest may be financial." He noted that "reducing the return to investors has not removed the interest of investors," and advocated a similar model for future SIBs. In another case, the Augsburg child welfare SIB was advertised by sponsors as being fully based on non-profit investment and very low maximum rates of return, and who emphasized that the model "reduces the often-legitimate concerns about profit-driven private investors" (Ruf 2014). The South Carolina Nurse Family Partnership PfS project is also fully financed by non-profit investors who have committed to reinvest any outcome payments to expand the program to additional clients (South Carolina 2016; Tse and Warner 2018). The Oklahoma Women in Recovery SIB is also based almost entirely on investment from a single charitable foundation, which committed to continual reinvestment in programming as outcomes payments are received (Oklahoma 2017). Other projects have emphasized that outcomes payments will be partially recycled (Third Sector Capital Partners 2014).

CASE STUDY
The South Carolina Nurse Family Partnership PfS Project:
Ensuring Public Value through SIB Design

Prior to February 2016, Nurse-Family Partnership (NFP) was an operational non-profit organization serving 1,200 families in pairing specially trained nurses with at-risk, first-time mothers to facilitate in-home support visits to improve health outcomes for children and mothers living in poverty (Social Finance 2016a). The NFP model was extensively researched using randomized control trials, demonstrating sizable and sustained beneficial effects from nurse home visits, motivating expansion of the program (Social Finance 2016a). In February 2016, the South Carolina Department of Health and Human Services (SCDHHS), Nurse-Family Partnership, and Social Finance as intermediary partnered in launching the United States' first statewide pay-for-success initiative, which expanded comprehensive, preventative home visiting services to 4,000 families starting in the second trimester of pregnancy through to the child's second birthday (Social Finance 2016a). Service delivery is being evaluated using a randomized control trial methodology designed by the J-PAL North America research centre, along four success outcomes that will calculate PfS payments: "reduction in child injury rates, reduction in pre-term births, increase in healthy birth intervals, and enrollment of moms from low-income zip codes" (Allin 2016, 3; see also Social Finance 2016a).

The SCDHHS received a Medicaid waiver that covered a portion of NFP's project costs, while also expanding the number of home visits permissibly billable (per mother-child pair) from two visits to forty (Allin 2016, 1). US$30 million was mobilized through the project: US$17 million from philanthropic funders and approximately US$13 million from Medicaid. South Carolina would make up to US$7.5 million in success payments if outcome targets were met (Social Finance 2016a; Urban Institute n.d.). Success payments will be calculated in year five and year six of the project, although J-PAL is conducting a "comprehensive, long-term evaluation of NFP's impact on mothers and children" beyond the PfS contract period, which is atypical for PfS projects, as they tend to focus on the "short-term benefits in mapping success metrics and payments" (Allin 2016, 2).

The South Carolina Nurse Family Partnership PfS project is a best-practice SIB in a number of regards. In addition to rigorous research and evaluation dedicated to improving service delivery for participants and demonstrating cost effectiveness, it is fully financed by non-profit investors who have committed to reinvest any outcome payments to expanding the program to additional clients (South Carolina 2016; Tse and Warner 2018). The SIB also focused on transitioning a demonstrated best practice from philanthropic to public funding, had a large-scale impact on vulnerable populations, and explicitly built in long-run systems change and financial sustainability beyond the SIB (Tse and Warner 2018).

Despite these examples, it does not, however, appear that the SIB model more generally is adopting these reforms. Based on the data we presented in Chapter 2, low-interest-rate SIBs appear to be the exception, although there is significant variation. Additionally, we could identify only 26 of the 122 SIB projects to date as funded solely by non-profit investors. This highlights a high potential for crowding out of intrinsic motivation.

Dynamic Selection

Strong reciprocity theory predicts that, dynamically, this crowding out will affect the balance of strong reciprocators in the community relative to rational egoists, further displacing intrinsic motivation. To the extent that SIBs communicate the notion that communities are incapable of properly managing their own affairs and that all public policy must be formulated by experts and professionals, this will further crowd out altruistic behaviour. SIBs also might undermine polycentric systems of governance by rewarding investors, as opposed to service providers, for success.

Even if SIBs are able to shift to a reliance on non-profit finance, genuine partnerships with service providers, and restricted interest rates, they still might be problematic for the composition of the service provider population over time. Non-profit social service delivery agents themselves are not homogeneous. One distinction often made is that between smaller, local community–based non-profits that deliver services but also are representative of their clients and engage in advocacy, and larger service delivery organizations that are more corporatized and bureaucratic in their structure. Large-scale service-based non-profits might have little resemblance to local community-based organizations and be more similar to for-profit organizations in how they structure their operations and administrative capacity.[29] Both large-scale non-profit and for-profit organizations in some countries have the size and influence to exert pressure on government policy in their interests, an ability local organizations might lack (Finn 2008, 8). As non-profits grow, particularly through increasing government revenue, there are concerns that this will compromise their commitment to the original mission and their ability to engage in advocacy for disadvantaged groups. There is also mixed evidence regarding the effectiveness of large non-profits relative to smaller organizations, with some studies demonstrating, counter to economies-of-scale arguments, that smaller non-profits are no less efficient in the proportion of revenues spent on programing and administration, and are more cost effective in fundraising (van der Heijden 2013).

It has been noted that relatively few organizations can deliver large-scale service interventions and also have the institutional capacity to

---

29 See Dees (1998, 60) for discussion of a spectrum of non-profit enterprise from "purely philanthropic" to "purely commercial."

handle the complex project management and tracking required by SIBs (Dear et al. 2016, 51) and that SIBs primarily have been engaging large non-profits to deliver services (Edmiston and Nicholls 2018, 73). The SIB model then might lead to a marginalization of smaller, community-based non-profits (Sinclair et al. 2014) that focus on addressing local concerns (Joy and Shields 2013), and "challenge … the values supporting the historic ways in which services have been delivered by public, non-profit and voluntary providers" (Fraser et al. 2018b, 8). National non-SIB PbR models face similar criticisms, but the evidence is mixed regarding provider composition (Albertson et al. 2018, 88–9)

With SIBs there are also related concerns that non-profit organizations will be driven from their mission and replaced by for-profit entities (Fraser et al. 2018b, 9) or more corporatized non-profits. There is historical precedent for this. For example, the earlier move to PbR in the United Kingdom in workforce development shifted service delivery away from secular, community-based non-profits to larger, religious-based organizations (Finn 2008, 22). In the Netherlands, the move to PbR contracting resulted in a shift in the type of workforce development services offered and a greater market share for for-profit entities; while, in Australia, community-based organizations had trouble competing (44–5). SIBs might place smaller non-profits under additional pressure in the context of the increasing dependence of the non-profit sector on government, which threatens to erode the role of non-profits as civil society organizations and lead them to change their mission and organizational structure to secure contracts and meet externally imposed targets, rather than the needs of their clients (McHugh et al. 2013).

Radical Critique

The proposed solutions to the problematic implications of SIBs suggest a shift of resources from public control to charitable foundation control, relative to conventional procurement. Some have argued that this model is regressive, since increasing private philanthropy has contradictory implications on socio-economic inequality, with the charitable model primarily reproducing power relations between dominant and popular classes. This critique is couched within a critical assessment of reliance on the voluntary and non-profit sectors more broadly (Roelofs 1995), and traces its roots back to Marx and Engels' ([1848] 1963) description of philanthropists and charity as the "redress[ing of] social grievances, in order to safeguard bourgeois society" (61).

Roelofs (2003), for example, notes that charitable foundations rely on and are accountable to their benefactors, who generally represent the dominant interests in society. The foundations themselves generally are established directly by corporations or individuals who trace their wealth back to ownership rights over private corporate enterprise. In the SIB context, for example, based on our compiled data, at least 34 per cent of non-profit investors were private individual or family foundations, and at least another 13 per cent were corporate foundations, such that nearly half of the non-profit investors in SIBs were accountable only back to these private stakeholders, as opposed to more collectivist community foundation models, where the influence of wealthy contributors is less transparent. Roelofs, in reviewing the historical evolution of foundations in the United States and criticism based on the early twentieth-century progressive movement, highlights the unaccountable and undemocratic nature of foundations and their potential to subvert democratic processes. She argues that the charitable foundation model is fundamentally undemocratic, that it enables and maintains an inequitable distribution of private wealth and power by facilitating tax avoidance through the transfer of wealth to trusts and foundations. The wealthy, in turn, exert their influence through the selection of social service delivery projects, as well as broader agenda setting through the funding of policy research.

From a critical political economy perspective, a larger non-profit service sector more broadly can also reflect and reinforce regressive tendencies that are indicative of class struggle outcomes in favour of "the middle class or landed political elites," while a large public service sector is more reflective of the greater influence of "labour movements and allied forces" (Kendall 2003, 4; Salamon and Anheier 1998). Within this framework, a large charitable sector can have a dissipating effect on social movements that advocate for more fundamental change aimed at addressing the root causes of high socio-economic inequality. It does this through various channels, including the paid employment of individuals who otherwise would focus on more radical social change, and the employment of labour displaced by increasingly capital-intensive production, while not driving down the rate of profit by contributing to surplus goods production (Roelofs 2003, 2). Within this framework, it is not surprising to see a parallel increase in philanthropic efforts and increasing socio-economic inequality, with rising interest in corporate social responsibility and adaptations such as venture philanthropy and philanthrocapitalism (see Appendix E) – operational philosophies that SIBs clearly advance (Joy and Shields 2018).

This critical perspective also highlights how the private, non-profit sector production of goods and services shares many of the workplace perils of private, for-profit production, with low unionization rates

and minimal job security, and workers who are subject to undemocratic workplace governance structures and whose jobs rely on the
vagaries of funders. From a macroeconomic perspective, SIBs and PbR
structures might be masking a more fundamental source of neoclassical "efficiency" gains, based on the labour extraction theory central
to the Marxian theory of surplus value creation (Stanford 2015, 107–
15). By introducing aggressive industrial management techniques and
intensive supervision into human services, workers are pushed to an
intensity of effort beyond what they otherwise would choose, and qualitatively experience greater alienation from their work such that control
as to how tasks are done, for what purpose, and how the workplace is
organized is further diminished (Rinehart 2006, 14–18).

In the end, within this critical political economy framework, at the
macro level the non-profit sector displaces and marginalizes more progressive change and popular movements based on universal access to
social programs, with paternalistic charity models focused on fixing
what are deemed individual failings, as opposed to looking at the structural nature of capitalist society, which generates increasing inequality, alienation, and social exclusion.[30] At the micro level, it is used as a
means to reduce costs and undermine the bargaining power of workers
to negotiate for better working conditions, wages, and benefits. If stakeholders in non-profit organizations subscribe to this radical perspective, they will not likely hold an affinity for the corporate and private
foundation sector, but will view the substitution of public control for
foundation control over resources negatively, preferring direct public
provision or a *social* or *solidarity economy* model based on state support
for more autonomous collectivist solutions.[31]

Arguably, however, this critical political economy framework under-
estimates the salience and persistence of non-self-regarding preferences
and their ability to generate effective alternative governance and economic institutions. True to Marx, this framework assumes that commu-
nal and cooperative norms will be swept away by capitalism; but they
have persisted, and community governance has proven an effective
and efficient counterpart to markets and the state both historically and

---

30 See Gürcan (2015) for an elaboration of this point and the radical critique of the non-
profit sector more broadly.
31 See Appendix E for discussion of the social-solidarity economy concepts. See also
Cooke (2007), working from a critical political economy perspective, who highlights
the importance of distinguishing between capitalist and non-capitalist private
ownership structures, such as cooperatives and non-profits, when assessing the
impact of privatization.

in modern times (Bowles 2004, 489–91). Although many foundations have ties to corporate interests that might sully the perception of their motives, many non-profit investors in SIBs appear to be community foundations with diffuse donor bases and genuine community-based relationships and motives, suggesting a range of diversity similar to that characterizing non-profit client service providers. Similarly, a number of the private investors in SIBs are organizations that seek to insert social values into investment practices to provide a socially responsible investment as an alternative to conventional savings vehicles. Although increased public provision of health, education, and other social services is likely defensible on numerous grounds, the ability of the community sector to make up for failings of both the market and government also appears to have its place in efficient public-good provision (Ostrom 2005; Salamon 1987, 38–42). For non-profits, compliance with government funding requirements can be burdensome (Evans, Richmond, and Shields 2005; McGregor-Lowndes and Ryan 2009), and although SIBs might be far from an ideal funding model from the non-profit perspective, they still might be viewed as an improvement over the status quo if appropriately structured in partnership with aligned organizations. There is certainly some truth in the radical critique outlined above, but there also appears to be a role and rationale for localized charitable models in addition to public support, ideally as part of a social-solidary economy approach.

The Hybridization Objection

A second potential objection to our proposed policy solution set and the non-profit versus for-profit analysis on which it rests is that it presents a false dichotomy. The delivery of social services and the broader addressing of social challenges have undergone massive reforms in both organizational form and practice, and there has been a convergence between non-profit and for-profit provision (Dees and Anderson 2003). For-profit corporations increasingly express commitment to corporate social responsibility (Graff Zivin and Small 2005, 1), non-profits increasingly embrace the ethos of private sector efficiency (Dees 1998), and social enterprises increasingly are being formed to pursue both social mission and profits (see Appendix E). The pursuit of social benefit, then, is no longer the exclusive realm of non-profits, and now there is the potential to benefit from the best of both worlds and the strong reciprocity that is present regardless of corporate form.

Although this challenge legitimately highlights the feasibility of the for-profit structure in achieving social purposes, it does not undermine the fundamental disadvantage the for-profit corporation faces. As Dees and Anderson (2003, 8) highlight, social impact is notoriously challenging to quantify and monitor, underpinning the economic rationale of the non-profit corporate form, summarized earlier in the chapter. Although a for-profit might leverage the good will and intrinsic motivations of workers and other stakeholders, the non-profit form is strategically constructed and positioned to better reassure donors that their contributions, in money, time, or effort, will be dedicated to social mission rather than to private gain.

Conclusion

In this chapter, we examined how private organizations and individuals within these organizations participating in SIBs respond to varying institutional contexts and incentive structures that are altered by policy interventions such as SIBs, based on payments by outcomes. Instead of focusing on the atomistic, self-regarding, payoff-maximizing agent at the centre of the principal-agent model and of mainstream economics more broadly, we presented evidence that frames individuals as socially embedded and other-regarding, with reflexive preferences that depend on context. We looked at the role of assumptions around self-regarding versus non-selfish behaviour, the distinction between instrumentalism and principle-driven actions, and the importance of understanding behaviour as contextual and adaptive to institutional settings. We attempted to demonstrate how a more complex, coherent, and empirically supported construction of motivation that incorporates the role of ethical considerations and intrinsic motivations raises further challenges for an efficiency-enhancing case made on behalf of SIBs.

Specifically, we drew upon the fact that the vast majority of service providers in SIBs are non-profit organizations, are likely to be driven by a social mission, and are more likely to have workers who are driven by intrinsic motivations, in addition to pecuniary concerns for themselves and their organization, to achieve outcomes for their clients and do their work well. This is particularly the case for smaller, community-based non-profits. We analysed the implications of the SIB model using the concept of strong reciprocity – the idea that a large proportion of individuals in any given situation is likely predisposed to cooperative behaviour, values intent and process in addition to outcomes, and will punish those who violate norms of cooperative behaviour. Based on the framework we presented in Chapter 4, this makes it even more challenging for SIBs to outperform conventional delivery.

We use these findings to inform some recommendations for the design of SIBs to minimize the displacement of the intrinsic motivations of non-profit stakeholders, including restricting investors to community-respected non-profit investors, offering rates of return below the cost of government borrowing, and/or earmarking profits for reinvestment in social service provision. We also recommend developing outcome targets in conjunction with non-profit service providers to ensure that targets reflect overall clients' well-being and success, as opposed just to government cost savings. Within this context, if incremental resources for valued activities are produced through SIBs by circumventing self-imposed budget constraints and tapping into CSR contributions from new partners, SIB models will more plausibly generate improvements over conventional procurement.

If SIBs continue to offer high interest rates to for-profit investors without expertise in social service delivery, and to set targets in isolation of the concerns of non-profit stakeholders, this has implications for the evolution of the model. If non-profits' employees are more likely to be dedicated to the well-being of their clients and less willing to compromise on holistic care they deem appropriate, but that is difficult to quantify for outcomes metrics, over time investors and intermediaries might decide they will have better a chance of hitting specified targets if they rely on for-profit providers. Alternatively, non-profit providers might shift their behaviour in response to a deemed violation of these norms, become disgruntled, and engage in strategic gaming (Albertson et al. 2018, 24). This is a specific instance of the idea in the strong reciprocity framework that controlling policy is likely to displace cooperative and altruistic behaviour. The work on strong reciprocity suggests that, from an efficiency perspective, this displacement risks inferior outcomes overall, and the quality of social services procured is likely to suffer. This implies that, in addition to reducing the capacity of the state for social service delivery, SIBs might structurally privilege for-profit providers over time, and shift activity away from non-profit providers while undermining the effectiveness of those that remain. Increased market share and profits did not appear in surveys of stakeholder motivation, but we suggest these are potential motivators and should be of concern. Within the non-profit sector itself, the SIB model structurally supports a reallocation of resources away from more activist community-based organizations to larger more conservative non-profits, further displacing more systematic change.

SIBs as currently being pursued, through their PbR structure and emphasis on paternalistic relationships with service providers, impose a self-seeking logic on social service delivery. Given the still current dominant position in social service provision of non-profit agencies with intrinsic motivation and social missions, there is a mismatch between the claims of the SIB model and its likely effects in practice. The centrality of pay-by-results might be just as likely to backfire as to have any meaningful positive effects relative to more conventional contracting forms such as implicit incentive contracts based on contingent renewal.

6 Government

Introduction

As the only commissioning agents and near-exclusive funders of outcome payments to date, government – and the broader public sector – arguably is the most essential institutional participant in Social Impact Bonds (Dear et al. 2016, 44). Despite ceding ground to the private sector and markets, governments remain central in SIBs (Berndt and Wirth 2018; Costa and Shah 2013). Since SIBs are often premised on reducing governments' future social expenditure obligations, and only governments can earmark these notional savings for upfront preventative interventions, without the participation of government such self-financing cannot proceed. A few other stakeholders reasonably can be seen to have the obligation to fund the costs associated with allowing social problems to persist, but with the exception of one SIB, all outcome payments have been either funded by government or by public sector or quasi-public institutions.[1] We therefore now focus on government, in this chapter examining the motivations and constraints faced by elected officials and civil servants.

In the previous chapter, one challenge we highlighted with the more orthodox principal-agent-based framework of SIBs was the assumption of a conflict of interests between governments and service providers. This was due to the motivational prominence of service providers'

---

1 A notable exception is private insurance providers, which have genuine contingent financial obligations to support individuals into the future. The only fully private sector–funded SIB we identified was issued by the Dutch De Amersfoortse health insurance company (ABN AMRO 2017). The two SIBs issued in Israel are the only other SIBs without a lead government outcome funder; instead, their funders were public universities and mandated non-profit health insurers.

self-interest, while given secondary prominence to alternative drivers such as intrinsic motivations or other-regarding preferences, beyond inclusion of a corporate social responsibility effect. A shortfall of the framework with respect to government is the opposite: that the government representative is presumed to be purely benevolent and as maximizing social welfare. As noted by Richard Musgrave (1999), this approach "is helpful to visualize how a correctly functioning public sector would perform ... to serve as standard" and that "the vision of a first-best solution is needed to identify a feasible second best" (35). This public finance or social welfare approach, however, has faced critiques on multiple fronts. Public Choice theorists, for example, have argued that rent seeking, where interest groups seek direct or indirect resource transfers at the expense of others, is endemic to the political process, and have challenged utilitarian social welfare analysis with notions of justice emphasizing property rights and freedom from interference, while Marxian theories of the state have long questioned the impartiality of the state and its depiction as neutral arbiter in capitalist societies.

Government, like the non-profit sector, is conducive to employment characteristics that attract strong reciprocators, validating an altruistic approach based on the public service motivation framework we reviewed in Chapter 5. With respect to SIBs, however, our analysis so far raises doubts about their potential SIBs to be cost effective relative to conventional procurement. Yet SIBs are proceeding and proliferating. In this chapter, we explore potential drivers of state participation in SIBs, beyond the assumption of efficiency reasons, with the state understood as a realm of competing interests.

Here we draw on four stylized theories of the state to frame and construct a model of government representatives of these interests in ongoing competition for control of the state. Strategic factors feature prominently in program and policy design once representatives hold decision-making power within of state institutions. In the first three theories, we follow and build on Chang (2002, 2003), using the categories of (neoclassical) welfare economics, neoliberal, and institutionalist political economy. To these three we add a Marxian theory of the state. Neoliberal, Marxian, and strands of institutionalist thinking all support a model of state decision making based on political competition for control of the state that we believe can provide some insight into the emergence of SIBs. We explore the proposition that state leaders can use SIBs to better their standing versus political competitors – specifically, the idea that SIBs can allow state leaders to reinforce their class-based political alliances and secure more potential support from voters in the medium term, while obfuscating the cost impact of these activities through off-budget accounting.

We begin by presenting a brief summary of survey-based evidence and other scholarship examining government motivations for participating in SIBs. We then recap what we call a *relative cost critique* of SIBs, motivating the development of an alternative, non-efficiency-based rationale of state engagement in SIBs. We follow this by summarizing four competing theories of the state in economics and discussing their implication for SIBs. We then offer policy recommendations to help mitigate the use of SIBs when alternative delivery could achieve targeted outcomes more efficiently, and present some final remarks in the conclusion.

Motivations of Government

It has been suggested that government representatives issuing an SIB will be concerned with a variety of factors, including how SIBs align both with overall government priorities and those of the specific department or agency assigned to implement and administer the SIB on behalf of government (Maier and Meyer 2017, 3). Publicly stated rationales of governments embarking on SIB projects generally echo the rhetoric of early proponents of the SIB model, highlighting the win-win scenario of cost savings financing the intervention or of not having to expend public funds on the project (see Chapter 1). In survey and interview data, government outcome funders echo reasons expressed by investors and service providers related to innovation, collaboration, and a focus on outcomes (Gustafsson-Wright, Gardiner, and Putcha 2015, 25). Government also might be motivated to engage with SIBs due to expected benefits of financial sector investment and insight (Liebman and Sellman 2013, 9). With outcomes-based commissioning more generally, efficiency enhancement through cost reductions and modifying behavioural incentives both inside and outside government have been common motivators (Albertson et al. 2018).

Political economic factors have also been noted as motivators (Maier and Meyer 2017, 3). In surveys, government stakeholders also have emphasized overcoming internal government constraints, restricted budgetary resources, and "budget silos, procurement issues, hurdles in the budgeting process, and political barriers" as motivations for the SIB model (Gustafsson-Wright, Gardiner, and Putcha 2015, 25). Government might engage with SIBs due to the ability to transfer risk (Liebman and Sellman 2013, 9), which allows them to pass off to private sector agents responsibility for high-profile program failures and resultant negative publicity.[2] All other things being equal, government values high-risk transfers and low financial returns to investors – the opposite of what investors are looking from a risk-financial rewards perspective (Giacomantonio 2017).

SIBs also might produce reputational benefits for governments, given their growing status as an innovative delivery method, and might be adopted because of a desire to "imitat[e] ... the actions of other governments that they regard highly" (Maier and Meyer 2017, 6–7). Governments might be interested in PbR schemes more generally, as success can convey competent governance and, at the local level, can leverage national government outcome payments, bringing additional resources to the region (Courty and Marschke 2011b, 71–2). Government austerity is also a widely referenced enabler of SIBs (see Chapter 7), which are helpful in this context and might enable government to initiate incremental social service programing while temporarily keeping the cost off government balance sheets, allowing governments to report lower projected deficits (see Chapter 3).

There are also indications that government stakeholders are not united in their embrace of the SIB model, as the interests of elected officials, civil service workers, senior management, and other public sector stakeholders might not be in alignment. Some such stakeholders – for example, unions representing civil servants – have opposed and been critical of SIBs, based on the bonds' privatization elements and questionable effectiveness. Clear opposition has been present in several leading SIB countries, including Australia (Community and Public Sector Union 2017; Public Services International et al. 2017), Canada (Canadian Union of Public Employees 2013, 2018; Malcolmson 2014; Ryan 2015, 2017; National Union of Public and General Employees 2012, 2017, 2018, 2019), and the United States (American Federation of State, County and Municipal Employees 2015; Blumgart 2014; Gregg and Bogdan 2014; Lester 2014, 2015; Tewfik 2015), as well as through at least one international union (European Public Service Union 2013).[3] The UK House of Lords (United Kingdom 2017c, 86) has also called into

---

2 As we discussed in Chapter 3, however, full risk transfer is challenging given the perceived end responsibility of governments to address social challenges (Fraser et al. 2018b, 15).

3 Based on an online search, unions in the United Kingdom do not appear to be particularly active in publicly opposing SIBs. However, one UNISON document did reference working in partnership with international labour organizations to oppose "the increasing threat of global Social Impact Bonds ... to fund public services (health, social care, prisons, probation and education) and the £1billion SIB market emerging in the UK" (UNISON 2016, 14).

question the UK government's emphasis on the model. There has been "vociferous opposition" (Dear et al. 2016, 44) to SIBs in certain other countries, leading to governments being more hesitant and restrained in adopting the model. This suggests that decision making around SIBs and the policy-making process more generally is a contested terrain with competing interests.

Relative Cost Critique

Several authors have argued that SIBs face some fundamental challenges on their own terms, questioning their ability to deliver the effectiveness and innovation proclaimed by proponents and undermining efficiency-based explanations of SIB emergence (Fox and Albertson 2011; Joy and Shields 2013; Lake 2015; Loxley 2013; Loxley and Puzyreva 2015; McHugh et al. 2013; McKay 2013a; Roy et al. 2017; Sinclair et al. 2014; Stid 2013; Warner 2013; Whitfield 2015). This literature situates SIBs within the broader neoliberal or New Public Management reforms of public administration, including contracting out, a focus on "value for money," and greater reliance on the private sector through vehicles such as public-private partnerships. These authors highlight that SIBs neglect the existing strengths and advantages of conventional non-profit and government provision, and in practice face at least three challenges with respect to delivering cost-effective public services.

One challenge is that SIBs face the added costs of having to cover the additional administrative and transaction costs associated with the rigid and high-stakes contracting structure inherent in the model. SIB contracts need to specify clearly in advance the targeted outcomes and metrics of evaluation, as well as all contingencies that might arise and the associated repayment terms for investors. Each party to the transaction needs to obtain specialized legal expertise to make sure their interests are properly reflected in the associated contracts between stakeholder groups. Doubts have been raised that SIBs can overcome these transaction costs given their current scale (see also KPMG 2014; Williams 2018, 2019).

A second challenge is that SIBs must cover the returns of successful investors over and above the government cost of borrowing – a cost not present in more conventional delivery models. From the investors' perspective, this profit margin is justified given the risk they face and the value added they bring to the project, but the veracity of these claims is tenuous. Expected and maximum rates of return on SIBs for investors on average are significantly above the government cost of borrowing and, based on the limited data that have been publicly released, SIBs appear mostly to be meeting their outcome targets, which suggests that minimal risk transfer might be occurring in practice (see Chapter 2). Governments, then, for the most part are presumably repaying investors as per the specified terms, meaning that additional public funds are required to cover incremental costs associated with the spread between government borrowing rates and investor returns. It is also unclear what expertise investors bring to the project other than financing and monitoring, given that the agencies hired mostly appear to have track records of successful social service delivery.

Third, SIBs could introduce inappropriate and detrimental incentive structures that might have unintended consequences for the behaviour of service organizations. The pay-by-results structure associated with SIBs has led to both concerns and accusations that strategic gaming has taken place in some SIBs, where, for example, client groups were selected because they were easy to serve and targets would be easily met (see also Edmiston and Nicholls 2018; Popper 2015). More generally, there is empirical evidence to support that workers in public and non-profit sectors self-select occupations based on a pro-social or altruistic-type commitment to public service, and that performance-based incentives might displace these motivations. This and other characteristics of the public service (see Dixit 2002) make it unlikely that crude performance-based incentives will have the desired effect, and in fact might be detrimental. In the SIB case, workers might see their programs and efforts diverted to meet narrowly defined indicators of success, as opposed to the broader needs of their clients, with money leaving the social service sector and going to for-profit investors (Edmiston and Nicholls 2018).

The above review raises significant doubts regarding the potential of SIBs to be cost effective relative to conventional procurement, motivating a search for alternative explanations of the emergence of SIBs. To understand why governments implement SIBs requires a theory of the state that frames how decisions are made and what motivates government stakeholders to select particular policy approaches over others.

Theories of the State

In this section, we summarize four traditions of economic thought that we use to frame our analysis of the motivations and behaviour of government in relation to SIBs. Two of these traditions, the neoclassical and neoliberal schools, are orthodox, and two, institutionalist and Marxian economics, are heterodox. Within our "neoclassical" category, we include welfare economics and public finance approaches, while our heterodox institutionalist approaches incorporate insights from the "old" institutionalist tradition and subsequent evolutionary and behaviourist approaches.

The Neoclassical School

Theories of the state can be classified into two broad categories – "contract theory" and a "predatory or exploitation theory" (North 1979, 250; 1981, 21) – that, in a manner, parallel the traditional equity versus efficiency distinction in mainstream economics.[4] The first category emphasizes the potential collective gains that government facilitates, and the subsequent incentives that individuals have to collaborate voluntarily. Unlike other approaches to the state that draw on elements of both, the neoclassical welfare economics school relies on a contract theory of the state, which is inextricably tied to two subsequent rationales. The first is the *public goods* rationale, where certain goods can be consumed collectively by many without additional cost or detriment to others once supplied, such as national defence; the second is the more straightforward benefits of coordination, such as determining on what side of the road to drive (Hardin 1997). The two contract theory rationales are distinguished by the potential incentive to free ride on public goods through the avoidance of payment, where, in the latter, once the norm has been established, there are minimal enforcement costs given the inherent benefit to all of abiding by the norm. In addition, the interaction of private actors in free markets might give rise to positive or negative externalities that are not incorporated into the incentive structure of private agents – in effect, a generalization of the public-good problem.

Public goods, gains from coordination, and the presence of externalities create space in a market system based on private ownership for government intervention to rectify market failures that result in Pareto-inefficient outcomes. This is a version of the state, combined with distributional considerations, that gives rise to the notion that society collectively can be represented by a social welfare function, and can be thought of as the public finance or welfare economics approach.[5] Within this broader framework, the state is presented "as an association of individuals engaged in a cooperative venture, formed to resolve problems of social coexistence and to do so in a democratic and fair

---

4 Note that, here, "contract theory" is distinct from the usage of term we presented in Chapter 4.

5 This approach originates with Bergson (1938) and Samuelson (1954).

fashion ... based on and reflecting the shared concerns of its individual members" (Musgrave 1999, 31). This *public finance* approach assumes as a starting point that government sets out to act in the best interests of its citizens as reflected by their individual preferences.

Public finance or welfare economics was the dominant theory of the state in the post-war era. Based on neoclassical theory, the theory emphasized how the real-world economy deviated significantly from the optimal scenario of Walrasian general equilibrium, thereby necessitating an active role for the state in managing and participating in economic affairs (Chang 2003). The neoclassical welfare economics theory of the state forms the basis of government action in the principal-agent approach we used in Chapter 3, in that the principal is a government representative selecting a delivery structure based on maximizing the net benefit to society of a given intervention.

The Neoliberal School

The neoliberal theory of the state is a semi-coherent combination of neo-classical economics augmented with Austrian-Libertarian political philosophy and economic ideas regarding individual freedom, the role of markets, and government officials, based on three central components (Chang 2003, 47–8). First, the theory adopts a *contractarian* perspective on the nature of the state, such that any role for the state beyond a basic enforcement of property rights specifically and the broader rule of law more generally is questionable from a moral or ethical perspective. Individuals' freedom to pursue their self-interest through market exchange and free from state intervention takes primacy over efficiency considerations.

Second, the neoliberal perspective views the market as an effective information processor that cannot be outdone by central planning (see also Mirowski 2015, 435). Although markets might not be perfect in the neoclassical sense, they are the most effective mechanism to coordinate the preferences and activities of autonomous individuals, given the high potential of government also to fail.[6] The state's ability to improve outcomes through intervention in the market economy is claimed to be highly limited due to information constraints, and within neoliberal state theory it is implausible for the state to identify market failure effectively as well as to intervene constructively to address it. Intertwined with this government failure approach, neoliberal state theory

---

6 See Becker (1958) for an early expression of this concern.

has worked to restrict the domain of genuine market failure to a few basic areas related to the enforcement of property rights and the rule of law and large-scale infrastructure projects.

Third, the neoliberal state models government as composed of rent-seeking and easily corruptible politicians and bureaucrats, and therefore emphasizes a predatory theory of the state. This is based on the work of the Public Choice school, whose study of government and politics is based on the "basic behavioral postulate ... that man is an egoistic, rational, utility maximizer" (Mueller 2003, 1–2). In this sense, the Public Choice approach is a natural extension of a narrow interpretation of neoclassical theory of the individual to state actors, where a single ruler has a natural monopoly on force at a particular geographic scale – and therefore on the enforcement of property rights – and seeks to maximize rent extraction (North 1981). With respect to the civil service, Public Choice assumes that imperfectly supervised government workers seek to maximize their power as reflected by the size of their budgets, and therefore will oversupply publicly provided goods (Bel, Fageda, and Warner 2010, 555; Letza, Smallman, and Sun 2004, 165). Public Choice also models politicians as vote maximizers who compete for votes and set their policies solely based on achieving this goal and, in turn, to access the benefits associated with holding office (Downs 1957). This latter approach generates the median voter theorem: the idea that politicians will converge to the preferences of the median voter if preferences and candidates are limited to a single dimensional metric – for example, rankings on a left-right political spectrum.[7]

This leads to a system of government that is highly responsive to the desires of voters when voters are well informed; however, the application of Public Choice's optimizing rational egoist model of human behaviour undermines this result. In this framework, voters vote

---

7 Hotelling (1929, 54–5) described the convergence of political platforms in a two-party system to maximize votes, a notion that was subsequently examined more systematically by Downs (1957) and Black (1958). Roemer (2006) examines the limitations of this approach and the challenges and implications of extending the model from a single dimension to multidimensional policy spaces, and from a deterministic framework to a probabilistic framework that introduces uncertainty with respect to voters' and politicians' knowledge of each other's characteristics. He also examines the implications of modelling politicians as having preferences over possible government practice and policy outcomes, instead of, or in addition to, the desire to hold decision-making power and its associated benefits. He highlights, however, that "probably 95% of the formal literature in political economy since Downs" has stayed within the deterministic, vote-maximizing, single-issue-dimension framework (Roemer 2006, 3).

based on self-interest. Given that the cost of voting is real in terms of the opportunity cost of time and effort, and that a single vote is highly unlikely to make any difference in the outcome of an election, rational egoists have little reason to vote or to pay much attention to politics in general. This leads to politicians' behaviour being open to the influence of interest groups that organize to redistribute – directly or, more commonly, indirectly – income and or/wealth to themselves through government policy change.[8] Interest groups in this framework support policy change in their favour by delivering votes and resources to politicians who, in turn, implement favoured policies to secure re-election.[9] Rational politicians in this framework then balance the benefit of catering to interest groups in return for campaign contributions and voter mobilization against the probability of alienating the much larger but less attentive group of voters who are not members of the interest groups in question (Austen-Smith 1987; Denzau and Munger 1986).

The conclusion arising from the Public Choice approach is that regulation, redistribution, and other interventionist government activity is even more detrimental to economic efficiency than is typically argued by neoclassical economists.[10] This is due to private sector actors now acting through interest groups, shifting resources away from production activity to unproductive redistributive efforts, seeking to generate transfers or economic rents from favourable policy (Buchanan and Tullock 1962; Tullock 1967). This is made possible, again, by the rational inattentiveness of self-regarding voters who assume such a small share of the burden, spread out among taxpayers as a whole, that it is not worth their time or effort to engage in countermobilization. Neoliberal state theory based on early Public Choice theory then cautions about the state's tendency to grow to the detriment of the public interest, and

---

8 For the seminal development of the Public Choice interest group approach, see Olson (1965), Stigler (1971), and Peltzman (1976). For another approach that fully and explicitly integrates voting processes with interest group behaviour, see Lindbeck and Weibull (1987).

9 Stigler (1971, 13) highlights, for example, how politicians hold stakes in private businesses, especially in law and finance (private service sectors that SIBs also employ extensively) and use them as vehicles for receiving perquisites from special interest groups.

10 These results hinge heavily on these questionable assumptions, and lead to some fundamentally misleading conclusions that are not consistent with the empirical evidence, with both the assumptions and the predictions of the theory facing challenges (Chernomas and Hudson 2017, 92–105; Pressman 2004; Quiggin 1987).

prescribes vigilance in this regard, particularly with respect to the damage caused by interest groups.[11]

Within this framework, state leaders that set policy and oversee the allocation of government resources will be pressured to deliver on commitments made to interest groups, and will adapt fiscal policy to accommodate them, where possible. This political competition also influences the development of government institutional structure, with elected officials changing bureaucratic institutions to their advantage (Moe 1990). Incumbents in the lead-up to elections will use fiscal policy to signal their political competence to deliver benefits to voters if re-elected (Rogoff 1990; Rogoff and Sibert 1988), usually taking the form of micro-level policies that concentrate benefits to favour targeted voters, sympathetic interest groups, and particular constituencies (Drazen and Eslava 2010; Wagner 1977).[12] There is also evidence that governments manipulate financial reporting, either through the flexibility afforded by accounting conventions or by not acknowledging liabilities,

---

11 This strictly critical assessment of interest groups is not equally held by the Chicago School of rational choice political economy, sometimes included in a broad definition of Public Choice (see, for example, Chernomas and Hudson 2017, 92–105), which also applies the rational egoist model of behaviour to the political system and interest groups. Peltzman (1976), building on Stigler (1971), highlights how the rational inattentiveness of voters sets limits on the ability of interest groups to capture public officials. Interest groups will stay small and concentrated, as large interest groups raise the ire of taxpayers as well as free-rider problems. Becker (1983, 1985) more clearly emphasizes how interest group competition can be beneficial when groups have equal access to political power, and that "the condemnation of special interest groups is excessive because competition among these groups contributes to the survival of policies that raise output" (344), a conclusion explicitly in contrast to the more classical Virginia School of Public Choice based on the work of Buchanan and Tullock. Wittman (1989) and Coughlin, Mueller, and Murrell (1990) take this approach even further, arguing that democratic political competition and effectively functioning interest groups can produce efficient outcomes in a manner similar to how market competition disciplines firms and produces Pareto-efficient outcomes.

12 Several studies note that deficit spending does not lead to electoral success and/ or that reducing deficits is associated with greater electoral success in some circumstances; see Alesina et al. (1998); Brender (2003); Brender and Drazen (2008); Drazen and Eslava (2010); Peltzman (1992). Alesina et al. (1998) argue explicitly that the lack of negative voter response to reduced spending and deficits is linked to preferences of voters for conservative fiscal policy. These constraints may result in politicians alternatively increasing spending on target constituencies in the lead up to elections by reallocating spending as opposed to increasing overall expenditure (Drazen and Eslava 2010).

particularly in election years, in order to present a more favourable fiscal picture of lower deficits or higher surpluses to the electorate.[13]

More recent studies loosely in the Public Choice tradition have used the descriptor *Machiavellian* to describe a related politically motivated form of strategic privatization and contracting out, which right-leaning political parties use as a means to cultivate the political support of centrist voting blocs and build broader support for privatization.[14] This type of procurement is not only about a government's catering to its base of support, but also about using procurement to shift the preferences and/or interests of undecided or unaligned groups towards those of the government in power and its core supporters. For example, right-leaning governments might privatize a state enterprise through the sale of undervalued shares, aiming to court target populations in favour of privatization and/or to manipulate the political identity of new shareholders towards business interests (Biais and Perotti 2002; Sundell and Lapuente 2012, 72).

The empirical literature on Machiavellian privatization, generally focused on local municipal service contracting, has proposed a number of variables to explain the degree of contracting out among different governments.[15] These can be grouped into the following categories, with an increase in the variable associated with a higher degree of privatization: (1) fiscal constraints; (2) economic efficiency or cost-reduction potential through economies of scale or increased competition; (3) relative power of interest groups, primarily categorized as those associated with capital and those with labour; (4) ideological commitment of the governing party to the "free market"; (5) positive opinion of the electorate regarding privatization; and (6) ease of political decision making

---

13 See Kido, Petacchi, and Weber (2012), who find that these effects are lesser in states where state auditors have greater independence. See also Sbragia (1996), who presents a compelling narrative of the political economy of US municipal finance focused on how municipalities have come up with innovative financing structures to circumvent state limits on spending through the establishment of authorities, embedded in an interest group framework.

14 See Bel and Fageda (2009), Biais and Perotti (2002) and Sundell and Lapuente (2012). There are at least two bodies of literature looking at the explanatory factors of privatization, one that is European based and focused on the privatization of state-owned enterprises, and a US-based literature looking at the contracting out of local government services (Bel and Fageda 2007). Also, Antellini-Russo and Zampino (2012) employ the Machiavellian procurement descriptor to explain the use of public-private partnerships.

15 See Bel and Fageda (2007, 2009) and Sundell and Lapuente (2012) for summary reviews of this literature.

in the given political governance structure.[16] Political competition also plays a mediating factor, depending on the ideology of the governing party.[17] Table 6.1 provides examples of indicators used to measure or proxy for these explanatory variables.

All of the above factors fit into a more generic model of political competition, where politicians use control over government resources to reinforce public support, subject to fiscal constraints and institutional structure. Ideological commitment identifies a centre or base of interest group support for a particular government, while the strength of these groups and, to a lesser extent, public opinion influence the balance of power within and between governing political parties and/or coalitions. Fiscal constraints and economic efficiency affect the ability of governments to respond to interest groups. Looking specifically at the SIB model, one would also likely seek a dependent variable associated with the degree of financialization, or the relative power or influence of the financial sector.

IMPLICATIONS

Within the broader neoliberal theory of the state and the specific notion of Machiavellian privatization, SIBs can be understood as a specific type of contracting out or privatization that might allow vote-maximizing politicians to garner the support of interest groups and inattentive

---

16 Note that this approach moves away from the more classical Public Choice approaches based on vote maximizing, and incorporates political parties and ideological considerations that, in turn, might incorporate other-regarding preferences. Kalt and Zupan (1984) note, however, that this still fits within broader rational choice, as other-regarding preferences are modelled as a consumption good based on ideological preferences. Alternatively, they note that ideology can be reduced to a strategic rule of thumb aligning with constituent interests, in a context of rational inattention and other information asymmetries, as originally noted by Downs (1957, 96–114). With respect to voters, Kalt and Zupan (1984) note that ideologically driven preference "poses no problems for the economic theory of politics. Publicly interested ideologues are just another special interest capable of capturing the political process, subject to the comparative statics of organizational costs and benefits" (281).

17 A significant positive interaction between (4) and (7) supports the presence of Machiavellian contracting, since, as political competitiveness intensifies and control of the state is threatened, right-wing governments will be motivated to increase their use of strategic privatization to get political support (Sundell and Lapuente 2012), while left-wing politicians will be more likely to contract out when they have a comfortable majority, since their interest group base is opposed to privatization. It has been noted that left-wing governments usually privatize to generate funds, seeking the highest financial gain, rather than for vote-gaining purposes (Biais and Perotti 2002), again producing a positive interaction effect.

Table 6.1. Variables Associated with the Degree of Contracting Out by Governments

Explanatory Variables	Rationale	Indicator or Proxy
(1) Fiscal constraints	Deficits are politically unpalatable ceteris paribus; privatization allows for shifting of expenses off-books and/or produces windfall gains from concession contracts or asset sales.	Borrowing rates or debt rating of government; debt-equity ratio of government*; tax levels†; legislated budget constraints†; funds from higher levels of government†.
(2) Economic efficiency	Potential cost savings permit deficit reduction or new spending on additional political priorities.	Population size being governed*†; number of registered stock companies*; geographic size of political unit*; measures of transaction costs†.
(3) Relative power of interest groups	Labour will oppose contracting out while capital will support.	Unionization rate†; percentage of workforce in public sector†; source of financial campaign contributions to politicians.
(4) Ideology of governing party	Right-wing political parties or individual politicians will support contracting out, left-wing politicians will oppose.	Number of seats of each party in legislature, ranked ideologically on left–right spectrum; indexes of survey-based ideological rankings of individual politicians*.
(5) Opinion of the electorate regarding privatization	Politicians, due to electoral competition, will be influenced by the will of the electorate.	Median annual income*; percentage of various income groups of total population†; votes cast for different politicians by ideology†.
(6) Political governance structure	Contracting out will be more likely where decision-making power is consolidated and change is easier to implement.	Number of veto players in government decision-making structure*.
(7) Degree of political competition	A higher intensity of political competition will drive politicians who benefit from politically motivated contracting out to do so at a higher rate.	Margin of victory of electoral mandate*; size of majority in legislature*.

† Noted as common regressors in Bel and Fageda (2007).

* Used by Sundell and Lapuente (2012).

voters, at least in the short term, by redirecting spending towards popular programs and improving the publicly reported budgetary indicators broadly interpreted as measures of government performance.[18] At the level of elected officials, the SIB model presents several advantages for public sector decision makers facing significant budgetary constraints who prioritize lower reported deficits and high-profile targeted spending over value-for-money considerations. This is consistent with a survey of government participants in SIBs who indicated that scaling up the proposed social service activities in the face of budgetary limitations was a recurring motivation (Gustafsson-Wright, Gardiner, and Putcha 2015, 25; Warner 2013, 11–12). As we discussed in Chapter 3, under their current accounting treatment, SIBs have the potential to go unaccounted for in public accounts until outcome payments are to be made, thus pushing off costs off, potentially to future governments. Within this context, and assuming the political competition approach, governments, investors, and service providers jointly have an incentive to construct SIB projects with outcome targets that are easily achieved and with excessive rates of return (Maier and Meyer 2017, 6–7), such that rates are higher than required to attract investors. This has been verified empirically by Hevenstone and von Bergen (2020, 212), who conclude that SIB "targets [are] set through collaborative political negotiations that have a strong potential to inflate government costs, with providers pushing for 'achievable' targets."

Aspects of the neoliberal theory of the state provide a degree of normative and positive support for the SIB model, but they also raise concerns. In general, Public Choice theory provides an underlying rationale for the proponents' case for SIBs based on the disparagement of government capabilities. In the neoliberal framework, SIBs might lead to greater efficiencies relative to bureaucratic administration because governments are prone to failure due to power-maximizing bureaucrats, and markets are the best mechanism to process information and allocate resources. The contracting out of project management activities in addition to service provision, the issuing of investment shares, and payment based on results all lead to better alignment of incentives, and might reduce the discretionary power of self-interested bureaucrats.

Although neoliberal theory provides an incremental rationale for SIBs, SIBs are only a partial solution, given the remaining centrality of the state in setting outcome metrics and the fact that SIBs use taxation

---

18 There is empirical evidence to suggest that voters are generally in favour of greater investment in preventative social services; see, for example, Lipsey and Cullen (2007, 316) and Public Health Association of Victoria and VicHealth (2011).

revenue to fund in-kind social services, undermining consumer sovereignty on both fronts. In this context, the Public Choice perspective raises concerns about the use of SIBs by investors and intermediaries to extract rents, and by politicians and bureaucrats to mask increased spending and inflate their sphere of influence – by temporarily skirting legislated budget constraints or exploiting information asymmetries and in turn increasing the tax burden on the population more broadly, targeting benefits strategically to support re-election.

The Heterodox Institutionalist Approach

Chang (2002, 2003) acknowledges that the Austrian information critique and the ignorance of the role of interest groups are genuine weaknesses in neoclassical welfare economics, but suggests this does not necessarily support a case against an active and interventionist state with respect to the economy. He notes cases where the state has been effective in constructing institutions that help mitigate risk arising from information deficiencies, and points to work with coalitions of interest groups to achieve developmental goals. He proposes an *Institutionalist Political Economy* (IPE) theory of the state in "the tradition of … Karl Marx, Thorstein Veblen, Joseph Schumpeter, Karl Polyani, Andrew Shonfield, and Herbert Simon" (Chang 2002, 551), as well as Kenneth Arrow (Chang 2003, 51). Chang's IPE approach is generally consistent overall with the heterodox institutionalist tradition, which also traces its roots to Veblen, as well as to John Commons and Wesley Mitchell, and more modern scholars such as Geoffrey Hodgson.

The heterodox institutionalist approach is similar to a welfare economics approach in that the theory lays out the theoretical basis for a strong role for the state in the economy. It departs, however, from the market-centric neoclassical framework of optimization, perfect information, and fixed property rights and technologies, with the state playing a leading entrepreneurial role as vision-setting coordinator, builder of institutions, and conflict manager (Chang 2003, 51–63). Within this institutionalist framework, market solutions might or might not be more effective; the market does not have an *a priori* privileged position, as in the neoclassical and welfare economics approach, with markets themselves being socially constructed institutions that often have had to be imposed violently with the backing of the state to displace traditional non-market institutions of provision and exchange. Political means have been and continue to be used in the assignment of property rights and other "rights-obligation structures" (Chang 2002, 550) that continually evolve and shape the determination of the institutional structure that is taken as given in neoclassical theory. Minimizing the state to avoid its politicized use is critiqued as a flawed normative prescription, as it does not speak to this continuous struggle, the political nature of the market, the relative demerits of non-intervention, and examples of successful state-led economic transformation. Within the heterodox institutionalist approach, there is no *a priori* natural boundary between the state and the market, and politics is the mechanism to engage and manage this contested delineation.

Since institutionalist economists focus on the social provisioning process more generally, with markets not having privileged status, the state and other institutions such as the family are viewed as important means of production and allocation. The state is privileged, however, in its ability to play a central role in purposefully influencing the development and evolution of other provisioning institutions (Whalen 1992). The state, in institutional economics, is "pragmatic," arising from the need for the "institutional coordination of collective problem solving" (Waller 2006, 32). In this sense, institutionalist economics advances a contract theory approach to the state. Linking back to the work of Veblen, however, the importance of power in economic relations and the economy is also a central concept in institutional economics, and the state as a central mechanism in allocating power is then an important institution of study, leading to a recognition of how dominant interests within the state reflect class power (Wunder and Kemp 2008, 40). Veblen's discussion of government pre-empted Public Choice in the broad sense of government and politics as a tool of special interests. But, for Veblen, the special interests that were served were those of the business class: rather than rational inattention, Veblen pointed to an irrational patriotic affinity of the common people towards the propertied classes of their nation (Leathers 1989, 295–6). Veblen also pre-empted the basic premise of Downsian-style political competition and the coming together of parties' policy proposals, but again these were tethered to the interests of the business class – although these ideas did not have longevity in Veblen's writings (Leathers 1989, 296–7).[19]

This critical view of the state as beholden to business interests is not consistent within the broader heterodox institutionalist tradition. More commonly, institutionalists speak to the need and ability of the state to

---

19 Leathers (1989) highlights how Veblen, while for the most part committed to the notion that government policy is driven by business interests, at times was not consistent on this point and had also suggested the potential of profiting off government by self-seeking government officials and businesses to lead to runaway growth of the state to the detriment of broader economic well-being.

manage competing interests and to formulate a shared vision for economic development and management. If one goes back to John Commons, it is through the conflict between interest groups that stability and popular consensus are generated, suggesting that equitable access to power through free association facilitates this process (Wunder and Kemp 2008, 400).[20] More generally, the institutionalist approach views the state as a constructive and progressive means for resolving conflict if based on democratic participation.

The institutionalist approach rejects the notion of the self-regarding rational egoist as an accurate reflection of human behaviour more generally, and specifically in the context of politicians and government, highlighting the clear empirical evidence of non-self-regarding behaviour, particularly in public life, based on "moral views and social norms" (Chang 2002, 549) and the endogenous adaptation to public service values through participation in collectivist institutions.[21] This is consistent with the broader commitment within the institutionalist approach to preferences as endogenous and socially constructed. The institutionalist approach highlights how many neoliberal prescriptions for regulating and motivating civil servants might be counterproductive and crowd out intrinsic motivation (Chang 2002, 549).

The heterodox institutionalist tradition primarily defines itself in relation to and distinct from neoclassical economics (see, for example, Hodgson 1993). While there is strong emphasis on modelling the economy as an evolutionary system, how the economy or institutions evolve over time in the broader heterodox institutionalist approach is highly context specific and/or path dependent, with institutionalists relying on the notion of "cumulative causation" (Hodgson 1993, 17–19). This notion aims to include "all relevant factors" that "can ... only be determined empirically," and "den[ies] the existence of a primary cause" (Berger 2008, 359), leading to accusations that institutionalism is atheoretical and only concerned with specific policy problems. Defenders of the approach dispute this claim (Hodgson 2000). Within the institutionalist evolutionary approach, temporal and geographic differences arising historically will result in a diversity of institutional governance structures.[22] Given this commitment to context and institutional speci-

---

20 This prescription is similar to the use by some mainstream theorists of neoclassical behavioural assumptions. See footnote 11 above.

21 Our discussion in Chapter 5 of public service motivation and strong reciprocity at a high level serves as possible foundations for these notions.

22 See Ebner (2006), who summarizes Schumpeter's theory of the state, which is firmly in this institutionalist tradition, where institutional diversity is emphasized,

ficity, institutionalist theory does not produce predictive tendencies of the state in "general or abstract," as such would be a "methodological contradiction" (Waller 2006, 14). This open-endedness, combined with its pragmatic approach to socio-economic provisioning and existentialist underpinnings emphasizing human agency, centres the institutionalist's instrumentalist approach on the feasibility and desirability of conscientious and purposeful policy reforms and economic leadership (Dugger 1988).

IMPLICATIONS

The institutionalist approach has ambiguous implications for understanding and evaluating the SIB model. More generally, heterodox institutionalism and, in particular Chang's IPE, is a theory of how state apparatus can function well, and of the potential for constructive state economic leadership if led by well-meaning social planners unwilling to shy away from constructive interventionism. In this sense, it suggests scepticism about the privileged status that SIBs provide markets and privatization. Based on strong empirical foundations, the institutionalist critique of human motivation and behaviour represented by optimization and self-interest fundamentally undermines the outcome implications of the Public Choice modelling of interest group behaviour, creating the potential for interest group advocacy and civil participation mediated by the state as a means for social progress. Together this undermines Public Choice's disparaging view of government capabilities.

The institutionalist epistemological framework is based, however, on a context of "dynamic and evolving social reality" (Whalen 1992, 63), with fundamental uncertainty and limits on our comprehension of the outcomes of social processes and interventions. Given an emphasis on the constructive role of the state in facilitating collaboration between different stakeholder groups with dispersed information to resolve social challenges, institutionalists, like neoliberals, then might provide some nominal support for SIBs. In this context, SIBs can be seen as a specific product realized from an environment of "democratic experimentalism," which beneficially reconciles activist governance features within delegated governance frameworks (Dorf and Sabel 1998, 267). SIBs fit similarly well into Roberto Unger's (2009) call for a "reconstructive Left," which would strive for "socially inclusive growth" based

---

with states varying from entrepreneurial and growth promoting to parasitic and retarding, emerging from both social contract and exploitative state types.

on the "experimental co-existence of different regimes of private and social property, as well as of different ways of relating governments to firms" (ix). In Unger's framework, "generalization of the work of venture capital beyond the confines of the private venture-capital industry" (91) would take place, with the goal to "democratize the market by extending the range of its legal and institutional forms" (92). Specifically with respect to government provision of social services, Unger argues that "the state should provide directly only those services that are too difficult, too expensive or simply too new to be provided by private providers" and that government's role should be to "act as a vanguard, developing experimentally new services or new ways of providing old services" through "experimental diversification on the basis of a loose set of associations between governmental and non-governmental initiatives" (86–7). At its foundation, these approaches recognize that "the cost of producing a good or service is not defined by a publicly-accessible production function but depends on the capabilities of the particular people who produce it," with these capabilities requiring coordination in a manner that does "not inhibit their continuing development" (Loasby 1998 157). In this context, SIBs might serve a discovery-type purpose in a dynamic setting with incomplete information regarding the social service delivery set and the optimal delivery structure that facilitates the agglomeration and application of dispersed knowledge and skills. Given this context of uncertainty, government representatives might in fact engage in SIBs from a place that genuinely reflects the pursuit of public interest.

The Marxian Approach

Although Chang's IPE approach references Marx as one of several sources of methodological inspiration, the heterodox institutionalist approach is generally seen as a separate school from Marxian state theory, which, while sharing some features with the institutionalist approach, is distinct in its analysis and implications. Based on the peripheral discussion of the state in Marx's original works, early Marxian state theory generated an eclectic collection of ideas, which in different contexts framed the state as: a parasitic and peripheral entity, a simple manifestation of class relations, a mediator of inter- and intra-class conflict, a tool of direct class domination, an apolitical set of institutions, and a more complex infrastructure not directly dominated by the ruling class but with tendencies to systematically advance and protect its interests in an indeterminate manner (Jessop 1990, 26–9).

Modern Marxian theories of the state build on this last conception, viewing the state as a social relation structured as an adaptive set of institutions that enable and facilitate commodity production and exchange that cannot be provided by individual capitalists or blocs of capital through decentralized competition. Government leaders create and manage state institutions with capital and, if successful, achieve the required conditions for capital accumulation and profitability in a non-deterministic or non-mechanical fashion (see Foley 1978; Jessop 1990). The state also coordinates relations between tranches of capital, organizing them into a semi-coherent alliance for this purpose. The form of state that emerges in a given context is historically specific and subject to pressure from class struggle and other broad-based popular movements, but with a pervasive tendency for the broader public interest to be framed in alignment with the interests of capital.[23]

Marxist analysis of the state has long argued, as have neoliberal approaches, that the state is not a neutral administrative body implementing technocratically determined, socially optimal policy (Wagner 1977). Modern Marxist theories of the state seek to emphasize the integral and functional nature that the state plays in capitalist reproduction without resorting to a deterministic *reductionist* view of the state as a simple "expression of capitalist class dominance," or a *functionalist* approach that "tries to explain phenomena by showing that they meet a need of the capitalist system as a whole or of the capitalist class in particular" (Foley 1978, 224; see also Jessop 1990). Like the institutionalist approaches, the modern Marxist theories of the state highlight its historical specificity, but reject the institutionalist's open-ended indeterminism, with dominant class relations of the economic system playing a defining role in the agenda of the state, which, under capitalism, is the capital-labour relationship.

Within this context, capital with its inherent advantages generally will see its interests reflected in state policy. With respect to fiscal policy, "the problems of capital have created the agenda for the modern state's expenditures and the conflict between classes and class fractions the primary pressures on state decisions" (Foley 1978, 225). Working within the Marxian framework, Foley (1978) highlights that most state decisions are not made through elections or referenda; rather, most state policy is set outside the political process, political positions are formed

---

23 This is based on Gramsci's theory of hegemony and is incorporated more explicitly into a theory of the state by Poulantzas; see Jessop (1985, 1990).

through intra-party competition, and electoral success is linked to the ability of political parties and candidates to leverage financial support.

In the Marxian framework, individuals are not deemed independent atomistic beings, as they are in the neoliberal framework, but hold identities derived from their class interests, either in a deterministic sense or more realistically as a strong influencer (Davis 2003, 109–10). Government workers and elected officials might have some agency, but since individuals are embedded in class relations, it is the class struggle that is the prime determinant, as opposed to subjective atomistic individual preferences. A class analysis approach also has normative implications for privatization. When privatization leads to the replacement of non-exploitative production with capitalist production methods based on exploitative class relations, this likely will have a negative effect on workers that is independent of the impact on wages (Cook 2007).

Like the Public Choice perspective and institutionalists focused on power, the Marxian theory of the state highlights the role of private interests in shaping policy to extract private benefits at the expense of the broader public interest, but adds an additional layer of analysis that informs the prioritization of interests. Specifically, it argues that solutions to perceived social problems are advanced within and shaped by the broader evolving dynamic of the reproduction of class relations, and the specific form that policy solutions take will be shaped by class struggle. Unlike neoliberal theory, which sees all interest groups as relatively equal in a liberal democratic society, Marxian theory highlights the privileged position of private capital in determinants of state policy. This arises out of the ability of capitalists to withhold and exclude others from the means of production either by shutting down or by relocating capital to another jurisdiction. This threat to withdraw capital gives capitalists leverage over politicians, who are more likely to be replaced when economic conditions subsequently deteriorate. Central to the policy development process, then, is the imperative to sustain the profitability of capital and to avert crises.

The ability and need of the working class, within these constraints, to shape policy in a manner more favourable to its interests is contested in Marxian tradition. Some, such as O'Connor (1973), emphasize the need of policy, in the form of the welfare state, to resolve the contradictions of capitalist development and facilitate ongoing capital accumulation. Here, class conflict is still the determining factor, but the outcome is more functionalist in nature. Alternatively, the "class mobilization thesis," as summarized by Esping-Andersen (1990, 16–17), argues that class conflict does matter, in the sense that a stronger working class has an impact, through alliances with other social groups such as farmers, on the degree of social distribution and decommodification through welfare state expenditures.[24] Within this social democratic version of the political competition thesis, the power of the working class and, in turn, the size of the welfare state, is based on its sustainable access to political resources – based on electoral success, trade union density, and alliances – relative to the power of countervailing forces. Duménil and Lévy (2011, 29) use a similar class-coalition framework when explaining the shift of alliances that has defined the neoliberal era, with the alliance between the "popular class" and non-financial management displaced by an alliance between management and finance.

IMPLICATIONS

The Marxian framework highlights the potential for SIBs, if scaled sufficiently, to facilitate reproduction of the social relations underpinning the capitalist system over time. This is to be accomplished by advancing financialization, generating profitable capital sinks through privatization, and producing opportunities for the financial sector to recover from the crisis of legitimacy stemming from its role in the Great Recession. SIBs do so in a manner that reflects the dominance of capital, relative to a hypothetical alternative based on progressive taxation, limits on financial capital, and the development of universal social programs – an institutional constellation more characteristic of the pre-neoliberal era. SIBs, then, can be understood as a means to continue to reshape state activity under neoliberalism in favour of the dominant tranches of capital – specifically, the financial sector and its beneficiaries.

Dowling and Harvie (2014), for example, highlight how the rise of SIBs, as part of the UK Conservative Party's Big Society agenda, is clearly linked to parallel crises of "capital accumulation … social reproduction, and the fiscal crisis of the state" (872). They note that the broader social investment market and SIBs, in particular, with their focus on quantifying outcomes and converting them into revenue streams for investors, help to resolve the social reproduction crisis by providing new profitable sinks for capital while addressing social issues that hinder the effective reproduction of labour power – that is, the health, education, and social development required to produce and maintain current and future workers. Dowling and Harvie (2014) then highlight how SIBs and social investment simultaneously take the social value that

---

24 See Howell (2003) for a summary of a similar contrast between the *varieties of capitalism* approach, which focuses on economic governance more broadly and places the needs of firms as the central explanatory factor in policy regime development, and more conflict-orientated, class-based approaches.

is produced outside capitalist relations of production, quantify it, and facilitate its transfer to investors.

Dowling (2017) further extends this research, again focusing on the UK context, linking together the government's support for financialization, neoliberalism, and austerity, and growing anger directed at finance in the wake of the crisis and government bailouts of the sector, with a redemptive "social turn" (305) of finance sought in the SIB model. The defensive manoeuvre is used to "legitimate the further expansion of financial markets ... to support continued neo-liberal welfare reform premised upon an austerity agenda ... without addressing the structural conditions of social and economic inequality" (305). In the end, for Dowling, the SIB, like other social investment products, is centred on the generation of profit, subjugating social outcomes, with finance again "privatising gains and socialising risks and costs" (306). Wiggan (2019, 118) similarly emphasizes how, through SIBs, "the state crafts ... new opportunities for value reallocation, appropriation and extraction from the commodification of social welfare by finance."

Cooper, Graham, and Himick (2016) similarly focus on how accounting in SIBs is used to "lay a neoliberal economic grid upon some of the most vulnerable in our society ... effac[ing] their humanity, replacing it with extreme rationality and quantification," while reformulating social value into financial returns. Ryan and Young (2018) echo the above arguments, highlighting the neoliberal tendencies of SIBs by expanding profitable opportunities for capital while further commodifying social reproduction and financializing publicly funded services. They note how, in some cases, SIB projects have generated an increased reliance on volunteers and led to more precarious working conditions for non-profit staff, advocating for better resourced conventional delivery as an alternative.

Joy and Shields (2017, 2018) also situate SIBs in this critical framework as being advanced by economists and business representatives – relative newcomers to the social services scene – who advocate for the marketization of social services, the generation of profit for investors, and the displacement of collectivist solutions aimed at addressing the root causes of poverty with individualist behaviouralist fixes.[25] In a more recent study, Joy and Shields (2020) delineate in greater detail how an SIB "economizes the social through the techniques of benchmarking,

---

25 Although not situated clearly in a critical political economy approach, others, such as Sinclair et al. (2014) and Tse and Warner (2018), make similar observations regarding the substitution of public values for financialized metrics and outcomes while highlighting the negative implications.

governance, devolution, and responsibilization" (191), thus continuing the damaging neoliberal trends undermining the comparative advantage of higher levels of government to address socio-economic challenges.

Implications for the Design and Regulation of Social Impact Bonds

In stark contrast to the neoclassical welfare economics underpinning the behavioural modelling of government in our contract theory framework constructed in Chapter 4, neoliberal, modern Marxian, and strands of institutionalist theories of the state all to various degrees put forward a vision of the state as a collection of institutions subject to manipulation by interest groups or classes in a manner contrary to the public interest. Past experience with privatization and contracting out raises concerns that this might be of particular concern for SIBs. Where senior public officials are acting in a strategic, self-serving manner, there is an abundance of motivation for SIBs with easy-to-achieve outcome targets and overcompensated investors. As Maier and Meyer (2017, 7) summarize, "all key actors will have an interest in setting success thresholds too low and agreeing on excessively generous terms. SIBs would then turn into a funding tool that harms the interest of taxpayers." Investors want SIBs to meet targets to recoup their investments, and service providers want SIBs to succeed because failure might have significant reputational effects (Giantris and Piakiewicz 2013). Public officials who prioritize reputational concerns might be overexuberant in their embrace of SIBs, given their abstract popularity and rhetorical attractiveness across the political spectrum (Maier and Meyer 2017). Loss- or failure-averse public officials are more likely to set soft or easily achievable targets.[26]

---

26 This assumes politicians view SIBs that do not meet their targets as a loss or failure and those that hit targets as a success. See Jervis (1992, 188–92) for an outline of the logic for assuming politicians are loss averse, noting that even relatively small failures can have a disproportionate effect on undermining confidence of the electorate, relative to successes. Alternatively, politicians might view failure as the status quo – for example, in an all-or-nothing SIB where government does not pay anything to investors if targets are not met. In this case, prospect theory (see Tversky and Kahneman 1992) predicts, based on the reflection effect, where individuals gamble on losses but are risk averse on gains, that politicians' risk aversion would lead again to overcompensation of investors. See Linde and Vis (2017), who find evidence of the reflection effect in an experiment with a sample of Dutch legislators; they do not find evidence of loss aversion, but qualify this finding. In our opinion, however, it is more plausible that an SIB that did not meet its targets would be

Given the complexity of the policy instrument and the marginal importance of SIBs for the vast majority of voters, it is unlikely that sufficient public attention or pressure will be generated through electoral consequences to ensure that SIBs are structured in the public interest. As Maier and Meyer (2017, 3) note, "very few voters even know what a SIB is. Even fewer voters will be informed about the details of a particular SIB contract. Specific information about SIBs, for example about their transaction costs, is never made public though it might be of interest for taxpayers." This does not necessarily mean a vacuum of accountability: as Wittman (1989, 1403) highlights, government structures such as committees can lead to a highly rigorous examination of specialized government policy and program areas that are incomprehensible and/or uninteresting to the general public, as well as structures that integrate the work of the more specialized forums responsible for annual budgeting exercises that examine aggregate spending composition and projected deficit measures. It is not clear that SIBs can be captured in these formal structures without legislative or regulatory changes, and such strutures or committees might not see the issue until the SIB investors are paid and deals have long since been negotiated, potentially deferring accountability, possibly to future governments.

Based on the potential for misapplication and obfuscation of the SIB model within our three alternative theories of the state, we suggest that increased independent oversight, transparency, and accountability mechanisms be implemented for SIBs. Specifically, we offer the following three recommendations to aid in monitoring and pre-empting the inappropriate application of the SIB model. First, SIBs should be subject to a transparent cost-benefit analysis that compares the merits and potential benefits of the model relative to alternative procurement methods, as opposed to rationalizing the model solely based on prospective cost savings or not at all (see Chapter 3 for further discussion). This should include some accounting for transaction and administration costs that are being covered outside the formal SIB structure or those committed in-kind.

Second, if the use of SIBs continues to grow and spending levels on them become a more meaningful proportion of government budgets, it

---

interpreted as a failure, given the in-kind resources, associated opportunity costs, and political capital invested. Additionally, despite efforts of proponents to frame failure in a positive light as a learning experience (see Anderson and Phillips 2015; Porter 2015), reporting on the prominent lack of achievement in the Riker's Island antirecidivism SIB was framed by multiple writers as a failure and indicator of the model's ineffectiveness (see Chen 2015; Cohen and Zelnick 2015; Farmer 2015).

might be prudent for government auditors to re-examine and develop standard practices for how SIBs are reported in public accounts, particularly if SIBs continue to hit their targets consistently and are repaying investors.

Third, a transparent selection process for investors should be used that seeks to achieve competitive rates of return and that explicitly accounts for the expected expertise and value added that investors bring to the effectiveness of social services delivery. Corporate social responsibility appears to be a significant motivation for many investors, so it is not clear why government should be paying market-based rates of return to SIB investors when it could be borrowing at below-market rates to self-finance projects, particularly if investors are not otherwise contributing to the project. To date, many SIBs appear to have been designed, constructed, and issued in a manner that would not stand the test of modern government procurement standards with respect to transparency or competition.

Conclusion

Proponents point to the new resources and efficiency enhancements obtainable through the SIB model. Here, we have presented an alternative explanation for the proliferation of the model. Available data on the historical development and evolution of the SIB model suggest that a significant proportion of SIBs are hitting their targets and paying out rates of return well above government costs of borrowing. Moreover, the use of SIBs is growing even though they face high administrative and transaction costs, in addition to the need to pay out returns to investors and are unlikely to be offset by any induced innovation. We are drawn, therefore, to seek an alternative explanation of the emergence and proliferation of SIBs: we propose that the SIB model is replacing conventional delivery models due to its alignment with the interests of finance and its consistency with the defining features of neoliberal governance.

In this chapter, we reviewed three stylized economic theories of the state – neoliberal, heterodox institutionalist, and Marxian – that contrast in their assumptions regarding the behaviour of public officials in the execution of their duties relative to neoclassical welfare economics, the approach that underlies government behaviour in the principal-agent model we set out in Chapter 4. These theories put forward a vision of political behaviour based on motives and outcomes not necessarily aligned with the public interest. In this context, governments might pursue SIBs even if the delivery mechanism is costlier and less efficient than traditional methods.

Neoliberal theory, relying heavily on the Public Choice approach, emphasizes how SIBs might be particularly helpful in competition for inattentive voters. SIBs, however, are obscure instruments to most voters, and they facilitate off-book costs that are difficult to monitor and spread out among many voters. At the same time, SIBs generate new spending focused on prevention that is easier for motivated voters and interest groups to detect, value, and potentially benefit from. Public Choice theory also highlights the role of interest groups in the process and how they can take advantage of voter inattentiveness, with the alignment of interests between government, investors, and service providers in SIBs potentially leading to overly generous payments with easily achievable targets when these stakeholders are primarily self-regarding. Although neoliberal theory in general supports moves such as SIBs towards privatization and market-based solutions, Public Choice also provides a framework to analyse the rent-seeking opportunities such schemes open up, with the theory pointing to the alternative of government's not being involved in social service provision at all.

Although Marxian theory also highlights the instrumentality of the state to advance sectoral interests, in this approach not all interest groups are equal, and power is of central concern. Marxian theory emphasizes the dominant role of capital in capitalist societies and that, within capitalism, it is the reproduction of the capital-labour relation and the sustainment of profitability, not the self-interest of politicians and civil servants, that anchor state activity. The form state intervention takes is shaped by class struggle. SIBs in this framework can be understood as a means to continue to reshape state activity under neoliberalism in favour of the dominant tranches of capital – specifically, the financial sector and its beneficiaries. We build on these insights in Chapter 7 as we situate SIBs in the broader historical context of neoliberalism.

Heterodox institutionalist theory is mixed in its potential insights and evaluation with respect to SIBs. The Veblen-inspired framework of governance in the interest of large corporations supported by irrational voters with an atavistic affinity for the business class has obvious parallels to Marxian theory as an exploitative view of the state, but other strands of institutionalist thinking have opposing views. More generally, heterodox institutionalists highlight how the underlying behavioural principles of Public Choice do not reflect observed reality either in terms of individual behaviour or in examples of successful state leadership in social and economic transformation. Institutionalists highlight how norms of public service and reciprocity can lead to state decision makers' prioritizing the public interest. Combined with the institutionalist evolutionary emphasis on the constructive role of the state as an entrepreneur, coordinator, and mediator, this line of inquiry opens up space for SIBs to be a reasonable organizational approach for social services, as a means for tapping into dispersed knowledge and capabilities. Typical of its indeterminism, the institutionalist tradition at the same time opens up the potential for SIBs to be a constructive solution while undermining anti-statist approaches that dismiss state-led conventional approaches due to ideological biases.

With respect to the relative merits of each of the above theories, early Public Choice theory has been challenged on multiple fronts, from both heterodox and mainstream economists, and empirically it has performed rather poorly, its behavioural assumptions regarding voters and politicians not standing up to testing (Chernomas and Hudson 2017, 92–105; Kalt and Zupan 1984; Pressman 2004). Overall, Public Choice has been accused of theoretical inconsistencies, resorting to degenerative ad hoc assumptions or substantial reformulation to rescue it (Quiggin 1987). For example, its treatment of government failure while idealizing the market is unbalanced, and as other rational choice–based approaches have pointed out, these conclusions regarding the political system are an artefact of the selective assumptions, even if individuals are modelled as purely self-regarding (Wittman 1989).

In this respect, the institutionalist and Marxian approaches fare better, partially due to their method of abstraction focusing on moving from the examination of concrete phenomena to theory, as opposed to relying on arbitrary first principles. This methodology helps inform their approaches, which are historically grounded and facilitate the examination of diverse institutional arrangements. The degree to which public institutions function effectively in the public interest as opposed to narrow vested interests – or, in Marxian terms, the degree to which the structure's progressivity or regressivity will reproduce class relations and conditions of profitability – will vary with historical circumstance (Duménil and Lévy 2004). The neoliberal period of the past forty years has been one of regressive change in terms of growing inequality and increasingly precarious work in most advanced economies. This change, however, has not been uniformly experienced. In the following chapter, we draw on institutionalist and Marxian approaches to identify contextually based factors that have given rise to this differential experience, and to suggest that the emergence of social impact bonds is linked to these broader trends.

7 The Political Economic Context of the Emergence of Social Impact Bonds

Introduction

This chapter examines the broader political economic context of the emergence of Social Impact Bonds within a combined Marxian- and Veblen-inspired heterodox institutionalist framework, two approaches that emphasize historical specificity, power relations, and recognition of the state as a site of conflicting interests. Within this framework, we situate SIBs as arrangements arising due to congruency with the interests of well-positioned classes – specifically, finance capital and those who derive increasing wealth from the sector. Our approach is also institutionalist in that it emphasizes institutional variation between countries arising from human agency, circumstance, and path dependence, and highlights how these differences can lead to significant variation in how countries respond to broader global political economic developments with respect to social and economic policy. Our approach is also Marxian in the sense that we argue that this variation is fundamentally a product of class struggle, but is constrained within capitalist societies, such that the systematic tendencies and crises that capitalist economies generate, paired with globalization, will shape and restrict governance options and create patterns and similarities across developed countries based on their integration in the global capitalist economic system.

Unlike Public Choice–based approaches founded on methodological individualism, this approach does not rely on a foundation of proponents with a conscious motivation to support the interests of finance and its beneficiaries. In fact, we believe that the movement behind SIBs arises from stakeholders' genuine concern to address the pressing issue of growing socio-economic inequality and from an acute frustration with current systems that neglect the high social returns to preventative investments in poverty reduction and social inclusion. What we are arguing is that the modern political economic structure of advanced capitalist economies – a consciously constructed political ideology and practice aimed at facilitating the restoration of profit and capital accumulation after the crises of the 1970s – has a particular logic embedded in its social structures and institutions that privileges certain solutions over others (Mirowski and Plehwe 2015). Here, there is also clear alignment with Gramsci's concept of cultural hegemony. This approach is consistent with heterodox economics more broadly in asserting that individuals are socially embedded, operating in a structure-agent framework, with institutionally shaped preferences (Davis 2003, 108–66).

The United Kingdom, the pioneer of SIBs, continues to be a leading nation with respect to their development as measured by number of projects. As we detailed in Chapter 2, the United Kingdom and the United States together account for 60 per cent of all SIBs launched to date and for approximately three-quarters of all participants and total investment in SIBs. When the liberal market economies of Australia, Canada, Israel, and New Zealand are added, this group makes up 74 per cent of all projects, 90 per cent of all participants, and 91 per cent of all investment in SIBs (Table 7.1).[1] In this chapter, we undertake a comparative analysis of these countries and countries operating under more interventionist economic frameworks and that have been more cautious and limited in their support and implementation of the SIB model.

Our comparative analysis focuses on the key defining and empirically observed elements of neoliberalism and financialization that have been identified in the literature, highlighting the greater intensity of these trends in what have been classified historically as liberal market economies. This analysis builds upon the fact that neoliberal restructuring has not been equally deep among the advanced developed nations (Kotz 2017b, 32), and upon the tiered nature of globalized financialization and its spread through global capitalist markets (Lapavitsas 2013). The United States and, to a lesser extent, the United Kingdom and other liberal market economies have led these trends, while continental European countries and the Nordic social democratic countries, while undertaking structural shifts, have maintained a relatively intact social model. This analysis also draws on the work of scholars who

---

1 This analysis is based on one less SIB than in our sample in Chapter 2 due to the exclusion here of the one South African SIB.

Table 7.1. Social Impact Bond Projects, Participants, and Investment, by Type of Governance Regime

Governance Regime	# of SIBs	%	# of Participants	%	Total Investment (US$ millions)	%
Liberal	90	74	116,877	90	341.7	91
Conservative	28	23	5,954	5	18.1	5
Social democratic	3	2	4,360	3	13.2	4

have identified distinct or ideal-type regimes of accumulation and welfare states across capitalist societies, suggesting that this institutional specificity has some staying power and acts to mediate the impact of broader global political economic developments and influences.

We begin by defining the concepts of neoliberalism and financialization, relying on the work of heterodox economists, primarily those working from what we label here as a critical political economy (CPE) perspective.[2] We then review the establishment of the institutional structures of supports for SIBs at the national level, tracing their emergence to broader neoliberal trends and financial sector actors. Following this, we present data on several characteristics and indicators illustrating the fundamental structural shifts in mature capitalist nations that have occurred under neoliberal and financialized capitalism, highlighting the differences between country groupings.

Defining Neoliberalism

The global economic system has undergone distinct phases of development, with varying institutional frameworks governing class relations,

---

2 Political economy is a contested term. It is used by those operating in the tradition of the classical political economists Adam Smith, David Ricardo, Thomas Malthus, and their critic Karl Marx, whose general framework placed class as the fundamental unit of analysis. Neoclassical and other mainstream economists use the term to encompass the imperialist practice within their respective research programs to apply ahistorical and deductive frameworks based on methodological individualism and instrumental rationality to the study of government and the state. In this chapter, we claim the term for the former use, with "critical" referring to the work of political economists who trace their origins primarily back to and emphasize the work of Marx. This application of the label by no means aims to diminish the competing perspectives and differences within this broader category, to which, given the scope of this chapter, we make only limited reference.

managing contradictions, and responding to endogenous crises, facilitating waves of capital accumulation (Kotz 1987). One theoretical approach that relates these phases directly back to profitability and capital accumulation, the central driving force of capitalist development, is the concept of the Social Structure of Accumulation (SSA). An SSA is a functional social structure and associated set of institutions that provides stability, manages class conflict, and facilitates long waves of robust capital accumulation and growth (Bowles, Gordon, and Weisskopf 1986). Successful SSAs facilitate capitalists' extraction from workers effort sufficient to generate surplus value, realize profits, manage international relations to maintain favourable terms of trade, and ensure that state activity, especially taxation and labour law, does not unduly undermine profitability (Bowles et al. 1986, 137). SSAs eventually succumb to their internal contradictions and tendency for the rate of profit to fall over time, generating instability and an increasing allocation of profits into financial sector activities instead of reinvestment in production, with new SSAs emerging in response to crises of profitability (Kotz 1987). In this manner, capitalism goes through discrete shifts in institutional regimes, with relatively brief transitions.

Neoliberalism has been identified as the most recent SSA, and described as both the acceptance of a particular logic and a set of institutional structural changes and policy outcomes (Kotz 2017b). These include: (a) trade liberalization and the elimination of restrictions on international capital mobility; (b) rejection of Keynesian demand management; (c) broad deregulation of corporate activity in production and consumer markets; greater tolerance for monopolistic dominance by industry; (d) reductions in the social safety net; (e) the substitution of private for public sector production and enterprise; (f) tax reductions for business and the wealthy; (g) attacks on unions and increasingly precarious working environments for workers; (h) more intense competition both between and within corporations; (i) an elite class of chief executives that circulate between companies; and (j) a disembedded financial sector with revised product and activity emphasis (Kotz 2017b, 42).

Duménil and Lévy (2004, 1–2) similarly define neoliberalism as a transformation of capitalism, reflecting a resurgence of the interests of finance, "a class of capitalist owners and the institutions in which their power is concentrated," with the objective "to restore ... the class's revenues and power, which had diminished since the Great Depression and World War II." Financial deregulation, labour market reforms, and globalization, as they have unfolded on neoliberal terms, are subordinate components of this larger project. As with the SSA approach, these changes are spurred by a decline in the rate of profit, triggering an endogenously generated structural crisis. Within the above description put forward by Duménil and Lévy, finance is taken to include not only the financial sector proper, but also the "complex of upper capitalist classes, whose property materializes in the holding of securities … and financial institutions" (Duménil and Lévy 2004, 16). In later work, they emphasize the shifting allegiances of "non-financial and government managers" away from the "popular classes" towards finance as central to understanding this transition (Duménil and Lévy 2011, 29).

Various other definitions of neoliberalism in the CPE approach are broadly consistent with these descriptions, and focus on a shift in the structure and institutions of capitalism to reflect a new set of ideas and practices. Harvey (2005, 2), for example, describes the neoliberal shift as prioritizing "a theory of political economic practices that proposes that human wellbeing can best be advanced by liberating individual entrepreneurial freedoms and skills within an institutional framework characterized by free markets, private property rights and free trade." The state still plays an important role in Harvey's definition, managing the money system, enforcing property rights, and constructing markets. As noted by Dowling (2017), Harvey offers some helpful concepts for framing SIBs from a CPE perspective, including "accumulation by dispossession" (Harvey 2003, 145–52), based on Marx's notion of primitive accumulation, where previously external productive resources are brought into the capitalist sphere of production. This generates "spatiotemporal fixes" (117–20) for excess money capital in response to an overaccumulation crisis, a description of crises distinct from the more classical Marxian explanations that rely on an endogenous tendency for the rate of profit to fall. SIBs, in this framework, can be thought of as a distinct form of privatization, privatizing the management and finance of publicly funded social programs – which is different in kind, if not in motivation, from the full privatization that was more common early in the neoliberal era – that could not be privatized earlier due to their inability to generate their own revenues without ongoing compensation from the state.

Like Harvey, Mirowski (2015) emphasizes the undiminished role of the state, but more heavily underscores its centrality in advancing neoliberal reform.[3] In his eleven tenets of neoliberalism, Mirowski highlights the divergence from classical liberal thought, including the centrality of the idea that neoliberalism must be constructed and advanced as a political project, requiring an alliance of active interests in academia, public policy, and business circles with a strong managerial

---

3 This is in contrast to Kotz (2017b), for example, who in some cases appears to equate neoliberalism with classical laissez-faire liberalism or free market fundamentalism (see 86–7), a premise Mirowski explicitly rejects.

state; and a growing acceptance that political democracy is not integral to the neoliberal project, and in practice might be a barrier. This leads to an element of discord where, in popular discourse, neoliberal rhetoric centres on democracy, freedom, and reduced government, but within the inner circles these ideas are restricted and bound by nuance and qualification. Mirowski also emphasizes the functional nature of inequality in neoliberal thought, as well as the view of markets as information processors that cannot be outdone by central planning, and the belief that markets can in all cases be constructed to resolve the problems apparently generated by markets themselves. In later work, Mirowski makes the explicit link to SIBs as part of a long-term shift by neoliberals from reliance on state finance as the source of market making and innovation. Here, credit-fuelled self-betterment is framed as the ultimate source of deliverance from individualized problems arising from the growing precariousness of workers under neoliberalism (Mirowski 2013, 350–5; see also Cooper et al. 2016). Under SIBs we have similar financialized solutions targeted at fixing supposedly deficient individuals, as opposed to addressing the root systematic causes and social conditions generating these social challenges.

Financialization

The rise of SIBs has been tied by critics to the broader financialization of public services (Lake 2015; Ryan and Young 2018; Whitfield 2015). Financialization can be considered as part of the broader transformation to a "post-industrial society" in advanced economies that has seen the ascendancy of services relative to industrial goods production (Krippner 2011, 2). As with neoliberalism, several, but congruent, definitions of financialization exist among heterodox/political economists. Epstein (2005), working more in the left–post-Keynesian tradition, for example, proposes an inclusive definition of financialization as "the increasing role of financial motives, financial markets, financial actors and financial institutions in the operation of the domestic and international economies" (3), characterized by "significant increases in financial transactions, real interest rates, the profitability of financial firms, and the shares of national income accruing to the holders of financial assets" (4).[4] Kotz (2017b, 33) also adopts this definition, and Levitt (2013, 186–8) proposes a similar one.

---

4 Although it is clear empirically that rising real interest rates have not persisted through the neoliberal era.

Krippner (2005), while acknowledging the multiple characteristics of Epstein's definition, proposes a more parsimonious meaning for financialization: "a pattern of accumulation in which profits accrue primarily through financial channels rather than through trade and commodity production" (181; see also Krippner 2011). Lapavitsas (2013), also working in the Marxian tradition, defines financialization as a "systematic transformation of advanced capitalist economies" (15), where non-financial corporations become increasingly involved in and internalize traditional financial sector functions and activities, diminishing the traditional reliance of the productive sector on bank finance; with banks deriving a greater portion of their profits from financial market transactions and household/consumer lending; and with consumers themselves increasingly using credit to meet their essential consumption needs and financial markets for retirement savings and insurance purposes. In earlier work, Lapavitsas (2012) emphasizes the link between financialization and the growing reliance of the working class on credit to access the means of subsistence as the state has withdrawn. As "social provision has retreated in the fields of housing, pensions, consumption, education," and "access to money increasingly dictates the ability to obtain basic goods," he highlights how workers are increasingly vulnerable and victim to financial expropriation through the expenses associated with accessing credit from strategically positioned lenders. Similarly, dos Santos (2012) demonstrates how these changes, which "pushed wage earners onto financial markets as an integral part of their basic reproduction," (85) have led to entrenched financial expropriation practices in the United States and the United Kingdom and their expansion to other advanced economies.

Although there is some debate regarding primacy, there is a general consensus among CPE analysts about the concurrent ascendance of finance with neoliberalism, at least in the later years. All of the definitions of neoliberalism reviewed above emphasize financialization explicitly or implicitly, at least to some extent. Kotz (2017b, 33–4), for example, highlights financialization as an important feature, but argues that it has, at best, second-order explanatory power, as the rise of finance was due to the financial deregulation spawned by neoliberal reforms, and the sector did not expand its share of profits significantly until the 1990s. Duménil and Lévy's (2005) definition of neoliberalism, on the other hand, assigns central prominence to the resurgence of the financial sector, defining neoliberalism as a product of financialization, and stating that "most, if not all of the Left now agree that neoliberalism is the ideological expression of the reasserted power of finance" (17).[5]

In addition to these Marxian-inspired analysts, the monopoly capital, or *Monthly Review*, school has embedded financialization as a core concept of its depiction of the current stage of capitalism, now referred to in the framework as *finance-monopoly capital* (Foster 2007). In the left/post-Keynesian school, Epstein refers to the era since the mid-1970s as one of "profound transformation ... characterized by the rise of neoliberalism, globalization, and financialization" (3), with post-Keynesian authors more broadly being active in analysing the ascendancy of financialization, drawing upon Keynes's critique of rentiers and emphasizing policy choice as opposed to endogenous crises of the Marxian variety (Lapavitsas 2013, 29–33).

The consensus among critical political economists also extends to the consequences of financialization, particularly in the exemplar of the United States. The increasing size of the financial sector there is evident according to various indicators, including the value of financial assets relative to net worth of the non-financial sector, and the share of finance in gross domestic product (GDP), leading to rising inequality, more intense crises, and tepid accumulation/economic growth in advanced economies.[6] Faced with a relatively stable economy-wide rate of profit over this period of growth, finance has managed to capture an increasingly large share of profits, in addition to a growing share of skilled labour at the expense of the real economy (Kneer 2013). The increasing reliance of the productive sector on internal finance and the ballooning financial liabilities of the household sector relative to GDP have also been dramatic.[7] After exhausting the ability to maintain a targeted,

---

5   Levitt (2013, 186–8), while accepting Kotz's timelines, holds a similar view, elevating "The Great Financialization" (186) as the source of the displacement of the golden era, decoupling capital from national interests and confinement, unleashing capital and crises around the globe, and undermining the discretion of the state while ushering in a host of neoliberal reforms.

6   For a review and discussion of these subsequent indicators of financialization, see Lapavitsas (2013, 205–44).

7   Lapavitsas (2013) argues that, although finance might be predatory, it is not parasitic, as the financial system is an essential component of advanced capitalism. He differentiates between two distinctive sources of financial profits: those arising through expropriation and those arising as a share of surplus value realized (151). Although contradictory forces are at play regarding the value of finance to productive enterprise, he argues that the financial transactions that take place between workers and capitalist firms are "exploitative ... but qualitatively distinct from exploitation in production" (143). Baragar and Chernomas (2012) demonstrate, however, that exploitation through the financial system does effectively raise the rate of exploitation

socially determined standard of living through increases in household labour supply, financialization permitted a significant component of the working class to maintain living standards through increasing debt, despite facing a prolonged period of stagnant or declining real wages since the 1970s (Saltis 2011). The financial crisis simultaneously removed this stop-gap measure of debt-financed consumption, thrust a large mass of workers into unemployment, insolvency, and highly precarious circumstances, and generated a populist backlash against the financial industry and a scramble by political leaders to resolve the crisis and restore legitimacy to the prevailing economic system.

The subsequent rescue of the financial industry with minimal support for the population more broadly was only the most acute example of finance's reliance on the state at the expense of the wider population.[8] This post-crash environment – with finance and the state facing a legitimation crisis, the growing fiscal crisis of government, and socialeconomic inequality becoming an increasingly salient topic of popular discourse – was the one in which SIBs emerged. This appearance of a financialized solution to a crisis of financialization links directly to Mirowski's definition of neoliberalism, but the parallels of SIB securitization with the very instruments that triggered the financial crisis still give one pause. Cooper et al. (2016, 80) draw attention to this in reference to a specific homelessness prevention SIB: "in the same way that individuals, securitized as mortgage holders in mortgage-backed securities, become particular market risks according to their payment and default patterns, homeless individuals' life experiences are now part of a pattern of risk to investors in the SIB scheme." But in the case of SIBs, rather than relying on the implicit guarantee that the state will underwrite risky behaviour, government payment of investors' returns is built directly into the model. SIBs, then, from this perspective, are an evolution of the growth of finance and its heavy reliance on the state, deepening the "vast public subsidy to the financial system characteristic of financialization" (Lapavitsas and Mendieta-Muñoz 2016, 49). At the core, it has been these rescued "urban financial elites who share not only common work experiences but also social and educational backgrounds" (Williams 2018, 6) that have been driving the development of SIBs.

---

as traditionally understood, but the resulting surplus value materializing as profits is not generally to the benefit of the productive capitalists, abstracting away from aggregate demand and credit market effects.

8 See Lapavitsas and Mendieta-Muñoz (2016) for a discussion of state support for the financial sector over the neoliberal era.

SIB Leaders and Followers: A Comparative Analysis

Scholars examining SIBs have often noted neoliberalism, New Public Management, and financialization as important contextual developments for understanding the emergence of SIBs (Berndt and Wirth 2018; Chiapello and Knoll 2020; Cooper et al. 2016; Dowling 2017; Dowling and Harvie 2014; Joy and Shields 2013, 2018, 2020; Sinclair, McHugh, and Roy 2019; Warner 2013; Wiggan 2019). Also key are the Great Recession and subsequent turn to austerity (Fraser et al. 2020; Heinrich and Kabourek 2018; Maier et al. 2018; Roy et al. 2017; Williams 2018). Critical scholars emphasize that it is this context – a result of broader of class struggle – and the centrality of maintaining profitability and resolving endogenous crises that best explain the emergence of privatized and financialized tools such as SIBs. From this perspective, efficiency considerations with respect to social program delivery are secondary. Despite these broader political economic trends, there remains significant diversity when it comes to economic governance and welfare state protections, with various traditions emphasizing a constellation of regimes using different categorical frameworks.

A number of classification frameworks have been developed over time through the examination of the socio-economic policy regimes of the advanced economies. Specifically, in regard to social policy, Titmuss (1974, 30–1) suggests three categories: the "industrial achievement-performance" model, which primarily linked benefits to labour market history and aligns with continental European models; the "residual welfare state model," based on a minimalist approach typical of the United States, for example; and the "institutional-redistributive model," which was more extensive and based on universal social programs, with Scandinavia being the exemplar. Esping-Andersen (1990, 3), building on these categories, classifies welfare states as "conservative, liberal and 'social democratic.'" Liberal regimes rely on lower levels of welfare spending and redistribution, with targeted benefits based on means testing, although over time they have also come to rely on refundable tax credits for low-income workers with labour market earnings (Esping-Andersen and Myles 2011, 646). Conservative and social democratic regimes are characterized by robust social insurance–based welfare state programs and centralized wage setting. Conservative and social democratic welfare states have significantly higher social benefits and worker protections than do liberal regimes, but the characters of these welfare states are historically distinct. Conservative regimes are distinguished primarily by the differentiation of benefit levels based on status hierarchies and reliance on the family unit to provide social care, supported by a household head income earner. Social democratic regimes, for their part, emphasize universalism and the opportunity for women to participate in the workforce. The distinction between the two regimes, however, has diminished in recent decades (Danforth 2014).

Salamon and Anheier (1998) use a similar approach to explain the shape of the non-profit sector in relation to the welfare state, with a 2 x 2 matrix classification of regimes based on social expenditures and size of the non-profit sector, and political economic factors shaping the degree to which they are compliments or substitutes. As with Esping-Andersen, different regimes emerge based on a power resource approach where the historical success of various classes and coalitions in establishing and shaping the modern welfare state persists over time. Here, conservative/corporatist regimes have both high welfare expenditures and large non-profit sectors due to ruling classes that collaborate with religiously founded service providers to mitigate against working-class pressures; social democratic regimes have high social expenditures and small non-profit sectors due to the reliance on pure public delivery arising from working-class governance; and liberal regimes end up with low welfare expenditures due to weak working-class movements, with a large, gap-filling philanthropic sector.

Two other approaches include those of Gordon (1994) and, more recently, Kleinknecht, Kwee, and Budyanto (2016), who emphasize differences in labour-management relations systems and more employer-centred liberal regimes versus European corporatist models, and the varieties-of-capitalism approach (Hall and Soskice 2001, 8), which makes a similar distinction between coordinated and liberal market systems for broader economic governance, highlighting the important mediating factor the needs of employers played in the composition of welfare states (Arts and Gelissen 2010, 574). [9]

Hajer (2020) compares the use of SIBs in the United Kingdom and the United States to that in Germany and France, and, using a governance regime approach, highlights the differences in political

---

9 Chiapello and Knoll (2020) also set out a welfare conventions approach to analyse SIB design. They identify eight welfare conventions – Philanthropy, Communitarian, Civic, Full Employment, Market, Entrepreneurial, Financial, and Behavioral – each with "its own political rationality supported by specific governmental technologies" (107). As opposed to the classification frameworks reviewed above and used in our analysis below, which aim to classify national regimes, the welfare conventions approach can be applied to examine particular welfare instruments, such as SIBs, drawing upon and blending competing conventions while marginalizing others. The relative strength of each convention then is used to help explain the variations in SIB design.

Table 7.2. Country Classification, by Type of Governance Regime

Governance Regime	Countries
Liberal	Australia, Canada, Israel, Ireland, New Zealand, United Kingdom, United States
Conservative	Austria, Belgium, France, Germany, Italy, Japan, South Korea, Netherlands, Portugal, Spain, Switzerland
Social democratic	Denmark, Finland, Norway, Sweden

Note: Population weighting is based on average of population in 2005, 2010, and 2015.

Source: Authors' calculations based on data from OECD (2018).

Table 7.3. Social Impact Bond Projects, Participants, and Investment, by Type of Governance Regime, Weighted by Population

Governance Regime	Bonds	Participants	Investment
		(per million persons)	
Liberal	0.20	264.8	0.77
Conservative	0.06	12.3	0.04
Social Democratic	0.12	173.5	0.53

economic context along various dimensions. He theorizes how these differences have supported the emergence of SIBs in the former two countries while hindering them in the latter two. Below we replicate Hajer's (2020) framework for selected indicators according to regime type. We use the original three categories of Esping-Andersen (1990), which required some discretion on our part, recognizing the diversity of opinion regarding their sufficiency and sustainability over time (for discussion, see Arts and Gelissen 2010, 574). Table 7.2 outlines our classification of countries by type of governance regime, while Table 7.3 presents the averages of a number of indicators used in Hajer (2020), which are drawn to represent a breadth of the noted approaches by regime.

It can be seen that SIBs are much more prominent in liberal governance regimes than elsewhere, in terms of bonds per head of population, participants in SIBs per head of population, and investment in SIBs per head of population. Their prevalence in social democratic regimes ranks second, but well behind liberal regimes on all three measures. Conservative regimes lag well behind in the usage of SIBs.

Table 7.4. Indicators in Hajer (2020) and Links to a Favourable Environment for Social Impact Bonds

Measure	Rationale
Income inequality (Gini)	Countries with high inequality will experience greater pressure to ameliorate associated social challenges, and will have more high net worth individuals with wealth to contribute to SIB projects, whether directly or through foundations.
Worker protections and benefits (active labour market program spending and collective bargaining coverage)	Countries with more precarious labour forces will have a greater need for targeted social interventions. The state will also experience greater cost savings by contracting out to a lower-wage workforce relative to public service delivery.
In-kind versus cash social public expenditure	Countries with higher social public expenditure delivered in-kind will be greater attractors of privatization interests.
Private versus public delivery (outsourcing, size of government, proportion voluntary private of total social public expenditure, and public sector employment)	Countries with a tradition of public delivery will have greater confidence in public sector capabilities and be more sceptical of privatization narratives.
Size of financial sector	More financialized economies will be more prone to financialized solutions that privilege and complement the financial sector.
Intensity of austerity in post-crisis era (deficit and government expenditure reductions)	Countries adopting more aggressive austerity measures since the financial crisis will be more prone to use SIBs.

Table 7.4 outlines the factors that Hajer (2020) advances as explanations for the tendency to adopt SIBs. Income inequality is predicted to be important to explain both the need for social intervention and the availability of private wealth to finance SIBs. Weak worker protections and lower bargaining power lead to a greater need for social intervention and a reduced capacity of labour to resist the contracting out of state activities. It is also predicted that interest in various forms of privatization will be higher in countries with greater financialization and higher post-crisis austerity measures, and higher social public expenditures delivered in-kind, while lower in countries with traditions of public sector service delivery. Table 7.5, showing quite clearly that liberal regimes, which have been the greatest users of the SIB model,

Table 7.5. Classification Indicators by Type of Governance Regime, Weighted by Population

Governance Regime	Inequality	Bargaining Power of Labour			Public versus Private Delivery			Financialization	Austerity Measures		
	Inequality, Gini Coefficient, Average of Various Years, 1985–2013	% of GDP Spent on Active Labour Market Programs, 1985–2013	Workforce Collective Bargaining Coverage, 1985–2016	Social Public Expenditure: In-kind as Proportion of Total, 1995–2015	Outsourcing as % of General Government Procurement 1995–2015	Share of Labour Force Employed in General Government and Public Corporations, Various Years, 2000–13	Voluntary Private Social Expenditure as % of Total Social Expenditure, 2000–15	Finance and Insurance activities as % of GDP, 1995–2015	Deficit as % GDP, 2009–13	Real Government Expenditure Growth, 2010–15	Change in General Government Expenditure as % of GDP, 2010–15
Liberal	0.353	0.78	22.0	48.1	27.5	15.8	30.1	6.8	8.7	-2.1%	-5.0
Conservative	0.305	1.72	63.7	39.0	33.6	*14.9	10.3	4.8	5.1	3.7%	-1.2
Social democratic	0.242	2.93	84.6	43.5	29.7	22.1	7.2	3.6	-1.0	9.1%	0.3

* Result is highly sensitive to the very low government employment levels in Japan and South Korea, with 7.7 per cent and 7.1 per cent, respectively. The average for the conservative grouping without South Korea and Japan is 19.1 per cent.

Source: Authors' calculations based on data from OECD (2018).

are aligned as predicted along most of these indicators.[10] Although this analysis demonstrates only a high congruency among types of governance regime, it is highly suggestive that the political economic context is playing an important role.

Side Note: The United Kingdom and the United States Compared

As highlighted in Hajer (2020), based on almost every measure, the United States is clearly the most neoliberal state, yet SIBs were not founded there but in the United Kingdom. In this note, we discuss why. Although a well-grounded evidentiary explanation would require a more rigorous ethnographic study of the policy-making context of the two national government that eventually initiated the development of SIBs, we sketch a suggestive path here. This contextual rationale is based on the recognition that, for new policy instruments to be implemented, a number of factors must align (Kingdon 2003): a problem must be articulated and recognized; a ready and feasible solution must be available and be conceptually well developed; and these must fit with the government priorities and agenda of the day. The governance culture and institutional specificities of each country then can mediate the specific shape and timing of how broader structural changes materialize in different institutional contexts.

First, the antecedents of the emergence of SIBs in the United Kingdom can be traced back to at least the early 2000s. These were the product of the political economic context and governance approaches of the government of the day, both of which were quite distinct from those of the United States. While both the Tony Blair and George W. Bush administrations pursued domestic neoliberal reforms, the shapes of these reforms were quite different. Bush's neoliberal polices were more conventional, including, for example, tax cuts for the wealthy and an extensive contracting out of military operations. Blair's Third Way neoliberalism, given his political vehicle, necessitated commitment to social justice in some form – and the form this took laid the

---

10 The key exception is procurement as a percentage of government expenditure, where liberal regimes have a lower tendency to outsource on average than do social democratic and conservative ones. This result is highly influenced by the United States' relatively lower rate of contracting out; without the United States, the liberal group is only one percentage point lower on this metric then the conservative group. High contracting out is also not unexpected for conservative regimes: as Salamon and Anheier (1998) note, one of the defining features of the welfare state in conservative regimes is the delegation of social service provision to faith-based non-profits.

groundwork and nurtured the policy infrastructure that would lead to the SIB model. Consistent with neoliberalism more broadly, there was a shift from traditional social democratic collectivism to an othering of the disadvantaged, an emphasis on personal responsibility and self-betterment for welfare recipients, and dismissal of the state's ability to address these issues directly. This was contrasted with the dynamic potential of local and private social economy organizations to deliver poverty-reduction programming and the power of skills training and other localized interventions as the solution to social exclusion (Amin, Cameron, and Hudson 2002, 22–8). The massive expansion of the Private Finance Initiative for public infrastructure projects and related privatization measures (Whitfield 2001, 2007), an emphasis on governance by performance indicators and measurement (Bevan and Hood 2006), and the widespread implementation of pay by results in health care and labour market programming (Finn 2009; United Kingdom 2008) all also contributed to a foundational expertise and mindset that led naturally to SIBs. An emphasis by the New Labour executive on new public administration governance systems to manage, measure, and deliver on political commitments (Barber 2007) likely facilitated the saturation of these ideas into the public service.

Arising from this, the first UK SIB project was eventually developed as a result of a 2007 call from the Labour government for ideas to promote public-private partnerships to address social issues (Eames et al. 2014, 7), and was subsequently advanced by the government's Council on Social Action (Whitfield 2015, 7). Social Finance, the entity that managed the first SIB project and subsequently went on to be the leading proponent of SIBs both in the United Kingdom and globally, was also the product of another New Labour social economy initiative.[11] Before the Labour government was defeated, David Cameron's Conservatives were already positioned with their "big society" vision, based on displacing "big government" through the localization of government service provision and greater reliance on community, volunteer, and non-profit organizations (Cohen 2013; Coote 2011, 1–2). A central

---

11 Social Finance initially focused on the establishment of a social investment fund seeded with the deposits in dormant bank accounts, with several founding members, including the chair, Sir Richard Cohen, having served on the government's Commission on Unclaimed Assets (Warrell 2008). These efforts eventually led to the launch of Big Society Capital, fulfilling an election commitment of the Cameron government, as part of the "big society" vision. Big Society Capital has since become a major investor in SIB projects, in some respects underpinning the SIB market in the United Kingdom (Williams 2018, 7).

campaign plank of the new Conservative government provided a framework for the continued development and expansion of the SIB model, and the Conservatives became reliable champions of SIBs over time, with Cameron even using his presidency of the 2013 G8 meetings to add social investment, including SIBs, to the agenda (United Kingdom 2013).

With the election of Barack Obama, the US executive was faced with satisfying a similar political stakeholder group as New Labour, marking the start of an administration that would be naturally more inclined to SIBs, particularly given the Democratic Party's increasing linkages with the financial sector. While the election was in the midst of the economic crisis, focusing the platform on the significant associated challenges, it did not take long for the Obama administration to embrace the SIB concept known as "Pay for Success." In 2009 it established the Office of Social Innovation and Civic Participation, which went on to become a leading voice and funder of SIB projects in the United States. Therefore, although the institutional and historical specificities of the two countries might have led to the rise of SIBs first in the United Kingdom, we suggest that the structural features of US political economy are even more promising in the long run.[12]

Conclusion

Proponents put forward SIBs as a multi-stakeholder win for governments, service providers, investors, and those in need, emphasizing their utilty as an efficiency-enhancing commissioning innovation. This chapter has put forward an opposing proposition: that SIBs may be replacing conventional delivery models due to their alignment with well-placed private interests and the broader political-economic context. Neoliberalism and financialization have led to a transformation of the state, reliant increasingly on the private sector, including in -social services. The penetration of these trends, however, is not universal, and countries continue to exhibit distinct governance regimes that produce signficant differences in inequality, collective bargaining coverage, social protection, financialization, and austerity. It is the deeply unequal, highly fincialized liberal regimes that are leading the way with SIBs – countries with weak welfare states and labour movements in decline, ill-positioned to counter privatization variants such as SIBs. Each of

---

12 A similar case could be made for public-private partnerships in infrastructure, which also saw significant growth under the Obama administration and was supported by federal policy interventions (Deye 2015).

these dimensions of difference individually align with environments more condusive to SIBs. Collectivelly, the governace regime comparisons raise a broader question as to what fundamentally will best address the interlinked socio-eoncomic ills targeted individually by SIBs. The fact that SIBs are proliferating in countries with weak welfare states sows further doubts regarding their motivations and potential for positive transformative change, and raises the question: are SIBs simply a costly distraction, diverting us from the essential public reinvestment and restructuring required? We pick up this question in Chapter 9.

8 Development Impact Bonds

Introduction

In the previous chapters, we focused our analysis on Social Impact Bonds in developed countries, and our data and discussion were mostly limited to those projects.[1] We defined the typical SIB as a public sector–issued procurement contract that enables the delivery of some preventative social service intervention, and that bundles together design, delivery, and project finance in a single package. The contract payment structure is based on the contractor's achieved outcomes, and private investment is used to finance the project, with investors facing at least some repayment and return risk contingent on the outcomes achieved.

Development Impact Bonds (DIBs) are a form of SIB that deviate slightly from this definition. In DIBs, as in SIBs, private (for-profit or non-profit) investors replace the upfront financing of social services and are repaid, with a premium, if the social service agency that is being funded reaches agreed-upon targets for service outcomes. They differ from SIBs in that it is primarily aid donors or foreign foundations that make repayments to investors and participate in setting performance targets, drawing up contracts, and setting parameters for service agencies – which are usually non-government organizations, but they could also be local private partners. Donors may partner with governments to perform this role, but, unlike in SIBs, the domestic government is not necessarily a central player or even involved. Figure 8.1 outlines the basic structure of a Development Impact Bond.

As with SIBs, DIBs are part of a larger trend towards payment by results in the administration of foreign aid, with large donors such as

---

1 In Chapter 5, however, we presented data on stakeholders that included SIBs and Development Impact Bonds.

Figure 8.1. Typical Development Impact Bond Structure

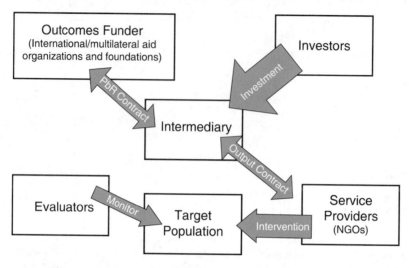

the United States Agency for International Development (USAID), the United Kingdom's Department for International Development (DFID), the United Nations Development Programme (UNDP), the World Bank, and the Canadian International Development Agency (CIDA) each promoting different forms of PbR in the proposed restructuring of their aid programs (Bhushan and Calleja 2015; Centre for Global Development 2015; DFID 2014; UNDP 2019; USAID 2017; World Bank 2011). Results-based aid has risen in recent years, but estimates by Bhushan and Calleja (2015) put it at between US$24 billion and US$47 billion, which amounts to no more than 1.7 per cent to 3.4 per cent of total foreign aid. DIBs represent a very minute portion of this.

DIBs are relatively few in number, and have emerged fairly recently. The first project, an agricultural-based workforce development DIB in Peru, was launched in January 2015. By August 2017 three DIBs had been contracted and were in operation, with a total cost of around US$30 million; one other had been contracted but was not yet in operation). By summer 2018, two more had been contracted, bringing the total cost to around US$44 million.[2] By January 2019, the Social Finance

---

2   Personal correspondence with Izzy Boggild-Jones, 24 January 2018. This total differs from that in the SIB database used in Table 8.1; it might include grants as well as investment costs.

Table 8.1. Development Impact Bonds, by Region, as of January 2019

Region		%	# of Partici-pants	%	Total Investment ($US millions)	%	Participants per Bond	US$ per Bond
Africa	3	38	61,830	6	31.4	82	20,610	10.47
India	3	38	918,000	94	6.8	18	306,000	2.26
South America	2	25	610	0	0.9	2	305	0.43
Total	8	75	979,830	100	38.2	100	122,479	4.77

Source: Social Finance (2018).

SIB database had eight projects listed as active, with nearly one million participants, the vast majority of whom were in two relatively large projects (see Table 8.1 and Appendix F). To date, participants in India have received less intensive or, at least, less costly interventions, while DIBs in Africa have been more intensive and have received the bulk of investment.

As of 2017, there were two dozen DIBs in design, and the expectation is that they will grow in number as aid agencies and recipient countries promote them (Gustafsson-Wright et al. 2017). A distinction has been made between SIBs in developing countries and DIBs, but it is not a clear one. For instance, of the twenty-six DIBs in design listed in Gustafsson-Wright et al. (2017, 76–7), ten are described as Social Impact Bonds. The Colombia Workforce Development project is listed as an SIB, yet it receives funding from both the Inter-American Development Bank and the Swiss State (61). The Brazil Secondary Education project is listed as an SIB, but hopes to receive funding from the Inter-American Development Bank and the International Finance Corporation (87). It is hard to know why these are not consistently classified as DIBs; in some parts of the Brookings document they are, in others they are listed as SIBs or simply as impact bonds. Meanwhile, of the four South African bonds counted in the twenty-six impending DIBs, three are unambiguously SIBs (two in early childhood development, one in workforce development), and have no involvement by foreign donors. A fourth, in HIV prevention and treatment, will receive US$3 million in Catalytic Funding from the Global Fund, but is also listed as an SIB (113).

Of the twenty-eight impact bonds identified as either contracted or in design, eleven (42 per cent) are for projects in the health sector, including the treatment of cataracts, nutritional education for pre-diabetic women, and improved maternity care (Gustafsson-Wright et al. 2017,

16). Employment (six), agriculture (five), and education (four) are the next largest sectors, while there are two DIBs in social welfare. This distribution contrasts with that for SIBs in high-income countries, where employment and social welfare dominate (16). These differences reflect not only differing policy priorities, as Gustafsson-Wright et al. (2017), but also different institutional structures in the two sets of countries.

Impact bonds in developing countries target marginalized or vulnerable groups, especially low-income individuals or families, those living in disadvantaged areas, and especially women and young people. There is a huge range of beneficiary coverage, from as few as 100 pre-diabetic women in the Palestine Type II Diabetes Mellitus (T2DM) DIB (Gustafsson-Wright et al. 2017, 102) to 600,000 mothers in the India (Rajasthan) Maternal and Newborn Health DIB (PSI 2017). The length of impact bond contract ranges from ten months to five years, with an average length of forty-two months and most being in the range of thirty to fifty months (Gustafsson-Wright et al. 2017, 17). They are, therefore, relatively short-term deals, which reduces risk for donors while also reducing funding and program guarantees for service deliverers. Most of the impact bonds implemented or under consideration in developing countries are relatively small by value. Of the three actually implemented by July 2017, one was for $110,000 (sustainable cocoa and coffee, Peru); one for around $400,000 (education for girls, India), and only one was of any size, US$27.6 million for a rehabilitation project of the International Committee of the Red Cross. Of the eleven projects for which there are data, the average up-front capital commitment was only US$2 million, with five impact bonds being under US$1 million, five between US$1 million and US$5 million, and only one over US$5 million (Gustafsson-Wright et al. 2017, 19). Because of their relatively small size and consequent relatively high transaction costs, there are proposals to bundle them together in what are called impact bond outcome funds. Outcome funds have been suggested for India and elsewhere in the fields of education and refugee services (Gustafsson-Wright et al. 2017, 12).

Expanding Enabling Fields

The bundling of impact bonds through the use of outcome funds is an example of an effort to expand the enabling field for DIBs, given their relatively large transaction costs. This recommendation for donors originated in the 2013 Report of the Development Impact Bond Working Group, published by the Centre for Global Development and Social Finance. The report recommended several other ways in which the major actors in DIBs, governments, foundations, aid donors, investors, intermediaries, and service deliverers might encourage their use. Thus, it was argued that investors might establish investment funds for this purpose, governments might make policy room to encourage DIBs, intermediaries might help bring parties together and promote data sharing, while service delivery agencies might be encouraged to develop DIB models and to prepare for results-based contracting.

In 2014, Instiglio, Trustlaw (of the Thomson Reuters Foundation), and the law firm Baker and McKenzie published A Legal Road Map for Social Impact Bonds in Developing Countries (Instiglio and Thomson Reuters Foundation 2014) that examines the legal challenges facing implementation of SIBs in seven essentially middle-income developing countries (Brazil, Chile, Colombia, India, Mauritius, Mexico, and South Africa). Instiglio had been created in 2012 precisely to expand the use of impact bonds: "to design pilot programs that test key aspects of social impact bonds, learn from these programs, and create a development funding model that … ties funding to results, in developing countries" (Instiglio and Thomson Reuters Foundation 2014, 3).

In Canada, the MaRS Centre for Impact Investing, established in 2011, has performed similar functions of promoting impact bonds and payment by results. Together with Social Finance UK, in 2017 it helped design the Cameroon Kangaroo Mother Care (KMC) DIB designed to assist "low birth weight and preterm infants, by funding the scale-up of quality KMC practices in target hospitals across Cameroon" (Gustafsson-Wright et al. 2017, 90).

Case Studies of Development Impact Bonds

Below we present summary descriptions of the first five DIBs to be launched.

Educate Girls DIB in India

The Educate Girls DIB, in Rajasthan, India, targets approximately 15,000 children, 9,000 of whom are girls, in 166 government schools. The object is to enrol out-of-school girls and improve the literacy of both girls and boys in English, Hindi, and math. Rajasthan has a very poor record of education, with low enrolments, high dropout rates, and low-quality achievement, which limits the life chances of both boys and girls, but especially girls.

The DIB was conceived in 2013 when UBS Optimus Foundation, the philanthropic arm of the UBS financial group, agreed to invest upfront capital in Educate Girls, the Indian non-governmental organization implementing the program. Instiglio helped design the DIB as well as a system to track outcomes. The UK Children's Investment Fund, a large charity with offices in London, New Delhi, and Nairobi, is the outcome payer. IDinsight was hired as independent evaluator of enrolments, which account for 20 per cent of outcome payments, and gains in improved achievement in English, Hindi, and math, which account for 80 per cent (Gungadurdoss 2016). IDinsight uses randomized control trials comparing schools with the intervention and those without. The targeted internal rate of return payable to pay UBS Optimus Foundation is 10 per cent per annum and the maximum is 15 per cent, with a single outcome payment between zero and US$412,000.

After two years of operation, the DIB had enrolled 69 per cent of the out-of-school girls identified and met 50 per cent of the target for improved achievement, and this after a delayed commencement of the project (Gustafsson-Wright et al. 2017, 81) and a shaky start in the teaching of mathematics (Gungadurdoss 2016). After year three, however, Educate Girls had enrolled 768 girls between the ages of seven and fourteen in 141 villages in Rajasthan, and offered supplementary learning to 7,318 children at 166 schools. After three years, learning levels in literacy and math were 28 per cent better than those of children who did not have support from Educate Girls. The result was that the UBS Optimus Foundation exceeded its target rate of return, earning a staggering 52 per cent profit, some of which was to be returned to Educate Girls (Mannion 2018).

The Rainforest Foundation and Cocoa in Peru

In 2015 the Rainforest Foundation UK (RFUK) raised US$110,000 for a ten-month DIB to assist 133 Indigenous Asháninka families in the Peruvian Amazon to improve both the quantity and the quality of their premium cocoa for international sale through their Kemito Producer Association, while at the same time reducing leaf rust disease, which was decimating small coffee plots (Gustafsson-Wright et al. 2017, 78–9). The outcome provider for this DIB was the Common Fund for Commodities, an intergovernmental financial institution under the United Nations, which saw it more or less as a pilot project or prototype, while the investor was a California-based private foundation that used the DIB "as an impact investment learning opportunity" (Gustafsson-Wright et al. 2017, 64). The outcome evaluator was KIT, the Royal Tropical Institute of Amsterdam.

This DIB did not carry a rate of return, but repaid the original committed capital according to four metrics: (1) a minimum 20 per cent increase in cocoa supplied to Kemito Ene by the members; (2) a minimum of 20 per cent of members to improve yields to 600 kilograms per hectare or more; (3) a minimum amount of 12 tonnes of cocoa bought and sold by the Association; and (4) a minimum of nineteen producers with 0.5 hectare of newly established coffee plots with leaf rust–resistant varieties (Gustafsson-Wright et al. 2017, 79). Outcome payments would be equal to US$27,500 per metric (US$110,000 in total) if the targets were reached 100 per cent, reducing to US$20,625 if 75 per cent of the target was achieved, US$13,750 if 50 per cent of target was achieved, and no payment if the target was not achieved at all. In the end, a total of US$75,625, or 68.8 per cent of the initial investment, was paid to the investor by the outcome funder, representing 75 per cent of target 1, 0 per cent of target 2, and 100 per cent each of targets 3 and 4 (Gustafsson-Wright et al. 2017, 79).

This project was also delayed in getting off the ground (Gustafsson-Wright et al. 2017, 64), but the expectation is that future scaling up would benefit from this pilot project.

The ICRC Program for Humanitarian Impact Investments

The ICRC Program for Humanitarian Impact Investments is a five-year US$26.7 million DIB that commenced in 2017 and is billed as the first humanitarian investment bond (ICRC 2017a). The money will be used to build and run three new physical rehabilitation centres in conflict and post-conflict countries of Africa – namely, Nigeria, Mali, and the Democratic Republic of Congo. Funding covers the cost of training new staff as well as the testing and implementation of new initiatives designed to improve efficiency. The services will be provided by the International Committee of the Red Cross, the outcome funders are the governments of Belgium, Switzerland, the United Kingdom, and Italy, together with la Caixa Foundation, a Spanish foundation established in 1997 to help eradicate poverty in low-income countries. The ICRC is the largest provider of physical rehabilitation in the world, operating in thirty-four countries, providing physiotherapy services and mobility devices to almost 330,000 people in 2016 (ICRC 2017a). The investors are European institutional investors and high-net-worth individuals, including New Re, part of Munich Re Group, and Bank Lombard Odier, and the outcome evaluator is Philanthropy Advisors. KOIS Invest acts as the structuring intermediary (Gustafsson-Wright et al. 2017, 85; ICRC 2017a).

The outcome metric will be the average efficiency of the new centres compared with that of existing centres, measured by "the number of beneficiaries having (re)gained mobility per local rehabilitation professional at the end of the intervention" (Gustafsson-Wright et al. 2017, 85). Payment will be by results and an annual return is promised, though the amount is as yet unknown, and some of the capital at least will be exposed to risk (ICRC 2017a). The Swiss government sees this as a "proof of concept," opening the door in the longer term to greater private sector participation in humanitarian relief through DIBs (ICRC 2017b).

The Village Enterprise Graduation Model

The Village Enterprise Graduation Model is a US$5.26 million, four-year DIB designed to help very poor families in Kenya and Uganda – those earning less than US$1.90 per day – by providing training and financial support for one family member with the goal of creating self-managed microfinanced enterprises. Village Enterprise is a US-based charity with Christian roots dating back to 1987 that operates on the basis of microfinancing and credit circles. It offers training programs, small amounts of seed money, and mentoring to the very poor. The DIB aims to help in excess of 12,000 families by setting up over 4,000 microenterprises (Village Enterprise 2017a; Gustafsson-Wright et al. 2017, 96).

Village Enterprise is the service deliverer, Global Development Incubator is the intermediary, acting as trustee and holding the outcomes fund, the outcome funders are USAID Development Innovation Ventures (DIV), UKAID (DFID), an anonymous philanthropic fund, the Global Development Incubator, Instiglio, and IDinsight. Upfront funding is provided by unspecified "socially motivated investors" (Village Enterprise 2017b, 7). Performance metrics will be based on increases in household consumption and assets using randomized control trials, but no further details are available.

The Utkrisht Maternal and Newborn Health DIB in India

The Utkrisht – Hindi for "excellence" – Maternal and Newborn Health DIB is a three-and-a-half-year, US$8 million project to raise the quality of 485 private facilities that provide 25 per cent of maternal and newborn health services in Rajasthan. That Indian state has among the highest rates of both maternal mortality and newborn mortality in the world, at 244 maternal deaths per 100,000 births and 47 infant deaths per 1,000 live births – 47 per cent and 14 per cent, respectively, higher than the national average in India (PSI 2017). If successful, this DIB will provide up to 600,000 pregnant women with improved care during delivery, and reduce maternal and newborn deaths by 10,000 over five years.

The service providers are the Hindustan Latex Family Planning Promotion Trust (HLFPPT) and Population Services International (PSI). Palladium acts as the intermediary, design agency and performance manager, while the outcome funders are USAID and Merck for Mothers, a foundation of the pharmaceutical giant, Merck. Of the funding, 80 per cent is provided by the UBS Optimus Foundation and the remainder by the implementation partnership of Palladium, PSI, and HLFPPT. Technical assistance is provided by a number of sources, including Instiglio and Social Finance (Gustafsson-Wright et al. 2017, 92).

The outcome metrics will be based on the extent to which the facilities reach or exceed national quality standards, with a potential maximum payment of US$18,000 per facility (Gustafsson-Wright and Boggild-Jones 2017). Payment details and the extent of guarantees are not available as of writing, but the maximum return is said to be 8 per cent per annum for the USB Optimus component and as much as 15 per cent for the implementation partnership. Independent evaluators had yet to be appointed (Gustafsson-Wright et al. 2017, 92).

Other Observations on Existing DIBs

Each of the first five DIBs draws on experienced and well-established service deliverers, which should bode well for successful outcomes. Each has or plans to have reputable independent evaluators, and each has knowledgeable and experienced intermediaries. Private foundations and socially motivated individuals supply most of the upfront investment money, as opposed to commercially inspired banks or investors. The outcome funders are mainly donor agencies, but private foundations play a role in four of the five.

In the two large DIBs by value, the Utkrisht and ICRC projects, there are multiple investors and multiple outcome funders. This helped facilitate financing the projects at both ends, but it also complicated putting the bids together and raised transaction costs. Inevitably, this lengthened the time between the start of feasibility studies and the start of service delivery: twenty-five months in the case of the Utkrisht DIB and thirty-three months for the ICRC project. Two of the other three DIBs were up and running within fourteen months and the third, the Rainforest Foundation DIB in Peru, was operational within seven months, despite acknowledged delays (Gustafsson-Wright et al. 2017).

It should be noted that, in several DIBs, additional grants or in-kind assistance covered certain aspects of design and/or evaluation, so that the actual cost of the DIB is above the declared cost. Thus, the Rainforest Foundation DIB in Peru obtained upfront grant money for feasibility, design, intermediation, and performance management from an undisclosed source, and legal fees and evaluation costs were financed directly by the outcome funder (Gustafsson-Wright et al. 2017, 79). In the case of the ICRC DIB, the Dutch government covered the design costs, including "ICRC staff costs and advisory support for design and structuring of the PHII" with an upfront grant (Gustafsson-Wright et al. 2017, 84). In the Utkrisht DIB, Merck for Mothers and USAID provided US$1 million for results verification and evaluation, Convergence provided US$0.7 million for design, rapid assessment, structuring, and coordination, while in-kind support was received for design from USAID, Merk for Mothers, UBSOF, Palladium, PSI, and HLFPPT, and for legal fees (Gustafsson-Wright et al. 2017, 93). Finally, in the Kenya and Uganda Graduation Model DIB, a total of US$0.82 million was received in grants to cover DIB design, process evaluation, randomized control trials, project management, reporting and disseminating, and trustee expenses (Gustafsson-Wright et al. 2017, 96). These are significant sums, covering administration and transaction costs, and should be factored into any eventual evaluation of the performance of these DIBs.

In none of the five DIBs was service innovation an obvious feature. All seem to continue established service provisions and several on a larger scale. As in the case of SIBs generally, most innovation appears to have been financial, with greater emphasis on measuring outcomes. Three of the five DIBs concentrate on strengthening private sector activities, be it micro enterprises, private clinics, or farmers.

A Closer Look at the Claimed Rationale of Results-based Aid and Its Challenges

The use of DIBs is justified partly by the argument that private funding increases the incentive to improve aid performance by focusing the attention of policy makers on outputs rather than on inputs. There is also the view that DIBs will bring greater transparency and accountability to government activities and that adaptation and learning will be encouraged by increasing the discretion of service deliverers over spending. DIBs, it is argued, will improve data collection and monitoring systems required for rigorous evaluation of performance (Center for Global Development (2015). These arguments are very similar to those advanced for the use of SIBs. What makes them more salient for DIBs, however, is the growing commitment to payment by results in the aid field and by the actual or threatened tightening up of aid flows in recent years (Food Sustainability Index 2018).

It would be unwise to generalize from the limited experience to date, but it does appear that large, well-established service deliverers are likely to be the main beneficiaries of the growth of DIBs and that the extension of existing services is likely to be more prevalent than innovation in service delivery. Again, this parallels findings with respect to SIBs (see Chapters 3 and 5).

It also cannot be assumed that there will always be outcome funders for proposed DIBs, even when they look promising in terms of delivering results. Thus, one of the first DIB proposals, to address sleeping sickness in Uganda, was scoped originally in 2011, had a successful pilot in 2014–15, and a feasibility study completed in 2015. It was promoted by DFID, which funded the pre-implementation phase and which was anticipating implementation in 2015 (DFID 2014, 14). The project has not progressed since, however, because of a failure to secure outcome funding (Gustafsson-Wright et al. 2017, 116). It is interesting that DFID itself did not offer to act as outcome funder. It goes to show, however, that departures from established ways of proceeding might not be that easy in the foreign aid field, and it might be difficult to divert aid flows in the direction of DIBs.

Otherwise, the cautions about DIBs are very similar to those about SIBs. There is an unstated assumption that political systems are open to increasing incentives to enhance private funding of state activities and/or to promote the provision of services by non-state entities. Outcome measurement of DIBs is critical, and there is the danger of stressing short-run outcomes at the expense of long-run ones, oversimplifying outcome criteria, and opening up performance evaluation to various gaming strategies and possible collusion among the various actors to maximize investor returns. But it is far too early to judge the likelihood, frequency, or severity of these problems, and the aid community is proceeding as if it will not come to characterize DIBs. One further possibility is that, if payment by results comes to characterize foreign aid, through DIBs or other instruments, then the flow of aid itself might become even more unpredictable than it is at the moment.

Are Development Impact Bonds the Future for Foreign Aid?

DIBs promise to reduce the costs and improve the quality of service delivery, which, if it came to be, would reduce the immediate demands of programs on scarce government funding and foreign aid dollars. They would take service delivery increasingly out of government hands and promote the kind of independent services model that Collier outlines in *The Bottom Billion* (Collier 2007, 118–19). Collier envisages this model of service delivery as best suited to situations where government delivery of such vital services as health and education has completely failed. Through this model, donors and governments would flow money using "competing channels of service delivery" that would be evaluated constantly and funded according to performance. Collier insists, however, that he sees these service authorities as an option only in the "worst settings" (Collier 2007, 119). The DIB model specifically and payment by results more generally, however, are being considered in countries where state performance in service delivery is not considered a complete failure.

DIBs to date appear to have relatively high transaction costs that are not always reflected in the investment costs associated with DIBs, with donors and others picking up these costs as extras. The assumption is that, as more DIBs are developed, transaction costs will decline. Given the complexity of the DIBs we have examined, this remains a moot point. Outcome funds and investment funds might be one way of scaling up DIB activity to reduce overall transaction costs, and one could argue that there are scaling elements similar to these in the two large DIBs discussed above, the ICRC and the Village Enterprise projects. But this does not characterize most of the planned DIBs, so small scale and relatively large transaction costs might continue to be a feature of DIBs for some time.

The likelihood is that DIBs will, at best, offer only a limited increase in outside funding, and donors are unlikely to come up with additional funds for them. DIBs might simply recast some existing aid if results prove promising. Successful pilots might offer suggestions for improved service delivery and aid effectiveness, and they will be examined carefully by donors and investors alike. The reality is, however, that the PbR mechanism constitutes a very miniscule proportion of current aid flows, and DIBs constitute a virtually negligible proportion of that. DIBs are likely to favour service deliverers with an established track record and a relatively tried and tested delivery model. They are unlikely to be the focus of innovation and creativity that proponents claim for them. Gungadurdoss (2016) has argued that it might be difficult for many service providers to meet the minimum standards likely to be set by future DIBs, and that "strong incentives combined with lower capacity can easily lead to attempts to game the system, cream-skimming, and even harm to the beneficiaries."

Table 8.2. Foreign Direct Investment, Foreign Aid, Debt Transfers, and Capital Flight, sub-Saharan Africa, 1970–2010

Period	Foreign Direct Investment (FDI)	Official Development Assistance (ODA)	Net Transfers on Debt	Capital Flight	Per cent of FDI + ODA (%)
		(constant US$ billions)			
1970–79	23.3	63.3	81.3	116.9	134.9
1980–89	18.7	132.6	62.1	205.4	135.8
1990–99	53.7	181.1	−20.1	138.4	59.0
2000–10	210.7	282.5	5.4	353.5	71.7
1970–2010	306.4	659.5	128.6	814.2	84.3
of which: oil-exporting countries (% of total)	165.1% (53.9%)	206.1% (31.2%)	12.1% (9.4%)	590.7% (72.5%)	172.9

Source: Boyce and Ndikumana (2012)

Development Impact Bonds and the Need for Foreign Aid

While donors concentrate on ways of improving the performance of aid, there is a more fundamental question of the need for foreign aid. Boyce and Ndikumana (2012) estimate that massive amounts of capital are fleeing countries in sub-Saharan Africa – well in excess of aid inflows or foreign direct investment, and in many years in excess of both (see Table 8.2). The cumulated capital flight has been much greater than debt flows. Capital outflows are particularly large in oil-producing countries, but are also very large in poorer countries that rely more heavily on foreign aid.

The findings of Boyce and Ndikumana have been echoed by research at the UNDP on illicit capital flows from the least developed countries (LDCs), most of which are in sub-Saharan Africa (UNDP 2011). They show that, between 1990 and 2008, for every US dollar the LDCs received in foreign aid (overseas development assistance, or ODA), fully 60 cents left the LDCs in illicit capital flows, with many countries having ratios well in excess of that. Thus, Equatorial Guinea lost $16.70 for every $1 of ODA, Angola $5.60, Myanmar $4.70, and Chad $2.90 for every dollar of aid received (UNDP 2011, 11).

In US dollars, the UNDP estimates conservatively that illicit flows have increased from $7.9 billion in 1990 to $20.2 billion in 2008 (UNDP 2011, 10). Cumulatively, the top ten exporters of illicit capital during the period were Bangladesh (cumulative outflow $34.8 billion), Angola ($34.0 billion), Lesotho ($16.8 billion), Chad ($15.4 billion), Yemen ($12.0 billion), Nepal ($9.1 billion), Uganda ($8.8 billion), Myanmar ($8.5 billion), Ethiopia ($8.4 billion), Zambia ($6.8 billion), and Sudan ($6.7 billion) (UNDP 2011, 12). All of these are significant recipients of foreign aid, and Uganda is the recipient of DIB attention.

It would seem, then, that the international donor community has much larger issues to face than improving the performance of foreign aid through the adoption of pay by results and Development Impact Bonds. Indeed, the challenges DIBs aim to address seem trivial in comparison to the challenge of dealing with illicit capital flows from developing countries.

9 Policy Recommendations, Reforms, and Alternatives

Introduction

This chapter concludes our book examining Social Impact Bonds as a new model for delivering social public programs. Our goal was to explain and describe the development and theoretical motivations of SIBs, to provide a solid foundation for future study of their effectiveness in practice over the short period of their existence. We also examined the relatively few Development Impact Bonds, and highlighted the challenges they face, which have many parallels with those facing SIBs, while others are specific to the international development context.

We begin this final chapter by reviewing our policy recommendations for structuring SIB projects, which we believe would help the SIB model realize some of its claimed potential. In the following two sections, we then take a step back and briefly examine the implications and potential of the SIB model in contrast to a more traditional social democratic approach to poverty reduction and social inclusion. We present what we call the micro alternative to SIBs: a reinvestment in the capacity of the state to be an entrepreneurial leader in generating social programs that better meet the needs of the disadvantaged and of society more generally. We then look at how SIBs are a continuation of the neoliberal trend away from universalism towards the targeting of social benefits, with negative implications for meaningful and widespread progress on social exclusion and inequality. Here, we review the framing effects of SIBs, and demonstrate how a focus on individualized responses, from a macroperspective, could marginalize large-scale collective approaches and societal changes to address systematic inequity and the recognition that poverty, disadvantage, and inequality are structural features of capitalism, which, if left unchecked, will grow in breadth and intensity.

Recap of Policy Recommendations

Our main finding is that the proponents' case for SIBs, while rhetorically strong, faces some fundamental weaknesses when systematically examined. As we summarized in Chapter 6, SIBs have built-in incremental costs relative to conventional publicly funded service delivery, and face significant inherent challenges in generating efficiencies sufficient to overcome these costs. At best, as currently structured, SIBs might claim to be better than a hypothetical, dysfunctional status quo. But even in here, the government leadership and structural reforms required to make SIBs happen suggest that this effort could be better spent on more straightforward improvements, without the added complexity and risks entailed in the SIB model. Overall, as currently operating, SIBs appear to be a pricy experiment in a context of restraint that is not generating much, if any, innovation, while further marginalizing the voices and status of vulnerable service users.

Despite our generally pessimistic central message, we note that SIBs have been successful in focusing attention and interest on evidence-based social program investment. This a welcome contrast to the inattention and regressive attitudes typical of the early neoliberal era. There is wide variation in how SIBs are being structured, and we believe these details are important in determining whether SIBs can be part of a constructive set of solutions to growing inequality and social exclusion, or an exacerbation of neoliberal reforms to social service delivery that only reinforce these ills.

Selecting the Procurement Model, and an Appropriate Counterfactual

Following the UK auditor general's (Morse 2015, 6–8, 33) recommendations on pay by results more broadly, we suggest that all SIBs would benefit from an explicit assessment of the model in the targeted program or policy area relative to conventional procurement or public delivery, and that it should be stated explicitly how value for money in these comparisons is to be measured. The relevant auditors general could implement and coordinate standardized reporting practices between departments and governments. These frameworks should account for the resources required within and outside government to develop and operate the SIB infrastructure needed to administer the project, track, and evaluate outcomes, and improve project management capacity.

On a related but distinct note, many SIBs rely on the use of existing publicly funded services or limited private sector opportunities without clearly accounting for the fact that use of these resources likely precludes their use by others. For example, some child welfare family preservation, homeless amelioration, and anti-recidivism SIBs rely on placing clients in existing social housing supports; other SIBs rely on existing apprenticeship/training opportunities and public health services. When generating the counterfactual for the evaluation of outcomes, the use of these existing services should be accounted for – specifically, whether access to the underlying public service or incremental SIB-specific supports is generating the outcomes, and if the SIB client's use of the service displaces use by another potential client. Given the preferential status given to SIB programming and investors, more focus should be placed on this attribution.

Since SIBs face higher transaction and administrative costs, governments should be explicit in identifying the full cost of each project and how the SIB model itself will generate the targeted outcomes more efficiently than alternative models. The appropriate counterfactual here would not be the status quo, but an equally resourced conventional model. One noted advantage of SIBs is that they help to overcome the underresourcing of management and evaluation capacity in service delivery organizations since resources for these activities are built into the model (Liebman and Feller 2014). A useful counterfactual for future research would be to fund conventional providers directly, with incremental resources for enhanced project management and administration equivalent to those made available through the SIB model to pay out investor returns and cover higher transaction costs (Whitfield 2015, 34).

Selecting the Outcome Target

A fundamental problem with pay by results is that objectives are multifaceted and challenging to measure, necessitating reliance on incomplete outcome measures. High-powered, incentive-based payment can distort service providers' behaviour in this context and compromise overall service quality by incentivizing the redirecting of effort from hard-to-measure, poorly monitored outcomes to ones more easily measured. Funding reforms based on PbR also can be interpreted as questioning the abilities and integrity of service providers, and might lead to the displacement of intrinsically motivated efforts and commitments to service quality. To improve the likelihood that SIBs lead to improvements, as opposed to declines, in service quality, we recommend that governments work with non-profit funders and service providers, including front-line staff, to set targets collaboratively with investors and the intermediary and to build program metrics that reflect clients' well-being, not just savings to government. This in all likelihood would see indicators diverge from those tied directly to cashable fiscal savings for government, and result in more elaborate compensation outcomes structures, but these would likely reduce the risk faced by investors, and thereby reduce the rates of return that would be otherwise required to secure investment. This participatory methodology should be applied to the broader program structure in addition to metrics, with the opportunity to adapt and innovate in response to program developments.

Selecting Investors, Rates of Return, and Proactive Disclosure

As part of the broader procurement selection process and to reduce the potential for excessive or inappropriately high rates of return and displacement of intrinsic and/or philanthropic efforts, we recommend SIBs institute a transparent investor selection process that evaluates and justifies the value added of investors to the project based on the nature of the organization providing funds, and that specifies any restrictions around the use of outcome payments. Our analysis shows that SIBs can provide meaningful improvements in social program efficiency only if financiers provide value added over and above the costs they add to the project. If investors are compensated above government borrowing rates, they should be required to generate efficiencies through project management and selection improvements that more than offset the differential between the expected rate of return and government borrowing rates if they are to provide value for money.

Since the construction of such an estimate might be challenging, some simple rules could be implemented to act as safeguards, such as restricting rates of return to or below the cost of government borrowing. This would help reassure that government is not transferring rents in the form of interest payments to private sector investors, but is attracting investors motivated primarily by corporate social responsibility concerns. It would also reassure non-profit stakeholders that the SIB is not diverting funds from social service delivery. Alternatively, governments could limit investors to non-profit investors with well-regarded reputations for social and fiduciary responsibility, based on a track record of supporting high-performing social service delivery, or government could require investors to commit explicitly that any returns will be reinvested in social service projects. The latter could require the establishment of an independent non-profit organization to receive and reallocate outcomes payments. Some SIB proponents' narratives implicitly suggest that private, for-profit investors should be adequately compensated for risk, and should receive a market rate of return on their investments in SIBs. We see no justification for this logic, given the philanthropic attributes and corporate social responsibility benefits associated with financial involvement in these projects.

We also recommend a standardized and transparent process for proactive public disclosure around SIB project outcomes, specifically including returns paid to investors in addition to outcomes for project participants. This would assist in determining whether public funds paid out as outcome payments are providing value for money relative to more conventional social service models, and whether the interest rates paid out to investors, apparently well above the cost of conventional public borrowing, are justified.

Pursuing "Common Sense" Improvements Independent of SIBs

The most promising attributes of the SIB model, in our opinion, are, first, the built-in central coordination within government to break down siloed decision making between departments in order to determine the net impact of a social service intervention, and in turn funding initiatives that are expected to produce a social return and potentially a financial return to government; and, second, the related incremental resources for research, evaluation, and performance management within service delivery agencies. As we saw in Chapter 1, the potential gains from this approach appear substantial, and example structures such as the Washington State Institute for Public Policy provide a template for a systematic approach to inform this type of process. This could be pursued independently of SIB development, realizing the core value of what is central to the SIB model and the underlying source of returns paid to investors. This forms the basis of our 'micro-alternative" explored below.

The Micro Alternative: Conventional Delivery through (Re)building State Capacity

Despite the potential for more positive variants, more generally we are pessimistic about the ability of SIBs to generate meaningful reductions in inequality and social exclusion. SIBs fit clearly into a logic of neoliberalism and financialization that has resulted in a reformulation of the state and reduced its capacity to intervene effectively to support equitable development. Public sector reforms based on neoliberal ideas and New Public Management have systematically reduced this capacity through contracting out, privatization, and a shift away from seeing government as a provider of service to seeing it as a procurer of service. This has generated an increasing role for the private sector in the delivery of public services, particularly in the United Kingdom, the United States, and other countries that are leading in SIB implementation. At its core, contracting out, whether to the for-profit or the non-profit sector, is fundamentally based on cost cutting, and undermines the logic and advantage of decommodified universal public delivery (Zullo 2019). SIBs further the transfer of responsibility and activity from the public to the private sector, undermining the clear advantages of public delivery. We suggest that the fundamental social problems motivating SIBs arise from precisely these trends, and that, in fact, the reverse is what is required.

The non-profit sector has both advantages and limitations when it comes to delivering public services. Its targeted specificity, flexibility, and adaptiveness, and ability to leverage voluntary contributions can lead to innovative, locally adapted service provision. While acknowledging these advantages, the weaknesses of the non-profit and charitable sectors have also been emphasized, with the emergence of the modern welfare state as a response to inherent limitations of the non-profit sector (Salamon 1987, 38–42). These limitations include resource constraints, small-scale operations of limited scope, the sector's uncoordinated and overlapping nature, and the lack of accountability and professionalization. The nature of civil service employment and capacities in many respects offers a solution to these challenges: a high degree of professionalization with the associated job ladders, career longevity, and accumulation of institutionalized knowledge and expertise; built-in formal structures of knowledge exchange through interjurisdictional associations; and a capacity to engage meaningfully with academics and other researchers over longer periods.

A focus on better contracts, on a foundation of the presumed superiority of private delivery, faces significant uphill challenges in resolving principal-agent problems, which are different in kind from those of public service delivery. Zullo (2019) captures this point by highlighting the fundamental discord between contracting out to the private sector and public service delivery: private markets are based on the principle of exclusion, with profits based on aligning products to markets as determined by their respective profitability, and the focus of the profit-maximizing contractor becomes the setting of bounds of service access and/or responsibility in order to minimize costs and maximize profits. Public services in the policy areas in which SIBs operate arise from a fundamentally different set of motivations: a political process, based on "a mandate toward inclusion [that] imposes a burden to accommodate any disadvantaged constituent" (Zullo 2019, 115), a characteristic that intensifies with genuine and broader democratic participation and engagement. The inclusive nature of public services themselves also then lead to unique production characteristics, including multidimensional, flexible, and responsive roles for workers in often unanticipated circumstances, where PbR-type structures actually would detract from high-quality service delivery. The complexity of the social problems at which many SIBs are aimed is simply too great to be addressed by simple PbR-based outcomes management. Rather, these problems require transformative social interventions that succeed best within a relational, personalized, and adaptive framework (Sinclair, McHugh, and Roy 2019).

Zullo (2019) highlights how, even with a non-profit provider, the financial vulnerability of the enterprise will lead to cost-minimizing and exclusionary behaviour, or will require forging the cost savings that underlie the justification for contracting out in the first place and engaging in open-ended relational contracting. Universalism, on the other hand, and the associated production techniques in themselves provide a solution to principal-agent problems by dissolving them in the first place through public employment, based on compressed pay scales, delegation of authority, and so on.

There is much to be said, then, for the unique position and ability of government to engage in constructive intervention in the economy to address social issues directly (Chang 2003, 51–63; Musgrave 1999, 34–6), but there is evidence that this capacity, particularly in liberal advanced economies – which have been leading the development of SIBs – has been systematically eroded. For example, Light (2016), in his examination of the US federal government, reviews the increasing number of "government breakdowns" and highlights how "government was not always so vulnerable" (1). He stresses the shift from the effective governance of the post-war era to the subsequent "disinvestment in government's capacity" (5) by the US Congress over time. This has led to previous successes in policy and program areas including anti-discrimination, voting rights, public health, and access to social services increasingly and intentionally being undermined and put at risk. He concludes that most of the breakdowns identified "were the predictable consequence of decisions made by Congress and the president," some of which were "carefully designed through backdoor budget cuts, hiring freezes, sequesters, duplication and overlap, and a host of administrative ills" (18).

Rhodes (1994) points to a similar disinvestment strategy in the United Kingdom that he terms the "hollowing out" of the state through civil service reductions, privatizations, contracting out, increased "managerial control reduc[ing] civil service discretion," (145) and "fragmentation" (147) that has damaged both the administrative capacity and effectiveness of the civil service. While recapping the negative consequences of such hollowing out, Pyper (2011) points to the emergence of a new generation of privatized management and policy consultants, often partisan in nature (see also O'Toole 2006). Reforms under Conservative governments saw reductions in the civil service, excluding the privatization of almost 30 per cent of Crown corporations between 1988 and 1994 (Clayton and Pontusson 1998, 82), while later austerity measures generated a new wave of reductions, with civil service numbers falling by 19 per cent between 2010 and 2017 (Freeguard, Adam, Andrews, and Boon 2017). Based on their interviews with a variety of public servants, Toynbee and Walker (2017, 9) speak of a "dismembered" government, where the "social state ... [is] threadbare, ... and other functions are dilapidated." Even within social democratic states, public sector employment reductions were significant. Sweden, for example, saw reductions in the early 1990s in the range of 12 per cent, with employment in health-related occupations falling by 7 per cent, in care services for the vulnerable by 10 per cent, and in education by 4 per cent. Large overall reductions also occurred in Australia, Belgium, Finland, and the Netherlands in the range of 2.5 to 9.9 per cent (Clayton and Pontusson 1998).

By contracting out strategic coordination, vision setting, and management, SIBs contract out the functions governments theoretically have a comparative advantage in delivering, further diminishing their capacity. There is growing acknowledgement that government needs to take leadership and build capacity in strategic planning – particularly the capacity to undertake structural change to support civil service delivery (see Barber 2007, 2014). These capabilities rely on traditional planning and Weberian bureaucratic benefits that have advantages over market-based processes – an approach that will be required if the high levels of economic inequalities generated by neoliberalism are to be reversed. Although the non-profit sector has increased its capacity throughout this era and has some advantages, in an age of austerity it is equally under pressure and continues to lack resources necessary to compensate for state retrenchment. Emphasis on further hollowing out through instruments such as SIBs comes at a cost. We suggest that efforts should focus on rebuilding the capacity of government to act as a strategic planner, coordinator, and active agent of social service delivery.

The Macro Alternative: Universalism versus Individualized Approaches

In addition to undermining state bureaucratic capacity, neoliberal retrenchment also resulted in undermining state provision of universal social programs and benefits and scaling back social insurance and assistance systems. Here, we propose that this is a driving factor of the growing social challenges SIBs aim to address; that rebuilding these programs is a more sensible approach to making progress on combatting these ills; and that SIBs are not aligned with this approach.

Over the twentieth century, significant welfare states were built up in many of the advanced western market economies. Universal health, education, pension, family benefits, and other social programs and collectivist solutions were developed and expanded in the post-war era, in a clear response to political pressure by workers' movements and the failure of capitalism to generate shared prosperity and development. Although there is significant variation in extent, this general trend towards development of universal social programs was present in both more liberal countries such as Canada and the United Kingdom and more paradigmatic, social democratic Nordic countries, including Sweden and Denmark (Béland, Blomqvist, Andersen, Palme, and Waddan 2014).

In the United Kingdom, for example, while early twentieth-century social welfare programming saw incremental growth through the launch and development of contribution-based social insurance programs for workers and the unemployed, the Second World War and the subsequent Beveridge report ushered in a leap to universalism. In the immediate post-war period, legislative initiatives generated a number of universal social programs that were available at no cost or without eligibility exclusions, including public health care through the National Health Service, access to primary and secondary education, and a cash family benefit (Barr 2004, 30–2). Building on previous systems, a more robust and compulsory social insurance system, paid for by joint employer-employee contributions, was also instituted to provide income support benefits in cases such as unemployment, maternity leave, illness, and retirement. The social insurance system, initially funded by a flat-rate contribution, was later based on earnings, and became redistributive both in its financing and distribution. A parallel system for means-tested benefits was also developed for those not sufficiently supported through the social insurance system. All of these programs saw growth and maturation over the three decades after the war (Barr 2004, 33–5).

Even in the United States, where commitment to state provision and universalism historically has been weak, the post-war expansion of public social programs era was significant, with the implementation of Medicare/Medicaid, Social Security, and expanded access to post-secondary education through measures such as the GI Bill and growing state public education systems. There were significant enhancements in the post-war period to the Social Security system's insurance-based benefits, launched in the 1930s, "to the point where, together with related programs, virtually all workers and their families were covered" (Barr 2004, 35), with benefit levels also becoming more generous and progressive. Although means-tested assistance programs under Social Security did not embrace universalism or expand to the degree they did in the United Kingdom, some expansion did occur, such as allowing for payments under the Aid to Dependent Children program where the father was unemployed, as opposed to absent or disabled.[1] In both the United Kingdom and the United States, then, there was a movement over the twentieth century away from stigmatization of benefit recipients and the need to demonstrate impoverishment to get access to support. Fundamentally underlying these social benefit programs during this period was a commitment to full employment as "the primary method of income support" (Barr 2004, 37), a measure included in broader definitions of the welfare state (Esping-Andersen 1990). This commitment, along with the associated high rates of labour force participation it can generate, led to the potential of establishing a quasi-universalist system of social benefits while having many programs still tied to employment, as was the case in Sweden in the 1970s and 1980s (Clayton and Pontusson 1998, 77).

The commitment to universalism was considered by some as a positive development for efficiency, social equality, and sustainability. As Sen (1992) recaps, targeting in social programs has many shortcomings, including the exclusion of the eligible due to informational challenges, the encouragement of perverse and unproductive behaviour to qualify, increased administrative costs, postponements in accessing service, intrusiveness, and stigmatization of the poor.[2] Also, as Sen

---

1 For further discussion of the history of the UK welfare state and, to a lesser extent, that of the US welfare state, see Barr (2004, 16–41).

2 Sen suggests that some targeting is inevitable in all social provision due to decisions about where to offer service and what particular social services to offer. He suggests that "capability-orientated" (19) targets, rather than income-targeted programs, are better at avoiding abuse, such as benefits based on disability and health status, for example. He notes that certain social services have strong self-selection attributes

notes, the political economy of social programs leads to a systematic trend of defunding, low quality, and insufficiency of targeted programming, while universal programming, due to broad-based consumption and resulting social solidarity, is more politically sustainable, effective, and robust. While neoliberal proponents rely on the case that targeting will lead to greater benefits to those who need them the most, others have argued that the opposite is true once the political factors around government budgetary allocation are considered (see also Gelbach and Pritchett 2002; Kidd 2015). This *paradox of redistribution* – that universalism will lead to greater redistribution relative to targeted programs due to greater political support and larger budgets for social programs – although challenged over time, continues to be empirically supported (Korpi and Palme 1998; Jacques and Noël 2018).

Since the late 1970s, increasing universalism through collectivist approaches has been halted for the most part and put on the defensive in many countries (Gilbert 2017; van Orschot 2002). Increased means testing and the introduction of private provision accessed primarily by the wealthy has created parallel private systems in some cases, with universalism in retrenchment in some policy areas (Béland et al. 2014). This, combined with the abandonment of full employment commitments, increasingly hostile environments for unions, and other neoliberal policy reforms, has led to growing income inequality and precariousness of work. Although the welfare state framework and program eligibility primarily endured in the face of ambitious regressive attempts at reform (Pierson 1994, 1996), the changing nature of work amplified the impact of successful scale-backs (Clayton and Pontusson 1998; Korpi and Palme 2003; Starke 2006). This materialized as significant reductions in benefit levels in many countries – for example, the income-replacement rates provided by social insurance in cases of unemployment or sickness (Pintelon 2012) – even though social public expenditures trended upward over time.

In the United Kingdom, the reforms initiated by the Thatcher government resulted in significant restrictions in eligibility and reduction in value of unemployment benefits, a retrenchment of social housing support, and reductions in the value of child benefits (Clayton and Pontusson 1998). Under a later Conservative government, McKee and Stuckler (2011, 2) describe "progressive exclusion of the middle classes

---

that mitigate abuse, such that those using the service must consume it directly and generally only if needed and well suited to receive it, such as health care, literacy, and employment-of-last-resort programs.

from the welfare state, through incremental erosion of universal benefits" in areas such as child benefits and post-secondary education.

In the United States, early in his tenure President Reagan instituted significant cuts to unemployment benefits and the Aid to Dependent Children program.[3] The 1990s, under the Clinton administration, saw significant reductions in and eligibility restrictions to the food stamp program, and a similarly aimed overhaul of the Aid to Dependent Children program with the introduction of funding caps, work requirements, and limits on years of eligibility (Clayton and Pontusson 1998). Countries with relatively larger welfare states saw similar reforms, with aggressive reductions in unemployment and social assistance benefits, and more tempered reductions in pension benefits. Sweden, the exemplar of social democracy, saw a similar trend, but with retrenchment more widely spread among the population, given the more universal nature of the country's social programs. Changes included the introduction of waiting periods for unemployment benefits, user fees in health care, and a downloading of sick leave benefits to employers (Clayton and Pontusson 1998). This was reflective of a broader trend of recommodification in the Nordic (and Western English-speaking) countries, while continental Europe remained relatively stable, at least with respect to social insurance programs (Pintelon 2012). In general, then, there was a sustained restructuring trend away from universalism towards social insurance, and from social insurance to means testing (Clayton and Pontusson 1998, 90–1).

Support for the disadvantaged has become increasingly targeted and individualized. In addition, economists and governments have focused more on "human capital" and individualized approaches that aim to "fix" people – framing poverty and disadvantage as individual failings as opposed to natural systematic outcomes of capitalist economies. A key example of this is in the area of income support benefits and the greater emphasis on labour market activation – that is, moving unemployed workers into jobs through individual-level programming and work-seeking obligations (Bonvin 2008; van Berkel 2009). In economics – particularly in the field of international development – there has been a turn towards randomized control trials and the application of "nudge" interventions aimed at tweaking or influencing individual behaviour among the poor to help them make better decisions about

---

3 There were some partially offsetting benefit increases later during Reagan's presidency through food stamps and the introduction of an earned income tax credit (Pierson 1996, 164–5), although these were limited, and the latter assisted only those with some employment earnings.

time allocation, investment in education, and so on. The underlying assumption of this approach, exemplified by the work of Banerjee and Duflo (2007, 2011), is that, although market failures such as a lack of access to credit or information play a role, the poor exhibit significant discretion with respect to how they allocate their resources and apparently make bad choices that lead to continuing impoverishment, and that small changes can lead to big differences "without changing the existing social and political structure" (Banerjee and Duflo 2011, 271).

This focus on small changes in individual behaviour at the expense of a broader discussion regarding about appropriate policy regimes and economic structures has been identified as problematic by Reddy (2012) from at least two perspectives. First, the macro-institutional context, including the political, historical, and economic, acts as a mediating and intervening force on micro interventions. This leads to impacts varying between contexts, bringing into question the validity of the approach and the presumption that scaling up the intervention will generate similar results in different jurisdictions. Second, and as Chernomas and Hudson (2017, 33–6) also emphasize, this approach sidelines structural reforms to economic and social policies and institutions, and the associated "impact of political dynamics and processes of social change" (Reddy 2012, 62). As Reddy (2012, 65) notes it is in fact this political and socio-economic context that generates the "causal relations." that are being tested in the first place.

Part of the shift towards targeted interventionism as opposed to universalism has been linked to the shifting political alliances that have more generally sustained support for the welfare state and social democracy, albeit in its third-way form. Gingrich and Häusermann (2015), for example, highlight the "pro-welfare" political coalition that emerged with the shift from industrial to post-industrial society and the reduced reliance on the "manual working class" (51), while drawing on new, higher-skilled, better-educated middle-class "interpersonal service workers" (53), many of whose jobs have resulted from an expanded welfare state. The growing importance of cultural issues at the expense of economic issues also led to a partial shift of the political support of the traditional, low-skilled working class. These shifts simultaneously led to a partial diffusion of support for the welfare state among political parties, with conservatives weakening their opposition to social insurance schemes, while social democratic parties adapted to their new supporting coalition by shifting away from universalist income replacement programs towards targeted programs and a focus on "social investment" (51) in health, education, and labour market activation. Gingrich and Häusermann (2015), however, highlight how these results are shaped by welfare regimes, and how welfare state stabilization through conservative support for social insurance has not been observed in liberal market economies.

SIBs continue this trend, leaving the origins of social ills unaddressed and "prioritizing individual-level measures over systemic ones" (Maier and Meyer 2017, 4; see also Joy and Shields 2018). This trend cuts across policy intervention areas, with resources often provided to connect participants with existing socially provided or subsidized programs and services, including housing, apprenticeship and work placements, and health services. SIB projects are adding incremental capacity to connect a small number of individuals to these services, as well as new coaching and psycho-social interventions such as cognitive behavioural therapy, to cope with and help manage the damage stemming from social disadvantage. Development Impact Bonds share the motivations of SIBs and suffer from many of that model's shortcomings. They reflect a desire by aid agencies to build pay by results into their activities as neoliberal policies of donors shrink or constrain aid budgets, and to replace governments that other actors see as inefficient. DIBs deflect from much more serious considerations that should be applied to foreign aid, such as the need for it within global exploitative relationships. Like SIBs, they also raise issues about targeted interventionism by donors and governments versus the provision of more universal programs.

More fundamentally, as Whitfield (2015) highlights, the root challenges, including "lack of jobs, low income, financial exploitation, overcrowded and poor living conditions, crime and violence, environmental hazards and ill health" (4) are not being addressed (see also Dowling 2017, 305; Joy and Shields 2018). He points, for example, to the preponderance of workforce development SIBs that focus on supply-side training and job placement measures, which neither create incremental jobs nor address systematic discrimination in labour markets. A similar critique could be levied against anti-recidivism SIBs, many of which are based on employment-related supports. Parallels exist in all other service areas targeted by SIBs: child welfare SIBs are not addressing the poverty, discrimination, and lack of or precarious employment faced by at-risk families that lead to family instability; health IBs do not address the social determinants of health and underlying environmental factors that lead to illness to begin with; and environmental SIB projects create flood mitigation infrastructure in response to climate change, which remains unaffected. While prevention is built into the language and mantra of SIBs, it is more often a diversionary approach for a small, select population, leaving the broader social hazards unaddressed and to impinge on other victims, while marginalizing the voices of vulnerable populations and their allies. In sum, SIBs reinforce an individualized and undemocratic approach, continuing the stigmatization and disempowerment that are part of neoliberalism and undermining collectivist and democratic approaches, such as universalism and broader commitments to full employment, that would help address the underlying sources of disadvantage.

The current socio-economic instability and the emergence of nationalist and populist movements based on insider-outsider politics have been linked by several heterodox economists to the evolution of neoliberalism and the associated growing insecurity and precariousness of a large portion of the working class, the dismantling of social safety nets, expired commitments to full employment, and an end to the normality of reliable full-time employment (Duroy 2014; Kotz 2017a; Standing 2012). Growing economic inequality and prejudice can be self-reinforcing, but countermeasures equally can generate synergies (Haight 2013). The reconstruction and renewal of a universalist welfare state approach, based on historical evidence, would be a better way to address the underlying root causes of growing inequality, precariousness, and social exclusion. The scale and urgency of addressing this growing inequality rooted in neoliberalism cannot reasonably rest on targeted residual social programs that feed the divisive othering and individualization of poverty and disadvantage. The contradictions inherent in SIBs suggest that this model cannot reach the scale or generate the structural institutional shifts required for meaningful and sustainable change. Rebuilding the broader welfare state based on notions of collectivism and the institutional supports required to implement and sustain such structural change is a more advisable approach to addressing these challenges meaningfully.

Conclusion

Our analysis challenges the broader assumptions behind the Social Impact Bond model and the solutions that are required. Proponents of SIBs argue that the socio-economic challenges we currently confront require "all hands on deck" – that the resources, diversity, innovation, and financing of the private sector are needed to address these growing challenges. There is some rationale in this claim. Targeted social service support is necessary for those who are acutely disadvantaged and require personalized assistance to overcome the multifaceted and integrated barriers associated with long-term impoverishment. SIBs, when reformed within the parameters we suggest, might have a limited role in helping the diffusion of targeted best practices in areas that currently attract significant philanthropic support, with governments playing a role in helping leverage and coordinate this investment more efficiently.

As portrayed by proponents, however, SIBs misframe what the private sector is capable of and well placed to deliver, as well as the broader socio-economic challenges society faces. SIBs divest governments of the coordination, planning, and dissemination responsibilities in social service delivery that they are structurally well positioned to deliver. SIBs face inherent costs, and have a weak *a priori* foundation for claims that they will generate sufficient improvements to overcome these disadvantages. In practice, even when viewed as a second-best and expensive solution to overcoming government funding and capacity constraints, the case for SIBs is underwhelming. In the post-crisis context of austerity, SIBs, as currently structured, with their apparently generous investor compensation rates, are more likely a drain on limited government allocations than a generator of incremental resources for social services. SIBs also do not appear to be generating innovations, but replicating existing models founded on prior public and philanthropic investment.

Social Impact Bonds continue the neoliberal trend that led to the massive increase in inequality now used to justify their necessity. Overcoming the challenges of growing inequality, however, will require structural changes based on a reinvestment in the civil service, the rebuilding of labour movements, and, ultimately, a reimagined welfare state. This is no doubt a monumental task, but to quote governance guru Michael Barber (2014, 24) somewhat out of context, "for a target to have real impact on the ground it has to be motivational, it has to have that moral purpose." Universal access to high-quality, well-funded public services that are available to all, we believe, provides such a calling.

Appendix A: Review of Meta-Analytical Studies on Common Social Impact Bond Policy Sectors

Anti-recidivism Programming

In the field of anti-recidivism programming, Lipsey and Cullen (2007) review an array of meta-analytical studies that are based on "hundreds" of articles on the subject, with few obtaining the ideal of large sample size, random assignment, high program treatment integrity, and low attrition, with many based on "quasi-experiments with nonrandomized control groups, modest sample sizes, and varying completion and attrition rates" (299). They conclude that correctional interventions such as supervision, increased monitoring, more severe penalties, and "tough love" approaches are not "especially effective in reducing the recidivism of the offenders to whom they are applied," and in some cases were associated with increases in recidivism (300), while rehabilitation services offer more promising outcomes.

Lipsey and Cullen (2007) find that supervision-based programs demonstrate recidivism reductions of between 2 per cent and 8 per cent, while greater sanctioning and punitive reform approaches lead to a range of predicted outcomes between an 8 per cent reduction to a 26 per cent increase in reoffence. Interventions focused on rehabilitation demonstrate consistently positive impacts, with meta-analysis average effects ranging from 10 per cent to 40 per cent reductions and most estimates centred near 20 per cent. Programs found to be the most successful focused on identifying and changing behaviour associated with criminal acts, but that could be altered through an intervention, and on maintaining program standards and implementation integrity.

One important caveat is that many of the published studies included in the meta-analyses were based on research projects designed and implemented by the researchers themselves, and these projects had outcomes that were up to twice as effective as those not designed by researchers, which would constitute the majority of those implemented in practice (Lipsey and Cullen 2007, 315). In general, Lipsey and Cullen note the large gap between programming shown to be effective in peer-reviewed research and program implementation in practice more broadly. This suggests that program integrity is not consistent or that projects with researchers involved benefit in some other manner.

MacKenzie and Farrington (2015) conduct a review of randomized control trials and meta-analyses undertaken since 2005, and their findings are broadly consistent with those of Lipsey and Cullen (2007). They note that "prison sentences, correctional boot camps, intensive community supervision and other interventions designed to increase control or make punishment more onerous are not effective in reducing recidivism … [and] there is little evidence that providing delinquents and offenders with opportunities in the community like jobs and housing is successful in reducing recidivism if these opportunities are not combined with some type of rehabilitation that focuses on thinking, problem solving, or cognitions." Moreover, interventions such as "cognitive skills training, drug treatment … and education" are effective at reducing recidivism (589).

Child Welfare

In the field of child welfare services, programs aimed at keeping at-risk children living safely at home with their families have shown promising results, motivated by the negative outcomes facing children taken into care.[1] Intensive family preservation services[2] – in particular, those following established models such as the Homebuilder program – have

---

1   Children entering foster care have significantly worse educational and health outcomes, are more likely to rely on social assistance, have addiction issues, and be involved in the criminal justice system later in life; and when compared to other children in marginal situations that might lead to their removal from their family and placement in foster care, fair even worse with respect to delinquency, teen pregnancy, and earnings outcomes than those who stay with their families (Doyle 2007). See also Social Finance (2014).

2   Intensive family preservation services are based on a combination of "case management and intensive therapy and other services; … small caseloads of two to six families; a team approach; 24-hour/7-days-per-week availability; a wide variety of helping options (from 'concrete' to clinical services); in-home services with maximum use of natural helping resources; individualized, empowering interventions; and intensive (6 to 15 hours per week) and time-limited (1 to 4 months) services" (Schweitzer et al. 2015, 424–5).

demonstrated success at keeping children with their families and reducing foster care placements (Schweitzer, Pecora, Nelson, Walters, and Blythe 2015, 424–5). A meta-analysis by Schweitzer et al. (2015) although limited to just four studies using control group counterfactuals, found three demonstrating significant treatment results, with placement in foster care rates reduced in the range of 27 per cent to 90 per cent. The remaining study saw statistically significant reductions in placement effects only for those under court petition, and suffered from deviations from prescribed program standards, which might have compromised treatment integrity. The evidence on intensive family preservation services is not unambiguous, however, with other meta-analyses with less restrictive scope and inclusion criteria – such as Al et al. (2012) and Fraser, Nelson, and Rivard (1997) – showing no impact on placement rates.

Multisystemic therapy, a therapy program for youth that has been used in both anti-recidivism and child welfare settings, including SIBs, has shown to be effective in reducing recidivism rates and in reducing foster care or other out-of-home placements, with treatment effects, as measured by the standardized mean difference, of 0.201 and 0.267, respectively (van der Stouwe, Asscher, Stams, Deković, and van der Laan 2014).[3]

Early Childhood Development

There is clear interdisciplinary evidence that the experiences of individuals in their early childhood years lay the foundation for future success and are formative in their impact on life outcomes, with negatives outcomes traced back to a "lack of cognitive and non-cognitive stimulation given to young children" more "than simply from the lack of financial resources" (Heckman 2006, 1900). In the area of early childhood development, Blau and Currie (2004) review four rigorously designed, randomized control trials with low attrition rates and high treatment integrity that analyse the impact of interventions for disadvantaged children in the United States on their future school performance and other outcomes – specifically, in "cognitive skills, school readiness, and social and emotional development" (40–1). They find support for the effectiveness of interventions, with the most intensive ones seeing the most marked results.

---

3 This is calculated as the difference in the mean between the control and treatment groups divided by the within-group or pooled standard deviation.

One of these studies, the Perry Preschool Project, which involved a two-year intervention with highly educated teachers and small student-to-teacher ratios, saw "positive effects on achievement test scores, grades, high school graduation rates, and earnings, as well as negative effects on crime rates and welfare use" (Blau and Currie 2004, 44). Heckman, Pinto, and Savelyev (2013) later showed that the success was based mostly on improved social skills as opposed to academic competency.

Another program, the Carolina Abecedarian Project, delivered through an augmented, full-time child care setting, starting at birth and continuing until the children entered school, saw children who received the intervention obtain "at age 15 ... higher scores on achievement tests (especially reading) and reductions in the incidence of grade retention and special education" and "at age 21 ... higher average tests scores and were twice as likely to still be in school or to have ever attended a four-year college" (Blau and Currie 2004, 43).

A third full-time child care–based study, the Milwaukee Project, with a relatively small sample size, saw statistically significant increases in IQ, and a second small sample study, the Early Training Project, with a less intensive intervention, saw "dramatic" reductions in special education placement once in school, with an 83 per cent reduction in the need for special education services relative to the control group (Blau and Currie 2004, 42).

Blau and Currie also note that the level of support provided through these experimental studies was significantly higher than that provided in practice through broad-based public programs – particularly the Head Start program in the United States, which has not been subjected to any randomized control studies. Still, a newer Early Head Start program aimed at better meeting the needs of infants and toddlers included a randomized control group component; early results show that participating children have "significantly higher scores on several tests of cognitive development, exhibit less aggressive behavior, and less negative behavior towards parents during play, and are also better able to devote sustained attention to an object during play" (Blau and Currie 2004, 55).

It is important to note that quality programming plays an integral role in the ability of child care interventions to deliver positive outcomes (Heckman 2013, 2059n22). Some studies of the $5-a-day universal child care program in Quebec, for example, suggest that the program had a negative impact on child outcomes with respect to behaviour and cognitive ability (Baker, Gruber, and Milligan 2008; Haeck, Lefebvre, and Merrigan 2015). Low quality due to rapid implementation was suggested as the cause, with the program relying heavily on home-based care, lack of observance of student/teacher ratios, and incentives that encouraged parents to leave very young children in child care for long periods (Haeck, Lefebvre, and Merrigan 2015).

Housing and Homelessness Prevention

The use of housing interventions for broader social benefit is an idea that has deep roots in urban social policy, with more recent research connecting low-quality and precarious housing and homelessness to lower educational outcomes for children and poor health outcomes (Mueller and Tighe 2007). The idea of placing homeless populations directly into stable, affordable, personal living accommodation, as opposed to addressing homelessness through temporary shelter or transitional housing, has gained momentum under the "housing first" model, which, in addition to providing stable permanent housing, is defined by the associated social supports either on- or off-site and no expectation that challenges such as addictions or mental health will already have been addressed (Aubry, Nelson, and Tsemberis 2015, 468; Ly and Latimer 2015, 476). Housing First is linked back to the Pathways to Housing model introduced in New York City in the early 1990s, and is based on the tenets of "immediate provision of housing and consumer-driven services; Separation of housing and clinical services; Providing supports and treatment with a recovery orientation; [and the] Facilitation of community integration" (Aubry, Nelson, and Tsemberis 2015, 469). In contrast, more traditional approaches emphasize "treatment first," with graduated programming suites and housing targeted at later stages of the intervention, and with inferior results (Aubry, Tsemberis, Adair, et al. 2015, 463). Early studies of the effectiveness of Housing First found that participants "obtained housing earlier and remained stably housed longer, showed greater reductions in use of health and social services, and reported higher levels of quality of life," although the evidence base was limited (463). More recent research, based on a multi-site randomized control trial in five Canadian cities, confirmed previous results, with 73 per cent of the treatment group obtaining stable housing compared to 31 per cent for the control group; "quality of life" and "community functioning" were also higher for the Housing First participants, with treatment effects of 0.31 and 0.25, respectively (Aubry, Tsemberis, Adair, et al. 2015, 465–6). The effectiveness of *permanent supportive housing*, a program model explicitly targeted at those with addictions and mental health challenges, and similar to but slightly broader than Housing First, has also shown to be effective with respect to "reduced homelessness, increased housing tenure, and decreased emergency room visits and hospitalization" (Rog et al. 2014, 287).

Active Labour Market Programs

Card, Kluve, and Weber (2010) conducted a meta-analysis of 97 studies and 199 "programme estimates" based on unique program-participant group pairings and individual-level data, examining the effectiveness of active labour market programs over various targeted outcomes and time horizons (F453). As opposed to the standard "effect size" estimate – referred to as the treatment effect in the previously referenced meta-analyses, which is most common in meta-analytic studies, the authors opted for reporting the number of statically positively significant, insignificant, and negatively significant variables in three time horizon categories of one, two, and three or greater years. The estimated effect size for a subsample, however, provided an equally informative analysis of program impact (F456–7). Only around 10 per cent of the studies were based on randomized control trials, with the two largest groups of studies using averages of like-type generated from administrative data as the comparison group. Card, Kluve, and Weber (2010) demonstrate, however, that results are robust across these variations, using "success in finding employment after the intervention" and "not being registered in unemployment benefit programs" as the outcome variables.

This meta-analysis reveals that a plurality of studies consistently show that active labour market program interventions have a positive effect, with the results becoming more convincing as the time frame of analysis increases. Specifically, short-term impacts are significant and positive in 39.1 per cent of cases when measured approximately one year after the intervention, growing to 45.4 per cent for evaluations approximately two years later, and to 52.9 per cent in studies with data around the three-year mark or later. These percentages are based on different program samples because of data availability, but growing effectiveness is also found within specific programs over time. For programs measuring effectiveness in the short run, job search programs had positive results more often than training programs. For the subset of programs that used probability of employment, in studies that found a statistically significant positive effect, the median effect size was 0.21 in the short run and 0.29 in the long run. With respect to outcomes variation among program types, job search assistance was more effective in the short run, while classroom or work experience training was more effective in the medium and/or long run, with subsidized public sector employment standing out as least effective.

Health

In the field of health care, there is wide and long-standing recognition that a healthy lifestyle focused on diet and physical activity plays an important role in preventing illness and conditions such as cardiovascular disease (Estruch et al. 2013; Sofi, Capalbo, Cesari, Abbate, and Gensini 2008) and Type 2 diabetes (Psaltopoulou, Ilias, and Alevizak 2010), with supporting evidence that programs focused specifically on prevention can lead to behavioural changes associated with reduced risk. For example, Dunkley et al. (2014) conduct a meta-analysis of twenty-four studies examining Type 2 diabetes prevention programs, and find a mean weight reduction of 2.6 kilograms twelve months after program completion. There is also evidence that infection rates for other diseases, such those sexually transmitted, can be reduced significantly through counselling interventions (Althoff et al. 2015; O'Connor et al. 2014).

There is also growing acknowledgment of the importance of the "social determinants of health" – the idea that "living and working conditions shaped by public policy are the primary factors that determine how long you live and whether you live well or ill while you are alive" (Raphael 2015, 8), with increasing life expectancy in advanced countries driven by "improving material conditions of early childhood, education, food availability, health and social services, housing, employment security, working conditions, and other [social determinants of health]" (12).[4]

---

4 See Chernomas and Hudson (2016, 95–101) for a summary and links to further literature on the social determinants of health.

Appendix B: Proportion of Social Impact Bonds by Sector and Country

Table B.1. Proportion of Social Impact Bonds by Sector and Country

	Child and Family Welfare	Criminal Justice	Educa- tion and Early Years	Environ- ment and Sustain- ability	Health	Housing/ Home- lessness	Work- force Devel- opment
	(%)						
Australia	33	22	0	0	11	33	0
Austria	0	0	0	0	0	0	100
Belgium	0	0	0	0	0	0	100
Canada	25	0	25	0	25	0	25
Finland	0	0	0	0	0	0	100
France	0	0	0	0	0	0	100
Germany	33	0	33	0	0	0	33
Israel	0	0	0	0	50	0	50
Japan	0	0	0	0	100	0	0
Netherlands	0	9	0	0	9	0	73
New Zealand	0	0	0	0	0	0	100
Portugal	25	0	25	0	0	0	50
South Africa	100	0	0	0	0	0	0
South Korea	0	0	50	0	0	0	50
Sweden	0	0	100	0	0	0	0
Switzerland	0	0	0	0	0	0	100
United Kingdom	13	2	6	0	17	33	29
United States	23	27	8	4	12	19	8
All SIBs	16	9	8	1	14	20	32

Appendix C: Reported and Estimated Maximum and Expected Investor Returns/ Interest Rates on Social Impact Bonds

Table C.1. Social Impact Bonds Launched as of January 2019

(1) Location	(2) Country	(3) Sector	(4) Date Launched	(5) Maximum Loss of Investment (%)	(6) Maximum Aggregate Interest Rate per annum[a] (%)	(7) Maximum Return per annum (%)	(8) Expected/ Target return (%)	(9) Investors repaid by Outcome Funder?[b]	(10) Source for Outcome Status
1. Peterborough	UK	Criminal justice	Sep. 2010	100	6.1	13.0	7.5	In full	Social Finance (2018)
2. West Midlands (Birmingham, Solihull)	UK	Workforce development	Apr. 2012	100	2.8			Partial+	DWP (2016, 6)
3. East London (Tower Hamlets, Islington, Hackney)	UK	Workforce development	Apr. 2012	100	43.3			In full	Social Finance (2018)
4. Greater Merseyside	UK	Workforce development	Apr. 2012	100	36.9			In full	Social Finance (2018)
5. Nottingham	UK	Workforce development	Apr. 2012	100	16.0			In full	Social Finance (2018)
6. East London (Stratford, Canning Town, Royal Docks, Cathall)	UK	Workforce development	Apr. 2012	100	43.2			Partial+	DWP (2016, 6)
7. Perth, Kinross	UK	Workforce development	Apr. 2012	100				Partial+	DWP (2016, 6)
8. New York	USA	Criminal justice	Aug. 2012	17	6.8	6.9	3.9	No	Social Finance (2018)
9. Cardiff, Newport	UK	Workforce development	Nov. 2012	100	53.9			Partial+	DWP (2016, 6)
10. London	UK	Housing/ homelessness	Nov. 2012	100	39.3			Partial	Social Finance (2018)
11. London	UK	Housing/ homelessness	Nov. 2012	100	26.0			Partial	Social Finance (2018)
12. Greater Manchester	UK	Workforce development	Nov. 2012	100	49.9			In full	Social Finance (2018)

	Location	Country	Sector	Date					Status	Source
13.	Essex	UK	Child and family welfare	Nov. 2012	100	10.7	12.0	10.0	Partial+	Social Finance (2018)
14.	Thames Valley	UK	Workforce development	Nov. 2012	100	49.8			In full	Social Finance (2018)
15.	West London	UK	Workforce development	Nov. 2012	100				Partial+	DWP (2016, 6)
16.	New South Wales	Australia	Child and family welfare	Jul. 2013	100	14.3	30.0		On track	Loxley (2017)
17.	Sydney	Australia	Child and family welfare	Aug. 2013	50	14.1	15.0	12.0	Partial+	Loxley (2017)
18.	Salt Lake County	USA	Education and early years	Sep. 2013	100		7.3		Partial+	Social Finance (2018)
19.	Augsburg	Germany	Workforce development	Sep. 2013	100	0.0	3.0		In full	Shaw (2017)
20.	United Kingdom	UK	Child and family welfare	Sep. 2013	100				On track	Big Society Capital (2017)
21.	Rotterdam	Netherlands	Workforce development	Dec. 2013	66	4.8	12.0		Partial+	Klaassen and Guus de Mari (2017)
22.	New York City, Rochester	USA	Criminal justice	Dec. 2013	90	8.9	12.5	7.0	Unknown	
23.	Boston, Chelsea, Springfield	USA	Criminal justice	Jan. 2014	100	6.0	14.5	3.5	Unknown	
24.	Brussels	Belgium	Workforce development	Apr. 2014	100	8.0	6.0		Unknown	
25.	Saskatoon	Canada	Child and family welfare	May 2014	100	5.4	5.0		On track	Loxley (2017)
26.	Manchester	UK	Child and family welfare	Jun. 2014	100				Unknown	
27.	Birmingham	UK	Child and family welfare	Jul. 2014	100				Unknown	
28.	Chicago	USA	Education and early years	Oct. 2014	100	19.5	6.0	6.0	Partial+	Sanchez (2016, 57)

(Continued)

Table C.1 Continued

(1) Location	(2) Country	(3) Sector	(4) Date Launched	(5) Maximum Loss of Investment (%)	(6) Maximum Aggregate Interest Rate per annum[a] (%)	(7) Maximum Return per annum (%)	(8) Expected/ Target return (%)	(9) Investors repaid by Outcome Funder?[b]	(10) Source for Outcome Status
29. Massachusetts	USA	Housing/ homelessness	Dec. 2014	100	9.4	5.3		Partial+	United Way of Massachusetts Bay and Merrimack Valley (2018)
30. Cuyahoga County	USA	Child and family welfare	Dec. 2014	100	4.6		2.3	Unknown	Social Finance (2018)
31. Gloucestershire	UK	Housing/ homelessness	Jan. 2015	100	67.2			Partial+	ICF Consulting Services (2017, 24)
32. Lisbon	Portugal	Education and early years	Jan. 2015	100			2.0	Partial	Maze (2017)
33. Liverpool, Knowsley	UK	Housing/ homelessness	Jan. 2015	100	29.7			Partial+	ICF Consulting Services (2017, 24)
34. Greenwich (Manchester, Oldham, Rochdale)	UK	Housing/ homelessness	Jan. 2015	100	37.2			Partial+	ICF Consulting Services (2017, 24)
35. Leicestershire, Derbyshire	UK	Housing/ homelessness	Jan. 2015	100	71.0			Partial+	ICF Consulting Services (2017, 24)
36. Birmingham	UK	Housing/ homelessness	Jan. 2015	100	28.8			Partial+	ICF Consulting Services (2017, 24)
37. West Yorkshire (Kirklees, Calderdale, Wakefield, Yorkshire and the Humber)	UK	Housing/ homelessness	Jan. 2015	100				Partial+	ICF Consulting Services (2017, 24)
38. Newcastle	UK	Health	Mar. 2015		8.5			On track	Social Finance (2018)

	Location	Country	Housing/homelessness	Date					Partial+	ICF Consulting Services (2017, 24)
39.	Newcastle, Northumberland, South Tyneside, North Tyneside, Gateshead, Durham, Sunderland	UK		Mar. 2015	100					
40.	Utrecht	Netherlands	Workforce development	Apr. 2015			6.0		Unknown	
41.	Greater Manchester	UK	Workforce development	Apr. 2015		0.0			On track	Social Finance (2018)
42.	London	UK	Workforce development	Apr. 2015					Unknown	
43.	Greater Merseyside	UK	Workforce development	Apr. 2015					Unknown	
44.	Sheffield	UK	Workforce development	Apr. 2015					Unknown	
45.	Bern	Switzerland	Workforce development	Jun. 2015	5		1.0		Unknown	
46.	Manchester, Lambeth	UK	Health	Jun. 2015				5.0	Unknown	
47.	Worcestershire	UK	Health	Jul. 2015		21.2	2.6		Unknown	
48.	Rotterdam	Netherlands	Workforce development	Sep. 2015			10.0		On track	Klaassen and Guus de Mari (2017)
49.	Upper Austria	Austria	Workforce development	Sep. 2015	100	0.0	1.0		Unknown	
50.	Santa Clara County	USA	Housing/ homelessness	Sep. 2015		2.5			Unknown	
51.	Haifa, Tel Aviv	Israel	Workforce development	Nov. 2015			10.0	5.0	Unknown	
52.	Utrecht	Netherlands	Workforce development	Nov. 2015			10.0		Unknown	

(*Continued*)

Table C.1 Continued

(1) Location	(2) Country	(3) Sector	(4) Date Launched	(5) Maximum Loss of Investment (%)	(6) Maximum Aggregate Interest Rate per annum[a] (%)	(7) Maximum Return per annum (%)	(8) Expected/ Target return (%)	(9) Investors repaid by Outcome Funder?[b]	(10) Source for Outcome Status
53. Helsinki	Finland	Workforce development	Nov. 2015				10.0	Not on track	Keltanen (2018)
54. Haringey, Staffordshire, Tower Hamlets	UK	Health	Jan. 2016		93.5			Unknown	
55. South Carolina	USA	Health	Feb. 2016		−18.5			Unknown	
56. Denver	USA	Housing/ homelessness	Feb. 2016		5.6		3.5	Partial+	Cunningham, Gourevitch, Pergamit, Gillespie, and Hanson (2018); Gaitan (2018)
57. Israel	Israel	Health	Mar. 2016					Unknown	
58. Norrkoping	Sweden	Education and early years	May 2016	60		4.7		Unknown	
59. Netherlands	Netherlands	Criminal justice	Jun. 2016		3.3	3.9		Unknown	
60. Adelaide	Australia	Housing/ homelessness	Jun. 2016		8.3	13.0	8.5	Unknown	
61. Eindhoven	Netherlands	Workforce development	Jun. 2016			3.2		Unknown	
62. New South Wales	Australia	Criminal justice	Jul. 2016					Unknown	
63. Seoul	South Korea	Education and early years	Jul. 2016					Unknown	
64. Kent County	USA	Health	Aug. 2016					Unknown	
65. Regina	Canada	Education and early years	Sep. 2016	100	3.0	1.3		Unknown	
66. Enschede	Netherlands	Workforce development	Sep. 2016		10.1	10.0		Unknown	

No.	Location	Country	Policy area	Date					Status	Source
67.	Connecticut	USA	Child and family welfare	Sep. 2016	100	7.2		5.9	Unknown	
68.	Washington, DC	USA	Environment and sustainability	Sep. 2016	13	0.2	6.4	3.4	Unknown	
69.	British Columbia, Saskatchewan, Ontario	Canada	Workforce development	Oct. 2016			15.0		Partial+	Colleges and Institutes Canada (2018)
70.	Toronto, Vancouver	Canada	Health	Oct. 2016	50		8.8		Unknown	
71.	Salt Lake County	USA	Criminal justice	Dec. 2016		9.2	10.2	3.5	Unknown	
72.	Salt Lake County	USA	Housing/homelessness	Dec. 2016		-1.1	11.1	3.5	Unknown	
73.	Rural	France	Workforce development	Jan. 2017					Unknown	
74.	Urban	France	Workforce development	Jan. 2017					Unknown	
75.	Auckland	New Zealand	Workforce development	Feb. 2017					Unknown	
76.	Lambeth	UK	Education and early years	Feb. 2017		71.0			Unknown	
77.	Greater Boston	USA	Workforce development	Mar. 2017		3.2		6.5	Unknown	
78.	North Somerset	UK	Child and family welfare	Mar. 2017					Unknown	
79.	Gyeonggi	South Korea	Workforce development	Mar. 2017					Unknown	
80.	Bristol	UK	Housing/homelessness	Mar. 2017		-3.6			Unknown	
81.	Tulsa, OK	USA	Criminal justice	Apr. 2017		7.1			Unknown	
82.	Kobe	Japan	Health	Apr. 2017				5.0	Partial+	Platt (2018)

(*Continued*)

Table C.1 Continued

(1) Location	(2) Country	(3) Sector	(4) Date Launched	(5) Maximum Loss of Investment (%)	(6) Maximum Aggregate Interest Rate per annum[a] (%)	(7) Maximum Return per annum (%)	(8) Expected/ Target return (%)	(9) Investors repaid by Outcome Funder?[b]	(10) Source for Outcome Status
83. Tokyo (Hachioji)	Japan	Health	Apr. 2017					Partial+	Platt (2018)
84. London	UK	Education and early years	Apr. 2017		39.1			Unknown	
85. London	UK	Health	Apr. 2017		4.8			Unknown	
86. Queensland	Australia	Child and family welfare	Jun. 2017	50		12.0	7.0	Unknown	
87. New South Wales	Australia	Health	Jun. 2017	0	15.2		7.5	Unknown	
88. Uusimaa, Southwest Finland	Finland	Workforce development	Jun. 2017		1.4		10.0	Unknown	
89. Fundao	Portugal	Workforce development	Jul. 2017					Unknown	
90. Porto	Portugal	Workforce development	Jul. 2017					Unknown	
91. Porto	Portugal	Child and family welfare	Jul. 2017					Unknown	
92. Osnabrück	Germany	Child and family welfare	Sep. 2017					Unknown	
93. Queensland	Australia	Housing/ homelessness	Sep. 2017	40		11.0	7.5	Unknown	
94. Brent, London	UK	Housing/ homelessness	Sep. 2017					Unknown	
95. Almeda County	USA	Criminal justice	Sep. 2017					Unknown	
96. Lincolnshire	UK	Housing/ homelessness	Sep. 2017					Unknown	
97. Mannheim	Germany	Education and early years	Sep. 2017					Unknown	

No.	Location	Country	Sector	Date					
98.	Los Angeles	USA	Housing/homelessness	Oct. 2017		2.8	2.8	2.3	Unknown
99.	Northamptonshire	UK	Housing/homelessness	Oct. 2017					Unknown
100.	Glouchestershire	UK	Housing/homelessness	Oct. 2017					Unknown
101.	Queensland	Australia	Criminal justice	Oct. 2017	40	23.4		7.5	Unknown
102.	Manchester	UK	Housing/homelessness	Nov. 2017		28.3			Unknown
103.	Ventura County, CA	USA	Criminal justice	Nov. 2017		1.9		5.7	Unknown
104.	Netherlands	Netherlands	Health	Nov. 2017		6.4	10.0		Unknown
105.	Bradford	UK	Education and early years	Nov. 2017					Unknown
106.	London, Boroughs of Lambeth, Southwark, Lewisham	UK	Health	Dec. 2017				2.0	Unknown
107.	Victoria	Australia	Housing/homelessness	Dec. 2017					Unknown
108.	London	UK	Child and family welfare	Jan. 2018		22.1			Unknown
109.	Newcastle, Gateshead	UK	Housing/homelessness	Mar. 2018					Unknown
110.	Devon	UK	Health	Jun. 2018					Unknown
111.	Delaware	USA	Health	Aug. 2018		3.6			Unknown
112.	South Africa	South Africa	Child and family welfare	Sep. 2018		37.4	16.0		Unknown
113.	Hillingdon, London	UK	Health	Sep. 2018		8.1		7.0	Unknown
114.	New York, Massachusetts	USA	Workforce development	Sep. 2018	100	5.6			Unknown
115.	Jefferson County	USA	Child and family welfare	Sep. 2018		0.9			Unknown

(Continued)

Table C.1 Continued

(1) Location	(2) Country	(3) Sector	(4) Date Launched	(5) Maximum Loss of Investment (%)	(6) Maximum Aggregate Interest Rate per annum[a] (%)	(7) Maximum Return per annum (%)	(8) Expected/ Target return (%)	(9) Investors repaid by Outcome Funder?[b]	(10) Source for Outcome Status
116. Antwerp	Belgium	Workforce development	Dec. 2018					Unknown	
117. The Hague	Netherlands	Poverty reduction	Jan. 2019					Unknown	
118. Veldhoven	Netherlands	Workforce development	Jan. 2019					Unknown	
119. Denver County	USA	Child and family welfare	Jan. 2019		1.1			Unknown	
120. Venlo	Netherlands	Workforce development	Jan. 2019					Unknown	
121. Colorado	USA	Child and family welfare	Jan. 2019		1.3			Unknown	
122. Oklahoma	USA	Child and family welfare	Jan. 2019		0.0			Unknown	

Note: Data sources include Gustafsson-Wright, Gardiner, and Putcha (2015), Nonprofit Finance Fund (2017), and Social Finance (2019). Project documentation such as fact sheets and stakeholder websites were consulted in some cases to confirm or verify interest rate and investor return details. Some figures are based on authors' calculations of annualized rates of return based on reported total returns on investment. Figures include both internal rate of return methodology and simple annualized return rates on total investment. In the case of multiple entries for return rates, a simple unweighted arithmetic mean of returns for differing investor classes is presented.

[a] The maximum aggregate interest rate per annum (I) is the annualized return rate based on reported maximum outcome payments available (P_{max}) and total funds invested (I), including in some cases grant funding. Letting t be the contract duration in months, it is calculated as

$$= \left(\frac{P_{max}}{I}\right)^{\frac{12}{t}} - 1.$$

[b] "Partial+" refers to the case where we were able to identify that the investors were at least partially repaid – for example, for some years of the project and/or some outcome realizations – but were unable to confirm if full repayment had been made.

Appendix D: Description of Value-for-Money Analysis in Applied Public Finance

Value-for-money (VfM) analysis is an applied analytical approach implemented to assist public sector decision makers faced with competing procurement options – specifically a public-private partnership (PPP) model and a conventional model. The VfM accounting framework was pioneered by the Private Finance Initiative in the United Kingdom and has been adopted extensively in Canada and other advanced industrialized countries (Loxley 2010, 60; Morallos and Amekudzi 2008; Burger and Hawkesworth 2011, 11–12). Both the VfM analysis and the framework above are specific and constrained forms of cost-benefit analysis. Cost-benefit analysis was first integrated with formal welfare economic analysis by Otto Eckstein in 1958, although the approach has a long tradition in applied public finance, with origins going back to at least 1808 (Hanley and Spash 1993). In this welfare economics context, cost-benefit analysis provides a decision rule for undertaking an action, generally an investment, in the presence of some form of market failure such that the present value of private gains from such an undertaking do not reflect the present value of social benefits because prices of inputs and/or outputs differ from the social value of benefits (Boadway and Bruce 1984, 26–7, 292–7). This process involves calculating the cost and benefits based on shadow prices that correct prices for deviations from market prices, determining and incorporating the effects of externalities, and applying present-value calculations.

As VfM analysis and the government procurement framework outlined above are forms of customized cost-benefit analysis, they have some similarities. Both either implicitly or explicitly provide decision rules for a government decision maker who is selecting between competing procurement models where a project can be delivered either by a single firm or by more than one firm. The approaches, however, are customized and constrained in different ways, and put emphasis on different attributes of the problem at hand. VfM analysis does not derive an *a priori* rationale for why one procurement model might be more efficient than another; it is an accounting framework to compare explicitly variations in categorized costs between the two models. In doing so, however, VfM analysis highlights the importance of costs either abstracted away from or de-emphasized in the typical incentive theory framework, including transaction costs and the cost of financing under the different procurement models. This less abstract methodology of VfM brings it closer to an applied decision-making context, where the policy debate around SIBs is taking place. The VfM analysis, in fact, focuses on cost differentials between delivery methods, and assumes the project outcome or benefit being delivered is fixed or predetermined. This makes VfM more of a "cost-effectiveness analysis" than a cost-benefit analysis.[1]

The VfM approach is a simple rules-based test implemented by public sector decision makers. The approach tallies an adjusted net present cost of a project under the conventional delivery model, called the *public sector comparator*, which is compared to a *shadow bid* based on the expected net present cost of delivery through the PPP framework. The difference between the public sector comparator and PPP shadow bid, if positive, is termed the *value for money* provided by the PPP delivery model. VfM analysis is highly general in the sense that it can encompass any type of PPP contract structure, be it one with user fees, state-contingent subsidies, minimum revenue guarantees, fixed or flexible term contracts, and so on, and various assumptions regarding contract enforceability and information asymmetry. Grout and Sonderegger (2006) outline the conditions under which a simple money-based test such as the cost-based VfM analysis would be equivalent to a full cost-benefit analysis. First, there must be no excess profits realized such that the financial cost to government of the project is equal to the private sector delivery cost. Second, the two delivery models must provide the same expected social benefit.[2] Finally, the same discount rate must be

---

1 See Weinrott, Jones, and Howard (1982, p. 179) and Welsh, Farrington, and Gowar (2015, pp. 457–8) who highlight this distinction.
2 Note that any savings generated to government as a result of the project or program would be captured as part of this benefit, so that restricting the choice set in the standard SIB framework to projects or programs that generate financial savings does not result in any additional positive impact on overall social welfare, as it is assumed to be accounted for.

applied when calculating the net present value of benefits delivered under each delivery model.

With these conditions met, the appropriate normative condition for determining whether a PPP is the superior delivery method reduces to whether the benefits from bundling under a PPP outweigh any increase in financing, transaction, or other costs. If a change in quality of service is to be expected, this should be accounted for as well. For a public sector decision maker seeking the socially optimal delivery contract for a social service, the problem again in general is the same: the SIB will be superior if it provides a better solution to agency problems, after accounting for any quality adjustments. This similarity allows for a standard VfM approach to be used to evaluate the public benefit of proceeding with an SIB.

Under a VfM accounting analysis, the total costs of the PPP and conventional model are subdivided into their various components.[3] *Value for money* is calculated as the difference between the cost of the public sector comparator, which assumes the conventional delivery method, and the cost of the shadow bid under the alternative delivery method. The shadow bid and the public sector comparator are equal to the sum of each delivery model's component costs to the public sector entity over the life of the project.[4] In a VfM analysis, costs are distributed over time, and calculated in expected present-value terms through the application of a discount rate.[5] VfM accounting generates the decision-making rule for the public sector entity *ex ante* to the project's being procured, and assumes the decision to undertake the project has been made based on a preliminary cost-benefit assessment; what remains is the determination of the appropriate delivery model.[6]

---

3 See HM Treasury Taskforce (1999), Morallos and Amekudzi (2008), and PPP Canada (2011) for descriptions of the value-for-money assessment process.

4 For simplicity this model compares a conventional model to a single alternative, but in practice multiple alternatives might be considered. In particular, in the PPP case, a design-build model provides an intermediate comparator, as would a PbR model based on equity or debt financing by the service provider in the SIB context.

5 The determination of the appropriate discount rate or rates is not necessarily a straightforward exercise, and the selection of the discount rate can carry significant weight in the outcome of VfM analysis. See Loxley (2011, 66–76) and Morallos and Amekudzi (2008, 122–3).

6 Although we assume that the administrators undertaking the analysis are doing so in good faith, it has been noted by others that public officials might have an incentive to misrepresent costs – for example, to secure funding for projects based on their individualized, non-altruistic preferences over projects being considered. See, for example, Maskin and Tirole (2008).

There exists some variation in how costs are categorized in VfM analyses, but generally the cost of the public sector comparator is calculated as the sum of total lifecycle costs, including the "retained risks" of delivering the service publicly, plus a competitive neutrality adjustment. Competitive neutrality accounts for any differences in taxes paid to government by the contractor under the conventional and alternative delivery models, as well as any indirect subsidy or in-kind support encompassed in the public sector delivery model that the private sector entity would not have access to in the alternative model.[7] The cost of service delivery can be broken down further into such components as: administrative costs, including transaction costs such as procurement costs, legal, technical and financial advisor fees and contract management expenses incurred by government;[8] financing costs; and transfers to the various service providers at differing stages of delivery – for example, at the design and construction stage versus the operations phase. The cost of the SIB is calculated as the expected costs under the PPP approach, including retained risks, administration, plus payments to the PPP consortium. These consortium payments can also be divided into their various components, including financing costs and transfers to the various service providers for differing stages of the project.

Retained risks feature prominently in VfM analyses, and it is often through risk transfer that PPPs from an *ex ante* standpoint are determined to provide value for money (Loxley 2010, 66–73; Morallos and Amekudzi 2008). Retained risk cost is the estimated monetary cost to the public sector entity in a given delivery framework produced by a quantitative risk assessment with respect to contingent obligations, weighted by the probability of their being realized. The treatment of risk in a VfM analysis is somewhat peculiar from a principal-agent modelling perspective, and the meaning of *risk* is not equivalent in the two contexts. In the principal-agent model, estimates of future costs are unbiased and the uncertainty associated with future contingencies imposes a cost only if the holder is risk averse. In VfM accounting, *retained risk* is assumed to impose a positive cost on government. This

---

7 Typically, the tax differential takes the form of taxes that would not be paid under the conventional delivery framework but would be paid if purchased by a private entity in a market transaction, but there are cases where this can work in the opposite direction as well (Loxley 2010, 63).

8 It is assumed that the government directly pays auxiliary costs in all contract structures. See Levin and Tadelis (2010) for further discussion of the higher transaction costs versus delivery efficiency trade-off entailed with contracting out government services.

implies either that estimates of other costs are negatively biased or that the government is risk averse. In the principal-agent framework, modelling a government as risk averse is not the norm, given the ability of government to self-insure and its powers to raise revenue through taxation (Hart 2003, C75).[9] In our framework, we dispense with the distinction between costs labelled as retained risk and the other expected service delivery costs, and assume the government is risk neutral. We also allow benefits to vary, making our model more closely tied to a full cost-benefit analysis as opposed to a VfM-type cost-effectiveness approach.

It should also be highlighted that a social service able to generate benefits in excess of its costs is not a universally accepted criterion for proceeding with service delivery. Standard economic theory calls for an adjustment based on the "opportunity cost" of the resources dedicated to implementation, approximated by some market-based assessment of returns on financial assets. Applying this particular cost-benefit method for projects that have impacts well into the future also relies, as noted, upon the selection of a discount rate to reduce the magnitude of future benefits and costs due to the fact that their impact is delayed and the assumption that humans naturally value the present more than they do the future.

Using this approach Heckman (2006, 1901), for example, highlights that, although investment in preschool, school, and post-secondary job training interventions all have positive social returns, only investments in early childhood development clearly generate a positive payoff above and beyond the opportunity costs of these investments – the benchmark for the economic efficiency of resource allocation. While recognizing that equity considerations also play a role in informing social expenditure decisions, Heckman uses these results to highlight the pitfalls of waiting "too long to compensate" for social inequity that is clearly linked to early childhood disadvantage (2006, 1901).

It should be noted, however, that the assumptions behind the opportunity-cost, discount-rate approach to cost-benefit analysis are

---

9 This is done through powers of taxation and debt issuance by spreading risk among a large number of people, relative to private firms, which are less able to do so and tend to be more risk averse (Arrow and Lind 1970; Chambers and Echenique 2012). Private profit-maximizing firms will not accept incremental risk through contract negotiations without compensation, and if they are risk averse, there is no gain from a Welfarist perspective by transferring risk from government to a private firm unless it is more than offset by some other source of efficiency gain from bundling as part of the risk transfer.

not universally accepted. At their root, these concepts are founded on neoclassical economic assumptions of human behaviour and aggregate supply-constrained theoretical perspectives on the functioning and limitations of how economies operate and evolve in response to shocks and interventions. Structuralist and post-Keynesian approaches (see, for example, Taylor 2010) emphasize the aggregate demand constrained nature of modern economies, and other heterodox economists have been critical of the role of discount-rate approaches that privilege current over future outcomes (see, for example, Stanford 2015, 86–8). Even if one accepts the discount-rate approach, the selection of the particular rate is a contentious issue, and has a large impact on cost-benefit analysis outcomes, placing heavy weight on a theoretically contested notion (Loxley 2010, 63–6).

Appendix E: Social Investment and Entrepreneurship Concepts

In this appendix we review a number of conceptual developments related to integration of social concerns with finance and the production of goods and services – including socially responsible investing, social entrepreneurship and innovation, venture philanthropy, philanthrocapitalism, social finance, the social economy, and social enterprise – that underpin the notion of a convergence or hybridization of the non-profit sector with for-profit corporate forms. Several of these concepts are used regularly by proponents of SIBs, and constitute useful terminology for discussing the motivations of SIB stakeholders.

Socially Responsible Investing

Parallel to the increasing prominence of corporate social responsibility has been the growth of what has been termed socially responsible investing (SRI), or impact investing. Schueth (2003) defines SRI in the US context "as the process of integrating personal values and societal concerns into investment decision-making" (190), and identifies three mechanisms through which this takes place: *screening*, which assesses companies based on CSR criteria or avoids companies with poor CSR track records; *shareholder advocacy* to change the practices of how corporations operate and to encourage greater CSR; and *community investing*, which "provides capital to people in low-income, at-risk communities who have difficulty accessing it through conventional channels" (191).

Within a neoclassical framework, Graff Zivin and Small (2005) highlight that the two hypotheses of CSR, "disguised profit maximization" and "managerial utility maximization" (8), do not explain why investors would demonstrate a particular preference for SRIs, which empirically have been shown not to outperform the market (9), as opposed to direct charitable contributions. They frame CSR activity as for-profit firms entering into competition with non-profit entities for philanthropic contributions and the satisfaction it brings to stakeholders who interact with the firm, including investors. The "socially responsible firm" effectively becomes a "hybrid [organization] – neither entirely profit-maximizing nor wholly philanthropic" (1). The distribution of investors' resources among profit-maximizing firms, SRI, and direct donations to charity in this framework is based on investors' beliefs regarding the effectiveness of direct charity versus CSR in achieving their philanthropic goals. If investors see both as equally capable, they will be indifferent between CSR and direct charitable contributions.

For CSR and SRI to be efficient in the neoclassical framework, then, they must have some comparative advantage over direct delivery by specialized non-profits. Among those proposed are that consumers benefit from and leverage the goodwill of the social entrepreneur who leads the CSR firm, who in turn forgoes some profit in exchange for social good; that of corporate charitable contributions are treated more favourably for tax purposes than are personal contributions; and that the CSR firm is able to be more efficient due to, for example, economies of scope (Baron 2007, 715–16).

Pauly and Swanson (2017) apply the above modelling approach to SIBs, and suggest that participation by investors in the management of the SIB project provides such efficiency enhancements. From this perspective, SIBs combine elements of CSR, social entrepreneurship, and venture philanthropic approaches. This lays the foundational hypothesis for the efficiency-enhancing potential of SIBs, upon which, we have argued, they must rest for the model's rationale as superior to conventional procurement models. The emphasis on CSR motivations, growing the SRI market, and rehabilitating the image of finance-led capitalism has been clearly referenced in the SIB literature (Fraser, Tan, Lagarde, and Mays 2018, 10).

Social Entrepreneurship and Social Innovation

Schumpeter (1947) identified entrepreneurship as a central mechanism in the driving of economic change, defining "the entrepreneur and his function … [as] simply the doing of new things or the doing of things that are already being done in a new way (innovation)" (151). The entrepreneur is distinguished from the capitalist or his or her designate, the manager, who might not be creative or innovative, and the inventor, who might never move beyond the stage of discovery (151–2). In fact, the entrepreneur might not be the inventor at all; the identity centres more on "getting new things done" (152) than on originality or unique ideas or practice. While highlighting that "the mechanisms of economic change in capitalist society pivot on entrepreneurial activity," Schumpeter noted that "the function itself is not absent from other forms of society" (151).

Social entrepreneurship, then, focuses on these other forms – in particular, the application of entrepreneurship to solving problems of a social nature that have more recently been addressed through government and the non-profit and philanthropic sectors in advanced economies. In a widely cited definition, Dees (1998b) says: "Social entrepreneurs play the role of change agents in the social sector, by: Adopting a mission to create and sustain social value (not just private value); Recognizing and relentlessly pursuing new opportunities to serve that mission; Engaging in a process of continuous innovation, adaptation, and learning; Acting boldly without being limited by resources currently in hand; and Exhibiting a heightened sense of accountability to the constituencies served and for the outcomes created" (4). He also notes that social entrepreneurship has been associated with breaking down transitional boundaries between the for-profit, non-profit, and public sectors, that "markets do not work as well for social entrepreneurs" (1), and that "these behaviors should be encouraged and rewarded in those who have the capabilities and temperament for this kind of work" (3), implying that some form of non-market stimulation or assistance is called for.

The idea of social entrepreneurship has generated significant interest and financial support, centred in the United States and Europe, both within and outside academia, including training initiatives, research programs, and dedicated foundations (Defourny and Nyssens 2010, 33; Chell, Nicolopoulou, and Karatas-Özkan 2010, 485). SIBs can be viewed as a tool to support social entrepreneurship and generate innovation in social service delivery.

Venture Philanthropy and Philanthrocapitalism

Although social innovation proponents advocate entrepreneurial approaches in social program design and delivery, some have advocated a parallel shift in the role of financiers of non-profit social programs who draw upon the practices of venture capitalists for inspiration (Letts, Ryan, and Grossman 1997). Labelled *venture philanthropy*, proponents argue that this new framework reframes the grantee-donor relationship along several dimensions, including: a more intensive involvement of the donor in strategic decisions as to how the receiving organization will use the funds; a longer-term commitment to funding the organization and/or initiative, with the objective often being systems change or social innovation, as described above; more interest in developing the capabilities and infrastructures of organizations receiving the funds; and a focus on metrics and outcomes, with an explicit statement of objectives and tracking over time to determine if progress is being made (van Slyke and Newman 2006, 347–8).[1] SIBs, then, fit very well with the venture philanthropy model. SIBs create a mechanism for venture philanthropists to recycle capital and transform what was previously a donation into equity, allowing them, if successful in meeting targets, to extract funds and move on to the next project, where previously they would have needed to raise new funds. They also implicitly rely upon the value added by investors in project management and service provider selection.

Philanthrocapitalism is a related but distinct concept from venture philanthropy that focuses on the establishment of foundations by highly successful entrepreneurs who use both their wealth and their business experience to generate social outcomes. It is similar to venture philanthropy in that it includes "the application of modern business techniques to giving but also the effort by a new generation of entrepreneurial philanthropists and business leaders to drive social and environmental progress by changing how business and government operate" (Bishop 2015, 474). Although not completely new, this model, which has been exported globally, apparently has scaled up significantly the amount of resources committed to philanthropy, both money and in-kind, by the mega-wealthy corporate elite. Bishop (2015) highlights how the Great Recession opened the window wider for philanthrocapitalists, since the wealthy were better positioned to emerge well placed while governments were burdened by fiscal pressures, giving them disproportionate leverage in setting the global social development agenda, relative to the amount of funds they contribute as a proportion of total spending, while at the same time benefiting from CSR-type effects discussed above.

While proponents celebrate the large-scale mobilization of private funds for public good, critics highlight a parallel with a century of corporate-funded philanthropy and how philanthrocapitalists use their

---

1 Katz (2005) questions how fundamental a shift venture philanthropy is from long standing practices in philanthropic circles, linking the concept back to notions of *strategic* and *effective* philanthropy focused on outcomes and prevention, which in turn have a long tradition in the American context, going back at least to the Robber Baron era of the early twentieth century.

influence to directly appropriate and indirectly deploy government resources in an undemocratic fashion (McGoey 2014).

Social Enterprises, Social Finance, and the Social/Solidarity Economy

Social enterprises are a vehicle of social entrepreneurship, and are generally defined as a revenue-generating business driven primarily by a social purpose (Chell et al. 2010, 486; Mendell 2010, 248). Social enterprises have been characterized as a hybrid of organizational forms, blending elements of for-profit, non-profit, civil society, and public institutional models and motivations (Mendell 2010, 245–6). The specific forms social enterprises take in practice vary. Some operate under traditional corporate for-profit/share capital or cooperative business forms, and may hold third-party certification to validate their adherence to social objectives.[2] Social enterprises also may be constituted as either for-profit subsidiaries of non-profit entities or independent non-profit organizations. In the case of for-profit provision, this has links to the neoclassical literature on the private provision of public goods (Bagnoli and Watts 2003; Bergstrom, Blume, and Varian 1986). Specific corporate forms for social enterprises designated in legislation also exist, such as the "social cooperative" (Defourny and Nyssens 2010, 33) in Italy, "Community Interest Corporations" (Chew 2010, 610) in the United Kingdom, and the "Benefit Corporation" in the United States (Hiller 2013), which has allowed corporations legally to set objectives other than maximizing shareholder value, a doctrine that has been enforced in the US legal system (Collins and Kahn 2016).

Some SRI funds focus exclusively on investing in organizational forms that are structurally committed to a social mission, such as social enterprises, cooperatives, charities, or projects explicitly aimed at achieving similar goals. This type of financing, which is specifically targeted at proactive support for social and environmental objectives, has been termed "social finance" (Moore, Westley, and Nicholls 2010, 116). The broader supply of goods and services by these organizations and the collective context in which they operate has been labelled the "social economy" (Amin, Cameron, and Hudson 2002, 1–2), a term that denotes not only a collective of business types, but also a broader philosophical and ideological commitment to solidarity, mutualism, and independence (Anheier and Salamon 2006, 71). More critical transformational

---

2 Examples include BCorp certification by the BLab organization in the United States (Hiller 2013, 290–1), Social Enterprise Mark (2018) in the United Kingdom, and the Buy Social certification in Canada (Common Good Solutions 2017).

perspectives more recently have come to use the expanded term "solidarity economy" or the combined "social and solidarity economy" to emphasize the foundational importance of mutualism, collectivism, and cooperative structures.

Our data show that SIBs primarily rely on social enterprises and social economy organizations as service delivery agents. As noted in Table 5.1, a large majority of service providers, intermediaries, and technical assistance providers are non-profit organizations. Out of the thirty-six for-profit service providers we identified, at least twenty were social enterprises in the sense that they had a clearly identifiable social mission. Many for-profit intermediaries also expressed a specific commitment to social innovation, social finance, and/or specialization in outcomes-focused social service delivery as part of their corporate identity. A greater proportion of for-profit evaluators and technical assistance providers, however, was drawn from more traditional finance, accounting and tax, wealth management, and traditional research firms.

Appendix F: Development Impact Bonds

Table F.1. Development Impact Bonds Launched as of January 2019

Location	Sector	Date Launched	No. of Participants	Upfront Investment (US$ millions)	Aggregate Interest Rate per annum (%)	Repaid by Outcome Funder?	Source for Outcome Status
Ene River, Peru	Workforce development	Jan. 2015	99	0.11	0.0	Partial	Gustafsson-Wright et al. (2017)
Rajasthan, India	Education and early years	Jun. 2015	18,000	0.27	4.7	In full	Boggild-Jones and Gustafsson-Wright (2018)
Colombia	Workforce development	Apr. 2017	511	0.75	n.a.	Unknown	
Mopti, Mali; Maiduguri, Nigeria; Kinshasa, Democratic Republic of Congo	Health	Sep. 2017	30,000	27.01	7.0	Unknown	
Cameroon	Health	Oct. 2017	18,000	2.00	n.a.	Unknown	
Rajasthan, India	Health	Nov. 2017	600,000	3.50	n.a.	Unknown	
Kenya and Uganda	Poverty reduction	Feb. 2018	13,830	2.40	20.5	Unknown	
India	Education and early years	Sep. 2018	300,000	3.00	36.4	Unknown	

References

ABN AMRO. 2017. "ABN AMRO invests in sixth Social Impact Bond." Retrieved from https://www.abnamro.com/en/newsroom/newsarticles/2017/abn-amro-invests-in-sixth-impact-bond.html.

ABN AMRO. n.d. "Social Impact Bonds." Retrieved from https://www.abnamro.com/en/sustainnable-banking/finance-and-investment/social-impact-bonds/index.html.

Adema, W., P. Fron, and M. Ladaique. 2011. "Is the European Welfare State Really More Expensive? Indicators on Social Spending 1980–2012; and a Manual to the OECD Social Expenditure Database (SOCX)." OECD Social, Employment and Migration Working Papers 124. Paris: Organisation for Economic Co-operation and Development.

Afik, Z., H. Katz, A. Levy, and R. Yosef. 2019. "New Development: Does Investment in Social Impact Bonds Affect Equity Prices? An Event Study." *Public Money & Management*. Published online 12 November. doi:10.1080/09540962.2019.1685263.

Ahmed, K. 2013, February 10. "Cameron to push G8 on finance bonds for new 'social investment.'" *Daily Telegraph*, 10 February. Retrieved from http://www.telegraph.co.uk/finance/newsbysector/banksandfinance/9859906/Cameron-to-push-G8-on-finance-bonds-for-new-social-investment.html.

Ainsworth, D. 2017. "Ten 'social impact bonds' worth up to £54m launched." *Civil Society*, 18 October. Retrieved from https://www.civilsociety.co.uk/news/ten-social-impact-bonds-worth-up-to-54m-launched.html.

Al, C.M.W., G.J.J.M. Stams, M.S. Bek, E.M. Damen, J.J. Asscher, and P.H. van der Laan. 2012. "A Meta-analysis of Intensive Family Preservation Programs: Placement Prevention and Improvement of Family Functioning." *Children and Youth Services Review* 34 (8): 1472–9. doi:10.1016/j.childyouth.2012.04.002.

Albertson, K., C. Fox, C. O'Leary, G. Painter, K. Bailey, and J. LaBarbera. 2018. *Payment by Results and Social Impact Bonds: Outcome-Based Payment Systems in the UK and US*. Bristol: Policy Press.

Albertson, K., C. Fox, C. O'Leary, and G. Painter. 2020. "*Towards a Theoretical Framework for Social Impact Bonds.*" *Nonprofit Policy Forum* 11 (2). Retrieved from https://doi.org/10.1515/npf-2019-0056.

Alesina, A., R. Perotti, J. Tavares, M. Obstfeld, and B. Eichengreen. 1998. "The Political Economy of Fiscal Adjustments." *Brookings Papers on Economic Activity* 1998 (1): 197–266. doi:10.2307/2534672.

Allin, S. 2016. "South Carolina Nurse Family Partnership Pay for Success Project Policy Brief." Harvard Kennedy School Government Performance Lab. Retrieved from https://govlab.hks.harvard.edu/files/govlabs/files/south_carolina_nfp_pfs.pdf.

Althoff, M.D., C.T. Grayson, L. Witt, J. Holden, D. Reid, and P. Kissinger. 2015. "A Meta-Analysis of the Efficacy of Behavioral Interventions to Reduce Risky Sexual Behavior and Decrease Sexually Transmitted Infections in Latinas Living in the United States." *Health Education & Behavior* 42 (6): 709–18. doi:10.1177/1090198114540461.

Ambler, B. 2016. *Request for Solution Outline (RFSO) Social Bonds Pilot Scheme Stage Probity Report*. Sydney: TressCox Lawyers. Retrieved from http://www.health.govt.nz/system/files/documents/pages/tresscox_report_redacted_final-july2016.pdf.

American Federation of State, County and Municipal Employees. 2015. "Outsourcing Social Services: Eliminating Public Watchdogs." Retrieved from https://m.afscme.org/news/publications/privatization/power-tools-to-fight-privatization/document/3-Outsourcing-Factsheet-.pdf.

Amin, A., A. Cameron, and R. Hudson. 2002. *Placing the Social Economy*. London: Routledge.

Anderson, J., and A. Phillips. 2015. "What we learned from the nation's first social impact bond." *Huffington Post*, 10 July. Retrieved from http://www.huffingtonpost.com/james-anderson/whatwe-learned-from-the-_1_b_7710272.htm.

Andreoni, J. 1989. "Giving with Impure Altruism: Applications to Charity and Ricardian Equivalence." *Journal of Political Economy* 97 (6): 1447–58. doi:10.1086/261662.

Andreoni, J. 1990. "Impure Altruism and Donations to Public Goods: A Theory of Warm-Glow Giving." *Economic Journal* 100 (401): 464–77. doi:10.2307/2234133.

Anheier, H.K., and L.M. Salamon. 2006. "The Nonprofit Sector in Comparative Perspective." In *The Nonprofit Sector: A Research Handbook*, ed. W.W. Steinberg and R. Powell, 89–116. New Haven, CT: Yale University Press.

Antellini-Russo, F., and R. Zampino. 2012. "Infrastructures, Public Accounts and Public-Private Partnerships: Evidence from the Italian Local Administrations." *Review of Economics and Institutions* 3 (1): 1–28. Retrieved from https://ssrn.com/abstract=1992392.

Antolin, P., S. Schich, and J. Yermo. 2011. "The Economic Impact of Protracted Low Interest Rates on Pension Funds and Insurance Companies." *Financial Market Trends* 2011 (1): 237–56. doi:10.1787/19952872.

Arena, M., I. Bengo, M. Calderini, and V. Chiodo. 2016. "Social Impact Bonds: Blockbuster or Flash in a Pan?" *International Journal of Public Administration* 39 (12): 927–39. doi:10.1080/01900692.2015.1057852.

Arrow, K.J., and R.C. Lind. 1970. "Uncertainty and the Evaluation of Public Investment Decisions." *American Economic Review* 60 (3): 364–78. doi:10.1016/B978-0-12-214850-7.50031-0.

Arts, W.A., and J. Gelissen. 2010. "Models of the Welfare State." In *The Oxford Handbook of the Welfare State*, ed. F.G. Castles, S. Leibfried, J. Lewis, H. Obinger, and C. Pierson, 569–83. Oxford: Oxford University Press.

Ascoli, U., and C. Ranci. 2002. *Dilemmas of the Welfare Mix: The New Structure of Welfare in an Era of Privatization*. New York: Kluwer Academic; Plenum.

Atkinson, A., S. Burgess, B. Croxson, P. Gregg, C. Propper, H. Slater, and D. Wilson. 2009. "Evaluating the Impact of Performance-Related Pay for Teachers in England." *Labour Economics* 16 (3): 251–61. doi:10.1016/j.labeco.2008.10.003.

Aubry, T., G. Nelson, and S. Tsemberis. 2015. "Housing First for People with Severe Mental Illness Who Are Homeless: A Review of the Research and Findings from the At Home/Chez-soi Demonstration Project." *Canadian Journal of Psychiatry* 60 (11): 467–74. doi:10.1177/070674371506001102.

Aubry, T., S. Tsemberis, C.E. Adair, S. Veldhuizen, D. Streiner, E. Latimer, J. Sareen, et al. 2015. "One-Year Outcomes of a Randomized Controlled Trial of Housing First with ACT in Five Canadian Cities." *Psychiatric Services* 66 (5): 463–9. doi:10.1176/appi.ps.201400167.

Auger, D.A. 1999. "Privatization, Contracting, and the States: Lessons from State Government Experience." *Public Productivity & Management Review* 22 (4): 435–54. doi:10.2307/3380929.

Austen-Smith, D. 1987. "Interest Groups, Campaign Contributions, and Probabilistic Voting." *Public Choice* 54 (2): 123–39. https://doi.org/10.1007/BF00123002.

Azemati, H., M. Belinsky, R. Gillette, J. Liebman, A. Sellman, and A. Wyse. 2013. "Social Impact Bonds: Lessons Learned So Far." *Community Development Investment Review* 9 (1): 2–33. Retrieved from https://ideas.repec.org/a/fip/fedfcr/y2013p23-33nv.9no.1.html.

Baber, W.R., and A.K. Gore. 2008. "Consequences of GAAP Disclosure Regulation: Evidence from Municipal Debt Issues." *Accounting Review* 83 (3): 565–92. doi:10.2308/accr.2008.83.3.565.

Backström, C. 2015. "New Nordic network for social impact bonds." 15 April. Retrieved from http://socialinnovation.se/new-nordic-network-for-social -impact-bonds/.

Backström, C. 2016. "Social impact bond moddellen testas i Norrköping." 18 February. Retrieved from http://socialinnovation.se/social-impact -bond-modellen-testas-i-norrkoping/.

Bagnoli, M., and S.G. Watts. 2003. "Selling to Socially Responsible Consumers: Competition and the Private Provision of Public Goods." *Journal of Economics & Management Strategy* 12 (3): 419–45. doi:10.1111/j.1430-9134.2003.00419.x.

Bailey, K., and J. LaBarbera. 2018. "Pay for Success and Social Impact Bonds in the US." In *Payment by Results and Social Impact Bonds: Outcome-Based Payment Systems in the UK and US*, by K. Albertson, C. Fox, C. O'Leary, G. Painter, K. Bailey, and J. LaBarbera, 61–82. Bristol: Policy Press.

Baker, M., J. Gruber, and K. Milligan. 2008. "Universal Child Care, Maternal Labor Supply, and Family Well-Being." *Journal of Political Economy* 116 (4): 709–45. doi:10.1086/591908.

Banerjee, A.V., and E. Duflo. 2007. "The Economic Lives of the Poor." *Journal of Economic Perspectives* 21 (1): 141–68. doi:10.1257/jep.21.1.141.

Banerjee, A.V., and E. Duflo. 2011. *Poor Economics: A Radical Rethinking of the Way to Fight Global Poverty*. New York: Public Affairs.

Baragar, F., and R. Chernomas. 2012. "Profits from Production and Profits from Exchange: Financialization, Household Debt and Profitability in 21st-Century Capitalism." *Science & Society* 76 (3): 319–39. doi:10.1521/siso .2012.76.3.319.

Barber, M. 2007. *Instruction to Deliver: Tony Blair, the Public Services and the Challenge of Achieving Targets*. London: Politicos.

Barber, M. 2014. *How to Run a Government: So that Citizens Benefit and Taxpayers Don't Go Crazy*. London: Penguin.

Barclay, L., and D. Mak. 2011. *A Technical Guide to Developing a Social Impact Bond: Vulnerable Children and Young People*. London: Social Finance. Retrieved from http://www.socialfinance.org.uk/a-technical-guide-to -developing-a-social-impact-bond-vulnerable-children-and-young-people/.

Baron, D.P. 2007. "Corporate Social Responsibility and Social Entrepreneurship." *Journal of Economics & Management Strategy* 16 (3): 683–717. doi:10.1111/j.1530-9134.2007.00154.x.

Baron, D.P. 2008. "Managerial Contracting and Corporate Social Responsibility." *Journal of Public Economics* 92 (1): 268–88. doi:10.1016/j.jpubeco .2007.05.008.

Baron, D.P. 2009. "A Positive Theory of Moral Management, Social Pressure, and Corporate Social Performance." *Journal of Economics & Management Strategy* 18 (1): 7–43. doi:10.1111/j.1530-9134.2009.00206.x.

Barr, N. 2004. Economics of the Welfare State. 4th ed. Oxford: Oxford University Press.

Barrow Cadbury Trust. 2017. "Peterborough Social Impact Bond shown to cut reoffending and make investor returns." News release, 27 July. Retrieved from https://www.barrowcadbury.org.uk/news/peterborough-sib-worlds -1st-social-impact-bond-shown-cut-reoffending-make-impact-investors -return/.

Becker, G.S. 1958. "Competition and Democracy." *Journal of Law and Economics* 1 (October): 105–9. doi:10.2307/1886017.

Becker, G.S. 1974. "A Theory of Social Interactions." *Journal of Political Economy* 82 (6): 1063–93. doi:10.1086/260265.

Becker, G.S. 1976. "Altruism, Egoism, and Genetic Fitness: Economics and Sociobiology." *Journal of Economic Literature* 14 (3), 817–26. Retrieved from https://www.jstor.org/stable/2722629.

Becker, G.S. 1983. "A Theory of Competition among Pressure Groups for Political Influence." *Quarterly Journal of Economics* 98 (3): 371–400. doi:10.2307/1886017.

Becker, G.S. 1985. "Public Policies, Pressure Groups, and Dead Weight Costs." *Journal of Public Economics* 28 (3): 329–47. doi:10.1016/0047-2727(85) 90063-5.

Bel, G., and X. Fageda. 2007. "Why Do Local Governments Privatise Public Services? A Survey of Empirical Studies." *Local Government Studies* 33 (4): 517–34. https://doi.org/10.1080/03003930701417528.

Bel, G., and X. Fageda. 2009. "Factors Explaining Local Privatization: A Meta-Regression Analysis." *Public Choice* 139 (1–2): 105–19. doi:10.1007/s11127 -008-9381-z.

Bel, G., X. Fageda, and M.E. Warner. 2010. "Is Private Production of Public Services Cheaper than Public Production? A Meta-Regression Analysis of Solid Waste and Water Services." *Journal of Policy Analysis and Management* 29 (3): 553–77. doi:10.1002/pam.20509.

Bel, G., and M. Warner. 2008a. "Challenging Issues in Local Privatization." *Environment and Planning C: Government and Policy* 26 (1): 104–9. doi:10.1016/j .polsoc.2008.09.001.

Bel, G., and M. Warner. 2008b. "Does Privatization of Solid Waste and Water Services Reduce Costs? A Review of Empirical Studies." *Resources, Conservation and Recycling* 52 (12): 1337–48. doi:10.1016/j.resconrec.2008 .07.014.

Béland, D., P. Blomqvist, J.G. Andersen, J. Palme, and A. Waddan. 2014. "The Universal Decline of Universality? Social Policy Change in Canada,

Denmark, Sweden and the UK." *Social Policy & Administration* 48 (7): 739–56. doi:10.1111/spol.12064.

Bellé, N. 2015. "Performance-related Pay and the Crowding Out of Motivation in the Public Sector: A Randomized Field Experiment." *Public Administration Review* 75 (2): 230–41. doi:10.1111/puar.12313.

Bellé, N., and P. Cantarelli. 2015. "Monetary Incentives, Motivation, and Job Effort in the Public Sector: An Experimental Study with Italian Government Executives." *Review of Public Personnel Administration* 35 (2): 99–123. doi:10.1177/0734371X13520460.

Bénabou, R., and J. Tirole. 2003. "Intrinsic and Extrinsic Motivation." *Review of Economic Studies* 70 (3): 489–520. doi:10.1111/1467-937X.00253.

Bénabou, R., and J. Tirole. 2006. "Incentives and Prosocial Behavior." *American Economic Review* 96 (5): 1652–78. doi:10.1257/aer.96.5.1652.

Benckiser Foundation. 2016. "Funding What Works: Juvat." Retrieved from http://www.benckiser-stiftung.org/juvat.

Benevolent Society. 2013. *The Benevolent Society Social Benefit Trust No. 1*. Paddington, NSW: Benevolent Society. Retrieved from https://www.osii.nsw.gov.au/assets/office-of-social-impact-investment/files/TBS-Information-Memorandum.pdf.

Bennett, J., and E. Iossa. 2006. "Delegation of Contracting in the Private Provision of Public Services." *Review of Industrial Organization* 29 (1–2): 75–92. doi:10.1007/s11151-006-9110-z.

Bentz, A., P. Grout, and M. Halonen. 2005. "What Should Governments Buy from the Private Sector: Assets or Services?" Institut Veolia. Retrieved from http://www.institut.veolia.org/fileadmin/medias/documents/Conference_Services_publics/What_Should_Governments_Buy_from_the_Private_Sector_Assets_or_Services_Discussed_by_REY_Patrick.pdf.

Benz, M. 2005. "Not for the Profit, but for the Satisfaction? Evidence on Worker Well-being in Non-profit Firms." *Kyklos* 58 (2): 155–76. doi:10.1111/j.0023-5962.2005.00283.x.

Berger, S. 2008. "Circular Cumulative Causation (CCC) à la Myrdal and Kapp: 'Political' Institutionalism for Minimizing Social Costs." *Journal of Economic Issues* 42 (2): 357–65. doi:10.1080/00213624.2008.11507144.

Bergson, A. 1938. "A Reformulation of Certain Aspects of Welfare Economics." *Quarterly Journal of Economics* 52 (2): 310–34. doi:10.2307/1881737.

Bergstrom, T.C., L. Blume, and H. Varian. 1986. "On the Private Provision of Public Goods." *Journal of Public Economics* 29 (1): 25–49. doi:10.1016/0047-2727(86)90024-1.

Bergstrom, T.C., and O. Stark. 1993. "How Altruism Can Prevail in an Evolutionary Environment." *American Economic Review* 83 (2), 149–55. Retrieved from https://www.jstor.org/stable/2117656.

Berndt, C., and M. Wirth. 2018. "Market, Metrics, Morals: The Social Impact Bond as an Emerging Social Policy Instrument." *Geoforum* 90: 27–35. doi:10.1016/j.geoforum.2018.01.019.

Besley, T., and M. Ghatak. 2005. "Competition and Incentives with Motivated Agents." *American Economic Review* 95 (3): 616–36. doi:10.1257/0002828054201413.

Besley, T., and M. Ghatak. 2006. "Sorting with Motivated Agents: Implications for School Competition and Teacher Incentives." *Journal of the European Economic Association* 4 (2–3): 404–14. doi:10.1162/jeea.2006.4.2-3.404.

Bevan, G., and C. Hood. 2006. "What's Measured Is What Matters: Targets and Gaming in the English Public Health Care System." *Public Administration* 84 (3): 517–38. doi:10.1111/j.1467-9299.2006.00600.x.

Bhattacharyya, T., A.A. Freiberg, P. Mehta, J.N. Katz, and T. Ferris. 2009. "Measuring the Report Card: The Validity of Pay-for-Performance Metrics in Orthopedic Surgery." *Health Affairs* 28 (2): 526–32. doi:10.1377/hlthaff.28.2.526.

Bhushan, A., and R. Calleja. 2015. "Paying for Impact: Results-based Approaches in Development Finance, Situating Canada's Efforts in a Global Context." Ottawa: Canadian International Development Platform. Retrieved from http://cidpnsi.ca/wp-content/uploads/2015/05/ResearchReport_PayingforImpact_v2.pdf.

Biais, B., and E. Perotti. 2002. "Machiavellian Privatization." *American Economic Review* 92 (1): 240–58. doi:10.1257/000282802760015694.

Big Issue. 2018. "Big Issue Invest: Outcomes fund begins with the homeless and vulnerable." 2 February. Retrieved from https://www.bigissue.com/latest/big-issue-invest-outcomes-fund-begins-with-the-homeless-and-vulnerable/.

Big Lottery Fund. 2017. "Publications: Learning about Social Investment and Social Enterprise. Retrieved from https://biglotteryfund.org.uk/research/social-investment/publications#.

Big Lottery Fund. 2018. "Commissioning Better Outcomes: Awards from July 2013 to November 2018." Retrieved from https://www.tnlcommunityfund.org.uk/funding/programmes/commissioning-better-outcomes-and-social-outcomes-fund#section-4.

Big Society Capital. 2017. "Governance." Retrieved from https://www.bigsocietycapital.com/about-us/governance.

Bishop, M. 2013. "Philanthrocapitalism: Solving Public Problems through Private Means." *Social Research* 80 (2): 473–90. https://www.jstor.org/stable/24385612.

Black, D. 1958. *The Theory of Committees and Elections*. Cambridge: Cambridge University Press.

Blanchette, C., and E. Tolley. 2001. *Public- and Private-Sector Involvement in Health-Care Systems: A Comparison of OECD Countries*. Ottawa: Parliamentary Research Branch.

Blau, D., and J. Currie. 2004. "Preschool, Day Care, and Afterschool Care: Who's Minding the Kids?" NBER Working Paper 10670. Cambridge, MA: National Bureau of Economic Research. https://doi.org/10.3386/w10670.

Bloomer, N. 2016. "Revealed: Homeless charities 'complicit' in rough sleeper deportations." *Politics.co.uk*, 15 September. Retrieved from http://www.politics.co.uk/news/2016/09/15/homeless-charities-complicit-in-rough-sleeper-deportations.

Blumgart, J. 2014. "Rhode Island union: Social impact bonds are about greed, not good." Next City, 25 June. Retrieved from https://nextcity.org/daily/entry/social-impact-bonds-work-rhode-island-opposed.

Boadway, R.W., and N. Bruce. 1984. *Welfare Economics*. Oxford: Basil Blackwell.

Boardman, A.E., and A.R. Vining. 1989. "Ownership and Performance in Competitive Environments: A Comparison of the Performance of Private, Mixed, and State-Owned Enterprises." *Journal of Law & Economics* 32 (1): 1–33. doi:10.1086/467167.

Boggild-Jones, I., and E. Gustafsson-Wright. 2018. "World's first development impact bond for education shows successful achievement of outcomes in its final year." Brookings Institution, 13 July. Retrieved from https://www.brookings.edu/blog/education-plus-development/2018/07/13/worlds-first-development-impact-bond-for-education-shows-successful-achievement-of-outcomes-in-its-final-year/.

Bolton, P., and M. Dewatripont. 2005. *Contract Theory*. Cambridge, MA: MIT Press.

Bonvin, J. 2008. "Activation Policies, New Modes of Governance and the Issue of Responsibility." *Social Policy and Society* 7 (3): 367–77. doi:10.1017/S1474746408004338.

Bowles, S. 2004. *Microeconomics: Behavior, Institutions, and Evolution*. Princeton, NJ: Princeton University Press.

Bowles, S., and H. Gintis. 1993. "The Revenge of Homo Economicus: Contested Exchange and the Revival of Political Economy." *Journal of Economic Perspectives* 7 (1): 83–102. doi:10.1257/jep.7.1.83.

Bowles, S., and H. Gintis. 2005. "Social Capital, Moral Sentiments and Community Governance." In *Moral Sentiments and Material Interests*, ed. H. Gintis, S. Bowles, R. T. Boyd, and E. Fehr, 379–98). Cambridge, MA: MIT Press.

Bowles, S., D.M., Gordon, and T.E. Weisskopf. 1986. "Power and Profits: The Social Structure of Accumulation and the Profitability of the Postwar US Economy." *Review of Radical Political Economics* 18 (1–2): 132–67. doi:10.1177/048661348601800107.

Bowles, S., and S. Hwang. 2008. "Social Preferences and Public Economics: Mechanism Design When Social Preferences Depend on Incentives." *Journal of Public Economics* 92 (8): 1811–20. doi:10.1016/j.jpubeco.2008.03.006.

Boyce, J.K., and L. Ndikumana. 2012. *Capital Flight from Sub-Saharan African Countries: Updated Estimates, 1970–2010.* Amherst, MA: Political Economy Research Institute. Retrieved from http://www.peri.umass.edu/fileadmin/pdf/ADP/SSAfrica_capitalflight_Oct23_2012.pdf.

Boyne, G.A. 1998. "Bureaucratic Theory Meets Reality: Public Choice and Service Contracting in U.S. Local Government." *Public Administration Review* 58 (6): 474–84. doi:10.2307/977575.

Brender, A. 2003. "The Effect of Fiscal Performance on Local Government Election Results in Israel: 1989–1998." *Journal of Public Economics* 87 (9): 2187–205. doi:10.1016/S0047-2727(02)00045-2.

Brender, A., and A. Drazen. 2008. "How Do Budget Deficits and Economic Growth Affect Reelection Prospects? Evidence from a Large Panel of Countries." *American Economic Review* 98 (5): 2203–20. doi:10.1257/aer.98.5.2203.

Broadbent, J., and R. Laughlin. 2005. "Government Concerns and Tensions in Accounting Standard-Setting: The Case of Accounting for the Private Finance Initiative in the UK." *Accounting and Business Research* 35 (3): 207–28. doi:10.1080/00014788.2005.9729988.

Broccardo, E., M. Mazzuca, and M.L. Frigotto. 2020. "Social Impact Bonds: The Evolution of Research and a Review of the Academic Literature." *Corporate Social Responsibility and Environmental Management* 27 (3): 1316–32. doi:10.1002/csr.1886.

Buchanan, J.M., and G. Tullock. 1962. *The Calculus of Consent: Logical Foundations of Constitutional Democracy.* Ann Arbor: University of Michigan Press.

Burand, D. 2012. "Globalizing Social Finance: How Social Impact Bonds and Social Impact Performance Guarantees Can Scale Development." *NYU Journal of Law and Business* 9 (1): 447–502. Retrieved from https://repository.law.umich.edu/articles/1087/.

Burand, D. 2020. "New Development: The Application of Incomplete Contract Theory to Documenting Social Impact Bonds." *Public Money & Management* 40 (3): 247–9. doi:10.1080/09540962.2020.1714317.

Burchardt, T. 1997. *Boundaries between Public and Private Welfare: A Typology and Map of Services.* London: Centre for Analysis of Social Exclusion.

Burchardt, T., J. Hills, and C. Propper. 1999. *Private Welfare and Public Policy.* London: London School of Economics and Political Science.

Burger, P., and I. Hawkesworth. 2011. "How to Attain Value for Money: Comparing PPP and Traditional Infrastructure Public Procurement." *OECD Journal on Budgeting* 11 (1): 91–146. doi:10.1787/16812336.

Burgess, S., C. Propper, M. Ratto, and E. Tominey. 2017. "Incentives in the Public Sector: Evidence from a Government Agency." *Economic Journal* 127 (605): F117–41. https://doi.org/10.1111/ecoj.12422.

Burwell, S.M. 2015. "Setting Value-based Payment Goals: HHS Efforts to Improve U.S. Health Care." *New England Journal of Medicine* 372 (10): 897–9. doi:10.1056/NEJMp1500445.

Butler, D., D., Bloom, and T. Rudd. 2013. "Using Social Impact Bonds to Spur Innovation, Knowledge Building and Accountability." *Community Development Investment Review* 9 (1): 57–62. Retrieved from https://www.mdrc.org/sites/default/files/SIB_SFFedReserve.pdf.

Callanan, L., and J. Law. 2013. "Pay for Success: Opportunities and Risks for Non-profits." *Community Development Investment Review* 9 (1): 79–84. doi:10.1007/s13142-015-0354-8.

Callanan, L., J., Law, and L. Mendonca. 2012. *From Potential to Action: Bringing Social Impact Bonds to the US*. New York: McKinsey & Company. Retrieved from https://www.mckinsey.com/industries/social-sector/our-insights/from-potential-to-action-bringing-social-impact-bonds-to-the-us.

Canada. 2015. "Social Finance." Ottawa: Government of Canada. Retrieved from https://www.canada.ca/en/employment-social-development/programs/social-finance.html.

Canadian Union of Public Employees. 2013. "Social impact bonds wrong model to address homelessness, unemployment and poverty." 6 April. Retrieved from https://cupe.ca/social-impact-bonds-wrong-model-address-homelessness-unemployment-and-poverty.

Canadian Union of Public Employees. 2018. "CUPE calls for federal strategy to strengthen, not privatize, social services." 3 April. Retrieved from https://cupe.ca/cupe-calls-federal-strategy-strengthen-not-privatize-social-services.

Card, D., J., Kluve, and A. Weber. 2010. "Active Labour Market Policy Evaluations: A Meta-analysis." *Economic Journal* 120 (548): F452–77. doi:10.1111/j.1468-0297.2010.02387.x.

Carmel, E., and J. Harlock. 2008. "Instituting the 'Third Sector' as a Governable Terrain: Partnership, Procurement and Performance in the UK." *Policy & Politics* 36 (2): 155–71. doi:10.1332/030557308783995017.

Carpenter, J., S. Bowles, H. Gintis, and S. Hwang. 2009. "Strong Reciprocity and Team Production: Theory and Evidence." *Journal of Economic Behavior & Organization* 71 (2): 221–32. doi:10.1016/j.jebo.2009.03.011.

Carter, E. 2019. "More than Marketised? Exploring the Governance and Accountability Mechanisms at Play in Social Impact Bonds." *Journal of Economic Policy Reform*, 1–17. doi:10.1080/17487870.2019.1575736.

Carter, E. 2020. "Debate: Would a Social Impact Bond by Any Other Name Smell as Sweet? Stretching the Model and Why It Might Matter." *Public Money & Management* 40 (3): 183–5. doi:10.1080/09540962.2020.1714288.

Carter, E., C. FitzGerald, R. Dixon, C. Economy, T. Hameed, and M. Airoldi. 2018. *Building the Tools for Public Services to Secure Better Outcomes: Collaboration, Prevention, Innovation.* Oxford, UK: Government Outcomes Lab.

Cassis, Y. 2016. "Infrastructure Investments and the Shaping of Modern Finance. In *Infrastructure Finance in Europe: Insights into the History of Water, Transport and Telecommunications,* ed. Y. Cassis, G. De Luca, and M. Florio, 81–94). Oxford: Oxford University Press.

CCPA-SK. 2015. *Privatization Nation: The Canada-wide Failure of Privatization, Outsourcing and Public-Private Partnerships.* Regina, SK: Canadian Centre for Policy Alternatives - Saskatchewan.

Centre for Global Development. 2015. "Investing in Social Outcomes: Development Impact Bonds: FAQs." Retrieved from https://www.cgdev.org/page/investing-social-outcomes-development-impact-bonds-0.

Centre for Global Development, and Social Finance. 2013. *Investing in Social Outcomes: Development Impact Bonds.* London: Centre for Global Development and Social Finance.

Centre for Social Impact. 2017. "About CSI." Retrieved from https://www.csi.edu.au/about-csi/.

Chambers, C.P., and F. Echenique. 2012. "When Does Aggregation Reduce Risk Aversion?" *Games and Economic Behavior* 76 (2): 582–95. doi:10.1016/j.geb.2012.07.015.

Chang, H. 2002. "Breaking the Mould: An Institutionalist Political Economy Alternative to the Neo-liberal Theory of the Market and the State." *Cambridge Journal of Economics* 26 (5): 539–59. doi:10.1093/cje/26.5.539.

Chang, H. 2003. *Globalisation, Economic Development, and the Role of the State.* New York: Zed Books.

Chell, E., K. Nicolopoulou, and M. Karataş-Özkan. 2010. "Social Entrepreneurship and Enterprise: International and Innovation Perspectives." *Entrepreneurship & Regional Development* 22 (6): 485–93. doi:10.1080/08985626.2010.488396.

Chen, M. 2015. "Goldman Sachs and Bloomberg Philanthropies' investment in prison reform failed: Why do they consider it a success?" *Nation,* 19 August. Retrieved from https://www.thenation.com/article/goldman-sachs-and-bloomberg-philanthropies-investment-in-prison-reform-failed-why-do-they-consider-it-a-success/.

Chen, T., K. Chung, I. Lin, and M. Lai. 2011. "The Unintended Consequence of Diabetes Mellitus Pay-for-Performance (P4P) Program in Taiwan: Are Patients with More Comorbidities or More Severe Conditions Likely to Be Excluded from the P4P Program?" *Health Services Research* 46 (1p1): 47–60. doi:10.1111/j.1475-6773.2010.01182.x.

Chernomas, R., and I. Hudson. 2016. *Economics in the Twenty-first Century: A Critical Perspective.* Toronto: University of Toronto Press.

Chernomas, R., and I. Hudson. 2017. *The Profit Doctrine: Economists of the Neo-liberal Era*. London: Pluto Press.

Chew, C. 2010. "Strategic Positioning and Organizational Adaptation in Social Enterprise Subsidiaries of Voluntary Organizations: An Examination of Community Interest Companies with Charitable Origins." *Public Management Review* 12 (5): 609–34. doi:10.1080/14719031003633961.

Chiapello, E., and L. Knoll. 2020. "The Welfare Conventions Approach: A Comparative Perspective on Social Impact Bonds." *Journal of Comparative Policy Analysis: Research and Practice* 22 (2): 100–15. https://doi.org/10.1080/13876988.2019.1695965.

Chokshi, D.A., and T.A. Farley. 2012. "The Cost-Effectiveness of Environmental Approaches to Disease Prevention." *New England Journal of Medicine* 367 (4): 295–7. doi:10.1056/NEJMp1206268.

Chong, E., F. Huet, S. Saussier, and F. Steiner. 2006. "Public-Private Partnerships and Prices: Evidence from Water Distribution in France." *Review of Industrial Organization* 29 (1): 149–69. doi:10.1007/s11151-006-9106-8.

Christianson, J., S. Leatherman, and K. Sutherland. 2007. *Financial Incentives, Healthcare Providers and Quality Improvements: A Review of the Evidence*. London: Health Foundation. Retrieved from http://www.health.org.uk/sites/health/files/FinancialIncentivesHealthcarePRovidersAndQuality Improvements.pdf.

Clarke, T., and C. Pitelis. 1993. *The Political Economy of Privatization*. London: Routledge.

Clayton, R., and J. Pontusson. 1998. "Welfare-State Retrenchment Revisited: Entitlement Cuts, Public Sector Restructuring, and Inegalitarian Trends in Advanced Capitalist Societies." *World Politics* 51 (1): 67–98. Retrieved from https://www.jstor.org/stable/25054066.

Cohen, D., and J. Zelnick. 2015. "What We Learned from the Failure of the Rikers Island Social Impact Bond." *Nonprofit Quarterly*, 7 August. Retrieved from https://nonprofitquarterly.org/2015/08/07/what-we-learned-from-the-failure-of-the-rikers-island-social-impact-bond/.

Cohen, R. 2013. "Social Impact Bonds in Big Society: A Bird's Eye View." *Nonprofit Quarterly*, 7 May. Retrieved from https://nonprofitquarterly.org/2013/05/07/social-impact-bonds-in-big-society-a-bird-s-eye-view/.

Cohen, R. 2015. "The 2016 Federal Budget: What Nonprofits Should Know." *Nonprofit Quarterly*, 4 February. Retrieved from https://nonprofitquarterly.org/policysocial-context/25554-the-2016-federal-budget-what-nonprofits-should-know.html.

Cohen, R. 2017. "Why 'Pay for Success' Financing Could Cost Taxpayers More than They Bargained For." *In These Times*, 30

May. Retrieved from http://inthesetimes.com/article/20174 /pay-for-success-private-investment-education.

Colander, D. 2000. "The Death of Neoclassical Economics." *Journal of the History of Economic Thought* 22 (2): 127–43. https://doi.org/10.1080 /10427710050025330.

Collard, D.A. 1978. *Altruism and Economy: A Study in Non-selfish Economics.* Oxford: Oxford University Press.

Colleges and Institutes Canada. 2018. "First Social Impact Bond Pilot Has Positive Impact on Unemployed Canadians." Retrieved from https://www .collegesinstitutes.ca/news-centre/news-release/first-social-impact-bond -pilot-has-positive-impact-on-unemployed-canadians/.

Collier, P. 2007. *The Bottom Billion: Why the Poorest Countries Are Failing and What Can Be Done about It.* New York: Oxford University Press.

Collins, J.L., and W.N. Kahn. 2016. "The Hijacking of a New Corporate Form? Benefit Corporations and Corporate Personhood." *Economy and Society* 45 (3–4): 325–49. doi:10.1080/03085147.2016.1239342.

Colorado. 2018. Office of State Planning and Budgeting. *Governor's Youth Pay for Success Initiative: Three Pay for Success Projects to Improve Outcomes for Colorado at-Risk Teens.* Denver: Office of State Planning and Budgeting.

Coltham, J.B. 1972. "Educational Accountability: An English Experiment and Its Outcome." *School Review* 81 (1): 15–34. doi:10.1086/443060.

Common Good Solutions. 2017. "Buy Social Canada." Retrieved from http://commongoodsolutions.ca/buy-social-canada/.

Community and Public Sector Union. 2017. "Social Impact Investing Discussion Paper: CPSU Submission." Melbourne: Community and Public Sector Union. Retrieved from https://treasury.gov.au/sites/default/files /2019-03/c2017-183167-CPSU.pdf.

Conrad, D.A., M. Vaughn, D. Grembowski, and M. Marcus-Smith. 2015. "Implementing Value-based Payment Reform: A Conceptual Framework and Case Examples." *Medical Care Research and Review* 73 (4): 437–57. doi:10.1177/1077558715615774.

Cooke, P. 2007. "Social Capital, Embeddedness, and Market Interactions: An Analysis of Firm Performance in UK Regions." *Review of Social Economy* 65 (1): 79–106. doi:10.1080/00346760601132170.

Cooper, C., C., Graham, and D. Himick. 2016. "Social Impact Bonds: The Securitization of the Homeless." *Accounting, Organizations and Society* 55 (C): 63–82. doi:10.1016/j.aos.2016.10.003.

Coote, A. 2011. "Big Society and the New Austerity." In *The Big Society Challenge,* ed. M. Stott, 82–94. Cardiff: Keystone Development Trust.

Corporation for National and Community Service. 2017. "Social Investment Fund: Pay for Success." Retrieved from https://www.nationalservice.gov /programs/social-innovation-fund/our-programs/pay-success.

Costa, K., and S. Shah. 2013. "Government's Role in Pay for Success." *Community Development Investment Review* 9 (1): 91–6. Retrieved from https://ideas.repec.org/a/fip/fedfcr/00008.html.

Coughlin, J., D.C. Mueller, and P. Murrell. 1990. "Electoral Politics, Interest Groups, and the Size of Government." *Economic Inquiry* 28 (4): 682–705. doi:10.1111/j.1465-7295.1990.tb00826.x.

Coulson, A. (2008). "Value for Money in PFI Proposals: A Commentary on the UK Treasury Guidelines for Public Sector Comparators." *Public Administration* 86 (2), 483–498. doi:10.1111/j.1467-9299.2008.00729.x.

Courty, P., C.J. Heinrich, G. Marschke, and J. Smith. 2011. "U.S. Employment and Training Programs and Performance Standards System Design." In *The Performance of Performance Standards*, ed. J.J. Heckman, C.J. Heinrich, P. Courty, G. Marschke, and J. Smith, 15–29. Kalamazoo, MI: W.E. Upjohn Institute for Employment Research.

Courty, P., D.H. Kim, and G. Marschke. 2011. "Curbing Cream-Skimming: Evidence on Enrolment Incentives." *Labour Economics* 18 (5): 643–55. https://doi.org/10.1016/j.labeco.2011.01.007.

Courty, P., and G. Marschke. 2011a. "Curbing Cream-Skimming: Evidence on Enrolment Incentives." *Labour Economics* 18 (5): 643–55. doi:10.1016/j.labeco.2011.01.007.

Courty, P., and G. Marschke. 2011b. "Measuring Government Performance." In J.J. Heckman, C.J. Heinrich, P. Courty, G. Marschke and J. Smith, 203–30. Kalamazoo, MI: W.E. Upjohn Institute for Employment Research.

Crain, W.M., and J.C. Miller III. 1990. "Budget Process and Spending Growth." *William & Mary Law Review* 31 (4): 1021–46. Retrieved from https://scholarship.law.wm.edu/wmlr/vol31/iss4/6.

Crory, P. 2013. "Social Impact Bonds: YMCA Scotland." 3 June. Retrieved from https://senscot.net/social-impact-bonds-2/.

Cuifo, G., and A. Jagelewski. 2014. *Social Impact Bonds in Canada: Investor Insights*. Toronto: Deloitte and MaRS Centre for Impact Investing. Retrieved from https://impactinvesting.marsdd.com/resource/social-impact-bonds-canada-investor-insights/.

Cunningham, M., R. Gourevitch, M. Pergamit, S. Gillespie, and D. Hanson. 2018. *Denver Supportive Housing Social Impact Bond Initiative: Housing Stability Outcomes*. Washington, DC: Urban Institute, Metropolitan Housing and Communities Policy Center. Retrieved from https://www.urban.org/research/publication/denver-supportive-housing-social-impact-bond-housing-stability-outcomes.

Daily Manila Shimbun. 2017. "Private funds to help solve social issues in Japan." 22 August. Retrieved from http://manila-shimbun.ph/japan_news/private-funds-to-help-solve-social-issues-in-japan.html.

Damberg, C.L. 2009. *Physician Pay for Performance*. Santa Monica, CA: RAND Corporation. Retrieved from https://www.rand.org/pubs/technical _reports/TR562z13.html.

Danforth, B. 2014. "Worlds of Welfare in Time: A Historical Reassessment of the Three-World Typology." *Journal of European Social Policy* 24 (2): 164–82. doi:10.1177/0958928713517919.

Davis, J.B. 2003. *The Theory of the Individual in Economics: Identity and Value*. London: Routledge.

Davis, J.B. 2007. "The Turn in Recent Economics and Return of Orthodoxy." *Cambridge Journal of Economics* 32 (3): 349–66. doi:10.1093/cje/bem048.

Davis, J.H., F.D. Schoorman, and L. Donaldson. 1997. "Toward a Steward-ship Theory of Management." *Academy of Management Review* 22 (1): 20–47. doi:10.5465/amr.1997.9707180258.

Davis, R. 2014. *Social Impact Bonds: Private Finance that Generates Social Returns*. Brussels: European Parliamentary Research Service. Retrieved from www .europarl.europa.eu/EPRS/538223-Social-impact-bonds-FINAL.pdf.

Dayson, C., A. Fraser, and T. Lowe. 2020. "A Comparative Analysis of Social Impact Bond and Conventional Financing Approaches to Health Service Commissioning in England: The Case of Social Prescribing." *Journal of Comparative Policy Analysis: Research and Practice* 22 (2): 153–69, doi:10.1080/1387 6988.2019.1643614.

Dear, A., A. Helbitz, R. Khare, R. Lotan, J. Newman, G.C. Simms, and A. Zaroulis. 2016. *Social Impact Bonds: The Early Years*. London: Social Finance. Retrieved from http://socialfinance.org/social-impact-bonds -the-early-years/.

Dee, T.S., and J. Wyckoff. 2015. "Incentives, Selection, and Teacher Perfor-mance: Evidence from IMPACT." *Journal of Policy Analysis and Management* 34 (2): 267–97. doi:10.1002/pam.21818.

Dees, J.G. 1998. "Enterprising Nonprofits." *Harvard Business Review* 76: 54–69. Retrieved from http://ezinarticles.com/?Essential-Qualities-Of-An -Entrepreneur&id=398886.

Dees, J.G., and B.B. Anderson. 2003. "For-profit Social Ventures." *International Journal of Entrepreneurship Education* 2 (1): 1–26. Retrieved from http://catcher.sandiego.edu/items/soles/DeesAndersonCase.pdf.

Defourny, J., and M. Nyssens. 2010. "Conceptions of Social Enterprise and Social Entrepreneurship in Europe and the United States: Conver-gences and Divergences." *Journal of Social Entrepreneurship* 1 (1): 32–53. doi:10.1080/19420670903442053.

de Gruyter, E.D., D. Petrie, N. Black, and P. Gharghori. 2020. "Attracting Investors for Public Health Programmes with Social Impact Bonds." *Public Money & Management* 40 (3): 225–36. doi:10.1080/09540962.2020.1714312.

DeHoog, R.H. 1990. "Competition, Negotiation, or Cooperation: Three Models for Service Contracting." *Administration & Society* 22 (3): 317–40. doi:10.1177/009539979002200303.

Delbanco, S.F., K.M. Anderson, C.E. Major, M.B. Kiser, and B.W. Toner. 2011. *Promising Payment Reform: Risk-Sharing with Accountable Care Organizations.* Washington, DC: Commonwealth Fund.

Deloitte. 2012. *Paying for Outcomes: Solving Complex Societal Issues through Social Impact Bonds.* Toronto: Deloitte & Touche. Retrieved from http://www2 .deloitte.com/ca/en/pages/insights-and-issues/articles/paying-for -outcomes-social-impact-bonds.html.

Denzau, A.T., and M.C. Munger. 1986. "Legislators and Interest Groups: How Unorganized Interests Get Represented." *American Political Science Review* 80 (1): 89–106. doi:10.2307/1957085.

Devon County Council. 2018. "Pioneering new programme shows Devon leading the way in diabetes prevention." Press release, 13 June. Retrieved from https://www.devonnewscentre.info/pioneering-new-programme -shows-devon-leading-the-way-in-diabetes-prevention/.

Deye, A. 2015. "U.S. infrastructure PPPs: Ready for takeoff?" World Bank, 25 September. Retrieved from http://www.worldbank.org/en/news/opinion /2015/09/25/us-infrastructure-ppps-ready-for-takeoff.

Dijkgraaf, E., and R.H. Gradus. 2013. "Cost Advantage Cooperations Larger than Private Waste Collectors." *Applied Economics Letters* 20 (7): 702–5. doi:10 .1080/13504851.2012.732682.

Disley, E., and J. Rubin. 2014. *Phase 2 Report from the Payment by Results Social Impact Bond Pilot at HMP Peterborough.* London: Ministry of Justice Analytical Series. Retrieved from https://www.gov.uk/government/publications /phase-2-report-from-the-payment-by-results-social-impact-bond-pilot-at -hmp-peterborough.

Dixit, A. 2002. "Incentives and Organizations in the Public Sector: An Interpretative Rreview." *Journal of Human Resources* 37 (4): 696–727. doi:10.2307/3069614.

Domberger, S., and P. Jensen. 1997. "Contracting Out by the Public Sector: Theory, Evidence, Prospects." *Oxford Review of Economic Policy* 13 (4): 67–78. doi:10.1093/oxrep/13.4.67.

Donaldson, D. 2015. "Newpin paves way for social impact bond expansion." *Mandarin*, 24 August. Retrieved from http://www.themandarin.com.au /49174-social-impact-bonds-good-results-newpin/?pgnc=1.

Donaldson, L., and J.H. Davis. 1991. "Stewardship Theory or Agency Theory: CEO Governance and Shareholder Returns." *Australian Journal of Management* 16 (1): 49–64. doi:10.1177/031289629101600103.

Dorf, M.C., and C.F. Sabel. 1998. "A Constitution of Democratic Experimentalism." *Columbia Law Review* 98 (2): 267–473. doi:10.2307/1123411.

dos Santos, L. 2012. "On the Content of Banking in Contemporary Capitalism." In *Financialisation in Crisis*, ed. C. Lapavitsas, 83–118. Leiden, Netherlands: Brill.

Dowd, L. 2013. "Adoption scheme to help 'overlooked' children." *Sky News*, 26 October. Retrieved from http://news.sky.com/story/1157264/adoption-scheme-to-help-overlooked-children.

Dowling, E. 2017. "In the Wake of Austerity: Social Impact Bonds and the Financialisation of the Welfare State in Britain." *New Political Economy* 22 (3): 294–310. doi:10.1080/13563467.2017.1232709.

Dowling, E., and D. Harvie. 2014. "Harnessing the Social: State, Crisis and (Big) Society." *Sociology* 48 (5): 869–86. doi:10.1177/0038038514539060.

Downs, A. 1957. *An Economic Theory of Democracy*. New York: Harper and Row.

Doyle, J.J. 2007. "Child Protection and Child Outcomes: Measuring the Effects of Foster Care." *American Economic Review* 97 (5): 1583–610. doi:10.1257/aer.97.5.1583.

Drazen, A., and M. Eslava. 2010. "Electoral Manipulation via Voter-Friendly Spending: Theory and Evidence." *Journal of Development Economics* 92 (1): 39–52. doi:10.1016/j.jdeveco.2009.01.001.

Dubno, J.A., R.H. Dugger, and M.R. Smith. 2013. *Financing Human Capital Development for Economically Disadvantaged Children: Applying Pay for Success Social Impact Finance to Early Child Development*. Washington, DC: ReadyNation. Retrieved from http://www.readynation.org/uploads/db_files/RN%20PFS%20Finance%20Dubno%20Dugger%20Smith%20Paper%20130610.pdf.

Dugger, W.M. 1988. "Radical Institutionalism: Basic Concepts." *Review of Radical Political Economics* 20 (1): 1–20. doi:10.1177/048661348802000101.

Duménil, G., and D. Lévy. 2004. *Capital Resurgent: Roots of the Neoliberal Revolution*. Cambridge, MA: Harvard University Press.

Duménil, G., and D. Lévy. 2005. "Costs and Benefits of Neoliberalism: A Class Analysis." In *Financialization and the World Economy*, ed. G.A. Epstein, 17–45. Cheltenham, UK: Edward Elgar.

Duménil, G., and D. Lévy. 2011. *The Crisis of Neoliberalism*. Cambridge, MA: Harvard University Press.

Dunkley, A.J., D.H. Bodicoat, C.J. Greaves, C. Russell, T. Yates, M.J. Davies, and K. Khunti. 2014. "Diabetes Prevention in the Real World: Effectiveness of Pragmatic Lifestyle Interventions for the Prevention of Type 2 Diabetes and of the Impact of Adherence to Guideline Recommendations." *Diabetes Care* 37 (4): 922–33. doi:10.2337/dc13-2195.

Duroy, Q. 2014. "Neoliberal Europe: Enabling Ethno-cultural Neutrality or Fueling Neo-nationalist Sentiment?" *Journal of Economic Issues* 48 (2): 469–76. doi:10.2753/JEI0021-362448022.

Eames, S., V. Terranova, L. Battaglia, I. Nelson, C. Riesenberg, and L. Rosales. 2014. "A Review of Social Impact Bonds: Financing Social Service Programs through Public-Private Partnerships." Retrieved from http://www .reentryroundtable.net/wp-content/uploads/2011/05/A-Review -of-Social-Impact-Bonds-Final.pdf.

Easton, S. 2019. "Coalition budget commits $20m to study and stimulate social impact investing." *Mandarin*, 11 April. Retrieved from https://www .themandarin.com.au/106896-coalition-budget-commits-20m-to -study-and-stimulate-social-impact-investing/.

Ebner, A. 2006. "Institutions, Entrepreneurship, and the Rationale of Government: An Outline of the Schumpeterian Theory of the State." *Journal of Economic Behavior & Organization* 59 (4): 497–515. doi:10.1016/j.jebo.2005.06.003.

Eckstein, O. 1958. *Water Resource Development: The Economics of Project Evaluation*. Cambridge, MA: Harvard University Press.

Ecorys UK and ATQ Consultants. 2015. *Reconnections Social Impact Bond, Reducing Loneliness in Worcestershire: An In-depth Review Produced as Part of the Commissioning Better Outcomes Evaluation*. London: Big Lottery Fund. Retrieved from https://www.biglotteryfund.org.uk/research /social-investment/publications.

Edmiston, D., and A. Nicholls. 2018. "Social Impact Bonds: The Role of Private Capital in Outcome-based Commissioning." *Journal of Social Policy* 47 (1): 57–76. doi:10.1017/S0047279417000125.

Engel, E., R. Fischer, and A. Galetovic. 2013. "The Basic Public Finance of Public-Private Partnerships." *Journal of the European Economic Association* 11 (1): 83–111. doi:10.1111/j.1542-4774.2012.01105.x.

Epstein, A.M., T.H. Lee, and M.B. Hamel. 2004. "Paying Physicians for High-Quality Care." *New England Journal of Medicine* 350 (4): 406–10. doi:10.1056 /NEJMsb035374.

Epstein, G.A. 2005. "Introduction: Financialization and the World Economy. In *Financialization and the World Economy*, ed. G.A. Epstein, 3–16. Cheltenham, UK: Edward Elgar.

Esping-Andersen, G. 1990. *The Three Worlds of Welfare Capitalism*. Princeton, NJ: Princeton University Press.

Esping-Andersen, G., and J. Myles. 2011. "Economic Inequality and the Welfare State." In *The Oxford Handbook of Economic Inequality*, ed. W. Salverda, B. Nolan, and T.M. Smeeding, 639–64. Oxford: Oxford University Press.

Estache, A. 2006. "PPI Partnerships vs. PPI Divorces in LDCs." *Review of Industrial Organization* 29 (1–2), 3–26. Retrieved from https://EconPapers.repec .org/RePEc:ulb:ulbeco:2013/43914.

Estruch, R., E. Ros, J. Salas-Salvadó, M. Covas, D., Corella, F. Arós, E. Gómez-Gracia, et al. 2013. "Primary Prevention of Cardiovascular Disease with a Mediterranean Diet." *New England Journal of Medicine* 368 (14): 1279–90. doi:10.1056/NEJMoa1200303.

European Public Service Union. 2013. "EPSU position on the Social Investment Package (SIP)." Retrieved from https://www.epsu.org/article/epsu-position-paper-social-investment-package.

Evans, B., T. Richmond, and J. Shields. 2005. "Structuring Neoliberal Governance: The Nonprofit Sector, Emerging New Modes of Control and the Marketisation of Service Delivery." *Policy and Society* 24 (1): 73–97. doi:10.1016/S1449-4035(05)70050-3.

Fabricant, M., and M. Fine. 2012. *Charter Schools and the Corporate Makeover of Public Education: What's at Stake?* New York: Teachers College Press.

Falk, A., and U. Fischbacher. 2004. "Modeling Strong Reciprocity." In *Moral Sentiments and Material Interests: The Foundations of Cooperation in Economic Life*, ed. H. Gintis, S. Bowles, R. Boyd, and E. Fehr, 193–215. Cambridge, MA: MIT Press.

Fang, X., D.S. Brown, C.S. Florence, and J.A. Mercy. 2012. "The Economic Burden of Child Maltreatment in the United States and Implications for Prevention." *Child Abuse & Neglect* 36 (2): 156–65. https://doi.org/10.1016/j.chiabu.2011.10.006.

Farmer, L. 2015. "Are governments 'paying for failure' with social impact bonds?" *Governing*, August. Retrieved from http://www.governing.com/topics/finance/gov-social-impact-bonds.html.

Farrington, D.P., and B.C. Welsh. 2014. "Saving Children from a Life of Crime: The Benefits Greatly Outweigh the Costs!" *International Annals of Criminology* 52 (1–2): 67–92. https://doi.org/10.1017/S0003445200000362.

Fehr, E., and U. Fischbacher. 2005. "The Economics of Strong Reciprocity." In *Moral Sentiments and Material Interests: The Foundations of Cooperation in Economic Life*, ed. H. Gintis, S. Bowles, R.T. Boyd, and E. Fehr, 151–91). Cambridge, MA: MIT Press.

Fehr, E., U. Fischbacher, and S. Gächter. 2002. "Strong Reciprocity, Human Cooperation, and the Enforcement of Social Norms." *Human Nature* 13 (1): 1–25. doi:10.1007/s12110-002-1012-7.

Fehr, E., and S. Gächter. 2000. "Cooperation and Punishment in Public Goods Experiments." *American Economic Review* 90 (4): 980–94. Retrieved from https://pubs.aeaweb.org/doi/pdf/10.1257/aer.90.4.980.

Fehr, E., and S. Gächter. 2002a. "Altruistic Punishment in Humans." *Nature* 415 (6868): 137–40. doi:10.1038/415137a.

Fehr, E., and S. Gächter. 2002b. "Do Incentive Contracts Undermine Voluntary Cooperation?" Working Paper 32. Zurich: University of Zurich, Institute for Empirical Research in Economics.

Fehr, E., A. Klein, and K.M. Schmidt. 2007. "Fairness and Contract Design." *Econometrica* 75 (1): 121–54. doi:10.1111/j.1468-0262.2007.00734.x.

Fehr, E., and K.M. Schmidt. 1999. "A Theory of Fairness, Competition, and Cooperation." *Quarterly Journal of Economics* 114 (3): 817–68. https://doi .org/10.1162/003355399556151.

Financial Crisis Inquiry Commission. 2011. *The Financial Crisis Inquiry Report: Final Report of the National Commission on the Causes of the Financial and Economic Crisis in the United States*. Washington, DC: US Government Printing Office.

Finland. 2017. Ministry of Economic Affairs and Employment. "New inputs to boost immigrants' employment." Press release. Helsinki, 2 June. Retrieved from https://tem.fi/en/article/-/asset_publisher/maahanmuuttajien -tyollistymista-nopeutetaan-uusilla-panostuksilla.

Finn, D. 2008. *The British "Welfare Market": Lessons from Contracting Out Welfare to Work Programmes in Australia and the Netherlands*. York, UK: Joseph Rowntree Foundation. Retrieved from https://www.jrf.org.uk/report/lessons -contracting-out-welfare-work-programmes-australia-and-netherlands.

Finn, D. 2009. "The 'Welfare Market' and the Flexible New Deal: Lessons from Other Countries." *Local Economy* 24 (1): 38–45. doi:10.1080/02690940802645471.

Floyd, D. 2017. *Social Impact Bonds: An Overview of the Global Market for Commissioners and Policymakers*. London: Social Spider CIC. Retrieved from http://socialspider.com/wp-content/uploads/2017/04/SS _SocialImpactReport_4.0.pdf.

Folbre, N. 1995. "'Holding hands at midnight': The Paradox of Caring Labor." *Feminist Economics* 1 (1): 73–92. doi:10.1080/714042215.

Foley, D.K. 1978. "State Expenditure from a Marxist Perspective." *Journal of Public Economics* 9 (2): 221–38. doi:10.1016/0047-2727(78)90044-0.

Food Sustainability Index. 2018. "Proposed Foreign Aid Cuts: The Impact on Global Food Sustainability." Retrieved from http://foodsustainability.eiu. com/proposed-foreign-aid-cuts-the-impact-on-global-food-sustainability/.

Foster, J.B. 2007. "The Financialization of Capitalism." *Monthly Review* 58 (11): 1–12. Retrieved from http://www.greeneconomics.net /Financialization.pdf.

Fox, C., and K. Albertson. 2011. "Payment by Results and Social Impact Bonds in the Criminal Justice Sector: New Challenges for the Concept of Evidence-based Policy?" *Criminology and Criminal Justice* 11 (5): 395–413. doi:10.1177/1748895811415580.

Fox, C., and S. Morris. 2019. "Evaluating Outcome-based Payment Programmes: Challenges for Evidence-based Policy." *Journal of Economic Policy Reform*. doi:10.1080/17487870.2019.1575217.

Francois, P. 2000. "'Public Service Motivation' as an Argument for Government Provision." *Journal of Public Economics* 78 (3): 275–99. doi:10.1016 /S0047-2727(00)00075-X.

Francois, P. 2003. "Not-for-Profit Provision of Public Services." *Economic Journal* 113 (486): C53–C61. doi:10.1111/1468-0297.00110.

Francois, P. 2007. "Making a Difference." *Rand Journal of Economics* 38 (3): 714–32. doi:10.1080/10495142.2012.679165.

Francois, P., and M. Vlassopoulos. 2008. "Pro-social Motivation and the Delivery of Social Services." *CESifo Economic Studies* 54 (1): 22–54. doi:10.1093/cesifo/ifn002.

Fraser, A., S. Tan, A. Boaz, and N. Mays. 2020. "Backing What Works? Social Impact Bonds and Evidence-Informed Policy and Practice." *Public Money & Management* 40 (3): 195–204. doi:10.1080/09540962.2020.1714303.

Fraser, A., S. Tan, K. Kruithof, M. Sim, E. Disley, C. Giacomantonio, M. Lagarde, and N. Mays. 2018a. *Evaluation of Social Impact Bond Trailblazers in Health and Social Care: Final Report.* PIRU Publication 2018–23. London: Policy Innovation Research Unit.

Fraser, A., S. Tan, M. Lagarde, and N. Mays. 2018b. "Narratives of Promise, Narratives of Caution: A Review of the Literature on Social Impact Bonds." *Social Policy & Administration* 52 (1): 4–28. doi:10.1111/spol.12260.

Fraser, M.W., K.E. Nelson, and J.C. Rivard. 1997. "Effectiveness of Family Preservation Services." *Social Work Research* 21 (3): 138–53. doi:10.1093/swr/21.3.138.

Freeguard, G., R. Adam, E. Andrews, and A. Boon. 2017. *Whitehall Monitor 2017: The Civil Service as It Faces Brexit (Summary).* London: Institute for Government.

Freeman, R.B. 2005. "Labour Market Institutions without Blinders: The Debate over Flexibility and Labour Market Performance." *International Economic Journal* 19 (2): 129–45. doi:10.1080/10168730500080675.

Freeman, R.B. 2010. "It's Financialization!" *International Labour Review* 149 (2): 163–83. doi:10.1111/j.1564-913X.2010.00082.x.

Frey, B.S. 1997. "A Constitution for Knaves Crowds Out Civic Virtues." *Economic Journal* 107 (443): 1043–53. doi:10.1111/j.1468-0297.1997.tb00006.x.

Frey, B.S., F. Homberg, and M. Osterloh. 2013. "Organizational Control Systems and Pay-for-Performance in the Public Service." *Organization Studies* 34 (7): 949–72. doi:10.1177/0170840613483655.

Frey, B.S., and F. Oberholzer-Gee. 1997. "The Cost of Price Incentives: An Empirical Analysis of Motivation Crowding-Out." *American Economic Review* 87 (4): 746–55. https://www.jstor.org/stable/2951373.

Friedman, M. 2007. "The Social Responsibility of Business Is to Increase Its Profits." In *Corporate Ethics and Corporate Governance,* ed. W.C. Zimmerli, K. Richter, and M. Holzinger, 173–8. Berlin: Springer.

Friedman, M. 2009. *Capitalism and Freedom.* Chicago: University of Chicago Press.

Fryshuset. 2014. "Fryshuset får innovationsstöd av Postkodlotteriet för utveckling av ny investeringsmodell för preventivt socialt arbete, social impact bonds." 18 November. Retrieved from http://fryshuset.se/kronika /fryshuset-far-innovationsstod-av-postkodlotteriet-for-utveckling-av-ny -investeringsmodell-for-preventivt-socialt-arbete-social-impact-bonds/.

Gailmard, S. 2010. "Politics, Principal-Agent Problems, and Public Service Motivation." *International Public Management Journal* 13 (1): 35–45. doi:10.1080/10967490903547225.

Gaitan, V. 2018. "Exciting interim results show Denver's supportive housing social impact bond is paying off." 12 December. Retrieved from https://pfs.urban.org/pay-success/pfs-perspectives/exciting-interim -results-show-denver-s-supportive-housing-social-impact.

Galloway, I. 2013. "Forward." *Community Development Investment Review* 9 (1): 3–4. doi:10.1080/00139157.2013.768076.

Gardiner, S., and E. Gustafsson-Wright. 2015. "Perspectives on Impact Bonds: Putting the 10 Common Claims about Impact Bonds to the Test." Brookings Institution, 2 September. Retrieved from https://www.brookings.edu/blog /education-plus-development/2015/09/02/perspectives-on-impact-bonds -putting-the-10-common-claims-about-impact-bonds-to-the-test/.

Gelbach, J.B., and L. Pritchett. 2002. "Is More for the Poor Less for the Poor? The Politics of Means-tested Targeting." *Topics in Economic Analysis & Policy* 2 (1): 6.1–6.26. doi:10.2202/1538-0653.1027.

Giacomantonio, C. 2017. "Grant-maximizing but not Money-making: A Simple Decision-Tree Analysis for Social Impact Bonds." *Journal of Social Entrepreneurship* 8 (1): 47–66. doi:10.1080/19420676.2016.1271348.

Giantris, K., and B. Piakiewicz. 2013. "Pay for Success: Understanding the Risk Trade-offs." *Community Development Investment Review* 9 (1): 35–9. Retrieved from https://www.frbsf.org/community-development/files /pay-for-success-understanding-risk-trade-offs.pdf.

Gilbert, N. 2017. *Targeting Social Benefits: International Perspectives and Trends.* New York: Routledge.

Gillam, S.J., A.N. Siriwardena, and N. Steel. 2012. "Pay-for-Performance in the United Kingdom: Impact of the Quality and Outcomes Framework, a Systematic Review." *Annals of Family Medicine* 10 (5): 461–8. doi:10.1370 /afm.1377.

Gingrich, J., and S. Häusermann. 2015. "The Decline of the Working-Class Vote, the Reconfiguration of the Welfare Support Coalition and Consequences for the Welfare State." *Journal of European Social Policy* 25 (1): 50–75. https://doi.org/10.1177/0958928714556970.

Gintis, H. 2000. "Strong Reciprocity and Human Sociality." *Journal of Theoretical Biology* 206 (2): 169–79. doi:10.1006/jtbi.2000.2111.

Gintis, H., S. Bowles, R.T. Boyd, and E. Fehr. 2005. "Moral Sentiments and Material Interests: Origins, Evidence, and Consequences." In *Moral Sentiments and Material Interests: The Foundations of Cooperation in Economic Life*, ed. H. Gintis, S. Bowles, R.T. Boyd, and E. Fehr, 3–39. Cambridge, MA: MIT Press.

Glaeser, E.L., and A. Shleifer. 2001. "Not-for-Profit Entrepreneurs." *Journal of Public Economics* 81 (1): 99–115. doi:10.1016/S0047-2727(00)00130-4.

Globerman, S., and A.R. Vining. 1996. "A Framework for Evaluating the Government Contracting-out Decision with an Application to Information Technology." *Public Administration Review* 56 (6): 577–86. doi:10.2307/977256.

Godeke, S. 2013. "Community Reinvestment Act Banks as Pioneer Investors in Pay for Success Financing." *Community Development Investment Review* 9 (1): 69–74. Retrieved from https://www.frbsf.org/community-development/files/community-reinvestment-act-banks-pioneer-investors-pay-for-success-financing.pdf.

Goldsmith, H. 2014. "The Long-Run Evolution of Infrastructure Services." Working Paper 5073. Munich: Center for Economic Studies and IFO Institute.

Gordon, D.M. 1994. "Bosses of Different Stripes: A Cross-national Perspective on Monitoring and Supervision." *American Economic Review* 84 (2): 375–9. Retrieved from https://www.jstor.org/stable/2117862.

Gottschalk, P., and T.M. Smeeding. 1997. "Cross-national Comparisons of Earnings and Income Inequality." *Journal of Economic Literature* 35 (2): 633–87. Retrieved from https://www.jstor.org/stable/2729789.

Government Outcomes Lab. 2017. "LCF Round One: Full Awards." Retrieved from https://golab.bsg.ox.ac.uk/basics/outcomes-funds/life-chances-fund-latest-news/.

Government Outcomes Lab. 2020. *Projects Database*. Retrieved from https://golab.bsg.ox.ac.uk/our-projects/.

Graff Zivin, J., and A. Small. 2005. "A Modigliani-Miller Theory of Altruistic Corporate Social Responsibility." *Topics in Economic Analysis & Policy* 5 (1): 10.1–10.2. doi:10.2202/1538-0653.1369.

Gramlich, E.M., and P. Koshel. 1975. "Is Real-World Experimentation Possible? The Case of Educational Performance Contracting." *Policy Analysis* 1 (3): 511–30. doi:10.1016/B978-0-12-756850-8.50011-8.

Greenblatt, J., and A. Donovan. 2013. "The Promise of Pay for Success." *Community Development Investment Review* 9 (1): 19–22. Retrieved from https://www.frbsf.org/community-development/files/promise-pay-for-success.pdf.

Greene, S.E., and D.B. Nash. 2009. "Pay for Performance: An Overview of the Literature." *American Journal of Medical Quality* 24 (2): 140–63. doi:10.1177/1062860608326517.

Gregg, K., and J. Bogdan. 2014. "Social impact bonds legislation advances in Senate despite strong union opposition." *Providence Journal*, 15 June. Retrieved from http://www.providencejournal.com/breaking-news /content/20140615-social-impact-bonds-legislation-advances-in -senate-despite-strong-union-opposition.ece.

Grout, A., and S. Sonderegger. 2006. "Simple Money-based Tests for Choosing between Private and Public Delivery: A Discussion of the Issues." *Review of Industrial Organization* 29 (1–2): 93–126. doi:10.1177/1062860608326517.

Guasch, J.L., J. Laffont, and S. Straub. 2006. "Renegotiation of Concession Contracts: A Theoretical Approach." *Review of Industrial Organization* 29 (1–2): 55–73. doi:10.1007/s11151-006-9109-5.

Gungadurdoss, A. 2016. "Lessons from a Development Impact Bond: A Results-based Financing Program to Improve Educational Access and Achievement in India Shows the Importance of Data-Driven Decision-making and Adaptive Leadership." *Stanford Social Innovation Review*, 19 August. Retrieved from https://ssir.org/articles/entry/lessons_from _a_development_impact_bond.

Gürcan, E.C. 2015. "The Nonprofit-Corporate Complex: An Integral Component and Driving Force of Imperialism in the Phase of Monopoly-Finance Capitalism." *Monthly Review* 66 (11): 37–54. doi:10.14452/MR-066-11 -2015-04_4.

Gustafsson-Wright, E., and I. Boggild-Jones. 2017. "Colombia Leads the Developing World in Signing the First Social Impact Bond Contracts." Brookings Institution, 31 March. Retrieved from https://www.brookings.edu/blog /education-plus-development/2017/03/31/colombia-leads-the-developing -world-in-signing-the-first-social-impact-bond-contracts/.

Gustafsson-Wright, E., I. Boggild-Jones, D. Segel, and J. Durland. 2017. *Impact Bonds in Developing Countries: Early Learning from the Field*. Washington, DC: Brookings Centre for Universal Education and Convergence. Retrieved from https://www.brookings.edu/wp-content/uploads/2017/09/impact -bonds-in-developing-countries_web.pdf.

Gustafsson-Wright, E., S. Gardiner, and V. Putcha. 2015. *The Potential and Limitations of Impact Bonds: Lessons from the First Five Years of Experience Worldwide*. Washington, DC: Brookings Global Economy and Development Program. Retrieved from http://www.brookings.edu/~/media/Research /Files/Reports/2015/07/social-impact-bonds-potential-limitations /Impact-Bondsweb.pdf?la=en.

Hacker, J.S. 2004. "Privatizing Risk without Privatizing the Welfare State: The Hidden Politics of Social Policy Retrenchment in the United States." *American Political Science Review* 98 (2): 243–60. Retrieved from https://www.jstor .org/stable/4145310.

Haeck, C., P. Lefebvre, and P. Merrigan. 2015. "Canadian Evidence on Ten Years of Universal Preschool Policies: The Good and the Bad." *Labour Economics* 36 (C): 137–57. doi:10.1016/j.labeco.2015.05.002.

Haight, A.D. 2013. "The Intolerance Multiplier: A Diagram." *Review of Radical Political Economics* 45 (4): 525–32. doi:10.1177/0486613412475193.

Hajer, J. 2018. "The Political Economy of Social Impact Bonds." PhD diss., The New School. Retrieved from https://search.proquest.com/openview/9c83c5342a06962ca137ea69541dc089/1?pq-origsite=gscholar&cbl=18750&diss=y.

Hajer, J. 2019. "Social Impact Bonds: A Costly Innovation." Ottawa: Canadian Centre for Policy Alternatives, 16 January. Retrieved from https://www.policyalternatives.ca/publications/commentary/fast-facts-social-impact-bonds.

Hajer, J. 2020. "The National Governance and Policy Context of Social Impact Bond Emergence: A Comparative Analysis of Leaders and Skeptics." *Journal of Comparative Policy Analysis: Research and Practice* 22 (2): 116–33. doi:10.1080/13876988.2019.1695924.

Hall, M.H., and B. Reed. 1998. "Shifting the Burden: How Much Can Government Download to the Non-profit Sector?" *Canadian Public Administration* 41 (1): 1–20. doi:10.1111/j.1754-7121.1998.tb01525.x.

Hall, A., and D.W. Soskice. 2001. *Varieties of Capitalism: The Institutional Foundations of Comparative Advantage*. Oxford: Oxford University Press.

Halpern, J., and D. Jutte. 2013. "The Ethics of Pay for Success." *Community Development Investment Review* 9 (1): 41–6. Retrieved from https://EconPapers.repec.org/RePEc:fip:fedfcr:y:2013:p:41-46:n:v.9no.1.

Hanley, N., and C.L. Spash. 1993. *Cost-Benefit Analysis and the Environment*. Cheltenham, UK: Edward Elgar.

Hansmann, H.B. 1980. "The Role of Nonprofit Enterprise." *Yale Law Journal* 89 (5): 835–901. doi:10.2307/796089.

Hansmann, H.B. 1981. "Nonprofit Enterprise in the Performing Arts." *Bell Journal of Economics* 12 (2): 341–61. doi:10.2307/3003560.

Harbaugh, W.T., U. Mayr, and D.R. Burghart. 2007. "Neural Responses to Taxation and Voluntary Giving Reveal Motives for Charitable Donations." *Science* 316 (5831): 1622–5. doi:10.1126/science.1140738.

Hardin, R. 1997. "Economic Theories of the State." In *Perspective on Public Choice: A Handbook*, ed. D.C. Mueller, 21–34. Cambridge: Cambridge University Press.

Harris, D., and M.F. Larsen. 2016. *The Effects of the New Orleans Post-Katrina School Reforms on Student Academic Outcomes*. New Orleans, LA: Education Research Alliance for New Orleans. Retrieved from https://educationresearchalliancenola.org/publications/what-effect-did-the-post-katrina-school-reforms-have-on-student-outcomes.

Hart, O. 2003. "Incomplete Contracts and Public Ownership: Remarks, and an Application to Public-Private Partnerships." *Economic Journal* 113 (486): C69–C76. doi:10.1111/1468-0297.00119.

Hart, O., A. Shleifer, and R.W. Vishny. 1997. "The Proper Scope of Government: Theory and an Application to Prisons." *Quarterly Journal of Economics* 112 (4): 1127–61. doi:10.1162/003355300555448.

Harvard Kennedy School Government Performance Lab. 2017. *Pay for Success: Social Impact Bonds*. Retrieved from http://govlab.hks.harvard.edu /social-impact-bond-la.b.

Harvey, D. 2003. *The New Imperialism*. New York: Oxford University Press.

Harvey, D. 2005. *A Brief History of Neoliberalism*. New York: Oxford University Press.

Hathaway, J. 2016. "National Conference of State Legislatures: Social Impact Bonds." Retrieved from http://www.ncsl.org/research/labor-and -employment/social-impact-bonds.aspx#Use%20at%20the%20State%20Level.

Heckman, J.J. 1992. "Randomization and Social Policy Evaluation." In *Evaluating Welfare and Training Programs*, ed. C.F. Manski and I. Garfinkel, 201–30. Cambridge, MA: Harvard University Press.

Heckman, J.J. 2006. "Skill Formation and the Economics of Investing in Disadvantaged Children." *Science* 312 (5782): 1900–2. doi:10.1126/science.1128898.

Heckman, J.J., C. Heinrich, and J. Smith. 2011a. "Do Short-run Performance Measures Predict Long-run Impacts?" In *The Performance of Performance Standards*, ed. J.J. Heckman, C.J. Heinrich, P. Courty, G. Marschke, and J. Smith, 273–304. Kalamazoo, MI: W.E. Upjohn Institute for Employment Research.

Heckman, J.J., C. Heinrich, and J. Smith. 2011b. "A Formal Model of a Performance Incentive System." In *The Performance of Performance Standards*, ed. J.J. Heckman, C.J. Heinrich, P. Courty, G. Marschke, and J. Smith, 29–64. Kalamazoo, MI: W.E. Upjohn Institute for Employment Research.

Heckman, J.J., C. Heinrich, and J. Smith. 2011c. "Lessons for Advancing Future Performance Standards Systems." In *The Performance of Performance Standards*, ed. J.J. Heckman, C.J. Heinrich, P. Courty, G. Marschke, and J. Smith, 305–10. Kalamazoo, MI: W.E. Upjohn Institute for Employment Research.

Heckman, J.J., C. Heinrich, and J. Smith. 2011d. "Performance Standards and the Potential to Improve Government Performance." In *The Performance of Performance Standards*, ed. J.J. Heckman, C.J. Heinrich, P. Courty, G. Marschke, and J. Smith, 1–14. Kalamazoo, MI: W.E. Upjohn Institute for Employment Research.

Heckman, J.J., R. Pinto, and P. Savelyev. 2013. "Understanding the Mechanisms through which an Influential Early Childhood Program Boosted Adult Outcomes." *American Economic Review* 103 (6): 2052–86. doi:10.1257 /aer.103.6.2052.

Heckman, J.J., and J. Smith. 2011. "Do the Determinants of Program Participation Data Provide Evidence of Cream Skimming?" In *The Performance of Performance Standards*, ed. J.J. Heckman, C.J. Heinrich, P. Courty, G. Marschke, and J. Smith, 125–202. Kalamazoo, MI: W.E. Upjohn Institute for Employment Research.

Hefetz, A., and M. Warner. 2004. "Privatization and Its Reverse: Explaining the Dynamics of the Government Contracting Process." *Journal of Public Administration Research and Theory* 14 (2): 171–90. doi:10.1093/jopart /muh012.

Heinrich, C.J. 2011. "Local Responses to Performance Incentives and Implications for Program Outcomes." In *The Performance of Performance Standards*, ed. J.J. Heckman, C.J. Heinrich, P. Courty, G. Marschke, and J. Smith, 231–72. Kalamazoo, MI: W.E. Upjohn Institute for Employment Research.

Heinrich, C.J., and S.E. Kabourek. 2018. "Pay for Success in the U.S.: Are Viable and Sustainable Models Emerging?" Nashville, TN: Vanderbilt University. Retrieved from https://my.vanderbilt.edu/carolynheinrich/cv/.

Heinrich, C.J., and G. Marschke. 2010. "Incentives and Their Dynamics in Public Sector Performance Management Systems." *Journal of Policy Analysis and Management* 29 (1): 183–208. doi:10.1002/pam.20484.

Hermann, C., and J. Flecker. 2013. *Privatization of Public Services: Impacts for Employment, Working Conditions, and Service Quality in Europe*. New York: Routledge.

Hevenstone, D., and M. von Bergen. 2020. "Public-Private Partnerships in Social Impact Bonds: Facilitating Competition or Hindering Transparency?" *Public Money & Management* 40 (3): 205–12. doi:10.1080/09540962.20 20.1714304.

Hickman, E. 2016. "In-depth Review Mental Health and Employment Partnership (MHEP) Social Impact Bond: Produced as part of the CBO Fund Evaluation." London: Big Lottery Fund. Retrieved from https://www .biglotteryfund.org.uk/research/social-investment/publications.

Hiller, J.S. 2013. "The Benefit Corporation and Corporate Social Responsibility." *Journal of Business Ethics* 118 (2): 287–301. doi:10.1007/s10551-012 -1580-3.

Hinchliffe, T. 2018. "The €55M Portugal Social Innovation Fund is 'paradigm changing.'" *PortugalStartups.com*, 15 March. Retrieved from https:// portugalstartups.com/2018/03/portugal-social-innovation-fund/.

HM Treasury, Public Service Transformation Network, and New Economy. 2014. *Supporting Public Service Transformation: Cost Benefit Analysis Guidance for Local Partnerships*. 2nd ed. London: HM Treasury. Retrieved from https://www.gov.uk/government/uploads/system/uploads/attachment _data/file/300214/cost_benefit_analysis_guidance_for_local_partner ships.pdf.

Hodge, G.A. 2000. *Privatization: An International Review of Performance*. Boulder, CO: Westview Press.

Hodge, G.A. 2004. "The Risky Business of Public Private Partnerships." *Australian Journal of Public Administration* 63 (4): 37–49. doi:10.1111/j.1467-8500.2004.00400.x.

Hodge, G.A., and C. Greve. 2005. "Introduction." In *The Challenge of Public-Private Partnerships: Learning from International Experience*, ed. G.A. Hodge and C. Greve, 1–21. Cheltenham, UK: Edward Elgar.

Hodge, G.A., and C. Greve. 2007. "Public-Private Partnerships: An International Performance Review." *Public Administration Review* 67 (3): 545–58. https://doi.org/10.1111/j.1540-6210.2007.00736.x.

Hodge, G.A., and C. Greve. 2017. "On Public-Private Partnership Performance." *Public Works Management and Policy* 22 (1): 55–78. doi:10.1177/1087724X16657830.

Hodges, R., and H. Mellett. 2012. "The U.K. Private Finance Initiative: An Accounting Retrospective." *British Accounting Review* 44 (4): 235–47. doi:10.1016/j.bar.2012.09.005.

Hodgson, G.M. 1993. "Institutional Economics: Surveying the 'Old' and the 'New.'" *Metroeconomica* 44 (1): 1–28. doi:10.1111/j.1467-999X.1993.tb00786.x.

Hodgson, G.M. 2000. "What Is the Essence of Institutional Economics?" *Journal of Economic Issues* 34 (2): 317–29. doi:10.1080/00213624.2000.11506269.

Hodgson, G.M. 2007." Evolutionary and Institutional Economics as the New Mainstream?" *Evolutionary and Institutional Economics Review* 4 (1): 7–25. doi:10.14441/eier.4.7.

Hodgson, G.M. 2014. "On Fuzzy Frontiers and Fragmented Foundations: Some Reflections on the Original and New Institutional Economics." *Journal of Institutional Economics* 10 (4): 591–611. doi:10.1017/S1744137414000307.

Horesh, R. 1988. "Social Policy Bonds." *Papers Presented at the New Zealand Branch of Australian Agricultural Economics Society Conference* 2 (121): 266–80. Retrieved from https://www.aeaweb.org/articles?id=10.1257/089533002760278776.

Hotelling, H. 1929. "Stability in Competition." *Economic Journal* 39 (153): 41–57. doi:10.1007/978-1-4613-8905-7_4.

Houle, S.K., F.A. McAlister, C.A. Jackevicius, A.W. Chuck, and R.T. Tsuyuki. 2012. "Does Performance-based Remuneration for Individual Health Care Practitioners Affect Patient Care? A Systematic Review." *Annals of Internal Medicine* 157 (12): 889–99. doi:10.7326/0003-4819-157-12-201212180-00009.

Howell, C. 2003. "Varieties of Capitalism: And Then There Was One?" *Comparative Politics* 36 (1): 103–24. doi:10.2307/4150162.

Humphries, K.W. 2014. "Not Your Older Brother's Bonds: The Use and Regulation of Social-Impact Bonds in the United States." *Law and Contemporary*

Problems 76 (3): 433–52. Retrieved from https://heinonline.org/HOL
/LandingPage?handle=hein.journals/lcp76&div=48&id=&page=.

Hurd, M.D., and S. Rohwedder. 2010. "Effects of the Financial Crisis and Great
Recession on American Households." NBER Working Paper 16407. Cambridge, MA: National Bureau of Economic Research.

ICF Consulting Services. 2017. *Evaluation of the Fair Chance Fund: Second In-*
terim Report. London: Department for Communities and Local Government.
Retrieved from https://www.gov.uk/government/publications
/fair-chance-fund-evaluation-interim-reports.

ICRC (International Committee of the Red Cross). 2017a. "The world's first
"Humanitarian Impact Bond" launched to transform financing of aid in
conflict-hit countries." Press release, 6 September. Retrieved from https://
www.icrc.org/en/document/worlds-first-humanitarian-impact-bond
-launched-transform-financing-aid-conflict-hit.

ICRC (International Committee of the Red Cross). 2017b. "Switzerland to
participate in the first impact investment in the humanitarian sector." Press
release, 8 September. Retrieved from https://www.admin.ch/gov/en
/start/documentation/media-releases.msg-id-68049.html.

IES - Social Business School. n.d. "History." Retrieved from https://www.ies
-sbs-en.org/history/.

Insite Research and Consulting. 2014. *Innovation Fund Pilots Qualitative Evalu-*
ation: Early Implementation Findings. London: Department of Work and Pensions. Retrieved from https://www.gov.uk/government/uploads
/system/uploads/attachment_data/file/329168/if-pilots-qual-eval
-report-880.pdf.

Instiglio, and Thomson Reuters Foundation. 2014. *A Legal Road Map for Social*
Impact Bonds in Developing Countries. London: Instiglio and Thomson
Reuters Foundation. Retrieved from http://www.instiglio.org/wp-content
/uploads/2015/02/Legal-Road-Map-for-SIBs-in-Developing-Countries.pdf.

Institute for Child Success. 2017. "Pay for Success Financing for Child Care:
Challenges and Opportunities." Retrieved from https://www.institutefor
childsuccess.org/research-policy/search/?_sft_publications-tag=
pay-for-success.

Iossa, E., and D. Martimort. 2015. "The Simple Microeconomics of Public-
Private Partnerships." *Journal of Public Economic Theory* 17 (1): 4–48.
doi:10.1111/jpet.12114.

Istrate, E., and R. Puentes. 2009. *Investing for Success.* Washington, DC: Brookings Institution.

Ito, K. 2019. "The Rise of Social Impact Bonds in Japan." *Japan Times,* 20 January.
Retrieved from https://www.japantimes.co.jp/esg-consortium/2019/01
/20/esg-consortium/rise-social-impact-bonds-japan/.

Jabbar, H. 2015. "How Do School Leaders Respond to Competition? Market-based Competition and School Leader Strategies." New Orleans, LA: Education Research Alliance for New Orleans. Retrieved from https://educationresearchalliancenola.org/publications/what-effect-did-the-post-katrina-school-reforms-have-on-student-outcomes.

Jack, A. 2018. "Table: The top global social impact bonds." *Financial Times*, 18 December. Retrieved from https://www.ft.com/content/99b49376-eea6-11e8-89c8-d36339d835c0.

Jackson, E.T. 2013. "Evaluating Social Impact Bonds: Questions, Challenges, Innovations, and Possibilities in Measuring Outcomes in Impact Investing." *Community Development* 44 (5): 608–16. doi:10.1080/15575330.2013.854258.

Jacques, O., and A. Noël. 2018. "The Case for Welfare State Universalism, or the Lasting Relevance of the Paradox of Redistribution." *Journal of European Social Policy* 28 (1): 70–85. doi:10.1177/0958928717700564.

Jagelewski, A. 2016. Presentation on social impact bonds at the Winnipeg Social Finance Forum, 15 November. Retrieved from https://ccednet-rdec.ca/en/event/2016/11/15/winnipeg-social-finance-forum-ccednet-event.

Jamieson, D., R. Wilson, M. Martin, T. Lowe, J. Kimmitt, J. Gibbon, and M. French. 2020. "Data for Outcome Payments or Information for Care? A Sociotechnical Analysis of the Management Information System in the Implementation of a Social Impact Bond." *Public Money & Management* 40 (3): 213–24. doi: 10.1080/09540962.2020.1714306.

Jaumotte, F., and C. Osorio Buitron. 2015. "Inequality and Labor Market Institutions." IMF Staff Discussion Note SDN/15/14. Washington, DC: International Monetary Fund.

Jervis, R. 1992. "Political Implications of Loss Aversion." *Political Psychology* 13 (2): 187–204. doi:10.2307/3791678.

Jespersen, S.T., J.R. Munch, and L. Skipper. 2008. "Costs and Benefits of Danish Active Labour Market Programmes." *Labour Economics* 15 (5): 859–84. doi:10.1016/j.labeco.2007.07.005.

Jessop, B. 1985. Nicos Poulantzas: Marxist Theory and Political Strategy. London: Macmillan.

Jessop, B. 1990. *State Theory: Putting the Capitalist State in Its Place*. University Park, PA: Penn State Press.

Jolliffe, D., and C. Hedderman. 2014. *Peterborough Social Impact Bond: Final Report on Cohort 1 Analysis*. Leicester, UK: University of Leicester. Retrieved from https://www.gov.uk/government/uploads/system/uploads/attachment_data/file/341684/peterborough-social-impact-bond-report.pdf.

Jooste, S.F., and W.R. Scott. 2012. "The Public-Private Partnership Enabling Field: Evidence from Three Cases." *Administration & Society* 44 (2): 149–82. doi:10.1177/0095399711413868.

Joy, M., and J. Shields. 2013. "Social Impact Bonds: The Next Phase of Third Sector Marketization?" *Canadian Journal of Nonprofit and Social Economy Research* 4 (2): 39–55. doi:10.22230/cjnser.2013v4n2a148.

Joy, M., and J. Shields. 2017. "Austerity and the Non-profit Sector: Austerity and Social Impact Bonds." In *The Austerity State*, ed. S. McBride and B.M. Evans, 309–30. Toronto: University of Toronto Press.

Joy, M., and J. Shields. 2018. "Austerity in the Making: Reconfiguring Social Policy through Social Impact Bonds." *Policy & Politics* 46 (4): 681–95. doi:10.1332/030557318X15200933925397.

Joy, M., and J. Shields. 2020. "Debate: How Do Social Impact Bonds Economize Social Policy?" *Public Money & Management* 40 (3):190–192. doi:10.1080/09540962.2020.1714300.

Kalt, J.P., and M.A. Zupan. 1984. "Capture and Ideology in the Economic Theory of Politics." *American Economic Review* 74 (3): 279–300. Retrieved from https://www.jstor.org/stable/1804008.

Katz, S.N. 2005. "What Does It Mean to Say That Philanthropy Is 'Effective'? The Philanthropists' New Clothes." *Proceedings of the American Philosophical Society* 149 (2): 123–30. https://www.jstor.org/stable/4598921.

Keltanen, T. 2017. "Government to use the SIB model: Effective, impact-based investments in well-being are under way." *Sitra*, 30 June. Retrieved from https://www.sitra.fi/en/news/government-use-sib-model/.

Keltanen, T. 2018. "What's happening with the occupational well-being SIB?" *Sitra*, 13 February. Retrieved from https://www.sitra.fi/en/news/whats-happening-occupational-well-sib/.

Kendall, J. 2003. *The Voluntary Sector: Comparative Perspectives in the UK*. New York: Routledge.

Kidd, S. 2015. "The Political Economy of 'Targeting' of Social Security Schemes." *Development Pathways* (19): 1–26. Retrieved from https://www.researchgate.net/profile/Stephen_Kidd3/publication/283498208_The_political_economy_of_targeting_of_social_security_schemes/links/563b3b7908ae405111a68137/The-political-economy-of-targeting-of-social-security-schemes.pdf.

Kido, N., R. Petacchi, and J. Weber. 2012. "The Influence of Elections on the Accounting Choices of Governmental Entities." *Journal of Accounting Research* 50 (2): 443–76. doi:10.1111/j.1475-679X.2012.00447.x.

Kingdon, J.W. 2003. *Agendas, Alternatives, and Public Policies*. 2nd ed. New York: Longman.

Kippy, J. 2013. "Innovation Needs Foundation Support: The Case of Social Impact Bonds." *Community Development Investment Review* 9 (1): 75–8. Retrieved from https://ideas.repec.org/a/fip/fedfcr/00005.html.

Kitzmueller, M. 2010. "Economics and Corporate Social Responsiblity." In *21st Century Economics: A Reference Handbook*, ed. R.C. Free, 785–95. London: SAGE.

Klaassen, K., and G. de Mari. 2017. *Social Impact Bond: The Development of SIB as an Alternative Financing Form*. The Hague: The Hague University of Applied Sciences. Retrieved from https://www.thehagueuniversity.com/docs/default-source/studie-kiezen/whitepapers/t17618-mpc-social-impact-bond_gb.pdf.

Klein, N. 2007. *The Shock Doctrine: The Rise of Disaster Capitalism*. Toronto: Knopf.

Kleinknecht, A., Z. Kwee, and L. Budyanto. 2016. "Rigidities through Flexibility: Flexible Labour and the Rise of Management Bureaucracies." *Cambridge Journal of Economics* 40 (4): 1137–47. doi:10.1093/cje/bev056.

Klitgaard, R. 1997. "Cleaning Up and Invigorating the Civil Service." *Public Administration and Development* 17 (5): 487–509. doi:10.1002/(SICI)1099-162X(199712)17:5<487::AID-PAD981>3.0.CO;2-1.

Kneer, C. 2013. "Finance as a Magnet for the Best and Brightest: Implications for the Real Economy." Working Paper 392. Amsterdam: De Nederlandsche Bank. Retrieved from http://papers.ssrn.com.libproxy.newschool.edu/sol3/papers.cfm?abstract_id=2321613.

Koning, P., and C.J. Heinrich. 2013. "Cream-skimming, Parking and Other Intended and Unintended Effects of High-powered, Performance-based Contracts." *Journal of Policy Analysis and Management* 32 (3): 461–83. doi:10.1002/pam.21695.

Koretz, D.M. 2002. "Limitations in the Use of Achievement Tests as Measures of Educators' Productivity." *Journal of Human Resources* 37 (4): 752–77. doi:10.2307/3069616.

Korpi, W., and J. Palme. 1998. "The Paradox of Redistribution and Strategies of Equality: Welfare State Institutions, Inequality, and Poverty in the Western Countries." *American Sociological Review* 63 (5): 661–87. https://doi.org/10.2307/2657333.

Korpi, W., and J. Palme. 2003. "New Politics and Class Politics in the Context of Austerity and Globalization: Welfare State Regress in 18 Countries, 1975–95." *American Political Science Review* 97 (3): 425–46. https://doi.org/10.1017/S0003055403000789.

Kotz, D.M. 1987. "Long Waves and Social Structures of Accumulation: A Critique and Reinterpretation." *Review of Radical Political Economics* 19 (4): 16–38. doi:10.1177/048661348701900403.

Kotz, D.M. 2017a. *The Rise and Fall of Neoliberal Capitalism*. Rev. ed. Cambridge, MA: Harvard University Press.

Kotz, D.M. 2017b. "Social Structure of Accumulation Theory, Marxist Theory, and System Transformation." *Review of Radical Political Economics* 49 (4): 534–42. https://doi.org/10.1177%2F0486613417699050.

KPMG. 2014. *Evaluation of the Joint Development Phase of the NSW Social Benefit Bonds Trial*. Sydney: KPMG.

Kreps, D.M. 1997. "Intrinsic Motivation and Extrinsic Incentives." *American Economic Review* 87 (2): 359–64. Retrieved from https://www.jstor.org/stable/2950946.

Krippner, G.R. 2005. "The Financialization of the American Economy." *Socio-Economic Review* 3 (2): 173–208. doi:10.1093/SER/mwi008.

Krippner, G.R. 2011. *Capitalizing on Crisis*. Cambridge, MA: Harvard University Press.

Kuan, L.H. 2009. "Public-Private Partnerships in Defense Acquisition Programs: Defensible?" Monterey, CA: Naval Postgraduate School, Graduate School of Business and Public Policy. Retrieved from http://oai.dtic.mil/oai/oai?verb=getRecord&metadataPrefix=html&identifier=ADA514416.

Laboratório de Investimento Social. 2017. "SIB Research Programme." Retrieved from http://investimentosocial.pt/the-lab/sib-research-programme/?lang=en.

Laffont, J. 1975. "Macroeconomic Constraints, Economic Efficiency and Ethics: An Introduction to Kantian Economics." *Economica* 42 (168): 430–7. doi:10.2307/2553800.

Laffont, J., and D. Martimort. 2002. *The Theory of Incentives: The Principal-Agent Model*. Princeton, NJ: Princeton University Press.

Laffont, J., and J. Tirole. 1988. "Repeated Auctions of Incentive Contracts, Investment, and Bidding Parity with an Application to Takeovers." *Rand Journal of Economics* 19 (4): 516–37. doi:10.2307/2555455.

Laffont, J., and J. Tirole. 1993. *A Theory of Incentives in Procurement and Regulation*. Cambridge, MA: MIT Press.

Lagarde, M., M. Wright, J. Nossiter, and N. Mays. 2013. "Challenges of Payment-for-Performance in Health Care and Other Public Services – Design, Implementation and Evaluation." London: Policy Innovation Research Unit.

Lake, R.W. 2015. "The Financialization of Urban Policy in the Age of Obama." *Journal of Urban Affairs* 37 (1): 75–8. doi:10.1111/juaf.12167.

Lampty, R. 2014. "Hägglund proposes social impact bonds." 17 February. Retrieved from http://socialinnovation.se/hagglund-foreslar-social-impact-bonds/.

Lapavitsas, C. 2012. "Financialised Capitalism: Crisis and Financial Expropriation." In *Financialisation in Crisis*, ed. C. Lapavitsas, 15–50. Leiden, Netherlands: Brill.

Lapavitsas, C. 2013. *Profiting without Producing: How Finance Exploits Us All*. Brooklyn, NY: Verso Books.

Lapavitsas, C., and I. Mendieta-Muñoz. 2016. "The Profits of Financialization." *Monthly Review* 68 (3): 49–62. Retrieved from https://pdfs.semanticscholar.org/76e9/7f568509f70e2e4d5490e46ade1eaf3b7d32.pdf.

Leaman, C.K. 1989. "Forgotten Fundamentals: Successes and Excesses of Direct Government." In *Beyond Privatization: The Tools of Government Action*, ed. L.M. Salamon and M.S. Lund, 53–92. Washington, DC: Urban Institute.

Leathers, C.G. 1989. "Thorstein Veblen's Theories of Governmental Failure: The Critic of Capitalism and Democracy Neglected Some Useful Insights, Hindsight Shows." *American Journal of Economics and Sociology* 48 (3): 293–306. doi:10.1111/j.1536-7150.1989.tb03179.x.

Leete, L. 2006. "Work and the Nonprofit Sector." In *The Nonprofit Sector: A Research Handbook*, ed. W.W. Powell and R. Steinberg, 159–79. New Haven, CT: Yale University Press.

Lester, P. 2014. "Chicago approves early childhood pay-for-success plan." *Social Innovation Research Center*, 6 November. Retrieved from http://www.socialinnovationcenter.org/archives/608.

Lester, P. 2015. "AFSCME, progressive groups criticize pay for success." *Social Innovation Research Center*, 15 December. Retrieved from http://www.socialinnovationcenter.org/archives/1825.

Lester, P. 2018. "Pay for success legislation becomes law." *Social Innovation Research Center*, 9 February. Retrieved from http://www.socialinnovationcenter.org/archives/3176.

Letts, C.W., W. Ryan, and A. Grossman. 1997. "Virtuous Capital: What Foundations Can Learn from Venture Capitalists." *Harvard Business Review* 75: 36–50. Retrieved from https://hbr.org/1997/03/virtuous-capital-what-foundations-can-learn-from-venture-capitalists.

Letza, S.R., C. Smallman, and X. Sun. 2004. "Reframing Privatisation: Deconstructing the Myth of Efficiency." *Policy Sciences* 37 (2): 159–83. doi:10.1023/B:OLIC.0000048530.30139.98.

Levin, J., and S. Tadelis. 2010. "Contracting for Government Services: Theory and Evidence from US Cities." *Journal of Industrial Economics* 58 (3): 507–41. doi:10.1111/j.1467-6451.2010.00430.x.

Levine, A. 2018. "DCF, Discover and Longwood pilot social impact investing with Blood Bank." Press release. 7 September. Retrieved from https://www.delcf.org/2018/09/dcf-discover-and-longwood-pilot-social-impact-investing-with-blood-bank/.

Levitt, K.P. 2013. *From the Great Transformation to the Great Financialization*." New York: ZED Books.

Liebman, J.B. 2011. "Social Impact Bonds: A Promising New Financing Model to Accelerate Social Innovation and Improve Government Performance." Washington DC: Center for American Progress. Retrieved from https://www.americanprogress.org/issues/open-government/report/2011/02/09/9050/social-impact-bonds/.

Liebman, J.B., and A. Feller. 2014. "The Economics and Econometrics of Social Impact Bonds." Cambridge, MA: Harvard University. Retrieved from

https://scholar.harvard.edu/feller/publications/economics-and
-econometrics-social-impact-bonds.

Liebman, J.B., and A. Sellman. 2013. "Social Impact Bonds: A Guide for State and Local Governments." Cambridge, MA: Harvard Kennedy School, Social Impact Bond Technical Assistance Lab. Retrieved from http://projects .iq.harvard.edu/files/siblab/files/social-impact-bonds-a-guide-for -state-and-local-governments.pdf.

Light, C. 2016. "The 2015 John Gaus Award Lecture: Vision + Action = Faithful Execution: Why Government Daydreams and How to Stop the Cascade of Breakdowns that Now Haunts It." *Political Science & Politics* 49 (1): 5–20. doi:10.1017/S1049096515001110.

Lindbeck, A., and J.W. Weibull. 1987. "Balanced-Budget Redistribution as the Outcome of Political Competition." *Public Choice* 52 (3): 273–97. https://doi .org/10.1007/BF00116710.

Linde, J., and B. Vis. 2017. "Do Politicians Take Risks Like the Rest of Us? An Experimental Test of Prospect Theory under MPs." *Political Psychology* 38 (1): 101–17. https://doi.org/10.1111/pops.12335.

Lipsey, M.W., and F.T. Cullen. 2007. "The Effectiveness of Correctional Rehabilitation: A Review of Systematic Reviews." *Annual Review of Law and Social Science* 3: 297–320. doi:10.1146/annurev.lawsocsci.3.081806.112833.

Lipsky, M. 2010. *Street-level Bureaucracy: Dilemmas of the Individual in Public Service*. New York: Russell Sage Foundation.

Lipsky, M., and S.R. Smith. 1989. "Nonprofit Organizations, Government, and the Welfare State." *Political Science Quarterly* 104 (4): 625–48. doi:10.2307/2151102.

Loasby, B.J. 1998. "The Organisation of Capabilities." *Journal of Economic Behavior & Organization* 35 (2): 139–60. https://doi.org/10.1016/S0167 -2681(98)00056-0.

Lowe, T. 2013. "New Development: The Paradox of Outcomes – the More We Measure, the Less We Understand." *Public Money & Management* 33 (3): 213–16. doi:10.1080/09540962.2013.785707.

Lowe, T. 2020. "Debate: The Cost of SIBs." *Public Money & Management* 40 (3): 185–8. doi: 10.1080/09540962.2020.1714289.

Lowe, T., and R. Wilson. 2017. "Playing the Game of Outcomes-based Performance Management: Is Gamesmanship Inevitable? Evidence from Theory and Practice." *Social Policy & Administration* 51 (7): 981–1001. doi:10.1111 /spol.12205.

Loxley, J. 2010. *Public Service, Private Profits: The Political Economy of Public-Private Partnerships in Canada*. Winnipeg: Fernwood.

Loxley, J. 2013. *Social Impact Bonds*. Winnipeg: Canadian Centre for Policy Alternatives – Manitoba. Retrieved from http://www.policyalternatives.ca /publications/reports/social-impact-bonds.

Loxley, J. 2017. Social Impact Bonds and the Financing of Child Welfare. Winnipeg: Canadian Centre for Policy Alternatives – Manitoba. Retrieved from https://www.policyalternatives.ca/publications/reports/social-impact-bonds-and-financing-child-welfare.

Loxley, J. 2020. *Social Impact Bonds and the Financing of Child Welfare Revisited.* Winnipeg: Canadian Centre for Policy Alternatives – Manitoba. Retrieved from https://www.policyalternatives.ca/sites/default/files/uploads/publications/Manitoba%20Office/2020/06/SIBs%20Financing%20Child%20Welfare%20revisited%202020.pdf.

Loxley, J., and J. Hajer. 2019. "Public-Private Partnerships, Social Impact Bonds and the Erosion of the State in Canada." *Studies in Political Economy* 100 (1): 18–40. https://doi.org/10.1080/07078552.2019.1612167.

Loxley, J., and M. Puzyreva. 2015. *Social Impact Bonds: An Update.* Winnipeg: Canadian Centre for Policy Alternatives – Manitoba. Retrieved from https://www.policyalternatives.ca/publications/reports/social-impact-bonds-0.

Lunes, R., R. Frissen, F. Vermeer, and A. Revenboer. 2013. *Social Impact Bonds.* The Hague: Society Impact Platform and Ernest and Young. Retrieved from https://www.societyimpact.nl/wp-content/uploads/2015/06/Social-Impact-Bonds-Society-Impact-2013-English.pdf.

Ly, A., and E. Latimer. 2015. "Housing First Impact on Costs and Associated Cost Offsets: A Review of the Literature." *Canadian Journal of Psychiatry* 60 (11): 475–87. doi:10.1177/070674371506001103.

MacDonald, D. 2013. "Social Impact Bonds." *Alberta Views* 16 (10): 29–32. doi:10.1016/j.aos.2016.10.003.

MacDonald, S., M. Wenban, and G. Ciufo. n.d. "Building Social Bonds: Investing for Impact in Ontario." Retrieved from https://www2.deloitte.com/ca/en/pages/public-sector/articles/building-social-bonds.html.

MacKenzie, D.L., and D.P. Farrington. 2015. "Preventing Future Offending of Delinquents and Offenders: What Have We Learned from Experiments and Meta-analyses?" *Journal of Experimental Criminology* 11 (4): 565–95. doi:10.1007/s11292-015-9244-9.

Maier, F., G.P. Barbetta, and F. Godina. 2018. "Paradoxes of Social Impact Bonds." *Social Policy & Administration* 52 (7): 1332–53. doi:10.1111/spol.12343.

Maier, F., and M. Meyer. 2017. "Social Impact Bonds and the Perils of Aligned Interests." *Administrative Sciences* 7 (3): 24. doi:10.3390/admsci7030024/.

Mair, V. 2016. "French government launching social impact bonds with Mirova's support: Call for proposals for 'social impact contracts' announced." *Responsible Investor*, 25 April. Retrieved from https://www.responsible-investor.com/home/article/french_government_launching_sib/.

Malcolmson, J.D. 2014. "Social Impact Bonds: Cleared for Landing in British Columbia." Burnaby, BC: Canadian Union of Pubic Employees Research Branch, British Columbia Region. Retrieved from http://cupe.ca /social-impact-bonds-cleared-landing-british-columbia.

Manitoba. 2019. "Manitoba announces first social impact bond." Press release, 7 January. Winnipeg. Retrieved from https://news.gov.mb.ca/news/index .html?item=44895.

Mannion, L. 2018. "UBS puts Indian girls into school – and makes a profit." *Thomson Reuters*, 13 July. Retrieved from https://www.reuters.com/article /us-india-education-investment/ubs-puts-indian-girls-into-school-and -makes-a-profit-idUSKBN1K31F3.

Margolis, H. 1982. *Selfishness, Altruism and Rationality*. Cambridge: Cambridge University Press.

Martimort, D., and J. Pouyet. 2008. "To Build or Not to Build: Normative and Positive Theories of Public-Private Partnerships." *International Journal of Industrial Organization* 26 (2): 393–411. doi:10.1016/j.ijindorg.2006.10.004.

Martin, L.L. 2007. "Performance-based Contracting for Human Services: A Proposed Model." *Public Administration Quarterly* 31 (2): 130–58. Retrieved from https://www.jstor.org/stable/41288286.

Martin, L.L. 2015. "Performance-based Contracting." In *Government Contracting: A Public Solutions Handbook*, ed. R.A. Shick, 61–74. New York: Routledge.

Marx, K., and F. Engels. [1848] 1963. *The Communist Manifesto*, ed. D. Ryazanoff. Reprint. New York: Russell and Russell. Retrieved from https:// heinonline.org/HOL/P?h=hein.cow/comanif0001&i=2.

Maskin, E., and J. Tirole. 2008. "Public–Private Partnerships and Government Spending Limits." *International Journal of Industrial Organization* 26 (2): 412–20. doi:10.1016/j.ijindorg.2007.05.004.

Mason, A., and M. Goddard. 2009. "Payment by Results in Mental Health: A Review of the International Literature and an Economic Assessment of the Approach in the English NHS." York, UK: Centre for Health Economics. Retrieved from http://www.york.ac.uk/che/pdf/rp50.pdf.

Maze. 2018. "The Launch of One Value." Retrieved from https://maze-impact .com/2018/06/20/the-launch-of-one-value/.

Mazzucato, M. 2015. *The Entrepreneurial State: Debunking Public vs. Private Sector Myths*. New York: Public Affairs.

McGoey, L. 2014. "The Philanthropic State: Market–State Hybrids in the Philanthrocapitalist Turn." *Third World Quarterly* 35 (1): 109–25. doi:10.1080/01436597.2014.868989.

McGregor-Lowndes, M., and C. Ryan. 2009. "Reducing the Compliance Burden of Non-profit Organisations: Cutting Red Tape." *Australian Journal of Public Administration* 68 (1): 21–38. doi:10.1111/j.1467-8500.2008.00607.x.

McHugh, N., S. Sinclair, M. Roy, L. Huckfield, and C. Donaldson. 2013. "Social Impact Bonds: A Wolf in Sheep's Clothing?" *Journal of Poverty & Social Justice* 21 (3): 47–57. doi:10.1332/204674313X13812372137921.

McKay, K. 2013a. "Debunking the Myths behind Social Impact Bond Speculation." *Stanford Social Innovation Review*, 8 April. Retrieved from http://www.ssireview.org/blog/entry/debunking_the_myths_behind _social_impact_bond_speculation.

McKay, K. 2013b. "Evaluating Social Impact Bonds as a New Reentry Financing Mechanism: A Case Study on Reentry Programming in Maryland." Annapolis, ML: Department of Legislative Services. Retrieved from http:// works.bepress.com/cgi/viewcontent.cgi?article=1002&context=kylemckay.

McKee, M., and D. Stuckler. 2011. "The Assault on Universalism: How to Destroy the Welfare State." *British Medical Journal* (Clinical research ed.) 343: d7973. doi:10.1136/bmj.d7973.

McWilliams, A., and D. Siegel. 2001. "Corporate Social Responsibility: A Theory of the Firm Perspective." *Academy of Management Review* 26 (1): 117–27. doi:10.5465/amr.2001.4011987.

Mehrotra, A., C.L. Damberg, M.E. Sorbero, and S.S. Teleki. 2009. "Pay for Performance in the Hospital Setting: What Is the State of the Evidence?" *American Journal of Medical Quality* 24 (1): 19–28. doi:10.1177/1062860608326634.

Mendell, M. 2010. "Reflections on the Evolving Landscape of Social Enterprise in North America." *Policy and Society* 29 (3): 243–56. doi:10.1016/j.polsoc .2010.07.003.

Menezes, F., and M. Ryan. 2015. "Default and Renegotiation in Public-Private Partnership Auctions." *Journal of Public Economic Theory* 17 (1): 49–77. doi:10.1111/jpet.12102.

Milner, J., E.C. Poethig, J. Roman, and K. Walsh. 2015. "Putting Evidence First: Learning from the Rikers Island Social Impact Bond." *Huffington Post*, 6 July. Retrieved from https://www.huffingtonpost.com/john-roman-phd /putting-evidence-first-le_b_7738994.html.

Mirowski, P. 2013. *Never Let a Serious Crisis Go to Waste: How Neoliberalism Survived the Financial Meltdown*. New York: Verso Books.

Mirowski, P. 2015. "Postface: Defining Neoliberalism." In *The Road from Mont Pelèrin: The Making of the Neoliberal Thought Collective*, ed. P. Mirowski and D. Plehwe, 417–55. Cambridge, MA: Harvard University Press.

Moe, T.M. 1990. "Political Institutions: The Neglected Side of the Story." *Journal of Law, Economics, and Organization* 6 (Special ed.): 213–53. https://doi .org/10.1093/jleo/6.special_issue.213.

Mollinger-Sahba, A., P. Flatau, D. Schepis, and S. Purchase. 2020. "New Development: Complexity and Rhetoric in Social Impact Investment." *Public Money & Management* 40 (3): 250–4. https://doi.org/10.1080/09540962.2020 .1714318.

Moore, M., F.R. Westley, and A. Nicholls. 2012. "The Social Finance and Social Innovation Nexus." *Journal of Social Entrepreneurship* 3 (2): 115–32. doi:10.1080/19420676.2012.725824.

Morallos, D., and A. Amekudzi. 2008. "The State of the Practice of Value for Money Analysis in Comparing Public-Private Partnerships to Traditional Procurements." *Public Works Management & Policy* 13 (2): 114–25. doi:10.1177/1087724X08326176.

Morley, J. 2019. "The Ethical Status of Social Impact Bonds." *Journal of Economic Policy Reform.* doi:10.1080/17487870.2019.1573681.

Morse, A. 2015. *Outcome-based Payment Schemes: Government's Use of Payment by Results.* London: National Audit Office.

Mueller, E.J., and J.R. Tighe. 2007. "Making the Case for Affordable Housing: Connecting Housing with Health and Education Outcomes." *Journal of Planning Literature* 21 (4): 371–85. doi:10.1177/0885412207299653.

Mueller, D.C. 2003. *Public Choice III.* Cambridge: Cambridge University Press.

Mulgan, G., N. Reeder, M. Aylott, and L. Bo'sher. 2011. *Social Impact Investment: The Challenge and Opportunity of Social Impact Bonds.* London: Young Foundation. Retrieved from http://youngfoundation.org/publications/social-impact-investment-the-opportunity-and-challenge-of-social-impact-bonds/.

Muñoz, P., and J. Kimmitt. 2019. "A Diagnostic Framework for Social Impact Bonds in Emerging Economies." *Journal of Business Venturing Insights* 12 (e00141): 1–9. https://doi.org/10.1016/j.jbvi.2019.e00141.

Murnane, R., and D. Cohen. 1986. "Merit Pay and the Evaluation Problem: Why Most Merit Pay Plans Fail and a Few Survive." *Harvard Educational Review* 56 (1): 1–18. doi:10.17763/haer.56.1.l8q2334243271116.

Musgrave, R.A. 1999. "The Nature of the Fiscal State: The Roots of My Thinking." In *Public Finance and Public Choice: Two Contrasting Visions of the State,* ed. J.M. Buchanan and R.A. Musgrave, 29–49. Cambridge, MA: MIT Press.

National Council of Nonprofits. 2016. "Pay for Success, Social Impact Bonds: Principles on New Funding Mechanisms." Retrieved from https://www.councilofnonprofits.org/trends-policy-issues/pay-success-social-impact-bonds-principles-new-funding-mechanisms.

National Union of Public and General Employees. 2012. "Social Impact Bonds: A New Way to Privatize Public Services." Ottawa: National Union of Public and General Employees. Retrieved from http://nupge.ca/sites/nupge.ca/files/Social_Impact_Bonds.pdf.

National Union of Public and General Employees. 2017. "Social Impact Bonds: Putting Profit before People." 27 July. Retrieved from https://nupge.ca/content/social-impact-bonds-putting-profit-people.

National Union of Public and General Employees. 2018. "Will It Be Social Finance or Anti-social Finance?" Retrieved from https://nupge.ca/content/will-it-be-social-finance-or-anti-social-finance.

National Union of Public and General Employees. 2019. "Social Impact Bond Announcements Short on Details." 23 January. Retrieved from https://nupge.ca/content/social-impact-bond-announcements-short-details.

Neal, D. 2011. "The Design of Performance Pay in Education." In *Handbook of the Economics of Education*, vol. 4, ed. E.A. Hanushek, S. Machin, and L. Woessmann, 495–550. Amsterdam: North-Holland. https://doi.org/10.1016/B978-0-444-53444-6.00006-7.

New Economy. 2015. "Unit Cost Database." Retrieved from https://golab.bsg.ox.ac.uk/knowledge-bank/resources/unit-cost-database/.

New South Wales. 2017. Office of Social Impact Investment. "Social Benefit Bonds." Sydney. Retrieved from http://www.osii.nsw.gov.au/initiatives/social-benefit-bonds/.

New Zealand. 2013. Office of the Minister of Health. "Social Bonds: Proposal for a New Zealand Pilot." Wellington: Ministry of Health. Retrieved from https://www.health.govt.nz/system/files/documents/pages/social-bonds-cabinet-paper-redacted-v1.pdf.

New Zealand. 2016. Treasury and Ministry of Health. "Joint Report: Social Bonds Pilot Procurement: Lessons Learned Review." Report T2016/1602. Wellington: New Zealand Treasury. Retrieved from http://www.treasury.govt.nz/publications/informationreleases/socialbonds.

New Zealand. 2017a. Office of the Ministry of Health. "Social Bonds: New Zealand Pilot." Wellington: Ministry of Health. Retrieved from https://www.health.govt.nz/our-work/preventative-health-wellness/social-bonds-new-zealand-pilot.

New Zealand. 2017b. Treasury and Ministry of Health. "*Joint Report: Draft SOC Paper on the First Social Bond.*" Report 20161925. Wellington: New Zealand Treasury. Retrieved from http://www.treasury.govt.nz/publications/informationreleases/socialbonds/sb-3693730.pdf.

Neyland, D. 2018. "On the Transformation of Children At-Risk into an Investment Proposition: A Study of Social Impact Bonds as an Anti-market Device." *Sociological Review* 66 (3): 492–510. doi:10.1177/0038026117744415.

Ng, I.C., R. Maull, and N. Yip. 2009. "Outcome-based Contracts as a Driver for Systems Thinking and Service-Dominant Logic in Service Science: Evidence from the Defence Industry." *European Management Journal* 27 (6): 377–87. doi:10.1016/j.emj.2009.05.002.

Nicholls, A., and E. Tomkinson. 2013. *The Peterborough Pilot Social Impact Bond*. Oxford: University of Oxford, Said Business School. Retrieved from https://emmatomkinson.files.wordpress.com/2013/06/case-study-the-peterborough-pilot-social-impact-bond-oct-2013.pdf.

Nippon Foundation. 2015. "Third pilot project for 'social impact bond' structure: Nippon foundation and Amagasaki City joining to support

employment for young persons." Retrieved from https://www.nippon
-foundation.or.jp/en/news/articles/2015/121.html.

Niskanen, J. 2017. *Bureaucracy and Representative Government*. Chicago: Aldine.

Nonprofit Finance Fund. 2017. "Dataset: PFS Project Matrix." Retrieved from
http://www.payforsuccess.org/projects/.

North, D.C. 1979. "A Framework for Analyzing the State in Economic History." *Explorations in Economic History* 16 (3): 249–59. Retrieved from
https://search.proquest.com/openview/fbdb5b8d0d3962f2362821cfe1d7c6
a0/1?pq-origsite=gscholar&cbl=1819326.

North, D.C. 1981. A Neoclassical Theory of the State." In *Structure and Change
in Economic History*, ed. D.C. North, 20–32. New York: W.W. Norton.

Nuckols, T.K., E. Keeler, S. Morton, L. Anderson, B.J. Doyle,. J. Pevnick, M.
Booth, et al. 2017. "Economic Evaluation of Quality Improvement Interventions Designed to Prevent Hospital Readmission: A Systematic Review and
Meta-analysis." *JAMA Internal Medicine* 177 (7): 975–85. doi:10.1111
/milq.12015.

O'Connor, E.A., J.S. Lin, B.U. Burda, J.T. Henderson, E.S. Walsh, and E.P. Whit-
lock. 2014. "Behavioral Sexual Risk-Reduction Counseling in Primary Care
to Prevent Sexually Transmitted Infections: A Systematic Review for the US
Preventive Services Task Force Behavioral Counseling to Prevent STIs." *Annals of Internal Medicine* 161 (12): 874–83. doi:10.7326/M14-0475.

O'Connor, J. 1973. *The Fiscal Crisis of the State*. London: St Martin's Press.

OECD (Organisation for Economic Co-operation and Development). 2017.
"Competition Issues in Public-Private Partnerships." Paris: OECD. Retrieved from http://www.oecd.org/competition/competitionissuesinpublic
-privatepartnerships.htm.

OECD (Organisation for Economic Co-operation and Development). 2018.
"OECD.Stat." Retrieved from http://stats.oecd.org/.

Oklahoma. 2017. "Gov. Fallin announces Oklahoma's first-ever pay for success
contract addressing female incarceration." Press release, 11 April. Oklahoma
City. Retrieved from www.socialfinance.org/content/uploads
/External-Fact-Sheet.pdf.

Olson, J., and A. Phillips. 2013. "Rikers Island: The First Social Impact Bond in
the United States." *Community Development Investment Review* 9 (1): 97–101.
Retrieved from https://ideas.repec.org/a/fip/fedfcr/00009.html.

Olson, M. 1965. *The Logic of Collective Action: Public Goods and the Theory of
Groups*. Cambridge, MA: Harvard University.

Ontario. 2017. "Social Impact Bonds." Toronto. Retrieved from https://www
.ontario.ca/page/social-impact-bonds.

Ormiston, J., M. Moran, E.I. Castellas, and E. Tomkinson. 2020. "Everybody
Wins? A Discourse Analysis of Competing Stakeholder Expectations in

Social Impact Bonds." *Public Money & Management* 40 (3): 237–46. doi:10.1080/09540962.2020.1714316.

Ostrom, E. 2005. "Policies that Crowd Out Reciprocity and Collective Action." In *Moral Sentiments and Material Interests: The Foundations of Cooperation in Economic Life*, ed. H. Gintis, S. Bowles, R.T. Boyd, and E. Fehr, 253–76. Cambridge, MA: MIT Press.

O'Toole, B.J. 2006. "The Emergence of a 'New' Ethical Framework for Civil Servants." *Public Money & Management* 26 (1): 39–46. https://doi.org/10.1111/J.1467-9302.2005.00499.X.

Overholser, G., and C. Whistler. 2013. "The Real Revolution of Pay for Success: Ending 40 Years of Stagnant Results for Communities." *Community Development Investment Review* 9 (1): 5–11. doi:10.1111/j.1467-9302.2005.00499.x.

Owen, R. 2017. "Our pioneering project has cut reoffending – and paid a 3% dividend." *Guardian*, 9 August. Retrieved from https://www.theguardian.com/public-leaders-network/2017/aug/09/social-impact-bond-reoffending-dividend.

Painter, G., K. Albertson, C. Fox, and C. O'Leary. 2018. "Social Impact Bonds: More than One Approach." *Stanford Social Innovation Review*, 28 December. Retrieved from https://ssir.org/articles/entry/social_impact_bonds_more_than_one_approach.

Palameta, B., K. Myers, and N. Conte. 2013. *Applying Performance Funding to Essential Skills: State of Knowledge Review*. Ottawa: Social Research and Demonstration Corporation.

Pandey, S., J.J. Cordes, S.K. Pandey, and W.F. Winfrey. 2018. "Use of Social Impact Bonds to Address Social Problems: Understanding Contractual Risks and Transaction Costs." *Nonprofit Management and Leadership* 28 (4): 511–28. doi:10.1002/nml.21307.

Pan-Impact Korea. n.d.a. "About Us." Retrieved from http://panimpact.kr/about_us/.

Pan-Impact Korea. n.d.b. "Seoul SIB Fact Sheet." Retrieved from http://panimpact.kr/seoul-sib-fact-sheet/.

Pape, U., T. Brandsen, J.B., Pahl, B. Pieli-ski, D. Baturina, N. Brookes, R. Chavez-Ávila, et al. 2019. "Changing Policy Environments in Europe and the Resilience of the Third Sector." *VOLUNTAS: International Journal of Voluntary and Nonprofit Organizations* 31: 238–49. doi:10.1007/s11266-018-00087-z.

Parker, D., and K. Hartley, 2003. "Transaction Costs, Relational Contracting and Public Private Partnerships: A Case Study of UK Defence." *Journal of Purchasing and Supply Management* 9 (3): 97–108. doi:10.1016/S0969-7012(02)00035-7.

Partnership for Public Procurement. 2012. "Public Procurement Practice: Performance based Contracting." Retrieved from http://216.22.26.112/wp-content/uploads/2013/04/PerformanceBased.pdf.

Pauly, M.V., and A. Swanson. 2014. "Social Impact Bonds: New Product or New Package?" NBER Working Paper 18991. Cambridge, MA: National Bureau of Economic Research. Retrieved from http://www.nber.org/papers/w18991.

Pauly, M.V., and A. Swanson. 2017. "Social Impact Bonds: New Product or New Package?" *Journal of Law, Economics, and Organization* 33 (4): 718–60. doi:10.1093/jleo/ewx012.

Peltzman, S. 1976. "Toward a More General Theory of Regulation." *Journal of Law and Economics* 19 (2): 211–40. doi:10.1086/466865.

Peltzman, S. 1992. "Voters as Fiscal Conservatives." *Quarterly Journal of Economics* 107 (2): 327–61. doi:10.2307/2118475.

Pendeven, B., Y. Nico, and B. Gachet. 2015. *Social Impact Bonds: un nouvel outil pour le financement de l'innovation sociale.* Paris: Institut de l'entreprise. Retrieved from http://www.institut-entreprise.fr/documents/WEB_NOTE_SIB_ET%20ANNEXES.pdf.

Pennell, T. 2014. "Fact Sheet: The Cuyahoga Partnering for Family Success Program." Cleveland, OH: Enterprise Community Partners. Retrieved from https://www.enterprisecommunity.org/sites/default/files/cuyahoga-pfs-fact-sheet.pdf.

Peretti, J. 2016. "How management consultants are cashing in on austerity." *Guardian,* 17 October. Retrieved from https://www.theguardian.com/business/2016/oct/17/management-consultants-cashing-in-austerity-public-sector-cuts.

Perry, J.L. 1996. "Measuring Public Service Motivation: An Assessment of Construct Reliability and Validity." *Journal of Public Administration Research and Theory: J-PART* 6 (1): 5–22. https://doi.org/10.1093/oxfordjournals.jpart.a024303.

Perry, J.L., and H.G. Rainey. 1988. "The Public-Private Distinction in Organization Theory: A Critique and Research Strategy." *Academy of Management Review* 13 (2): 182–201. doi:10.1093/oxfordjournals.jpart.a024303.

Perry, J.L., and W. Vandenabeele. 2015. "Public Service Motivation Research: Achievements, Challenges, and Future Directions." *Public Administration Review* 75 (5): 692–9. doi:10.1111/puar.12430.

Perry, J.L., and L.R. Wise. 1990. "The Motivational Bases of Public Service." *Public Administration Review* 50 (3): 367–73. doi:10.2307/976618.

Petersen, L., A. LeChauncy, D. Woodard, T. Urech, C. Daw, and S. Sookanan. 2006. "Does Pay-for-Performance Improve the Quality of Health Care?" *Annals of Internal Medicine* 145 (4): 265–72. https://doi.org/10.7326/0003-4819-146-7-200704030-00015.

Petersen, O.H., U. Hjelmar, and K. Vrangbæk. 2017. "Is Contracting Out of Public Services Still the Great Panacea? A Systematic Review of Studies on Economic and Quality Effects from 2000 to 2014." *Social Policy & Administration* 52 (1): 130–57. doi:10.1111/spol.12297.

Pettijohn, S.L. 2013a. *Federal Government Contracts and Grants for Nonprofits.* Washington, DC: Urban Institute.

Pettijohn, S.L. 2013b. *The Nonprofit Sector in Brief: Public Charities, Giving and Volunteering 2013.* Washington, DC: Urban Institute.

Picot, A., M. Florio, N. Grove, and J. Kranz. 2016. "Public Infrastructure Provisioning: Foundations and Challenges." In *The Economics of Infrastructure Provisioning: The Changing Role of the State*, ed. A. Picot, M. Florio, N. Grove, and J. Kranz, 3–22. Cambridge, MA: MIT Press.

Pierson, P. 1994. *Dismantling the Welfare State? Reagan, Thatcher and the Politics of Retrenchment.* Cambridge: Cambridge University Press.

Pierson, P. 1996. "The New Politics of the Welfare State." *World Politics* 48 (2): 143–79. doi:10.1353/wp.1996.0004.

Pintelon, O. 2012. "Welfare State Decommodification: Concepts, Operationalizations and Long-Term Trends." Working Paper 12/10. Antwerp: Herman Deleeck Centre for Social Policy.

Pioneers Post. 2019. "Numbers for Good announces closure." 21 February. Retrieved from https://www.pioneerspost.com/news-views/20190221/numbers-good-announces-closure.

Platt, E. 2018. "Japan's social impact bonds attract healthy support." *Financial Times*, 18 November. Retrieved from https://www.ft.com/content/7d6877ec-ce16-11e8-8d0b-a6539b949662.

Podgursky, M.J., and M.G. Springer. 2007. "Teacher Performance Pay: A Review." *Journal of Policy Analysis and Management* 26 (4), 909–50. Retrieved from https://www.jstor.org/stable/30162809.

Popper, N. 2015. "Success metrics questioned in school program funded by Goldman." *New York Times*, 3 November. Retrieved from https://www.nytimes.com/2015/11/04/business/dealbook/did-goldman-make-the-grade.html.

Le portail de l'Économie. 2016. "Michel Sapin et Martine Pinville ont signé les deux premiers contrats à impact social en présence du Président de la République." Le portail de l'Économie, des Finances, de l'Action et des Comptes publics, 23 November. Retrieved from https://www.economie.gouv.fr/signature-deux-contrats-impact-social.

Porter, E. 2015. "Wall St. money meets social policy at Rikers Island." *New York Times*, 28 July. Retrieved from https://www.nytimes.com/2015/07/29/business/economy/wall-st-money-meets-social-policy-at-rikers-island.html.

PPP Canada. 2011. "PPP Business Case Development Guide." Ottawa: PPP Canada. Retrieved from http://www.p3canada.ca/_files/P3%20Business %20Case%20Development%20Guide.pdf.

Prendergast, C. 1999. "The Provision of Incentives in Firms." *Journal of Economic Literature* 37 (1): 7–63. doi:10.1257/jel.37.1.7.

Press, J. 2019. "Liberals set to unveil social-finance strategy, including $755M in new fund." *CTV News*, 12 June. Retrieved from https://www.ctvnews .ca/politics/liberals-set-to-unveil-social-finance-strategy-including-755m -in-new-fund-1.4462630.

Pressman, S. 2004. "What Is Wrong with Public Choice." *Journal of Post Keynesian Economics* 27 (1): 3–18. doi:10.1080/01603477.2004.11051423.

Preston, A.E. 1989. "The Nonprofit Worker in a For-profit World." *Journal of Labor Economics* 7 (4): 438–63. Retrieved from https://www.journals .uchicago.edu/doi/abs/10.1086/298216.

Prevista. 2017. "Social Impact Bonds." Retrieved from http://www.prevista .co.uk/funder/.

Pro Bono Economics and Frontier Economics. 2010. "St Giles Trust 'Through the Gates' Report: An Analysis of Economic Impact." Retrieved from https://www.probonoeconomics.com/sites/default/files/files/St%20 Giles%20Trust%20%27Through%20the%20Gates%27%20report.pdf.

Psaltopoulou, T., I. Ilias, and M. Alevizaki. 2010. "The Role of Diet and Lifestyle in Primary, Secondary, and Tertiary Diabetes Prevention: A Review of Meta-analyses." *Review of Diabetic Studies: RDS* 7 (1): 26–35. doi:10.1900 /RDS.2010.7.26.

PSI. 2017. "The Utkrisht Impact Bond." 17 November. Retrieved from https:// www.psi.org/2017/11/new-development-impact-bond-will-save-lives/.

Public Health Association of Victoria and VicHealth. 2011. *Healthy Australia: Public Support for Prevention Strategies*. Deakin and Carlton, Australia: Victorian Health Promotion Foundation and Public Health Association of Australia.

Public Services International, New South Wales Nurses and Midwives Association, Community and Public Sector Union, Australia Services Union, Electrical Trades Union, Act!onaid, et al. 2017. "Taking Back Control: A Community Response to Privatisation." Melbourne: Community and Public Sector Union. Retrieved from https://www.cpsucsa.org/peoplesinquiry.

Pyper, R. 2011. "Decentralization, Devolution and the Hollowing Out of the State." In *International Handbook on Civil Service Systems*, ed. A. Massey. 74–103. Cheltenham, UK: Edward Elgar.

Queensland. 2017. "Queensland's second social benefit bond to reduce youth reoffending." Press release. 1 June. Brisbane. Retrieved from http://statements.qld.gov.au/Statement/2017/6/1/queenslands -second-social-benefit-bond-to-reduce-youth-reoffending.

Quiggin, J. 1987. "Egoistic Rationality and Public Choice: A Critical Review of Theory and Evidence." *Economic Record* 63 (1): 10–21. doi:10.1111/j.1475 -4932.1987.tb00633.x.

Ragin, L.J., and T. Paladjian. 2013. "Social Impact Bonds: Using Impact Investment to Expand Effective Social Programs." *Community Development Investment Review* 9 (1): 63–7. Retrieved from https://www.frbsf.org /community-development/files/social-impact-bonds-impact -investment-expand-effective-social-programs.pdf.

Rahman, A. 1999. "Micro-credit Initiatives for Equitable and Sustainable Development: Who Pays?" *World Development* 27 (1): 67–82. doi:10.1016 /S0305-750X(98)00105-3.

Rainey, H.G., and P. Steinbauer. 1999. "Galloping Elephants: Developing Elements of a Theory of Effective Government Organizations." *Journal of Public Administration Research and Theory* 9 (1): 1–32. doi:10.1093/oxfordjournals .jpart.a024401.

Ramsden, P., A. Noya, and S. Galitopoulou. 2016. "Social Impact Bonds: State of Play and Lessons Learnt." OECD Working Paper. Paris: Organisation for Economic Co-operation and Development. Retrieved from https://www .oecd.org/cfe/leed/SIBs-State-Play-Lessons-Final.pdf.

Raphael, D. 2015. "Making Sense of the Social Determinants of Health in Canada." In *The Social Determinants of Health in Manitoba*. 2nd ed., ed. L. Fernandez, S. MacKinnon, and J. Silver, 7–30. Winnipeg: Canadian Centre for Policy Alternatives – Manitoba.

Reddy, S.G. 2012. "Randomise This! On Poor Economics." *Review of Agrarian Studies* 2 (2): 60–73. Retrieved from https://ideas.repec.org/a/fas/journl /v2y2012i2p60-73.html.

Rees, J., R. Taylor, and C. Damm. 2013. "Does Sector Matter? Understanding the Experiences of Providers in the Work Programme." Working Paper 92. Birmingham: University of Birmingham, Third Sector Research Centre. Retrieved from https://www.birmingham.ac.uk/Documents/college-social -sciences/social-policy/tsrc/working-papers/working-paper-92.pdf.

Rees, J., A. Whitworth, and E. Carter. 2014. "Support for All in the UK Work Programme? Differential Payments, Same Old Problem." *Social Policy & Administration* 48 (2), 221–39. doi:10.1111/spol.12058.

Reinvestment Fund. 2017. "First-of-its-kind $10 million pay for success fund announced." Press release, 31 May. Retrieved from https://www.reinvest ment.com/news/2017/05/31/first-kind-10-million-pay-success -fund-announced/.

Reuters. 2017. "Japan's 'social impact bond' gets first batch of investors." 20 July. Retrieved from http://www.reuters.com/article/us-japan-economy -socialimpact-bonds/japans-social-impact-bond-gets-first-batch-of -investors-idUSKBN1A50HJ?il=0.

Rhodes, R.A. 1994. "The Hollowing Out of the State: The Changing Nature of the Public Service in Britain." *Political Quarterly* 65 (2): 138–51. doi:10.1111 /j.1467-923X.1994.tb00441.x.

Rinehart, J.W. 2006. *The Tyranny of Work: Alienation and the Labour Process.* 5th ed. Toronto: Thompson Nelson.

Rittenhouse, D.R., S.M. Shortell, and E.S. Fisher. 2009. "Primary Care and Accountable Care: Two Essential Elements of Delivery-System Reform." *New England Journal of Medicine* 361 (24): 2301–3. doi:10.1056 /NEJMp0909327.

Rizzello, A., and R. Carè. 2016. "Insight into the Social Impact Bond Market: An Analysis of Investors." *ACRN Oxford Journal of Finance and Risk Perspectives* 5 (3): 145–71. Retrieved from https://www.researchgate.net /profile/Alessandro_Rizzello/publication/314114943_Insight_into_the _Social_Impact_Bond_market_an_analysis_of_investors/links /58b6073b45851591c5d18a60/Insight-into-the-Social-Impact-Bond -market-an-analysis-of-investors.pdf.

Robbins, K.C. 2006. "The Nonprofit Sector in Historical Perspective: Traditions of Philanthropy in the West." In *The Nonprofit Sector: A Research Handbook,* ed. W.W. Powell, and R. Steinberg, 13–31. New Haven, CT: Yale University Press.

Roelofs, J. 1995. "The Third Sector as a Protective Layer for Capitalism." *Monthly Review* 47 (4): 16–25. Retrieved from https://go.gale.com/ps/anon ymous?id=GALE%7CA17338537&sid=googleScholar&v=2.1&it=r&linkacce ss=abs&issn=00270520&p=AONE&sw=w.

Roelofs, J. 2003. *Foundations and Public Policy: The Mask of Pluralism.* Albany: State University of New York Press.

Roemer, J.E. 2006. *Political Competition: Theory and Applications.* Cambridge, MA: Harvard University Press.

Rog, D.J., T. Marshall, R.H. Dougherty, P. George, A.S. Daniels, S.S. Ghose, and M. Delphin-Rittmon. 2014. "Permanent Supportive Housing: Assessing the Evidence." *Psychiatric Services* 65 (3): 287–94. doi:10.1176/appi.ps.201300261.

Rogoff, K.S. 1990. "Equilibrium Political Budget Cycles." *American Economic Review* 80 (1): 21–36. Retrieved from https://pubs.aeaweb.org/doi/pdf /10.1257/aer.99.2.466.

Rogoff, K.S., and A. Sibert. 1988. "Elections and Macroeconomic Policy Cycles." *Review of Economic Studies* 55 (1): 1–16. doi:10.2307/2297526.

Romer, D. 2006. *Advanced Macroeconomics.* 3rd ed. New York: McGraw-Hill.

Ronicle, J., T. Fox, and N. Stanworth. 2016. *Commissioning Better Outcomes Fund Evaluation: Update Report Summary Report Targeted at Service Providers.* London: Commissioning Better Outcomes Fund.

Ronicle, J., and N. Stanworth. 2015. *Ways to Wellness Social Impact Bond: The UK's First Health SIB – A Deep Dive Report Produced as Part of the*

Commissioning Better Outcomes Fund Evaluation. London: Big Lottery Fund. Retrieved from https://www.biglotteryfund.org.uk/research/social -investment/publications.

Rose, S. 2016. "Social impact investment market to get a boost in 2016." *Sydney Morning Herald*, 3 January. Retrieved from http://www.smh.com.au /business/social-impact-investment-market-to-get-a-boost-in -2016-20151223-gltxgg.html.

Rose-Ackerman, S. 1996. "Altruism, Nonprofits, and Economic Theory." *Journal of Economic Literature* 34 (2): 701–28. Retrieved from https://www.jstor .org/stable/2729219.

Rosenthal, M.B., R.G. Frank, Z. Li, and A.M. Epstein. 2005. "Early Experience with Pay-for-Performance: From Concept to Practice." *JAMA* 294 (14): 1788–93. retrieved from https://jamanetwork.com/journals/jama /article-abstract/201673.

Ross, W., and P. Navarro. 2016. "Trump versus Clinton on Infrastructure." 27 October. Retrieved from peternavarro.com/sitebuildercontent /sitebuilderfiles/infrastructurereport.pdf.

Rothschild, S. 2013. "Human Capital Performance Bonds." *Community Development Investment Review* 9 (1): 103–8. Retrieved from https://www .frbsf.org/community-development/files/human-capital-performance -bonds.pdf.

Rowthorn, B., and H. Chang. 1992. "The Political Economy of Privatisation." *Economic and Labour Relations Review* 3 (2): 1–17. doi:10.1177/103530469200300201.

Roy, M.J., N. McHugh, and S. Sinclair. 2017. "Social Impact Bonds: Evidence-based Policy or Ideology?" In *The Handbook of Social Policy*, ed. B. Greve, 263–78. Northampton, MA: Edward Elgar.

Roy, M.J., N. McHugh, and S. Sinclair. 2018. "A Critical Reflection on Social Impact Bonds." *Stanford Social Innovation Review*, 1 May. Retrieved from https://ssir.org/articles/entry/a_critical_reflection_on_social_ impact_bonds#.

Ruf, N. 2014. "The First German Social Impact Bond (SIB): The Augsburg Pilot Project." 12 August. Retrieved from http://www.benckiser-stiftung.org /blog/overview-pilot-project-in-augsburg.

Ruf, N. 2017. "Second German SIB Started." 10 September. Retrieved from http://www.benckiser-stiftung.org/blog/second-german-sib-started.

Rutherford, M. 1996. *Institutions in Economics: The Old and the New Institutionalism*. Cambridge: Cambridge University Press.

Ryan, S. 2015. "Social Impact Bonds: The Next Horizon of Privatization." 21 December. Ottawa: Canadian Union of Public Employees. Retrieved from https://cupe.ca/social-impact-bonds-next-horizon -privatization.

Ryan, S. 2017. "Economics 101: Decoding Social Impact Bonds." 23 March. Ottawa: Canadian Union of Public Employees. Retrieved from https://cupe.ca/economics-101-decoding-social-impact-bonds.

Ryan, S., and M. Young. 2018. "Social Impact Bonds: The Next Horizon of Privatization." *Studies in Political Economy* 99 (1): 42–58. doi:10.1080/07078552.2018.1440985.

Sacred Heart Mission. 2018. "Victoria's first Social Impact Investment helping 180 people experiencing homelessness." St Kilda, Australia, 17 August. Retrieved from https://www.sacredheartmission.org/news-media/media-centre/media-releases/victoria-s-first-social-impact-investment-helping-180-people-experiencing-homelessness.

Salamon, L.M. 1987. "Of Market Failure, Voluntary Failure, and Third-Party Government: Toward a Theory of Government-Nonprofit Relations in the Modern Welfare State." *Journal of Voluntary Action Research* 16 (1–2): 29–49. https://doi.org/10.1177/089976408701600104.

Salamon, L.M. 1993. "The Marketization of Welfare: Changing Nonprofit and For-Profit Roles in the American Welfare State." *Social Service Review* 67 (1): 16–39. doi:10.1086/603963.

Salamon, L.M. 2015. *The Resilient Sector Revisited: The New Challenge to Nonprofit America.* Washington, DC: Brookings Institution Press.

Salamon, L.M., and H.K. Anheier. 1998. "Social Origins of Civil Society: Explaining the Nonprofit Sector Cross-nationally." *Voluntas: International Journal of Voluntary and Nonprofit Organizations* 9 (3): 213–48. doi:10.1023/A:1022058200985.

Salamon, L.M., and M.S. Lund. 1989. *Beyond Privatization: The Tools of Government Action.* Washington, DC: Urban Institute.

Salamon, L.M., and S.W. Sokolowski. 2017. "Explaining Civil Society Development I: Preference and Sentiment Theories." In *Explaining Civil Society Development: A Social Origins Approach*, ed. L.M. Salamon, S.W. Sokolowski, and M. Haddock, 45–73. Baltimore: Johns Hopkins University Press.

Salamon, L.M., S.W. Sokolowski, and M. Haddock, eds. 2017. *Explaining Civil Society Development: A Social Origins Approach.* Baltimore: Johns Hopkins University Press.

Saldinger, A. 2017. "DevExplains: Development Impact Bonds." 5 June. Retrieved from https://www.devex.com/news/devexplains-development-impact-bonds-90424.

Saltis, Z.A. 2011. *The Economic Consequences of Declining Real Wages in the United States 1970–2010.* Saarbrücken, Germany: Lambert.

Samuelson, A. 1954. "The Pure Theory of Public Expenditure." *Review of Economics and Statistics* 36 (4): 387–9. doi:10.2307/1925895.

Sanchez, M. 2016. "Investors Earn Maximum Initial Payment from Chicago's Social Impact Bond." *Education Digest* 82 (1): 57. Retrieved from https://

search.proquest.com/openview/fb50b0955e27bccd1777bede67006c8e/1
.pdf?pq-origsite=gscholar&cbl=25066.

Sanger, T. 2017. "Creating a Canadian Infrastructure Bank in the Public Inter-est." Ottawa: Canadian Centre for Policy Alternatives. Retrieved from https://www.policyalternatives.ca/publications/reports /creating-canadian-infrastructure-bank-public-interest.

Sappington, D.E.M., and J.E. Stiglitz. 1987. "Privatization, Information and Incentives." *Journal of Policy Analysis and Management* 6 (4): 567–82. doi:10.2307/3323510.

Sbragia, A.M. 1996. *Debt Wish: Entrepreneurial Cities, US Federalism, and Eco-nomic Development.* Pittsburgh: University of Pittsburgh Press.

Schueth, S. 2003. "Socially Responsible Investing in the United States." *Journal of Business Ethics* 43 (3): 189–94. doi:10.1023/A:1022981828869.

Schumpeter, J.A. 1947. "The Creative Response in Economic History." *Journal of Economic History* 7 (2): 149–59. doi:10.1017/S0022050700054279.

Schweitzer, D.D., J. Pecora, K. Nelson, B. Walters, and B.J. Blythe. 2015. "Build-ing the Evidence Base for Intensive Family Preservation Services." *Journal of Public Child Welfare* 9 (5): 423–43. doi:10.1080/15548732.2015.1090363.

Scott, A., P. Sivey, D.A. Ouakrim, L. Willenberg, L. Naccarella, J. Furler, and D. Young. 2011. "The Effect of Financial Incentives on the Quality of Health Care Provided by Primary Care Physicians." *Cochrane Database of Systematic Reviews* 9 (September). https://doi.org/10.1002/14651858.CD008451.pub2.

Sen, A.K. 1977. "Rational Fools: A Critique of the Behavioral Foundations of Economic Theory." *Philosophy and Public Affairs* 6 (4): 317–44. Retrieved from www.ibiblio.org/philecon/General%20Information_files/rationalfools.pdf.

Sen, A.K. 1992. *The Political Economy of Targeting.* Washington, DC: World Bank.

Shaoul, J. 2005. "The Private Finance Initiative or the Public Funding of Private Profit." In *The Challenge of Public–Private Partnerships: Learning from International Experience,* ed. G.A. Hodge, and C.J. Greaves, 190–206. Chelten-ham, UK: Edward Elgar.

Shaw, S. 2016. "A Difficult Birth: Lessons from the First Social Impact Bond in Germany." 27 September. Retrieved from http://www.benckiser-stiftung .org/blog/a-difficult-birth-lessons-from-the-first-social-impact-bond-in -germany.

Shergold, P., C. Kernot, and L. Hems. 2011. "Report on the NSW Social Impact Bond Pilot." Sydney: Centre for Social Impact. Retrieved from http://www .csi.edu.au/research/project/report-nsw-social-impact-bond-pilot/.

Shiller, R.J. 2013. "Capitalism and Financial Innovation." *Financial Analysts Journal* 69 (1): 21. doi:10.2469/faj.v69.n1.4.

Simon, H.A. 1991. "Organizations and Markets." *Journal of Economic Perspec-tives* 5 (2): 25–44. doi:10.1257/jep.5.2.25.

Sin, C.H., and I. Tsukamoto. 2018. "Japan highlights innovative Asia Pacific model for Social Impact Bonds." 14 May. Retrieved from http://blogs.lshtm.ac.uk/piru/2018/05/14/japan-highlights-innovative-asia-pacific-model-for-social-impact-bonds/.

Sinclair, S., N. McHugh, L. Huckfield, M. Roy, and C. Donaldson. 2014. "Social Impact Bonds: Shifting the Boundaries of Citizenship." In *Social Policy Review 26: Analysis and Debate in Social Policy*, ed. K. Farnsworth, Z. Irving, and M. Fenger, 119–36. Bristol: Policy Press.

Sinclair, S., N. McHugh, and M.J. Roy. 2019. "Social Innovation, Financialisation and Commodification: A Critique of Social Impact Bonds." *Journal of Economic Policy Reform*. doi:10.1080/17487870.2019.1571415.

SITRA. 2017. "About SITRA." Retrieved from https://www.sitra.fi/en/themes/about-sitra/#sitra-at-50.

Smith, V.L. 2003. "Constructivist and Ecological Rationality in Economics." *American Economic Review* 93 (3): 465–508. doi:10.1257/000282803322156954.

Social Enterprise Mark. 2018. "Enabling Social Enterprises through Independent Accreditation." Retrieved from https://www.socialenterprisemark.org.uk/.

Social Finance. (2011). "A Technical Guide to Commissioning Social Impact Bonds." London: Social Finance. Retrieved from https://www.socialfinance.org.uk/sites/default/files/publications/technical-guide-to-commissioning-social-impact-bonds1.pdf.

Social Finance. 2014. *The Essex Social Impact Bond: A Year in Review*. London: Social Finance.

Social Finance. 2016a. "Fact Sheet: South Carolina Nurse-Family Partnership Pay for Success Project." London: Social Finance. Retrieved from https://socialfinance.org/wp-content/uploads/2016/02/021616-SC-NFP-PFS-Fact-Sheet_vFINAL.pdf.

Social Finance. 2016b. "Global Network." London: Social Finance. Retrieved from http://socialfinance.org/global-network/.

Social Finance. 2018. "Impact Bond Database." London: Social Finance. Retrieved from http://www.socialfinance.org.uk/database/.

Social Finance US. n.d. "Outcomes Rate Cards." Retrieved from http://socialfinance.org/how-pay-for-success-works/outcomes-rate-card/.

Social Innovation and Finance Strategy Co-creation Steering Group. 2018. *Inclusive Innovation – New Ideas and New Partnerships for Stronger Communities*. Ottawa: Employment and Social Development Canada.

Social Ventures Australia. 2013. "Information Memorandum: Newpin Social Benefit Bond." Brisbane: Social Ventures Australia.

Social Ventures Australia. 2017. "Newpin Queensland Social Benefit Bond Information Memorandum." Brisbane: Social Ventures Australia. Retrieved

from http://www.socialventures.com.au/assets/Newpin-Qld-SBB
-Information-Memorandum-web.pdf.

Social Ventures Australia. 2018. "Who We Are and What We Do." Retrieved
from http://www.socialventures.com.au/who-we-are/.

Society Impact. 2017. "Over ons." Retrieved from https://www.society
impact.nl/over-ons/.

Sofi, F., A. Capalbo, F. Cesari, R. Abbate, and G.F. Gensini. 2008. "Physical
Activity during Leisure Time and Primary Prevention of Coronary Heart
Disease: An Updated Meta-analysis of Cohort Studies." *European Journal of
Cardiovascular Prevention & Rehabilitation* 15 (3): 247–57. doi: 10.1097
/HJR.0b013e3282f232ac.

Solding, L. 2015. "Social impact bonds introduceras i sverige." 2 July.
Retrieved from http://www.socialinnovation.se/social-impact
-bonds-introduceras-i-sverige/.

South Carolina. 2016. Department of Health and Human Services.
"Fact Sheet: South Carolina Nurse-Family Partnership Pay for Success
Project." Columbia. Retrieved from http://www.payforsuccess.org/sites
/default/files/resource-files/2-16-16-SC-NFP-PFS-Fact-Sheet_3.pdf.

Specking, H. 2015. "Social impact bonds made in Switzerland: Finally!" *Alliance*, 24 August. Retrieved from http://www.alliancemagazine.org/blog
/social-impact-bonds-made-in-switzerland-finally/.

Standing, G. 2012. "The Precariat: From Denizens to Citizens?" *Polity* 44 (4):
588–608. doi:10.1057/pol.2012.15.

Stanford, J. 2015. *Economics for Everyone: A Short Guide to the Economics of
Capitalism.* Ottawa: Canadian Centre for Policy Alternatives.

Starke, P. 2006. "The Politics of Welfare State Retrenchment: A Literature
Review." *Social Policy & Administration* 40 (1): 104–20. doi:10.1111/j.1467
-9515.2006.00479.x.

Starr, P. 2014. "The Meaning of Privatization." In *Privatization and the Welfare
State*, ed. S.B. Kamerman and A.J. Kahn, 15–48. Princeton, NJ: Princeton
University Press.

Start Foundation. 2016a. "About Us." Retrieved from http://www
.startfoundation.nl/english/about_us.

Start Foundation. 2016b. "Social Impact Bonds." Retrieved from http://www
.startfoundation.nl/activiteiten/sibboekje.

Steinberg, R. 2006. "Economic Theories of Nonprofit Organizations." In *The
Nonprofit Sector: A Research Handbook,* ed. W.W. Powell and R. Steinberg,
117–39. New Haven, CT: Yale University Press.

Stid, D. 2013. "Pay for Success Is Not a Panacea." *Community Development
Investment Review* 9 (1): 13–18. Retrieved from https://www.frbsf.org
/community-development/files/pay-for-success-not-panacea.pdf.

Stigler, G.J. 1971. "The Theory of Economic Regulation." *Bell Journal of Economics and Management Science* 2 (1): 3–21. doi:10.2307/3003160.

Stiglitz, J.E. 2008. "Foreword." In *Privatization: Successes and Failures*, ed. G. Roland, iv–xix. New York: Columbia University Press.

Stiglitz, J.E. 2013. *The Price of Inequality: How Today's Divided Society Endangers Our Future*. Rev. ed. New York: W.W. Norton.

Stiglitz, J.E. 2015. "Leaders and Followers: Perspectives on the Nordic Model and the Economics of Innovation." *Journal of Public Economics* 127 (July): 3–16. doi:10.1016/j.jpubeco.2014.09.005.

Stott, M. 2011. "The Big Society in Context." In *The Big Society Challenge*, ed. M. Stott, 1–26. Cardiff: Keystone Development Trust Publications. Retrieved from http://www.keystonetrust.org.uk/wp-content/uploads/2015/05/big-society-challenge.pdf.

Stuckler, D., and S. Basu. 2013. *The Body Economic: Why Austerity Kills*. New York: Basic Books.

Sturla, K., B. Shah, and J. McManus. 2018. "The Great DIB-ate: Measurement for Development Impact Bonds." *Stanford Social Innovation Review*, 21 November. Retrieved from https://ssir.org/articles/entry/the_great_dib_ate_measurement_for_development_impact_bonds.

Sugden, R. 1984. "Reciprocity: The Supply of Public Goods through Voluntary Contributions." *Economic Journal* 94 (376), 772–87. Retrieved from http://www.jstor.org/stable/2232294.

Sun, Y., W. You, F. Almeida, P. Estabrooks, and B. Davy. 2017. "The Effectiveness and Cost of Lifestyle Interventions including Nutrition Education for Diabetes Prevention: A Systematic Review and Meta-analysis." *Journal of the Academy of Nutrition and Dietetics* 117 (3): 404–21. doi:10.1111/1467-937X.00253.

Sundell, A., and V. Lapuente. 2012. "Adam Smith or Machiavelli? Political Incentives for Contracting Out Local Public Services." *Public Choice* 153 (3–4): 469–85. https://doi.org/10.1007/s11127-011-9803-1.

Switzerland. 2018. State Secretariat for Economic Affairs. "Impact Bonds Conference." Zurich. Retrieved from https://www.seco-cooperation.admin.ch/secocoop/en/home/about-us/events/archiv-events/social-impact-bond-conference-in-zurich1.html.

Syal, R. 2012. "A4e employee forged signatures to boost job placement numbers." *Guardian*, 6 March. Retrieved from https://www.theguardian.com/uk/2012/mar/06/a4e-employee-forged-signatures-teesside.

Tan, S., A. Fraser, C. Giacomantonio, K. Kruithof, M. Sim, M. Lagarde, E. Disley, et al. 2015. *An Evaluation of Social Impact Bonds in Health and Social Care: Interim Report*. London: London School of Tropical Hygiene. Retrieved from http://researchonline.lshtm.ac.uk/2391521/.

Tan, S., A. Fraser, N. McHugh, and M. Warner. 2019. "Widening Perspectives on Social Impact Bonds." *Journal of Economic Policy Reform*. doi:10.1080/17487870.2019.1568249

Taylor, E.S., and J.H. Tyler. 2012. "The Effect of Evaluation on Teacher Performance." *American Economic Review* 102 (7): 3628–51. doi:10.1257/aer.102.7.3628.

Taylor, L. 2010. *Maynard's Revenge.* Cambridge, MA: Harvard University Press.

Tewfik, O. 2015. "Communities Deserve Services, Not Schemes." 10 December. Retrieved from https://www.afscme.org/now/communities-deserve -services-not-schemes.

Thames Reach. 2015. "Social Impact Bond for Entrenched Rough Sleepers: Key Areas of Learning." London: Thames Reach. Retrieved from https:// thamesreach.org.uk/wp-content/uploads/2017/11/Social-Impact-Bond -for-Ennched-Rough-Sleepers.pdf.

Third Sector. 2014. "Why the Social Impact Bond at Peterborough Prison is being halted." 21 May. Retrieved from http://www.thirdsector.co.uk /why-social-impact-bond-peterborough-prison-halted/finance /article/1294813?utm_source=website&utm_medium=social.

Third Sector Capital Partners. 2014. "Fact Sheet: The Massachusetts Juvenile Justice Pay for Success Initiative." Retrieved from http://www .goldmansachs.com/our-thinking/trends-in-our-business/massachusetts -social-impact-bond/MA-juvenile-justice-pay-for-success-initiative.pdf.

Third Sector Capital Partners. 2017. "We Are Accelerating America's Transition to a Performance-Driven Social Sector." Retrieved from https://www .thirdsectorcap.org/.

Thompson, H.A. 2012. "The Prison Industrial Complex: A Growth Industry in a Shrinking Economy." *New Labor Forum* 21 (3): 39–47. https://doi.org/10.4 179%2FNLF.213.0000006.

Titmuss, R.M. 1974. *Social Policy.* London: Allen & Unwin.

Tomkinson, E. 2012. *Perspectives from the Social Finance Forum 2012: An Australian Snapshot Social Impact Bonds.* Sydney: Centre for Social Impact. Retrieved from https://www.csi.edu.au/media/uploads/Social_Impact _Bonds_-_An_Australian_Snapshot_-_November_2012.pdf.

Tomkinson, E. 2014. "Rotterdam Experiments with Social Impact Bond." 14 October. Retrieved from https://emmatomkinson.com/2014/10/15 /rotterdam-experiments-with-social-impact-bond/.

Town, R., R. Kane, P. Johnson, and M. Butler. 2005. "Economic Incentives and Physicians' Delivery of Preventive Care: A Systematic Review." *American Journal of Preventive Medicine* 28 (2): 234–40. doi:10.1016/j.amepre .2004.10.013.

Toynbee, P., and D. Walker. 2017. *Dismembered: How the Attack on the State Harms Us All.* London: Guardian Faber.

Tse, A.E., and M.E. Warner. 2018. "The Razor's Edge: Social Impact Bonds and the Financialization of Early Childhood Services." *Journal of Urban Affairs* 42 (6): 1–17. doi:10.1080/07352166.2018.1465347.

Tse, A.E., and M.E. Warner. 2019. "A Policy Outcomes Comparison: Does SIB Market Discipline Narrow Social Rights?" *Journal of Comparative Policy Analysis: Research and Practice* 22 (2): 134–52. doi:10.1080/13876988.2019.160 9789.

Tsukamoto, I. 2017. "Emerging SIBs in Japan and Yokohama: Social Impact Measurement Pilot Project." Retrieved from http://www.city.yokohama .lg.jp/seisaku/forum2.4.1.pdf.

Tullock, G. 1967. "The Welfare Costs of Tariffs, Monopolies, and Theft." *Economic Inquiry* 5 (3): 224–32. https://doi.org/10.1111/j.1465-7295.1967 .tb01923.x.

Tversky, A., and D. Kahneman. 1992. "Advances in Prospect Theory: Cumulative Representation of Uncertainty." *Journal of Risk and Uncertainty* 5 (4): 297–323. https://www.jstor.org/stable/41755005.

UNDP (United Nations Development Programme). 2011. *Illicit Financial Flows from the Least Developed Countries: 1990–2008.* New York: United Nations Development Program. Retrieved from http://content-ext.undp.org /aplaws_publications/3273649/IFFs_from_LDCs_web.pdf.

UNDP. 2019. "Social and Development Impact Bonds (Results-based Financing)." New York: UNDP. Retrieved from http://www.sdfinance.undp.org /content/sdfinance/en/home/solutions/social-development-impact -bonds.html#mst-6.

Unger, R.M. 2009. *The Left Alternative.* New York: Verso.

UNISON. 2016. *UNISON Annual Report 2015/16.* London: UNISON.

United Kingdom. 1999. HM Treasury Taskforce. "Technical Note 5: How to Construct a Public Sector Comparator." London: HM Treasury.

United Kingdom. 2005. Audit Commission. "Early Lessons from Payment by Results." London: Audit Commission. Retrieved from http://webarchive .nationalarchives.gov.uk/20150421134146/http://archive.audit-commission .gov.uk/auditcommission/subwebs/publications/studies/studyPDF /3289.pdf.

United Kingdom. 2008. Audit Commission. "The Right Result? A Review of Payment by Results 2003–07." London: Audit Commission. Retrieved from http://webarchive.nationalarchives.gov.uk/20150421134146/http:// archive.audit-commission.gov.uk/auditcommission/subwebs /publications/studies/studyPDF/3431.pdf.

United Kingdom. 2010. Ministry of Justice. "Social Impact Bond Launched." London: Ministry of Justice. Retrieved from http://webarchive.national archives.gov.uk/20100911070445/http://www.justice.gov.uk/news /announcement100910a.htm.

United Kingdom. 2011a. Office for Budget Responsibility. *Fiscal Sustainability Report.* London: Office for Budget Responsibility. Retrieved from http:// budgetresponsibility.independent.gov.uk/wordpress/docs/FSR2011.pdf.

United Kingdom. 2011b. *Open Public Services White Paper*. London: Stationery Office. Retrieved from https://www.gov.uk/government/publications /open-public-services-white-paper.

United Kingdom. 2012. Treasury. *A New Approach to Public Private Partnerships*. London: HM Treasury. Retrieved from https://www.gov.uk/government /uploads/system/uploads/attachment_data/file/205112/pf2_infra structure_new_approach_to_public_private_parnerships_051212.pdf.

United Kingdom. 2013. Cabinet Office. "Social Impact Investment Forum." London. Retrieved from https://www.gov.uk/government/news /social-impact-investment-forum.

United Kingdom. 2014a. Cabinet Office. "Youth Engagement Fund: Prospectus." London. Retrieved from https://www.gov.uk/government /publications/youth-engagement-fund-prospectus.

United Kingdom. 2014b. Department for International Development. *Sharpening Incentives to Perform: DFID's Strategy for Payment by Results*. London: Department for International Development.

United Kingdom. 2016. Cabinet Office. *Charities (Protection and Social Investment) Act 2016 Chapter 4*. Norwich: Stationary Office. Retrieved from http:// www.legislation.gov.uk/ukpga/2016/4/pdfs/ukpgaen_20160004_en.pdf.

United Kingdom. 2017a. Cabinet Office, and Department for Digital, Culture, Media & Sport. "Guidance: Social Impact Bonds." London. Retrieved from https://www.gov.uk/guidance/social-impact-bonds.

United Kingdom. 2017b. Department for Digital, Culture, Media & Sport. "Government improves life chances across the country: 22 projects will receive a proportion of the £48 million Life Chances Fund." 7 September. Retrieved from https://www.gov.uk/government/news/government -improves-life-chances-across-the-country.

United Kingdom. 2017c. House of Lords Select Committee on Charities. "Report of Session 2016–17: Stronger Charities for a Stronger Society." HL Paper 133. London: House of Lords.

United Kingdom. 2018. House of Commons Public Accounts Committee. *Private Finance Initiatives Inquiry*. Public Accounts Committee HC 894. London: House of Commons. Retrieved from https://www.parliament.uk /business/committees/committees-a-z/commons-select/public -accounts-committee/inquiries/parliament-2017/private -finance-initiatives-17–19/.

United Kingdom. 2019. Department for Education. "New schemes to help care leavers access education and employment: Education Secretary welcomes innovative approaches being trialled to reduce the number of care leavers 'Not in Education, Employment or Training.'" Press release, 9 January. London. Retrieved from https://www.gov.uk/government/news/new -schemes-to-help-care-leavers-access-education-and-employment.

United States. 2013. Department of Labor. "US labor department awards nearly $24 million in pay for success grants." Press release, 23 September. Washington, DC. Retrieved from http://www.dol.gov/opa/media/press/eta/ETA20131936.htm.

United States. 2016a. Office of Social Innovation and Civic Participation. "Pay for Success: An Opportunity to Find and Scale What Works." Washington, DC. Retrieved from https://obamawhitehouse.archives.gov/administration/eop/sicp/initiatives/pay-for-success.

United States. 2016b. White House. "Improving Outcomes through Pay for Success." Washington, DC. Retrieved from https://obamawhitehouse.archives.gov/sites/default/files/omb/budget/fy2016/assets/fact_sheets/improving-outcomes-through-pay-for-success.pdf-outcomes-through-pay-for-success.pdf&usg=AOvVaw1AclEV8s5LKipaEaxch1s1.

United Way of Massachusetts Bay and Merrimack Valley. 2018. "Pay for success initiative to reduce chronic individual homelessness exceeds goals; Issues first dividend payments to investors." Retrieved from https://unitedwaymassbay.org/news/pay-for-success-initiative-to-reduce-chronic-individual-homelessness-exceeds-goals-issues-first-dividend-payments-to-investors/.

Urban Institute. n.d. "South Carolina Nurse-Family Partnership Project." Urban Institute - Pay for Success Initiative. Retrieved from https://pfs.urban.org/pfs-project-fact-sheets/content/south-carolina-nurse-family-partnership-project.

USAID. 2017. "Ensuring Effective Development." 10 October. Retrieved from https://blog.usaid.gov/2017/10/ensuring-effective-development/.

Valentinov, V. 2011. "The Meaning of Nonprofit Organization: Insights from Classical Institutionalism." *Journal of Economic Issues* 45 (4): 901–16. doi:10.2753/JEI0021–3624450408.

Valentinov, V. 2012. "The Economics of the Nonprofit Sector: Insights from the Institutionalism of John R. Commons." *Social Science Journal* 49 (4): 545–53. doi:https://doi-org.libproxy.newschool.edu/10.1016/j.soscij.2012.06.002.

van Berkel, R. 2010. "The Provision of Income Protection and Activation Services for the Unemployed in 'Active' Welfare States: An International Comparison." *Journal of Social Policy* 39 (1): 17–34. https://doi.org/10.1017/S0047279409990389.

van der Heijden, H. 2013. "Small Is Beautiful? Financial Efficiency of Small Fundraising Charities." *British Accounting Review* 45 (1): 50–7. https://doi-org.libproxy.newschool.edu/10.1016/j.bar.2012.12.004.

van der Stouwe, T., J.J. Asscher, G.J.J. Stams, M. Deković, and P.H. van der Laan. 2014. "The Effectiveness of Multisystemic Therapy (MST): A Meta-analysis." *Clinical Psychology Review* 34 (6): 468–81. https://doi.org/10.1016/j.cpr.2014.06.006.

van Oorschot, W.J.H. 2002. "Targeting Welfare: On the Functions and Dysfunctions of Means-Testing in Social Policy." In *World Poverty: New Policies to Defeat an Old Enemy*, ed. P. Townsend and D. Gordon, 171–93. Bristol: Policy Press.

van Slyke, D.M. 2003. "The Mythology of Privatization in Contracting for Social Services." *Public Administration Review* 63 (3): 296–315. https://doi.org/10.1111/1540-6210.00291.

van Slyke, D.M. 2006. "Agents or Stewards: Using Theory to Understand the Government-Nonprofit Social Service Contracting Relationship. *Journal of Public Administration Research and Theory* 17 (2): 157–87. https://doi.org/10.1093/jopart/mul012.

van Slyke, D.M., and H.K. Newman. 2006. "Venture Philanthropy and Social Entrepreneurship in Community Redevelopment." *Nonprofit Management and Leadership* 16 (3): 345–68. https://doi.org/10.1002/nml.111.

Vera Institute for Justice. 2015. "Impact Evaluation of the Adolescent Behavioral Learning Experience (ABLE) Program at Rikers Island: Summary of Findings." New York: Vera Institute for Justice. Retrieved from http://archive.vera.org/sites/default/files/resources/downloads/adolescent-behavioral-learning-experience-evaluation-rikers-island-summary.pdf.

Vickers, J., and G.K. Yarrow. 1988. *Privatization: An Economic Analysis*. Cambridge, MA: MIT Press.

Vickers, J., and G.K. Yarrow. 1991. "Economic Perspectives on Privatization." *Journal of Economic Perspectives* 5 (2): 111–32. doi:10.1257/jep.5.2.111.

Village Enterprise. 2017a. *Annual Report 2017*. San Carlos, CA: Village Enterprise. Retrieved from http://villageenterprise.org/wp-content/uploads/2018/01/VE_AR_2017_WEB.pdf.

Village Enterprise. 2017b. "The Village Enterprise Development Impact Bond." San Carlos, CA: Village Enterprise. Retrieved from http://villageenterprise.org/our-impact/development-impact-bond/.

Villalonga, B. 2000. "Privatization and Efficiency: Differentiating Ownership Effects from Political, Organizational, and Dynamic Effects." *Journal of Economic Behavior & Organization* 42 (1): 43–74. https://doi.org/10.1016/S0167-2681(00)00074-3.

Vining, A.R., and A.E. Boardman. 2008. "Public-Private Partnerships in Canada: Theory and Evidence." *Canadian Public Administration* 51 (1): 9–44. https://doi.org/10.1111/j.1754-7121.2008.00003.x.

Vining, A.R., A.E. Boardman, and F. Poschmann. 2005. "Public–Private Partnerships in the US and Canada: 'There are no free lunches.'" *Journal of Comparative Policy Analysis: Research and Practice* 7 (3): 199–220. https://doi.org/10.1080/13876980500209363.

Vlaams minister van Werk. 2018. "Innovatieve manier om jongeren aan een job te helpen." Retrieved from https://philippemuyters.prezly.com /innovatieve-manier-om-jongeren-aan-een-job-te-helpen#.

Wagner, R.E. 1977. "Economic Manipulation for Political Profit: Macroeconomic Consequences and Constitutional Implications." *Kyklos* 30 (3): 395–410. https://doi.org/10.1111/j.1467-6435.1977.tb02200.x.

Waller, W. 2006. "The Pragmatic State: Institutionalist Perspectives on the State." In *Alternative Theories of the State*, ed. S. Pressman, 13–33. London: Palgrave Macmillan.

Warner, M.E. 2008. "Reversing Privatization, Rebalancing Government Reform: Markets, Deliberation and Planning." *Policy and Society* 27 (2): 163–74. https://doi.org/10.1016/j.polsoc.2008.09.001.

Warner, M.E. 2012. "Privatization and Urban Governance: The Continuing Challenges of Efficiency, Voice and Integration." *Cities* 29 (December): S38–43. https://doi.org/10.1016/j.cities.2012.06.007.

Warner, M.E. 2013. "Private Finance for Public Goods: Social Impact Bonds." *Journal of Economic Policy Reform* 16 (4): 303–19. https://doi.org/10.1080/174 87870.2013.835727.

Warner, M.E. 2015. "Profiting from Public Value? The Case of Social Impact Bonds." In *Creating Public Value in Practice*, ed. J. Bryson, B. Crosby, and L. Bloomberg, 143–60). New York: Taylor and Francis.

Warner, M.E., and G. Bel. 2008. "Competition or Monopoly? Comparing Privatization of Local Public Services in the US and Spain." *Public Administration* 86 (3): 723–35. https://doi.org/10.1111/j.1467-9299.2008.00700.x.

Warner, M.E., and A. Hefetz. 2008. "Managing Markets for Public Service: The Role of Mixed Public–Private Delivery of City Services." *Public Administration Review* 68 (1): 155–66. https://www.researchgate.net/deref /http%3A%2F%2Fdx.doi.org%2F10.1111%2Fj.1540-6210.2007.00845.x.

Warrell, H. 2008. "New firm to prepare ground for social investment bank." *Third Sector*, 21 April. Retrieved from http://www.thirdsector.co.uk /new-firm-prepare-ground-social-investment-bank/finance/article/803427.

Warren, R.K. 2007. *Evidence-based Practice to Reduce Recidivism: Implications for State Judiciaries*. Washington, DC: US Department of Justice, National Institute of Corrections.

Weakley, K. 2016. "'Social impact bond market could be worth £1bn', says minister." *Civil Society Media*, 14 January. Retrieved from https://www .civilsociety.co.uk/news/-social-impact-bond-market-could-be-worth-1bn -says-minister.html.

Weakley, K. 2018. "Government commits up to £48m of funding to social impact bond projects." *Civil Society Media*, 7 September. Retrieved from

https://www.civilsociety.co.uk/news/government-commits-up-to-48m
-funding-to-social-impact-bond-projects.html.

Wedel, K.R. 1976. "Government Contracting for Purchase of Service." *Social Work* 21 (2): 101–5. doi:10.1007/978-3-662-30309-2_1.

Weinrott, M.R., R.R. Jones, and J.R. Howard. 1982. "Cost-Effectiveness of Teaching Family Programs for Delinquents: Results of a National Evaluation." *Evaluation Review* 6 (2): 173–201. doi:10.1177/0193841X8200600202.

Weisbrod, B.A. 1988. *The Nonprofit Economy*. Cambridge, MA: Harvard University Press.

Weisbrod, B.A. 1989. "Rewarding Performance that Is Hard to Measure: The Private Nonprofit Sector." *Science* 244 (4904): 541–6. doi:10.1126/science.244.4904.541.

Welsh, B.C., D.P. Farrington, and B.R. Gowar. 2015. "Benefit-Cost Analysis of Crime Prevention Programs." *Crime and Justice* 44 (1): 447–516. Retrieved from https://www.journals.uchicago.edu/doi/abs/10.1086/681556.

Wettenhall, R. 2005. "The Public-Private Interface: Surveying the History." In *The Challenge of Public–Private Partnerships: Learning from International Experience*, ed. G.A. Hodge and C. Greve, 22–43. Cheltenham, UK: Edward Elgar.

Whalen, C.J. 1992. "Schools of Thought and Theories of the State: Reflections of an Institutional Economist." In *The Stratified State: Radical Institutionalist Theories of Participation and Duality*, ed. W.M. Dugger and W. Waller, 55–86. New York: Routledge. Retrieved from https://www.taylorfrancis.com/books/stratified-state-william-dugger-william-walle r/e/10.4324/9781315487090.

Whiteside, H. 2013. "Stabilizing Privatization: Crisis, Enabling Fields, and Public-Private Partnerships in Canada." *Alternate Routes: A Journal of Critical Social Research* 24: 85–107. http://www.alternateroutes.ca/index.php/ar/article/view/19219.

Whitfield, D. 2001. *Private Finance Initiative and Public Private Partnerships: What Future for Public Services?* Newcastle, UK: Centre for Public Services.

Whitfield, D. 2007. *Financing Infrastructure in the 21st Century: The Long Term Impact of Public Private Partnerships in Britain and Australia*. Adelaide: Don Dunstan Foundation.

Whitfield, D. 2015. *Alternatives to Private Finance of the Welfare State: A Global Analysis of Social Impact Bond, Pay-for-Success and Development Impact Bond Projects*. Adelaide: University of Adelaide, Australian Workplace Innovation and Social Research Centre.

Whitfield, D. 2017. "PFI/PPP Buyouts, Bailouts, Terminations and Major Problem Contracts." *ESSU Research Report* 9. https://doi.org/10.13140/RG.2.2.14558.23369.

Wiggan, J. 2019. "Financialisation, Social Impact Bonds and the Making of New Market Spaces in Social Policy." In *Towards a Spatial Social Policy*, ed.

A. Whitworth, 103–26. Bristol: Bristol University Press. https://doi
.org/10.2307/j.ctvs1g92b.10.

Williams, J.W. 2018. "Surveying the SIB Economy: Social Impact Bonds, 'Local' Challenges, and Shifting Markets in Urban Social Problems." *Journal of
Urban Affairs* 42 (6): 907–19. doi:10.1080/07352166.2018.1511796.

Williams, J.W. 2019. "From Visions of Promise to Signs of Struggle:
Exploring Social Impact Bonds and the Funding of Social Services
in Canada, the US and the UK." Retrieved from https://golab.bsg.ox.ac
.uk/news-events/blogs/visions-promise-signs-struggle-social
-impact-bonds-canada-us-and-uk/.

Williamson, O.E. 1981. "The Economics of Organization: The Transaction Cost
Approach." *American Journal of Sociology* 87 (3): 548—77. https://www.jstor
.org/stable/2778934.

Williamson, O.E. 1999. "Public and Private Bureaucracies: A Transaction Cost
Economics Perspective." *Journal of Law, Economics, and Organization* 15 (1):
306–42. https://doi.org/10.1093/jleo/15.1.306.

Williamson, O.E. 2002. "The Theory of the Firm as Governance Structure:
From Choice to Contract." *Journal of Economic Perspectives* 16 (3): 171–95.
https://www.jstor.org/stable/3216956.

Willis, P., and M. Tyler. 2018. "Implementing a social outcomes fund in Australia." *Mandarin*, 3 September. Retrieved from https://www.themandarin
.com.au/97738-implementing-a-social-outcomes-fund-in-australia/.

Wilson, R., A. Fraser, J. Kimmitt, S. Tan, N. McHugh, T. Lowe, M. Warner, et al.
2020. "Theme: Futures in Social Investment? Learning from the Emerging
Policy and Practice of Social Impact Bonds (SIBs)." *Public Money & Management* 40 (3): 179–82. https://doi.org/10.1080/09540962.2020.1714287.

Witkin, N. 2019. "A Theory of Impact Bonds as an Alternative to Pigouvian
Tax and Public Provision: Application for Climate Change." *Journal of Applied Business and Economics* 21 (5): 139–53.

Wittman, D. 1989. "Why Democracies Produce Efficient Results."
Journal of Political Economy 97 (6): 1395–424. https://doi.org/10.1086
/261660.

Wong, J., A. Ortmann, A. Motta, and L. Zhang. 2016. "Understanding Social
Impact Bonds and Their Alternatives: An Experimental Investigation." In
Experiments in Organizational Economics, ed. S.J. Goerg and J.R. Hamman,
39–83. Bingley, UK: Emerald Group. https://doi.org/10.1108
/S0193-230620160000019011.

World Bank. 2011. "A New Instrument to Advance Development Effectiveness: Program-for-Results Financing." Washington, DC: World Bank.
Retrieved from http://documents.worldbank.org/curated
/en/687711468325286151/A-new-instrument-to-advance
-development-effectiveness-program-for-results-financing.

World Bank. 2017. "Private Participation in Infrastructure Database." Washington, DC: World Bank. Retrieved from https://ppi.worldbank.org/.

WSIPP (Washington State Institute for Public Policy). 2017. "Benefit-Cost Technical Documentation." Olympia: Washington State Institute for Public Policy. Retrieved from http://www.wsipp.wa.gov/TechnicalDocument ation/WsippBenefitCostTechnicalDocumentation.pdf.

Wunder, T., and T. Kemp. 2008. "Institutionalism and the State: Founding Views Reexamined." *Forum for Social Economics* 37 (1): 27–42. https://doi .org/10.1007/s12143-008-9012-y.

Zullo, R. 2019. "Explaining Privatization Failure: The Vice of Sweet Carrots and Hard Sticks." *Review of Radical Political Economics* 51 (1): 111–28. https://doi.org/10.1177%2F0486613417718527.

Index

The letter *f* following a page number denotes a figure; the letter *n* a footnote; the letter *t* a table.